Docker Certified As
(DCA): Exam Guide

Enhance and validate your Docker skills by gaining
Docker certification

Francisco Javier Ramírez Urea

BIRMINGHAM - MUMBAI

Docker Certified Associate (DCA): Exam Guide

Copyright © 2020 Packt Publishing

Commissioning Editor: Vijin Boricha
Acquisition Editor: Rohit Rajkumar
Content Development Editor: Romy Dias
Senior Editor: Arun Nadar
Technical Editor: Sarvesh Jayant
Copy Editor: Safis Editing
Language Support Editor: Safis Editing
Project Coordinator: Neil Dmello
Proofreader: Safis Editing
Indexer: Priyanka Dhadke
Production Designer: Aparna Bhagat

First published: September 2020

Production reference: 1280820

Published by Packt Publishing Ltd.
Livery Place
35 Livery Street
Birmingham
B3 2PB, UK.

ISBN 978-1-83921-189-8

www.packt.com

To my wife, Raquel; my kids, Jorge and Andrea; and my friends at Hopla! Software
for their patience, love, and support.

– Francisco Javier Ramírez Urea

Packt.com

Subscribe to our online digital library for full access to over 7,000 books and videos, as well as industry leading tools to help you plan your personal development and advance your career. For more information, please visit our website.

Why subscribe?

- Spend less time learning and more time coding with practical eBooks and Videos from over 4,000 industry professionals

- Improve your learning with Skill Plans built especially for you

- Get a free eBook or video every month

- Fully searchable for easy access to vital information

- Copy and paste, print, and bookmark content

Did you know that Packt offers eBook versions of every book published, with PDF and ePub files available? You can upgrade to the eBook version at www.packt.com and as a print book customer, you are entitled to a discount on the eBook copy. Get in touch with us at customercare@packtpub.com for more details.

At www.packt.com, you can also read a collection of free technical articles, sign up for a range of free newsletters, and receive exclusive discounts and offers on Packt books and eBooks.

Contributors

About the author

Francisco Javier Ramírez Urea is a technology enthusiast and professional. He is a Docker Captain, casual developer, open source advocate, certified technology trainer, solutions architect, and technical book writer and reviewer.

He is also a Kubernetes Certified Administrator, a Docker Certified Associate, a Docker Certified Instructor, and a Docker MTA program consultant, as well as a Docker/Kubernetes and NGINX expert and DevOps/CI-CD solutions integrator.

He currently works as a solutions architect focused on containers and microservices technologies. He really enjoys teaching others everything he knows and continuous learning is his life's main motivation.

I want to give special thanks to my wife, Raquel, and my kids, Jorge and Andrea, for helping me remain focused on this book every day. I stole a lot of time from them to write this book. I also want to give thanks to my friends at Hopla! Software, the Docker community, and the Packt editors who had infinite patience helping me in this process.

Dear reader, I hope you enjoy this book. If you are preparing for the DCA exam, you need to be comfortable with the Docker Enterprise platform and review all proposed labs and questions. After that, I am sure you will be ready for your goal. Keep calm, read the questions carefully, and take a breath before answering. I wish you all the best of luck for the exam.

About the reviewer

Morten Nilsen is VP Principal DevOps Engineer at BNY Mellon. In 2016, after 12 years in finance, including as a hedge fund manager, he made a career change to IT. He began using Docker while developing the skills needed to be a DevOps engineer. At the time, Docker was gaining traction, and learning Docker gave him a leg up on the competition for his first consultancy with a company servicing e-commerce sites. In 2017, he was among the first to obtain a Docker Certified Associate certification. He's built new DevOps teams for start-ups and has improved SDLC automation and IaC for established teams. Docker is an important tool in his role on an API platform team supporting hundreds of APIs, thousands of services, and tens of thousands of containers.

Packt is searching for authors like you

If you're interested in becoming an author for Packt, please visit `authors.packtpub.com` and apply today. We have worked with thousands of developers and tech professionals, just like you, to help them share their insight with the global tech community. You can make a general application, apply for a specific hot topic that we are recruiting an author for, or submit your own idea.

Table of Contents

Section 3 - Docker Enterprise

Preface

Microservices and containers have changed the way developers create new applications. Microservice architectures allow us to decouple applications in their components, and today we have tools that can provide them with orchestrated and seamless interactions. Also, containers have changed the deployment artifacts for applications. We have moved from binaries to container images. This new development workflow helps developers to build applications faster and more securely, and ensures that the final product will work as intended, anywhere, without many modifications. Applications deployed as containers will follow general code versioning rules, which helps us to keep track of component releases and behavior.

This book will introduce microservices and containers and will help us to learn the key concepts of these technologies. We will learn how containers work, see how networks are implemented in different scenarios, and explore Docker Swarm and Kubernetes orchestration strategies and environments. We will also cover all the Docker Enterprise components and features required to implement Container as a Service platforms in production. All the topics covered in this book, with sample questions and detailed answers, will help you to learn the knowledge required to pass the official Docker Certified Associate exam.

Who this book is for

This book is intended for people who want to learn about container technology and who are preparing for the Docker Certified Associate exam. This book was also written as a guide for Docker Enterprise products and serves as an introduction to Kubernetes' terminology and features.

Good Linux and Windows user knowledge is required, and some networking skills will help you to understand container networking and the use of load balancers and proxies to provide a full-featured Container as a Service environment.

The labs in this book are focused on Linux hosts because most current Docker Enterprise components are deployed on Linux operating systems. Windows hosts can be part of Docker Swarm and Kubernetes clusters, but control planes are deployed using Linux hosts.

What this book covers

Chapter 1, *Modern Infrastructures and Applications with Docker*, introduces the microservices architecture and containers as the perfect match for modern infrastructures. It also covers Docker Engine concepts.

Chapter 2, *Building Docker Images*, presents the Docker image-building process, command-line tools, and best practices for creating good and secure images.

Chapter 3, *Running Docker Containers*, shows how Docker helps us to run containers in our systems and explains how these processes are isolated from Docker Engine hosts.

Chapter 4, *Container Persistency and Networking*, explains how to manage data out of the containers' life cycles, as well as how containers interact with internal and external resources.

Chapter 5, *Deploying Multi-Container Applications*, explains how we can deploy applications in which components are based on containers. We will learn how to manage an application's components with Infrastructure as Code files.

Chapter 6, *Introduction to Docker Content Trust*, shows how we can improve security in container-based environments, ensuring image ownership, immutability, and provenance.

Chapter 7, *Introduction to Orchestration*, reviews orchestration concepts before diving into Docker Swarm and Kubernetes as orchestrators.

Chapter 8, *Orchestration Using Docker Swarm*, covers Docker Swarm's features and implementation, explaining how to implement applications using this orchestrator.

Chapter 9, *Orchestration Using Kubernetes*, introduces basic Kubernetes concepts and compares this orchestrator with Docker Swarm to help you implement the best solution for different applications or infrastructures.

Chapter 10, *Introduction to the Docker Enterprise Platform*, introduces Docker Enterprise components and explains how Docker creates a production-ready Container as a Service platform.

Chapter 11, *Universal Control Plane*, explains Docker Enterprise's control plane component. We will learn how to implement Universal Control Plane in production and how to manage the Docker Enterprise platform.

Chapter 12, *Publishing Applications in Docker Enterprise*, reviews different methods for publishing applications and shows how to secure our Docker Swarm and Kubernetes platforms using Interlock and Ingress Controller.

Chapter 13, *Implementing an Enterprise-Grade Registry with DTR*, explains how Docker Enterprise provides a production-ready registry to manage and store Docker images.

Chapter 14, *Summarizing Important Concepts*, presents a summary of the most important concepts learned in the previous chapters. This chapter will help us to prepare for the Docker Certified Associate exam.

Chapter 15, *Mock Exam Questions and Final Notes*, contains some mock Docker Certified Associate exam questions and explains the basics of the exam process.

To get the most out of this book

In order to follow the book's labs and examples, it is recommended to have Docker Engine installed on your computer. A set of virtual environments is provided for you to allow you to run all the labs without modifying your computer. There are also many labs in which you have to deploy clusters, with many nodes involved. The labs will deploy virtual machines so you don't have to install many nodes, although you can deploy all the labs on your own infrastructure of hosts.

The provided virtual environments require Vagrant (https://www.vagrantup.com/) and VirtualBox (https://www.virtualbox.org/) to be installed on your computer. Docker images and software will be downloaded from the internet, so internet connectivity is also required. The following table shows the computer resources required to run all of the book's labs. You will free up resources by destroying environments once all the labs from each section or chapter are completed.

Software/hardware covered in the book	Chapters	OS requirements for running virtual environments
Docker standalone platform (Docker Engine)	1 to 7	2 vCPU, 4 GB of RAM, and 10 GB of disk space.
Docker Swarm cluster platform	8	4 vCPU, 8 GB of RAM, and 50 GB of disk space.
Kubernetes cluster platform	9	4 vCPU, 8 GB of RAM, and 50 GB of disk space.
Docker Enterprise platform	11, 12, and 13	8 vCPU, 16 GB of RAM, and 100 GB of disk space.

The labs from chapters 1 to 6 require one node. A minimum of 2 vCPUs and 4 GB of RAM is required. The labs from chapter 8 and chapter 9 will deploy 4 and 3 virtual nodes respectively, and more local resources are required. In these cases, you will need at least 4 vCPUs and 8 GB of RAM on your computer. The Docker Enterprise labs require more resources because the platform has quite large CPU and memory requirements per virtual node. These labs will run smoothly with at least 8 vCPUs and 16 GB of RAM because the Vagrant environment will deploy 4 virtual nodes with 4 GB of RAM per node.

In terms of disk space, your computer should have at least 100 GB of free disk for the biggest environment.

The minimum required Vagrant version is 2.2.8, while the minimum required version of VirtualBox is 6.0.0. The labs can be executed on macOS, Windows 10, and Linux. The labs were tested on the Ubuntu Linux 18.04 LTS and Windows 10 Pro operating systems during the writing of this book.

All labs can be executed on Docker Swarm, Kubernetes, and Docker Enterprise, although it is recommended to use virtual environments to execute all the labs' steps, including installation procedures.

If you are using the digital version of this book, we advise you to type the code yourself or access the code via the GitHub repository (link available in the next section). Doing so will help you avoid any potential errors related to the copying and pasting of code.

Before taking the exam, ensure that you understand and can answer all the questions in Chapter 15, *Mock Exam Questions and Final Notes*. The questions in this chapter are quite close to the ones currently present in Docker Certified Associate exam.

Download the example code files

You can download the example code files for this book from your account at www.packt.com. If you purchased this book elsewhere, you can visit www.packtpub.com/support and register to have the files emailed directly to you.

You can download the code files by following these steps:

1. Log in or register at www.packt.com.
2. Select the **Support** tab.
3. Click on **Code Downloads**.
4. Enter the name of the book in the **Search** box and follow the onscreen instructions.

Once the file is downloaded, please make sure that you unzip or extract the folder using the latest version of:

- WinRAR/7-Zip for Windows
- Zipeg/iZip/UnRarX for Mac
- 7-Zip/PeaZip for Linux

The code bundle for the book is also hosted on GitHub at `https://github.com/PacktPublishing/Docker-Certified-Associate-DCA-Exam-Guide`. In case there's an update to the code, it will be updated on the existing GitHub repository.

We also have other code bundles from our rich catalog of books and videos available at `https://github.com/PacktPublishing/`. Check them out!

Code in Action

Code in Action videos for this book can be viewed at `https://bit.ly/34FSiEp`.

Download the color images

We also provide a PDF file that has color images of the screenshots/diagrams used in this book. You can download it here: `http://www.packtpub.com/sites/default/files/downloads/9781839211898_ColorImages.pdf`.

Conventions used

There are a number of text conventions used throughout this book.

`CodeInText`: Indicates code words in text, database table names, folder names, filenames, file extensions, pathnames, dummy URLs, user input, and Twitter handles. Here is an example: "We can configure the shared storage we need to execute the `reconfigure` action."

A block of code is set as follows:

```
apiVersion: networking.k8s.io/v1beta1
kind: Ingress
metadata:
  name: test-ingress
  annotations:
    nginx.ingress.kubernetes.io/rewrite-target: /
```

When we wish to draw your attention to a particular part of a code block, the relevant lines or items are set in bold:

```
services:
  colors:
    image: codegazers/colors:1.16
    deploy:
      replicas: 3
```

Any command-line input or output is written as follows:

```
$ sudo mount -t nfs 10.10.10.11:/data /mnt
$ sudo cp -pR /var/lib/docker/volumes/dtr-registry-c8a9ec361fde/_data/*
/mnt/
```

Bold: Indicates a new term, an important word, or words that you see onscreen. For example, words in menus or dialog boxes appear in the text like this. Here is an example: "The screenshot shows the **Garbage collection** configuration page."

Warnings or important notes appear like this.

Tips and tricks appear like this.

Get in touch

Feedback from our readers is always welcome.

General feedback: If you have questions about any aspect of this book, mention the book title in the subject of your message and email us at customercare@packtpub.com.

Errata: Although we have taken every care to ensure the accuracy of our content, mistakes do happen. If you have found a mistake in this book, we would be grateful if you would report this to us. Please visit www.packtpub.com/support/errata, selecting your book, clicking on the Errata Submission Form link, and entering the details.

Piracy: If you come across any illegal copies of our works in any form on the Internet, we would be grateful if you would provide us with the location address or website name. Please contact us at copyright@packt.com with a link to the material.

If you are interested in becoming an author: If there is a topic that you have expertise in and you are interested in either writing or contributing to a book, please visit authors.packtpub.com.

Reviews

Please leave a review. Once you have read and used this book, why not leave a review on the site that you purchased it from? Potential readers can then see and use your unbiased opinion to make purchase decisions, we at Packt can understand what you think about our products, and our authors can see your feedback on their book. Thank you!

For more information about Packt, please visit packt.com.

Section 1 - Key Container Concepts

1

This first section focuses on key container concepts. We will learn their main features, how to create images, how to provide networking and persistent storage features, and how containers help us to improve security in relation to processes. You will also learn how to create and deploy container-based applications on Linux and Windows environments.

This section comprises the following chapters:

- Chapter 1, *Modern Infrastructures and Applications with Docker*
- Chapter 2, *Building Docker Images*
- Chapter 3, *Running Docker Containers*
- Chapter 4, *Container Persistency and Networking*
- Chapter 5, *Deploying Multi-Container Applications*
- Chapter 6, *Introduction to Docker Content Trust*

1
Modern Infrastructures and Applications with Docker

Microservices and containers have probably been the most frequently mentioned buzzwords in recent years. These days, we can still hear about them at conferences across the globe. Although both terms are definitely related when talking about modern applications, they are not the same. In fact, we can execute microservices without containers and run big monolithic applications in containers. In the middle of the container world, there is a well-known word that comes to mind when we find ourselves talking about them – Docker.

This book is a guide to passing the Docker Certified Associate exam, which is a certification of knowledge pertaining to this technology. We will cover each topic needed to pass this exam. In this chapter, we will start with what microservices are and why they are important in modern applications. We will also cover how Docker manages the requirements of this application's logical components.

This chapter will guide you through Docker's main concepts and will give you a basic idea of the tools and resources provided to manage containers.

In this chapter, we will cover the following topics:

- Understanding the evolution of applications
- Infrastructures
- Processes
- Microservices and processes
- What are containers?
- Learning about the main concepts of containers
- Docker components
- Building, shipping, and running workflows
- Windows containers

- Customizing Docker
- Docker security

Let's get started!

Technical requirements

In this chapter, we will learn about various Docker Engine concepts. We'll provide some labs at the end of this chapter that will help you understand and learn about the concepts shown. These labs can be run on your laptop or PC using the provided Vagrant standalone environment or any already deployed Docker host that you own. You can find additional information in this book's GitHub repository: `https://github.com/PacktPublishing/Docker-Certified-Associate-DCA-Exam-Guide.git`

Check out the following video to see the Code in Action:

`"https://bit.ly/3jikiSl"`

Understanding the evolution of applications

As we will probably read about on every IT medium, the concept of microservices is key in the development of new modern applications. Let's go back in time a little to see how applications have been developed over the years.

Monolithic applications are applications in which all components are combined into a single program that usually runs on a single platform. These applications were not designed with reusability in mind, nor any kind of modularity, for that matter. This means that every time a part of their code required an update, all the applications had to be involved in the process; for example, having to recompile all the application code in order for it to work. Of course, things were not so strict then.

Applications grew in number in terms of tasks and functionalities, with some of these tasks being distributed to other systems or even other smaller applications. However, the core components were kept immutable. We used this model of programming because running all application components together, on the same host, was better than trying to find some required information from other hosts. Network speed was insufficient in this regard, however. These applications were difficult to scale and difficult to upgrade. In fact, certain applications were locked to specific hardware and operating systems, which meant that developers needed to have the same hardware architectures at development stages to evolve applications.

We will discuss the infrastructure associated with these monolithic applications in the next section. The following diagram represents how the decoupling of tasks or functionalities has evolved from monolithic applications to **Simple Object Access Protocol (SOAP)** applications and the new paradigm of microservices:

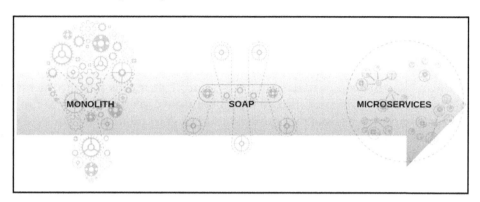

In trying to achieve better application performance and decoupling components, we moved to three-tier architectures, based on a presentation tier, an application tier, and a data tier. This allowed different types of administrators and developers to be involved in application updates and upgrades. Each layer could be running on different hosts, but components only talked to one another inside the same application.

This model is still present in our data centers right now, separating frontends from application backends before reaching the database, where all the requisite data is stored. These components evolved to provide scalability, high availability, and management. On occasion, we had to include new middleware components to achieve these functionalities (thus adding to the final equation; for example, application servers, applications for distributed transactions, queueing, and load balancers). Updates and upgrades were easier, and we isolated components to focus our developers on those different application functionalities.

This model was extended and it got even better with the emergence of virtual machines in our data centers. We will cover how virtual machines have improved the application of this model in more detail in the next section.

As Linux systems have grown in popularity, the interaction between different components, and eventually different applications, has become a requirement. SOAP and other queueing message integration have helped applications and components exchange their information, and networking improvements in our data centers have allowed us to start distributing these elements in different nodes, or even locations.

Microservices are a step further to decoupling application components into smaller units. We usually define a microservice as a small unit of business functionality that we can develop and deploy standalone. With this definition, an application will be a compound of many microservices. Microservices are very light in terms of host resource usage, and this allows them to start and stop very quickly. Also, it allows us to move application health from a high availability concept to resilience, assuming that the process dies (this can be caused by problems or just a component code update) and we need to start a new one as quickly as possible to keep our main functionality healthy.

Microservices architecture comes with stateless in mind. This means that the microservice state should be managed outside of its own logic because we need to be able to run many replicas for our microservice (scale up or down) and run its content on all nodes of our environment, as required by our global load, for example. We decoupled the functionality from the infrastructure (we will see how far this concept of "run everywhere" can go in the next chapter).

Microservices provide the following features:

- Managing an application in pieces allows us to substitute a component for a newer version or even a completely new functionality without losing application functionality.
- Developers can focus on one particular application feature or functionality, and will just need to know how to interact with other, similar pieces.
- Microservices interaction will usually be effected using standard HTTP/HTTPS API **Representational State Transfer** (**REST**) calls. The objective of RESTful systems is to increase the speed of performance, reliability, and the ability to scale.
- Microservices are components that are prepared to have isolated life cycles. This means that one unhealthy component will not wholly affect application usage. We will provide resilience to each component, and an application will not have full outages.
- Each microservice can be written in different programming languages, allowing us to choose the best one for maximum performance and portability.

Now that we have briefly reviewed the well-known application architectures that have developed over the years, let's take a look at the concept of modern applications.

A modern application has the following features:

- The components will be based on microservices.
- The application component's health will be based on resilience.
- The component's states will be managed externally.
- It will run everywhere.
- It will be prepared for easy component updates.
- Each application component will be able to run on its own but will provide a way to be consumed by other components.

Let's take a look.

Infrastructures

For every described application model that developers are using for their applications, we need to provide some aligned infrastructure architecture.

On monolithic applications, as we have seen, all application functionalities run together. In some cases, applications were built for a specific architecture, operating system, libraries, binary versions, and so on. This means that we need at least one hardware node for production and the same node architecture, and eventually resources, for development. If we add the previous environments to this equation, such as certification or preproduction for performance testing, for example, the number of nodes for each application would be very important in terms of physical space, resources, and money spent on an application.

For each application release, developers usually need to have a full production-like environment, meaning that only configurations will be different between environments. This is hard because when any operating system component or feature gets updated, changes must be replicated on all application environments. There are many tools to help us with these tasks, but it is not easy, and the cost of having almost-replicated environments is something to look at. And, on the other hand, node provision could take months because, in many cases, a new application release would mean having to buy new hardware.

Third-tier applications would usually be deployed on old infrastructures using application servers to allow application administrators to scale up components whenever possible and prioritize some components over others.

With virtual machines in our data centers, we were able to distribute host hardware resources between virtual nodes. This was a revolution in terms of node provision time and the costs of maintenance and licensing. Virtual machines worked very well on monolithic and third-tier applications, but application performance depends on the host shared resources that are applied to the virtual node. Deploying application components on different virtual nodes was a common use case because it allowed us to run these virtually everywhere. On the other hand, we were still dependent on operating system resources and releases, so building a new release was dependent on the operating system.

From a developer's perspective, having different environments for building components, testing them side by side, and certificating applications became very easy. However, these new infrastructure components needed new administrators and efforts to provide nodes for development and deployment. In fast-growing enterprises with many changes in their applications, this model helps significantly in providing tools and environments to developers. However, agility problems persist when new applications have to be created weekly or if we need to accomplish many releases/fixes per day. New provisioning tools such as Ansible or Puppet allowed virtualization administrators to provide these nodes faster than ever, but as infrastructures grew, management became complicated.

Local data centers were rendered obsolete and although it took time, infrastructure teams started to use computer cloud providers. They started with a couple of services, such as **Infrastructure as a Service (IaaS)**, that allowed us to deploy virtual nodes on the cloud as if they were on our data center. With new networking speeds and reliability, it was easy to start deploying our applications everywhere, data centers started to get smaller, and applications began to run on distributed environments on different cloud providers. For easy automation, cloud providers prepared their infrastructure's API for us, allowing users to deploy virtual machines in minutes.

However, as many virtualization options appeared, other options based on Linux kernel features and its isolation models came into being, reclaiming some old projects from the past, such as chroot and jail environments (quite common on **Berkeley Software Distribution (BSD)** operating systems) or Solaris zones.

The concept of process containers is not new; in fact, it is more than 10 years old. Process containers were designed to isolate certain resources, such as CPU, memory, disk I/O, or the network, to a group of processes. This concept is what is now known as **control groups** (also known as **cgroups**).

This following diagram shows a rough timeline regarding the introduction of containers to enterprise environments:

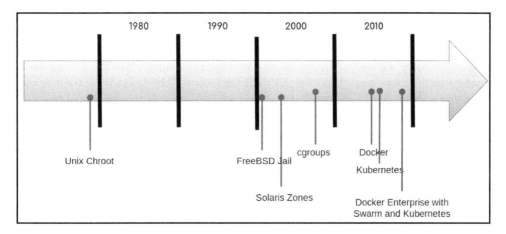

A few years later, a container manager implementation was released to provide an easy way to control the usage of cgroups, while also integrating Linux namespaces. This project was named **Linux Containers (LXC)**, is still available today, and was crucial for others in finding an easy way to improve process isolation usage.

In 2013, a new vision of how containers should run on our environments was introduced, providing an easy-to-use interface for containers. It started with an open source solution, and Solomon Hykes, among others, started what became known as Docker, Inc. They quickly provided a set of tools for running, creating, and sharing containers with the community. Docker, Inc. started to grow very rapidly as containers became increasingly popular.

Containers have been a great revolution for our applications and infrastructures and we are going to explore this area further as we progress.

Processes

A process is a way in which we can interact with an underlying operating system. We can describe a program as a set of coded instructions to execute on our system; a process will be that code in action. During process execution, it will use system resources, such as CPU and memory, and although it will run on its own environment, it can share information with another process that runs in parallel on the same system. Operating systems provide tools that allow us to manipulate the behavior of this process during execution.

Each process in a system is identified uniquely by what is called the process identifier. Parent-child relations between processes are created when a process calls a new one during its execution. The second process becomes a subprocess of the first one (this is its child process) and we will have information regarding this relationship with what is called the parent PID.

Processes run because a user or other process launched it. This allows the system to know who launched that action, and the owner of that process will be known by their user ID. Effective ownership of child processes is implicit when the main process uses impersonation to create them. New processes will use the main process designated user.

For interaction with the underlying system, each process runs with its own environment variables and we can also manipulate this environment with the built-in features of the operating system.

Processes can open, write, and close files as needed and use pointers to descriptors during execution for easy access to this filesystem's resources.

All processes running on a system are managed by operating system kernels and have also been scheduled on CPU by the kernel. The operating system kernel will be responsible for providing system resources to process and interact with system devices.

To summarize, we can say that the kernel is the part of the operating system that interfaces with host hardware, using different forms of isolation for operating system processes under the definition of **kernel space**. Other processes will run under the definition of **user space**. Kernel space has a higher priority for resources and manages user space.

These definitions are common to all modern operating systems and will be crucial in understanding containers. Now that we know how processes are identified and that there is isolation between the system and its users, we can move on to the next section and understand how containers match microservices programming.

Microservices and processes

So far, we have briefly reviewed a number of different application models (monolith, SOAP, and the new microservices architecture) and we have defined microservices as the minimum piece of software with functionality that we can build as a component for an application.

With this definition, we will associate a microservice with a process. This is the most common way of running microservices. A process with full functionality can be described as a microservice.

An application is composed of microservices, and hence processes, as expected. The interaction between them will usually be made using HTTP/HTTPS/API REST.

This is, of course, a definition, but we recommend this approach to ensure proper microservice health management.

What are containers?

So far, we have defined microservices and how processes fit in this model. As we saw previously, containers are related to process isolation. We will define a container as a process with all its requirements isolated with kernel features. This package-like object will contain all the code and its dependencies, libraries, binaries, and settings that are required to run our process. With this definition, it is easy to understand why containers are so popular in microservices environments, but, of course, we can execute microservices without containers. On the contrary, we can run containers with a full application, with many processes that don't need to be isolated from each other inside this package-like object.

In terms of multi-process containers, what is the difference between a virtual machine and containers? Let's review container features against virtual machines.

Containers are mainly based on cgroups and kernel namespaces.

Virtual machines, on the other hand, are based on hypervisor software. This software, which can run as part of the operating system in many cases, will provide sandboxed resources to the guest virtualized hardware that runs a virtual machine operating system. This means that each virtual machine will run its own operating system and allow us to execute different operating systems on the same hardware host. When virtual machines arrived, people started to use them as sandboxed environments for testing, but as hypervisors gained in maturity, data centers started to have virtual machines in production, and now this is common and standard practice in cloud providers (cloud providers currently offer hardware as a service, too).

In this schema, we're showing the different logic layers, beginning with the machine hardware. We will have many layers for executing a process inside virtual machines. Each virtual machine will have its own operating system and services, even if we are just running a single process:

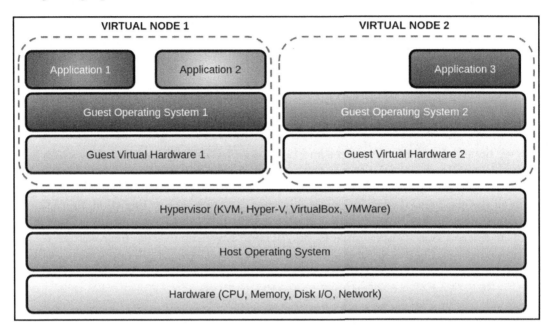

Each virtual machine will get a portion of resources and guest operating systems, and the kernel will manage how they are shared among different running processes. Each virtual machine will execute its own kernel and the operating system running on top of those of the host. There is complete isolation between the guest operating systems because hypervisor software will keep them separated. On the other hand, there is an overhead associated with running multiple operating systems side by side and when microservices come to mind, this solution wastes numerous host resources. Just running the operating system will consume a lot of resources. Even the fastest hardware nodes with fast SSD disks require resources and time to start and stop virtual machines. As we have seen, microservices are just a process with complete functionality inside an application, so running the entire operating system for just a couple of processes doesn't seem like a good idea.

On each guest host, we need to configure everything needed for our microservice. This means access, users, configurations, networking, and more. In fact, we need administrators for these systems as if they were bare-metal nodes. This requires a significant amount of effort and is the reason why configuration management tools are so popular these days.

Ansible, Puppet, Chef, and SaltStack, among others, help us to homogenize our environments. However, remember that developers need their own environments, too, so multiply these resources by all the required environments in the development pipeline.

How can we scale up on service peaks? Well, we have virtual machine templates and, currently, almost all hypervisors allow us to interact with them using the command line or their own administrative API implementations, so it is easy to copy or clone a node for scaling application components. But this will require double the resources – remember that we will run another complete operating system with its own resources, filesystems, network, and so on. Virtual machines are not the perfect solution for elastic services (which can scale up and down, run everywhere, and are created on-demand in many cases).

Containers will share the same kernel because they are just isolated processes. We will just add a templated filesystem and resources (CPU, memory, disk I/O, network, and so on, and, in some cases, host devices) to a process. It will run sandboxed inside and will only use its defined environment. As a result, containers are lightweight and start and stop as fast as their main processes. In fact, containers are as lightweight as the processes they run, since we don't have anything else running inside a container. All the resources that are consumed by a container are process-related. This is great in terms of hardware resource allocation. We can find out the real consumption of our application by observing the load of all of its microservices.

 Containers are a perfect solution for microservices as they will run only one process inside. This process should have all the required functionality for a specific task, as we described in terms of microservices.

Similar to virtual machines, there is the concept of a template for container creation called Image. Docker images are standard for many container runtimes. They ensure that all containers that are created from a container image will run with the same properties and features. In other words, this eliminates the *it works on my computer!* problem.

Docker containers improve security in our environments because they are secure by default. Kernel isolation and the kind of resources managed inside containers provide a secure environment during execution. There are many ways to improve this security further, as we will see in the following chapters. By default, containers will run with a limited set of system calls allowed.

This schema describes the main differences between running processes on different virtual machines and using containers:

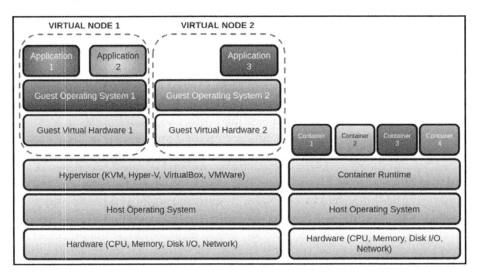

Containers are faster to deploy and manage, lightweight, and secure by default. Because of their speed upon execution, containers are aligned with the concept of resilience. And because of the package-like environment, we can run containers everywhere. We only need a container runtime to execute deployments on any cloud provider, as we do on our data centers. The same concept will be applied to all development stages, so integration and performance tests can be run with confidence. If the previous tests were passed, since we are using the same artifact across all stages, we can ensure its execution in production.

In the following chapters, we will dive deep into Docker container components. For now, however, just think of a Docker container as a sandboxed process that runs in our system, isolated from all other running processes on the same host, based on a template named Docker Image.

Learning about the main concepts of containers

When talking about containers, we need to understand the main concepts behind the scenes. Let's decouple the container concept into different pieces and try to understand each one in turn.

Container runtime

The runtime for running containers will be the software and operating system features that make process execution and isolation possible.

Docker, Inc. provides a container runtime named Docker, based on open source projects sponsored by them and other well-known enterprises that empower container movement (Red Hat/IBM and Google, among many others). This container runtime comes packaged with other components and tools. We will analyze each one in detail in the *Docker components* section.

Images

We use images as templates for creating containers. Images will contain everything required by our process or processes to run correctly. These components can be binaries, libraries, configuration files, and so on that can be a part of operating system files or just components built by yourself for this application.

Images, like templates, are immutable. This means that they don't change between executions. Every time we use an image, we will get the same results. We will only change configuration and environment to manage the behavior of different processes between environments. Developers will create their application component template and they can be sure that if the application passed all the tests, it will work in production as expected. These features ensure faster workflows and less time to market.

Docker images are built up from a series of layers, and all these layers packaged together contain everything required for running our application process. All these layers are read-only and the changes are stored in the next upper layer during image creation. This way, each layer only has a set of differences from the layer before it.

Layers are packaged to allow ease of transport between different systems or environments, and they include meta-information about the required architecture to run (will it run on Linux or Windows, or does it require an ARM processor, for example?). Images include information about how the process should be run, which user will execute the main process, where persistent data will be stored, what ports your process will expose in order to communicate with other components or users, and more.

Images can be built with reproducible methods using Dockerfiles or store changes made on running containers to obtain a new image:

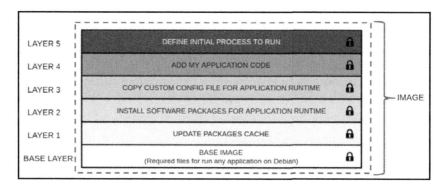

This was a quick review of images. Now, let's take a look at containers.

Containers

As we described earlier, a container is a process with all its requirements that runs separately from all the other processes running on the same host. Now that we know what templates are, we can say that containers are created using images as templates. In fact, a container adds a new read-write layer on top of image layers in order to store filesystem differences from these layers. The following diagram represents the different layers involved in container execution. As we can observe, the top layer is what we really call the container because it is read-write and allows changes to be stored on the host disk:

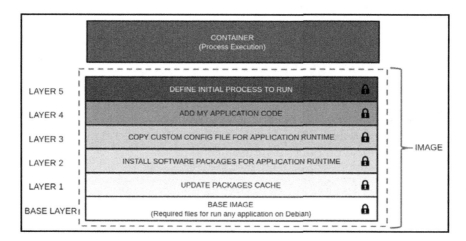

All image layers are read-only layers, which means all the changes are stored in the container's read-write layer. This means that all these changes will be lost when we remove a container from a host, but the image will remain until we remove it. Images are immutable and always remain unchanged.

This container behavior lets us run many containers using the same underlying image, and each one will store changes on its own read-write layer. The following diagram represents how different images will use the same image layers. All three containers are based on the same image:

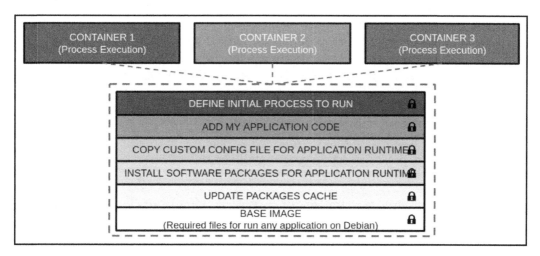

There are different approaches to managing image layers when building and container layers on execution. Docker uses storage drivers to manage this content, on read-only layers and read-write ones. These drivers are operating system-dependent, but they all implement what is known as copy-on-write filesystems.

A storage driver (known as **graph-driver**) will manage how Docker will store and manage the interactions between layers. As we mentioned previously, there are different drivers integrations available, and Docker will choose the best one for your system, depending on your host's kernel and operating system. **Overlay2** is the most common and preferred driver for Linux operating systems. Others, such as aufs, overlay, and btfs, among others, are also available, but keep in mind that overlay2 is recommended for production environments on modern operating systems.

Devicemapper is also a supported graph driver and it was very common on Red Hat environments before overlay2 was supported on modern operating system releases (Red Hat 7.6 and above). Devicemapper uses block devices for storing layers and can be deployed in observance of two different strategies: `loopback-lvm` (by default and only for testing purposes) and `direct-lvm` (requires additional block device pool configurations and is intended for production environments). This link provides the required steps for deploying: `direct-lvm`: `https://docs.docker.com/storage/storagedriver/device-mapper-driver/`

As you may have noticed, using copy-on-write filesystems will make containers very small in terms of disk space usage. All common files are shared between the same image-based containers. They just store differences from immutable files that are part of image layers. Consequently, container layers will be very small (of course, this depends on what you are storing on containers, but keep in mind that good containers are small). When an existing file in a container has to be modified (remember a file that comes from underlying layers), the storage driver will perform a copy operation to the container layer. This process is fast, but keep in mind that everything that is going to be changed on containers will follow this process. As a reference, don't use copy-on-write with heavy I/O operations, nor process logs.

Copy-on-write is a strategy for creating maximum efficiency and small layer-based filesystems. This storage strategy works by copying files between layers. When a layer needs to change a file from another underlaying layer, it will be copied to this top one. If it just needs read access, it will use it from underlying layers. This way, I/O access is minimized and the size of the layers is very small.

A common question that many people ask is whether containers are ephemeral. The short answer is *no*. In fact, containers are not ephemeral for a host. This means that when we create or run a container on that host, it will remain there until someone removes it. We can start a stopped container on the same host if it is not deleted yet. Everything that was inside this container before will be there, but it is not a good place to store process state because it is only local to that host. If we want to be able to run containers everywhere and use orchestration tools to manage their states, processes must use external resources to store their status.

As we'll see in later chapters, Swarm or Kubernetes will manage service or application component status and, if a required container fails, it will create a new container. Orchestration will create a new container instead of reusing the old one because, in many cases, this new process will be executed elsewhere in the clustered pool of hosts. So, it is important to understand that your application components that will run as containers must be logically ephemeral and that their status should be managed outside containers (database, external filesystem, inform other services, and so on).

The same concept will be applied in terms of networking. Usually, you will let a container runtime or orchestrator manage container IP addresses for simplicity and dynamism. Unless strictly necessary, don't use fixed IP addresses, and let internal IPAMs configure them for you.

Networking in containers is based on host bridge interfaces and firewall-level NAT rules. A Docker container runtime will manage the creation of virtual interfaces for containers and process isolation between different logical networks creating mentioned rules. We will see all the network options provided and their use cases in Chapter 4, *Container Persistency and Networking*. In addition, publishing an application is managed by the runtime and orchestration will add different properties and many other options.

Using volumes will let us manage the interaction between the process and the container filesystem. Volumes will bypass the copy-on-write filesystem and hence writing will be much faster. In addition to this, data stored in a volume will not follow the container life cycle. This means that even if we delete the container that was using that volume, all the data that was stored there will remain until someone deletes it. We can define a volume as the mechanism we will use to persist data between containers. We will learn that volumes are an easy way to share data between containers and deploy applications that need to persist their data during the life of the application (for example, databases or static content). Using volumes will not increase container layer size, but using them locally will require additional host disk resources under the Docker filesystem/directory tree.

Process isolation

As we mentioned previously, a kernel provides namespaces for process isolation. Let's review what each namespace provides. Each container runs with its own kernel namespaces for the following:

- **Processes**: The main process will be the parent of all other ones within the container.
- **Network**: Each container will get its own network stack with its own interfaces and IP addresses and will use host interfaces.

- **Users**: We will be able to map container user IDs with different host user IDs.
- **IPC**: Each container will have its own shared memory, semaphores, and message queues without conflicting other processes on the host.
- **Mounts**: Each container will have its own root filesystem and we can provide external mounts, which we will learn about in upcoming chapters.
- **UTS**: Each container will get its own hostname and time will be synced with the host.

The following diagram represents a process tree from the host perspective and inside a container. Processes inside a container are namespaced and, as a result, their parent PID will be the main process, with its own PID of 1:

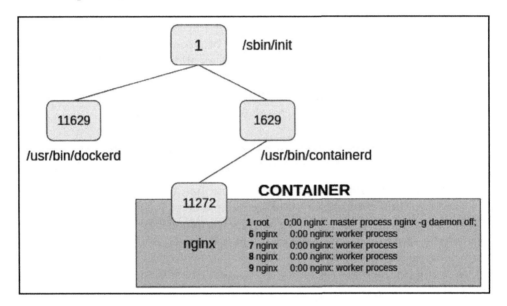

Namespaces have been available in Linux since version 2.6.26 (July 2008), and they provide the first level of isolation for a process running within a container so that it won't see others. This means they cannot affect other processes running on the host or in any other container. The maturity level of these kernel features allows us to trust in Docker namespace isolation implementation.

Networking is isolated too, as each container gets its own network stack, but communications will pass through host bridge interfaces. Every time we create a Docker network for containers, we will create a new network bridge, which we will learn more about in Chapter 4, *Container Persistency and Networking*. This means that containers sharing a network, which is a host bridge interface, will see one another, but all other containers running on a different interface will not have access to them. Orchestration will add different approaches to container runtime networking but, at the host level, described rules are applied.

Host resources available to a container are managed by control groups. This isolation will not allow a container to bring down a host by exhausting its resources. You should not allow containers with non-limited resources in production. This must be mandatory in multi-tenant environments.

Orchestration

This book contains a general chapter about orchestration, Chapter 7, *Introduction to Orchestration*, and two specific chapters devoted to Swarm and Kubernetes, respectively, Chapter 8, *Orchestration Using Docker Swarm*, and Chapter 9, *Orchestration Using Kubernetes*. Orchestration is the mechanism that will manage container interactions, publishing, and health in clustered pools of hosts. It will allow us to deploy an application based on many components or containers and keep it healthy during its entire life cycle. With orchestration, component updates are easy because it will take care of the required changes in the platform to accomplish a new, appropriate state.

Deploying an application using orchestration will require a number of instances for our process or processes, the expected state, and instructions for managing its life during execution. Orchestration will provide new objects, communication between containers running on different hosts, features for running containers on specific nodes within the cluster, and the mechanisms to keep the required number of process replicas alive with the desired release version.

Swarm is included inside Docker binaries and comes as standard. It is easy to deploy and manage. Its unit of deployment is known as a **service**. In a Swarm environment, we don't deploy containers because containers are not managed by orchestration. Instead, we deploy services and those services will be represented by tasks, which will run containers to maintain its state.

Currently, Kubernetes is the most widely used form of orchestration. It requires extra deployment effort using a Docker community container runtime. It adds many features, multi-container objects known as **pods** that share a networking layer, and flat networking for all orchestrated pods, among other things. Kubernetes is community-driven and evolves very fast. One of the features that makes this platform so popular is the availability to create your own kind of resources, allowing us to develop new extensions when they are not available.

We will analyze the features of pods and Kubernetes in detail in Chapter 9, *Orchestration Using Kubernetes*.

Docker Enterprise provides orchestrators deployed under Universal Control Plane with high availability on all components.

Registry

We have already learned that containers execute processes within an isolated environment, created from a template image. So, the only requirements for deploying that container on a new node will be the container runtime and the template used to create that container. This template can be shared between nodes using simple Docker command options. But this procedure can become more difficult as the number of nodes grows. To improve image distribution, we will use image registries, which are storage points for these kinds of objects. Each image will be stored in its own repository. This concept is similar to code repositories, allowing us to use tags to describe these images, aligning code releases with image versioning.

An application deployment pipeline has different environments, and having a common point of truth between them will help us to manage these objects through the different workflow stages.

Docker provides two different approaches for registry: the community version and Docker Trusted Registry. The community version does not provide any security at all, nor role-based access to image repositories. On the other hand, Docker Trusted Registry comes with the Docker Enterprise solution and is an enterprise-grade registry, with included security, image vulnerability scanning, integrated workflows, and role-based access. We will learn about Docker Enterprise's registry in Chapter 13, *Implementing an Enterprise-Grade Registry with DTR*.

Docker components

In this section, we are going to describe the main Docker components and binaries used for building, distributing, and deploying containers in all execution stages.

Docker Engine is the core component of container platforms. Docker is a client-server application and Docker Engine will provide the server side. This means that we have the main process that runs as a daemon on the host, and a client-side application that communicates with the server using REST API calls.

 Docker Engine's latest version provides separate packages for the client and the server. On Ubuntu, for example, if we take a look at the available packages, we will have something like this:
   - `docker-ce-cli` – Docker CLI: The open source application container engine
   - `docker-ce` – Docker: The open source application container engine

The following diagram represents Docker daemon and its different levels of management:

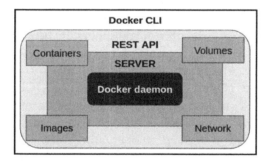

Docker daemon listens for Docker API requests and will be responsible for all Docker object actions, such as creating an image, list volumes, and running a container.

 Docker API is available using a Unix socket by default. Docker API can be used from within code-using interfaces that are available for many programming languages. Querying for running containers can be managed using a Docker client or its API directly; for example, with `curl --no-buffer -XGET --unix-socket /var/run/docker.sock http://localhost/v1.24/containers/json`.

When deploying cluster-wide environments with Swarm orchestration, daemons will share information between them to allow the execution of distributed services within the pool of nodes.

On the other hand, the Docker client will provide users with the command line required to interact with the daemon. It will construct the required API calls with their payloads to tell the daemon which actions it should execute.

Now, let's deep dive into a Docker daemon component to find out more about its behavior and usage.

Docker daemon

Docker daemon will usually run as a systemd-managed service, although it can run as a standalone process (it is very useful when debugging daemon errors, for example). As we have seen previously, `dockerd` provides an API interface that allows clients to send commands and interact with this daemon. `containerd`, in fact, manages containers. It was introduced as a separate daemon in Docker 1.11 and is responsible for managing storage, networking, and interaction between namespaces. Also, it will manage image shipping and then, finally, it will run containers using another external component. This external component, `RunC`, will be the real executor of containers. Its function just receives an order to run a container. These components are part of the community, so the only one that Docker provides is `dockerd`. All other daemon components are community-driven and use standard image specifications (**Open Containers Initiative – OCI**). In 2017, Docker donated `containerd` as part of their contribution to the open source community and is now part of the **Cloud Native Computing Foundation (CNCF)**. OCI was founded as an open governance structure for the express purpose of creating open industry standards around container formats and runtimes in 2015. The CNCF hosts and manages most of the currently most-used components of the newest technology infrastructures. It is a part of the nonprofit Linux Foundation and is involved in projects such as Kubernetes, Containerd, and The Update Framework.

By way of a summary, `dockerd` will manage interaction with the Docker client. To run a container, first, the configuration needs to be created so that daemon triggers `containerd` (using gRPC) to create it. This piece will create an OCI definition that will use `RunC` to run this new container. Docker implements these components with different names (changed between releases), but the concept is still valid.

Docker daemon can listen for Docker Engine API requests on different types of sockets: `unix`, `tcp`, and `fd`. By default, Daemon on Linux will use a Unix domain socket (or IPC socket) that's created at `/var/run/docker.sock` when starting the daemon. Only root and Docker groups can access this socket, so only root and members of the Docker group will be able to create containers, build images, and so on. In fact, access to a socket is required for any Docker action.

Docker client

Docker client is used to interact with a server. It needs to be connected to a Docker daemon to perform any action, such as building an image or running a container.

A Docker daemon and client can run on the same host system, or we can manage a connected remote daemon. The Docker client and daemon communicate using a server-side REST API. This communication can be executed over UNIX sockets (by default) or a network interface, as we learned earlier.

Docker objects

The Docker daemon will manage all kinds of Docker objects using the Docker client command line.

The following are the most common objects at the time of writing this book:

- IMAGE
- CONTAINER
- VOLUME
- NETWORK
- PLUGIN

There are other objects that are only available when we deploy Docker Swarm orchestration:

- NODE
- SERVICE
- SECRET

- CONFIG
- STACK
- SWARM

The Docker command line provides the actions that Docker daemon is allowed to execute via REST API calls. There are common actions such as list (or `ls`), `create`, `rm` (for remove), and `inspect`, and other actions that are restricted to specific objects, such as `cp` (for coping).

For example, we can get a list of running containers on a host by running the following command:

```
$ docker container ls
```

 There are many commonly used aliases, such as `docker ps` for `docker container ls` or `docker run` for `docker container run`. I recommend using a long command-line format because it is easier to remember if we understand which actions are allowed for each object.

There are other tools available on the Docker ecosystem, such as `docker-machine` and `docker-compose`.

Docker Machine is a community tool created by Docker that allows users and administrators to easily deploy Docker Engine on hosts. It was developed in order to fast provision Docker Engine on cloud providers such as Azure and AWS, but it evolved to offer other implementations, and nowadays, it is possible to use many different drivers for many different environments. We can use `docker-machine` to deploy `docker-engine` on VMWare (over Cloud Air, Fusion, Workstation, or vSphere), Microsoft Hyper-V, and OpenStack, among others. It is also very useful for quick labs, or demonstration and test environments on VirtualBox or KVM, and it even allows us to provision `docker-engine` software using SSH. `docker-machine` runs on Windows and Linux, and provides an integration between client and provisioned Docker host daemons. This way, we can interact with its Docker daemon remotely, without being connected using SSH, for example.

On the other hand, Docker Compose is a tool that will allow us to run multi-container applications on a single host. We will just introduce this concept here in relation to multi-service applications that will run on Swarm or Kubernetes clusters. We will learn about `docker-compose` in Chapter 5, *Deploying Multi-Container Applications*.

Building, shipping, and running workflows

Docker provides the tools for creating images (templates for containers, remember), distributing those images to systems other than the one used for building the image, and finally, running containers based on these images:

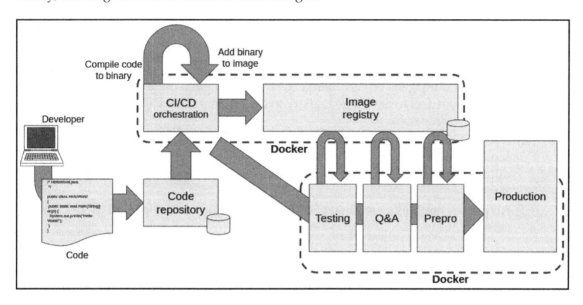

Docker Engine will participate in all workflow steps, and we can use just one host or many during these processes, including our developers' laptops.

Let's provide a quick review of the usual workflow processes.

Building

Building applications using containers is easy. Here are the standard steps:

1. The developer usually codes an application on their own computer.
2. When the code is ready, or there is a new release, new functionalities, or a bug has simply been fixed, a commit is deployed.
3. If our code has to be compiled, we can do it at this stage. If we are using an interpreted language for our code, we will just add it to the next stage.
4. Either manually or using continuous integration orchestration, we can create a Docker image integrating compiled binary or interpreted code with the required runtime and all its dependencies. Images are our new component artifacts.

We have passed the building stage and the built image, with everything included, must be deployed to production. But first, we need to ensure its functionality and health (Will it work? How about performance?). We can do all these tests on different environments using the image artifact we created.

Shipping

Sharing created artifacts is easier with containers. Here are some of the new steps:

1. The created image is on our build host system (or even on our laptop). We will push this artifact to an image registry to ensure that it is available for the next workflow processes.
2. Docker Enterprise provides integrations on Docker Trusted Registry to follow separate steps from the first push, image scanning to look for vulnerabilities, and different image pulls from different environments during continuous integration stages.
3. All pushes and pulls are managed by Docker Engine and triggered by Docker clients.

Now that the image has been shipped on different environments, during integration and performance tests, we need to launch containers using environment variables or configurations for each stage.

Running

So, we have new artifacts that are easy to share between different environments, but we need to execute them in production. Here are some of the benefits of containers for our applications:

- All environments will use Docker Engine to execute our containers (processes), but that's all. We don't really need any portion of software other than Docker Engine to execute the image correctly (naturally, we have simplified this idea because we will need volumes and external resources in many cases).
- If our image passed all the tests defined in the workflow, it is ready for production, and this step will be as simple as deploying the image built originally on the previous environment, using all the required arguments and environment variables or configurations for production.

- If our environments were orchestration-managed using Swarm or Kubernetes, all these steps would have been run securely, with resilience, using internal load balancers, and with required replicas, among other properties, that this kind of platform provides.

As a summary, keep in mind that Docker Engine provides all the actions required for building, shipping, and running container-based applications.

Windows containers

Containers started with Linux, but nowadays, we can run and orchestrate containers on Windows. Microsoft integrated containers on Windows in Windows 2016. With this release, they consolidated a partnership with Docker to create a container engine that runs containers natively on Windows.

After a few releases, Microsoft decided to have two different approaches to containers on Windows, these being the following:

- **Windows Server Containers (WSC)**, or process containers
- Hyper-V Containers

Because of the nature of Windows operating system implementation, we can share kernels but we can't isolate processes from the system services and DLLs. In this situation, process containers need a copy of the required system services and many DLLs to be able to make API calls to the underlying host operating system. This means that containers that use process container isolation will run with many system processes and DLLs inside. In this case, images are very big and will have a different kind of portability; we will only be able to run Windows containers based on the same underlying operating system version.

As we have seen, process containers need to copy a portion of the underlying operating system inside in order to run. This means that we can only run the same operating system containers. For example, running containers on top of Windows Server 2016 will require a Windows Server 2016 base image.

On the other hand, Hyper-V containers will not have these limitations because they will run on top of a virtualized kernel. This adds overhead, but the isolation is substantially better. In this case, we won't be able to run these kinds of containers on older Microsoft Windows versions. These containers will use optimized virtualization to isolate the new kernel for our process.

The following diagram represents both types of MS Windows container isolation:

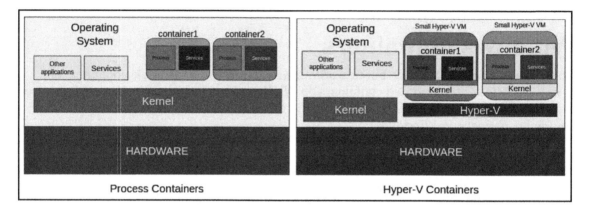

Process Containers   Hyper-V Containers

 Process isolation is a default container isolation on Windows Server, but Windows 10 Pro and Enterprise will run Hyper-V isolation. Since the Windows 10 October 2018 update, we can choose to use old-style process isolation with the `--isolation=process` flag on Windows 10 Pro and Enterprise.
Please check the Windows operating system's portability because this is a very common problem on Windows containers.

Networking in Windows containers is different from Linux. The Docker host uses a Hyper-V virtual switch to provide connectivity to containers and connects them to virtual switches using either a host virtual interface (Windows Server containers) or a synthetic VM interface (Hyper-V containers).

Customizing Docker

Docker behavior can be managed at daemon and client levels. These configurations can be executed using command-line arguments, environment variables, or definitions on configuration files.

Customizing the Docker daemon

Docker daemon behavior is managed by various configuration files and variables:

- **key.json**: This file contains a unique identifier for this daemon; in fact, it is the daemon's public key that uses the JSON web key format.
- **daemon.json**: This is the Docker daemon configuration file. It contains all its parameters in JSON format. It has a key-value (or list of values) format in which all the daemon's flags will be available to modify its behavior. Be careful with configurations implemented on the `systemd` service file because they must not conflict with options set via the JSON file; otherwise, the daemon will fail to start.
- **Environment variables**: HTTPS_PROXY, HTTP_PROXY, and NO_PROXY (or using lowercase) will manage the utilization of Docker daemon and the client behind the proxies. The configuration can be implemented in the Docker daemon `systemd` unit config files using, for example, `/etc/systemd/system/docker.service.d/http-proxy.conf`, and following the content for HTTPS_PROXY (the same configuration might be applied to HTTP_PROXY):

```
[Service]
Environment="HTTPS_PROXY=https://proxy.example.com:443/"
"NO_PROXY=localhost,127.0.0.1,docker-registry.example.com,.corp"
```

Be careful with the `key.json` file while cloning virtual machines because using the same keys on different daemons will result in strange behaviors. This file is owned by system administrators, so you will need to use a privileged user to review its content. This JSON file contains Docker Daemon's certificate in JSON Web Key format. We can just review the `key.json` file's content using the `cat` and `jq` commands (`jq` is not required, but I used it to format output. This command will help with JSON files or JSON output):

```
$ sudo cat /etc/docker/key.json |jq
{
  "crv": "P-256",
  "d": "f_RvzIUEPu3oo7GLohd9cxqDlT9gQyXSfeWoOnM0ZLU",
  "kid": "QP6X:5YVF:FZAC:ETDZ:HOHI:KJV2:JIZW:
         IG47:3GU6:YQJ4:YRGF:VKMP",
  "kty": "EC",
  "x": "y4HbXr4BKRi5zECbJdGYvFE2KtMp9DZfPL81r_qe52I",
  "y": "ami9cOOKSA8joCMwW-y96G2mBGwcXthYz3FuK-mZe14"
}
```

The daemon configuration file, `daemon.json`, will be located by default at the following locations:

- `/etc/docker/daemon.json` on Linux systems
- `%programdata%\docker\config\daemon.json` on Windows systems

In both cases, the configuration file's location can be changed using `--config-file` to specify a custom non-default file.

Let's provide a quick review of the most common and important flags or keys we will configure for Docker daemon. Some of these options are so important that they are usually referenced in the Docker Certified Associate exam. Don't worry; we will learn about the most important ones, along with their corresponding JSON keys, here:

Daemon argument	JSON key	Argument description
`-b, --bridge` string	`bridge`	Attach containers to a network bridge. This option allows us to change the default bridge behavior. In some cases, it's useful to create your own bridge interfaces and use the Docker daemon attached to one of them.
`--cgroup-parent` string	`cgroup-parent`	Set the parent cgroup for all containers.
`-D, --debug`	`debug`	This option enables debug mode, which is fundamental to resolving issues. Usually, it's better to stop Docker service and run the Docker daemon by hand using the `-D` option to review all `dockerd` debugging events.
`--data-root` string	`data-root`	This is the root directory of the persistent Docker state (default `/var/lib/docker`). With this option, we can change the path to store all Docker data (Swarm KeyValue, images, internal volumes, and so on).
`--dns` list	`dns`	This is the DNS server to use (default [ ]). These three options allow us to change the container DNS behavior, for example, to use a specific DNS for the container environment.
`--dns-opt` list	`dns-opt`	These are the DNS options to use (default [ ]).
`--dns-search` list	`dns-search`	These are the DNS search domains to use (default [ ]).
`--experimental`	`experimental`	This enables experimental features; don't use it in production.
`-G, --group` string	`group`	This is the group for the Unix socket (default `docker`).

`-H, --host` list	`host`	This is the option that allows us to specify the socket(s) to use.
`--icc`	`icc`	This enables inter-container communication (default `true`). With this option, we can disable any container's internal communications.
`--ip` IP	`ip`	This is the default IP when binding container ports (default `0.0.0.0`). With this option, we can ensure that only specific subnets will have access to container-exposed ports.
`--label` list	`label`	Set key=value labels to the daemon (default `[ ]`). With labels, we can configure environment properties for container location when using a cluster of hosts. There is a better tagging method you can use when using Swarm, as we will learn in `Chapter 8`, *Orchestration Using Docker Swarm*.
`--live-restore`	`live-restore`	This enables the live restoration of Docker when containers are still running.
`--log-driver` string	`log-driver`	This is the default driver for container logs (default `json-file`) if we need to use an external log manager (ELK framework or just a Syslog Server, for example).
`-l, --log-level` string	`log-level`	This sets the logging level (`debug`, `info`, `warn`, `error`, `fatal`) (default `info`).
`--seccomp-profile` string	`seccomp-profile`	This is the path to the seccomp profile if we want to use anything other than the default option.
`--selinux-enabled`	`selinux-enabled`	Enables SELinux support. This option is crucial for production environments using Red Hat Linux/CentOS. It is disabled by default.
`-s, --storage-driver` string	`storage-driver`	This is the storage driver to use. This argument allows us to change the default driver selected by Docker. In the latest versions, we will use `overlay2` because of its stability and performance. Other options include `aufs`, `btrfs`, and `devicemapper`.
`--storage-opt` list	`storage-opts`	Storage driver options (default `[ ]`). Depending on the storage driver used, we will need to add options as arguments, for example, using `devicemapper` or for specifying a maximum container size on `overlay2` or Windows filter (MS Windows copy-on-write implementation).
`--tls`	`tls`	This option enables TLS encryption between client and server (implied by `--tlsverify`).

--tlscacert string	tlscacert	Trust certs signed only by this CA (default ~/.docker/ca.pem).
--tlscert string	tlscert	This is the path to the TLS certificate file (default ~/.docker/cert.pem).
--tlskey string	tlskey	This is the path to the TLS key file (default ~/.docker/key.pem).
--tlsverify	tlsverify	Use TLS and verify the remote.

Logging information in container environments can be deployed using different layers of knowledge. As shown in the previous table, Docker daemon has its own logging configuration using --log-driver. This configuration will be applied to all containers by default if we do not specify any configuration during container execution. Therefore, we can redirect all container logs to some remote logging system using the ELK framework, for example (https://www.elastic.co/es/what-is/elk-stack), while some specific containers can be redirected to another logging backend. This can also be applied locally using different logging drivers.

Docker client customization

The client will store its configuration under the users' home directory on .docker. There is a config file where the Docker client will look for its configurations ($HOME/.docker/config.json on Linux or %USERPROFILE%/.docker/config.json on Windows). In this file, we will set a proxy for our containers if it's needed to connect to the internet or other external services, for example.

If we need to pass proxy settings to containers upon startup, we will configure the proxies key in .docker/config.json for our user, for example, using my-company-proxy:

```
"proxies":
{
    "default":
    {
        "httpProxy": "http://my-company-proxy:3001",
        "httpsProxy": "http://my-company-proxy:3001",
        "noProxy": "*.test.example.com, .example2.com"
    }
}
```

These configurations can be added as arguments when starting up the Docker container, as follows:

```
--env HTTP_PROXY="http://my-company-proxy:3001"
--env HTTPS_PROXY="https://my-company-proxy:3001"
--env NO_PROXY="*.test.example.com,.example2.com"
```

We will see what "environment option" means in Chapter 3, *Running Docker Containers*. Just keep in mind that, sometimes, our corporate environment will need applications to use proxies and that there are methods to configure these settings, either as user variables or using client configurations.

Other client features, such as experimental flags or output formatting, will be configured in the config.json file. Here is an example of some configurations:

```
{
  "psFormat": "table {{.ID}}\\t{{.Image}}\\t{{.Command}}\\t{{.Labels}}",
  "imagesFormat": "table
{{.ID}}\\t{{.Repository}}\\t{{.Tag}}\\t{{.CreatedAt}}",
  "statsFormat": "table {{.Container}}\t{{.CPUPerc}}\t{{.MemUsage}}"
}
```

Docker security

There are many topics related to container security. In this chapter, we will review the ones related to the container runtime.

As we have seen, Docker provides a client-server environment. From the client side, there are a few things that will improve the way in which we will be able to access the environment.

Configuration files and certificates for different clusters on hosts must be secured using filesystem security at the operating system level. However, as you should have noticed, a Docker client always needs a server in order to do anything with containers. Docker client is just the tool to connect to servers. With this picture in mind, client-server security is a must. Now, let's take a look at different kinds of access to the Docker daemon.

Docker client-server security

The Docker daemon will listen on system sockets (unix, tcp, and fd). We have seen that we can change this behavior and that, by default, the daemon will listen on the /var/run/docker.sock local Unix socket.

Giving users RW access to `/var/run/docker.sock` will add access to the local Docker daemon. This allows them to create images, run containers (even privileged, root user containers, and mount local filesystems inside them), create images, and more. It is very important to know who can use your Docker engine. If you deployed a Docker Swarm cluster, this is even worse because if the accessed host has a master role, the user will be able to create a service that will run containers across the entirety of the cluster. So keep your Docker daemon socket safe from non-trusted users and only allow authorized ones (in fact, we will look at other advanced mechanisms to provide secure user access to the container platform).

 Docker daemon is secure by default because it does not export its service. We can enable remote TCP accesses by adding `-H tcp://<HOST_IP>` to the Docker daemon start process. By default, port `2375` will be used. If we use 0.0.0.0 as the host IP address, Docker daemon will listen on all interfaces.

We can enable remote access to Docker daemon using a TCP socket. By default, communication will not be secure and the daemon will listen on port `2375`. To ensure that the client-to-daemon connection is encrypted, you will need to use either a reverse proxy or built-in TLS-based HTTPS encrypted socket. We can allow the daemon to listen on all host interface IP addresses or just one using this IP when starting the daemon. To use TLS-based communications, we need to follow this procedure (assuming your server hostname is in the `$HOST` variable):

1. Create a **certificate authority** (**CA**). The following commands will create its private and public keys:

```
$ openssl genrsa -aes256 -out ca-key.pem 4096
 Generating RSA private key, 4096 bit long modulus
.......................................................................................
.......................................................................................
.........................................................++
.......++
 e is 65537 (0x10001)
 Enter pass phrase for ca-key.pem:
 Verifying - Enter pass phrase for ca-key.pem:
 $ openssl req -new -x509 -days 365 -key ca-key.pem -sha256 -out
ca.pem
 Enter pass phrase for ca-key.pem:
 You are about to be asked to enter information that will be
incorporated
 into your certificate request.
 What you are about to enter is what is called a Distinguished Name
or a DN.
 There are quite a few fields but you can leave some blank
```

```
For some fields there will be a default value,
If you enter '.', the field will be left blank.
-----
Country Name (2 letter code) [AU]:
State or Province Name (full name) [Some-State]:Queensland
Locality Name (eg, city) []:Brisbane
Organization Name (eg, company) [Internet Widgits Pty Ltd]:Docker
Inc
Organizational Unit Name (eg, section) []:Sales
Common Name (e.g. server FQDN or YOUR name) []:$HOST
Email Address []:Sven@home.org.au
```

2. Create a server CA-signed key, ensuring that the common name matches the hostname you use to connect to Docker daemon from the client:

```
$ openssl genrsa -out server-key.pem 4096
Generating RSA private key, 4096 bit long modulus
.............................................................
..++
.............................................................
................................++
e is 65537 (0x10001)

$ openssl req -subj "/CN=$HOST" -sha256 -new -key server-key.pem -
out server.csr
 $ echo subjectAltName = DNS:$HOST,IP:10.10.10.20,IP:127.0.0.1 >>
extfile.cnf
 $ echo extendedKeyUsage = serverAuth >> extfile.cnf
 $ openssl x509 -req -days 365 -sha256 -in server.csr -CA ca.pem -
CAkey ca-key.pem \
 -CAcreateserial -out server-cert.pem -extfile extfile.cnf

Signature ok
 subject=/CN=your.host.com
Getting CA Private Key
Enter pass phrase for ca-key.pem:
```

3. Start Docker daemon with TLS enabled and use arguments for the CA, server certificate, and CA-signed key. This time, Docker daemon using TLS will run on port 2376 (which is standard for the daemon TLS):

```
$ chmod -v 0400 ca-key.pem key.pem server-key.pem
$ chmod -v 0444 ca.pem server-cert.pem cert.pem
$ dockerd --tlsverify --tlscacert=ca.pem --tlscert=server-cert.pem
--tlskey=server-key.pem \
 -H=0.0.0.0:2376
```

4. Using the same CA, create a client CA-signed key, specifying that this key will be used for client authentication:

```
$ openssl genrsa -out key.pem 4096
Generating RSA private key, 4096 bit long modulus
.....................................................++
...............++
e is 65537 (0x10001)
$ openssl req -subj '/CN=client' -new -key key.pem -out client.csr
$ echo extendedKeyUsage = clientAuth > extfile-client.cnf
$ openssl x509 -req -days 365 -sha256 -in client.csr -CA ca.pem -
CAkey ca-key.pem \
-CAcreateserial -out cert.pem -extfile extfile-client.cnf
Signature ok
subject=/CN=client
Getting CA Private Key
Enter pass phrase for ca-key.pem:
```

5. We will move generated client certificates to the client's host (the client's laptop, for example). We will also copy the public CA certificate file. With its own client certificates and the CA, we will be able to connect to a remote Docker daemon using TLS to secure the communications. We will use the Docker command line with `--tlsverify` and other arguments to specify the server's same CA, the client certificate, and its signed key (the daemon's default port for TLS communications is `2376`). Let's review an example using `docker version`:

```
$ docker --tlsverify --tlscacert=ca.pem --tlscert=cert.pem --
tlskey=key.pem -H=$HOST:2376 version
```

All these steps should be done to provide TLS communications, and *steps 4* and *5* should be undertaken for all client connections if we want to identify their connections (if you don't want to use a unique client certificate/key pair, for example). On enterprise environments, with hundreds or even thousands of users, this is ungovernable and Docker Enterprise will provide a better solution with all these steps included automatically, thereby providing granulated accesses.

Since Docker version 18.09, we can interact with Docker daemon using the `$ docker -H ssh://me@example.com:22 ps` command, for example. To use the SSH connection, you need to set up an ssh public key authentication.

Docker daemon security

Docker container runtime security is based on the following:

- Security provided by the kernel to containers
- The attack surface of the runtime itself
- Operating system security applied to the runtime

Let's take a look at these in more detail.

Namespaces

We have been talking about kernel namespaces and how they implement the required isolation for containers. Every container runs with the following namespaces:

- `pid`: Process isolation (**Process ID – PID**)
- `net`: Manages network interfaces (**Networking – NET**)
- `ipc`: Manages access to IPC resources (**InterProcess Communication – IPC**)
- `mnt`: Manages filesystem mount points (**Mount – MNT**)
- `uts`: Isolates kernel and version identifiers (**Unix Timesharing System – UTS**)

As each container runs with its own `pid` namespace, it will only have access to the listed process on this namespace. The `net` namespace will provide its own interfaces, which will allow us to start many processes using the same port on different containers. Container visibility is enabled by default. All containers will have access to external networks using host bridge interfaces.

A complete root filesystem will be inside each container, and it will use this as a standard Unix filesystem (with its own `/tmp`, and network files such as `/etc/hosts` and `/etc/resolv.conf`). This dedicated filesystem is based on copy-on-write, using different layers from images.

Namespaces provide layers of isolation for the container, and control groups will manage how many resources will be available for the container. This will ensure that the host will not get exhausted. In multi-tenant environments, or just for production, it is very important to manage the resources of containers and to not allow non-limited containers.

The attack surface of the daemon is based on user access. By default, Docker daemon does not provide any role-based access solution, but we have seen that we can ensure an encrypted communication for external clients.

As Docker daemon runs as root (the experimental mode will allow us to run rootless), all containers will be able to, for example, mount any directory on your host. This can be a real problem and that is why it's so important to ensure that only required users have access to the Docker socket (local or remote).

 As we will see in `Chapter 3`, *Running Docker Containers*, containers will run as root if we don't specify a user on image building or container startup. We will review this topic later and improve this default user usage.

It is recommended to run just Docker daemon on server-dedicated hosts because Docker can be dangerous in the wrong hands when it comes to other services running on the same host.

User namespace

As we've already seen, Linux namespaces provide isolation for processes. These processes just see what cgroups and these namespaces offer, and for these processes, they are running along on their own.

We always recommend running processes inside containers as non-root users (`nginx`, for example, does not require root to be running if we use upper ports), but there are some cases where they must be run as root. To prevent privilege escalation from within these root containers, we can apply user remapping. This mechanism will map a root user (UID 0) inside the container, with the user's non-root (UID 30000).

User remapping is managed by two files:

- `/etc/subid`: This sets the user ID range for subordinates.
- `/etc/subgid`: This sets the group ID range for subordinates.

With these files, we set the first sequence ID for users and groups, respectively. This is an example format for the subordinate ID, `nonroot:30000:65536`. This means that UID 0 inside the container will be mapped as UID `30000` on the Docker host and so forth.

We will configure Docker daemon to use this user remapping with the `--userns-remap` flag or the `userns-remap` key in JSON format. In special cases, we can change the user namespace behavior when running the container.

Kernel capabilities (seccomp)

By default, Docker starts containers with a restricted set of capabilities. This means that containers will run unprivileged by default. So, running processes inside containers improves application security by default.

These are the 14 capabilities available by default to any container running in your system: `SETPCAP`, `MKNOD`, `AUDIT_WRITE`, `CHOWN`, `NET_RAW`, `DAC_OVERRIDE`, `FOWNER`, `FSETID`, `KILL`, `SETGID`, `SETUID`, `NET_BIND_SERVICE`, `SYS_CHROOT`, and `SETFCAP`.

The most important thing to understand at this point is that we can run processes inside a container listening on ports under 1024 because we have `NET_BIND_SERVICE` capability, for example, or that we can use ICMP inside containers because we have `NET_RAW` capability enabled.

On the other hand, there are many capabilities not enabled by default. For example, there are many system operations that will need `SYS_ADMIN` capability, or we will need `NET_ADMIN` capability to create new interfaces (running `openvpn` inside Docker containers will require it).

Processes will not have real root privileges inside containers. Using seccomp capabilities, it is possible to do the following:

- Deny `mount` operations
- Deny access to raw sockets (to prevent packet spoofing)
- Deny access to some filesystem operations, such as file ownership
- Deny module loading, and many others

The permitted capabilities are defined using a default `seccomp` profile. Docker uses `seccomp` in filter mode, disabling all non-whitelisted calls defined on its own JSON format in profile files. There is a default profile that will be used when running containers. We can use our own `seccomp` profile using the `--security-opt` flag on launch. So, manipulating allowed capabilities is easy during container execution. We will learn more about how to manipulate the behavior of any container at the start of `Chapter 3`, *Running Docker Containers*:

```
$ docker container run --cap-add=NET_ADMIN--rm -it --security-opt
seccomp=custom-profile.json alpine sh
```

This line will run our container, adding the NET_ADMIN capability. Using a custom seccomp profile, we will be adding even more, as defined on custom-profile.json. For security reasons, we can even use --cap-drop to drop some of the default capabilities if we are sure that we don't need them.

> Avoid using the --privileged flag as your container will run unconfined, which means that it will run nearly with the same access to the host as processes running outside containers on the host. In this case, resources will be unlimited for this container (the SYS_RESOURCE capability will be enabled and limit flags will not be used). Best practice for users would be to remove all capabilities except those required by the process to work.

Linux security modules

Linux operating systems provide tools to ensure security. In some cases, they come installed and configured by default in out-of-the-box installations, while in other cases, they will require additional administrator interaction.

AppArmor and SELinux are probably the most common. Both provide finer-grained control over file operations and other security features. For example, we can ensure that only the allowed process can modify some special files or directories (for example, /etc/passwd).

Docker provides templates and policies that are installed with the product that ensures complete integration with these tools to harden Docker hosts. Never disable SELinux or AppArmor on production and use policies to add features or accesses for your processes.

We can review which security modules are enabled in our Docker runtime by looking at the SecurityOptions section of the Docker system info output.

> We can easily review Docker runtime features using docker system info. It is good to know that the output can be displayed in JSON format using docker system info --format '{{json .}}' and that we can filter by using the --filter option. Filtering allows us, for example, to retrieve only security options applied to the docker system info --format '{{json .SecurityOptions}}' daemon.

By default, Red Hat flavor hosts will not have SELinux enabled, but, on the other hand, Ubuntu will run by default with AppArmor.

> There is a very common issue when we move the default Docker data root path to another location in Red Hat Linux. If SELinux is enabled (by default on these systems), you will need to add a new path to the allowed context by using `# semanage fcontext -a -e /var/lib/docker _MY_NEW_DATA-ROOT_PATH` and then `# restorecon -R - v _MY_NEW_DATA-ROOT_PATH`.

Docker Content Trust

Docker Content Trust is the mechanism provided by Docker to improve content security. It will provide image ownership and verification of immutability. This option, which is applied at Docker runtime, will help to harden content execution. We can ensure that only certain images can run on Docker hosts. This will provide two different levels of security:

- Only allow signed images
- Only allow signed images by certain users or groups/teams (we will learn about the concepts that are integrated with Docker UCP in Chapter 11, *Universal Control Plane*)

We will learn about volumes, which are the objects used for container persistent storage, in Chapter 4, *Container Persistency and Networking*.

Enabling and disabling Docker Content Trust can be managed by setting the `DOCKER_CONTENT_TRUST=1` environment variable in a client session, in the `systemd` Docker unit. Alternatively, we can use `--disable-content-trust=false` (true by default) on image and container operations.

With any of these flags enabling content trust, all Docker operations will be trusted, which means that we won't be able to download and execute any non-trusted flags (signed images).

Chapter labs

We will use CentOS 7 as the operating system for the node labs in this book, unless otherwise indicated. We will install Docker Community Edition now and Docker Enterprise for the specific chapters pertaining to this platform.

Deploy `environments/standalone-environment` from this book's GitHub repository (`https://github.com/PacktPublishing/Docker-Certified-Associate-DCA-Exam-Guide.git`) if you have not done so yet. You can use your own CentOS 7 server. Use `vagrant up` from the `environments/standalone-environment` folder to start your virtual environment.

If you are using a standalone environment, wait until it is running. We can check the statuses of the nodes using `vagrant status`. Connect to your lab node using `vagrant ssh standalone`. `standalone` is the name of your node. You will be using the `vagrant` user with root privileges using `sudo`. You should get the following output:

```
Docker-Certified-Associate-DCA-Exam-Guide/environments/standalone$ vagrant
up
Bringing machine 'standalone' up with 'virtualbox' provider...
==> standalone: Cloning VM...
==> standalone: Matching MAC address for NAT networking...
==> standalone: Checking if box 'frjaraur/centos7' version '1.4' is up to
date...
==> standalone: Setting the name of the VM: standalone
...
==> standalone: Running provisioner: shell...
  standalone: Running: inline script
  standalone: Delta RPMs disabled because /usr/bin/applydeltarpm not
installed.
Docker-Certified-Associate-DCA-Exam-Guide/environments/standalone$ vagrant
status
Current machine states:
standalone running (virtualbox)
...
Docker-Certified-Associate-DCA-Exam-Guide/environments/standalone$
```

We can now connect to a standalone node using `vagrant ssh standalone`. This process may vary if you've already deployed a standalone virtual node before and you just started it using `vagrant up`:

```
Docker-Certified-Associate-DCA-Exam-Guide/environments/standalone$ vagrant
ssh standalone
[vagrant@standalone ~]$
```

Now, you are ready to start the labs.

Installing the Docker runtime and executing a "hello world" container

This lab will guide you through the Docker runtime installation steps and running your first container. Let's get started:

1. To ensure that no previous versions are installed, we will remove any `docker*` packages:

   ```
   [vagrant@standalone ~]$ sudo yum remove docker*
   ```

2. Add the required packages by running the following command:

   ```
   [vagrant@standalone ~]$ sudo yum install -y yum-utils    device-mapper-persistent-data    lvm2
   ```

3. We will be using a stable release, so we will add its package repository, as follows:

   ```
   [vagrant@standalone ~]$ sudo yum-config-manager \
   --add-repo https://download.docker.com/linux/centos/docker-ce.repo
   ```

4. Now, install Docker packages and `containerd`. We are installing the server and client on this host (since version 18.06, Docker provides different packages for `docker-cli` and Docker daemon):

   ```
   [vagrant@standalone ~]$ sudo yum install -y docker-ce docker-ce-cli containerd.io
   ```

5. Docker is installed, but on Red Hat-like operating systems, it is not enabled on boot by default and will not start. Verify this situation and enable and start the Docker service:

   ```
   [vagrant@standalone ~]$ sudo systemctl enable docker
   [vagrant@standalone ~]$ sudo systemctl start docker
   ```

6. Now that Docker is installed and running, we can run our first container:

   ```
   [vagrant@standalone ~]$ sudo docker container run hello-world
   Unable to find image 'hello-world:latest' locally
   latest: Pulling from library/hello-world
   1b930d010525: Pull complete
   Digest:
   sha256:b8ba256769a0ac28dd126d584e0a2011cd2877f3f76e093a7ae560f2a530
   1c00
   Status: Downloaded newer image for hello-world:latest
   ```

```
Hello from Docker!

This message shows that your installation appears to be working
correctly. To generate this message, Docker took the following
steps:
1. The Docker client contacted the Docker daemon.
2. The Docker daemon pulled the "hello-world" image from the Docker
Hub. (amd64)
3. The Docker daemon created a new container from that image that
runs the executable, which produces the output you are currently
reading.
4. The Docker daemon streamed that output to the Docker client,
which sent it to your terminal.

To try something more ambitious, you can run an Ubuntu container
with:
$ docker run -it ubuntu bash

Share images, automate workflows, and more with a free Docker ID:
https://hub.docker.com/.

For more examples and ideas, visit:
https://docs.docker.com/get-started/.
```

This command will send a request to Docker daemon to run a container based on the `hello-world` image, located on Docker Hub (`http://hub.docker.com`). To use this image, Docker daemon downloads all the layers if we have not executed any container with this image before; in other words, if the image is not present on the local Docker host. Once all the image layers have been downloaded, Docker daemon will start a `hello-world` container.

This book is a guide for the DCA exam and is the simplest lab we can easily deploy. However, you should be able to understand and describe this simple process, as well as think about all the common issues that we may encounter. For example, what happens if the image is on your host and is different, but with the same name and tags? What happens if one layer cannot be downloaded? What happens if you are connected to a remote daemon? We will review some of these questions at the end of this chapter.

7. As you should have noticed, we are always using `sudo` to root because our user has not got access to the Docker UNIX socket. This is the first security layer an attacker must bypass on your system. We usually enable a user to run containers in production environments because we want to isolate operating system responsibilities and management from Docker. Just add our user to the Docker group, or add a new group of users with access to the socket. In this case, we will just add our lab user to the Docker group:

```
[vagrant@standalone ~]$ docker container ls
Got permission denied while trying to connect to the Docker daemon
socket at unix:///var/run/docker.sock: Get
http://%2Fvar%2Frun%2Fdocker.sock/v1.40/containers/json
: dial unix /var/run/docker.sock: connect: permission denied

[vagrant@standalone ~]$ sudo usermod -a -G docker $USER

[vagrant@standalone ~]$ newgrp docker

[vagrant@standalone ~]$ docker container ls -a
CONTAINER ID IMAGE COMMAND CREATED STATUS PORTS NAMES
5f7abd49b3e7 hello-world "/hello" 19 minutes ago Exited (0) 19
minutes ago   festive_feynman
```

Docker runtime processes and namespace isolation

In this lab, we are going to review what we learned about process isolation and Docker daemon components and execution workflow. Let's get started:

1. Briefly review the Docker `systemd` daemon:

```
[vagrant@standalone ~]$ sudo systemctl status docker
● docker.service - Docker Application Container Engine
   Loaded: loaded (/usr/lib/systemd/system/docker.service; enabled;
vendor preset: disabled)
   Active: active (running) since sáb 2019-09-28 19:34:30 CEST;
25min ago
     Docs: https://docs.docker.com
 Main PID: 20407 (dockerd)
    Tasks: 10
   Memory: 58.9M
   CGroup: /system.slice/docker.service
           └─20407 /usr/bin/dockerd -H fd:// --
containerd=/run/containerd/containerd.sock
```

```
 sep 28 19:34:30 centos7-base dockerd[20407]:
time="2019-09-28T19:34:30.222200934+02:00" level=info
msg="[graphdriver] using prior storage driver: overlay2"
 sep 28 19:34:30 centos7-base dockerd[20407]:
time="2019-09-28T19:34:30.234170886+02:00" level=info msg="Loading
containers: start."
 sep 28 19:34:30 centos7-base dockerd[20407]:
time="2019-09-28T19:34:30.645048459+02:00" level=info msg="Default
bridge (docker0) is assigned with an IP a... address"
 sep 28 19:34:30 centos7-base dockerd[20407]:
time="2019-09-28T19:34:30.806432227+02:00" level=info msg="Loading
containers: done."
 sep 28 19:34:30 centos7-base dockerd[20407]:
time="2019-09-28T19:34:30.834047449+02:00" level=info msg="Docker
daemon" commit=6a30dfc graphdriver(s)=over...n=19.03.2
 sep 28 19:34:30 centos7-base dockerd[20407]:
time="2019-09-28T19:34:30.834108635+02:00" level=info msg="Daemon
has completed initialization"
 sep 28 19:34:30 centos7-base dockerd[20407]:
time="2019-09-28T19:34:30.850703030+02:00" level=info msg="API
listen on /var/run/docker.sock"
 sep 28 19:34:30 centos7-base systemd[1]: Started Docker
Application Container Engine.
 sep 28 19:34:43 centos7-base dockerd[20407]:
time="2019-09-28T19:34:43.558580560+02:00" level=info msg="ignoring
event" module=libcontainerd namespace=mo...skDelete"
 sep 28 19:34:43 centos7-base dockerd[20407]:
time="2019-09-28T19:34:43.586395281+02:00" level=warning
msg="5f7abd49b3e75c58922c6e9d655d1f6279cf98d9c325ba2d3e53c36...
```

This output shows that the service is using a default systemd unit configuration and that dockerd is using the default parameters; that is, it's using the file descriptor socket on /var/run/docker.sock and the default docker0 bridge interface.

2. Notice that dockerd uses a separate containerd process to execute containers. Let's run some containers in the background and review their processes. We will run a simple alpine with an nginx daemon:

```
[vagrant@standalone ~]$ docker run -d nginx:alpine
 Unable to find image 'nginx:alpine' locally
 alpine: Pulling from library/nginx
 9d48c3bd43c5: Already exists
 1ae95a11626f: Pull complete
 Digest:
sha256:77f340700d08fd45026823f44fc0010a5bd2237c2d049178b473cd2ad977
d071
```

```
Status: Downloaded newer image for nginx:alpine
dcda734db454a6ca72a9b9eef98aae6aefaa6f9b768a7d53bf30665d8ff70fe7
```

3. Now, we will look for the `nginx` and `containerd` processes (process IDs will be completely different on your system; you just need to understand the workflow):

```
[vagrant@standalone ~]$ ps -efa|grep -v grep|egrep -e containerd -e
nginx
root       15755     1  0 sep27 ?        00:00:42
/usr/bin/containerd
root       20407     1  0 19:34 ?        00:00:02 /usr/bin/dockerd -
H fd:// --containerd=/run/containerd/containerd.sock
root       20848 15755  0 20:06 ?        00:00:00 containerd-shim -
namespace moby -workdir
/var/lib/containerd/io.containerd.runtime.v1.linux/moby/dcda734db45
4a6ca72a9
  b9eef98aae6aefaa6f9b768a7d53bf30665d8ff70fe7 -address
/run/containerd/containerd.sock -containerd-binary
/usr/bin/containerd -runtime-root /var/run/docker/runtime-runc
root       20863 20848  0 20:06 ?        00:00:00 nginx: master
process nginx -g daemon off;
101        20901 20863  0 20:06 ?        00:00:00 nginx: worker
process
```

4. Notice that, at the end, the container started from `20848` PID. Following the `runtime-runc` location, we discover `state.json`, which is the container state file:

```
[vagrant@standalone ~]$ sudo ls -laRt /var/run/docker/runtime-
runc/moby
 /var/run/docker/runtime-runc/moby:
 total 0
 drwx--x--x. 2 root root 60 sep 28 20:06
dcda734db454a6ca72a9b9eef98aae6aefaa6f9b768a7d53bf30665d8ff70fe7
 drwx------. 3 root root 60 sep 28 20:06 .
 drwx------. 3 root root 60 sep 28 13:42 ..
 /var/run/docker/runtime-
runc/moby/dcda734db454a6ca72a9b9eef98aae6aefaa6f9b768a7d53bf30665d8
ff70fe7:
 total 28
 drwx--x--x. 2 root root     60 sep 28 20:06 .
 -rw-r--r--. 1 root root 24966 sep 28 20:06 state.json
 drwx------. 3 root root     60 sep 28 20:06 ..
```

This file contains container runtime information: PID, mounts, devices, capabilities applied, resources, and more.

5. Our NGINX server runs under PID `20863` and the `nginx` child process with PID `20901` on the Docker host, but let's take a look inside:

```
[vagrant@standalone ~]$ docker container exec dcda734db454 ps -ef
PID USER TIME COMMAND
1 root 0:00 nginx: master process nginx -g daemon off;
6 nginx 0:00 nginx: worker process
7 root 0:00 ps -ef
```

Using `docker container exec`, we can run a new process using a container namespace. This is like running a new process inside the container.

As you can observe, inside the container, `nginx` has PID 1 and it is the worker process parent. And, of course, we see our command, `ps -ef`, because it was launched using its namespaces.

We can run other containers using the same image and we will obtain the same results. Processes inside each container are isolated from other containers and host processes, but users on the Docker host will see all the processes, along with their real PIDs.

6. Let's take a look at `nginx` process namespaces. We will use the `lsns` command to review all the host-running process's namespaces. We will obtain a list of all running processes and their namespaces. We will look for `nginx` processes (we will not use `grep` to filter the output because we want to read the headers):

```
[vagrant@standalone ~]$ sudo lsns
NS TYPE NPROCS PID USER COMMAND
. . . . . . . . . . . . .
. . . . . . . . . . . . .
 4026532197 mnt 2 20863 root nginx: master process nginx -g daemon
off
 4026532198 uts 2 20863 root nginx: master process nginx -g daemon
off
 4026532199 ipc 2 20863 root nginx: master process nginx -g daemon
off
 4026532200 pid 2 20863 root nginx: master process nginx -g daemon
off
 4026532202 net 2 20863 root nginx: master process nginx -g daemon
off
```

This lab demonstrated process isolation within a process running inside containers.

Docker capabilities

This lab will cover seccomp capability management. We will launch containers using dropped capabilities to ensure that, by using seccomp to avoid some system calls, processes in containers will only execute allowed actions. Let's get started:

1. First, run a container using the default allowed capabilities. During the execution of this alpine container, we will change the ownership of the /etc/passwd file:

   ```
   [vagrant@standalone ~]$ docker container run --rm -it alpine sh -c
   "chown nobody /etc/passwd; ls -l /etc/passwd"
    -rw-r--r-- 1 nobody root 1230 Jun 17 09:00 /etc/passwd
   ```

   As we can see, there is nothing to stop us from changing whatever file ownership resides inside the container's filesystem because the main process (in this case, /bin/sh) runs as the root user.

2. Drop all the capabilities. Let's see what happens:

   ```
   [vagrant@standalone ~]$ docker container run --rm -it --cap-
   drop=ALL alpine sh -c "chown nobody /etc/passwd; ls -l /etc/passwd"
    chown: /etc/passwd: Operation not permitted
    -rw-r--r-- 1 root root 1230 Jun 17 09:00 /etc/passwd
   ```

   You will observe that the operation was forbidden. Since containers run without any capabilities, the chown command is not allowed to change file ownership.

3. Now, just add the CHOWN capability to allow a change of ownership for files inside the container:

   ```
   [vagrant@standalone ~]$ docker container run --rm -it --cap-
   drop=ALL --cap-add CHOWN alpine sh -c "chown nobody /etc/passwd; ls
   -l /etc/passwd"
    -rw-r--r-- 1 nobody root 1230 Jun 17 09:00 /etc/passwd
   ```

Summary

In this chapter, we have seen how modern applications are based on microservices. We learned what containers are and their benefits, and how microservices and containers match when we associate a process with specific functionality or a task (microservice) and we run it inside a container. We reviewed container concepts. Then, we talked about images, containers, and the mechanisms that isolate processes from the host. We introduced orchestration and registries as requirements for deploying applications with resilience on cluster environments and the ways in which we can manage images.

We then have learned about Docker's main components and how Docker Client interacts with Docker Engine securely. We introduced the most common Docker objects and the workflow we will use to create, share, and deploy new applications based on containers.

Nowadays, we can use containers on Microsoft Windows, but this all started with Linux. We compared both approaches to understand the similarities and differences between them and the advanced methods used to isolate processes on Windows using Hyper-V.

Finally, we reviewed how to configure Docker Engine using JSON files and environment variables, learned that containers are secure by default, and reviewed the different mechanisms used to accomplish this.

In the next chapter, we will build images using different methods and learn the processes and primitives necessary to create good images.

Questions

1. Is it true that we can only run one process per container? (select which sentences are true)

   a) We cannot execute more than one process per container. This is a limitation.
   b) We can run more than one process per container, but it is not recommended.
   c) We will only run one process per container to follow microservices logic.
   d) All of the above sentences are false.

2. What kernel facilities provide host CPU resource isolation on containers?

    a) Kernel namespaces.
    b) Cgroups (control groups).
    c) Kernel domains.
    d) None of them. It is not possible to isolate host resources.

3. Which of the following sentences are true?

    a) All containers will run as root by default.
    b) The user namespace will allow us to map UID 0 to another one on our host system, controlled and without any non-required privileges.
    c) As the Docker daemon runs as root, only root users can run containers on Docker hosts.
    d) All of the above sentences are false.

4. What have we learned about Windows Docker hosts?

    a) Linux containers can run on Windows hosts too.
    b) Windows Hyper-V containers will run a small virtual machine, providing the required resources for containers and do not have any Windows operating system dependencies.
    c) Windows Process Isolation requires system DLLs and services on containers to run properly, and do not provide complete portability.
    d) Windows images are bigger than Linux ones because Windows operating system component integrations are required in many cases to run even small processes.

5. Which of the following sentences are true regarding the Docker daemon configuration?

    a) We will configure Docker daemon on Linux using JSON format keys and values on `/etc/docker/daemon.json` or `systemd` unit files.
    b) On Windows hosts, we will use `%programdata%\docker\config\daemon.json` to configure Docker daemon.
    c) By default, the Docker client connection to the remote Docker daemon is insecure.
    d) None of the above sentences are true.

Further reading

- What are microservices?: `https://microservices.io/`
- What is a container?: `https://www.docker.com/resources/what-container`
- What is Docker?: `https://www.redhat.com/en/topics/containers/what-is-docker`
- Docker Engine installation and configuration: `https://docs.docker.com/engine/`
- Docker storage drivers: `https://docs.docker.com/storage/storagedriver/`

2
Building Docker Images

Building images is the first step in deploying your own container-based applications. It is a simple process and anyone can build images from scratch, but it is not easy to create images with sufficient quality and security for production. In this chapter, we will learn all the basics and tips and tricks for creating good, production-ready images. We will review the requirements for saving and distributing our work, as well as how to improve these processes to get better performance when the number of images and releases is substantial in enterprise environments.

In this chapter, we will cover the following topics:

- Building Docker images
- Understanding copy-on-write filesystems
- Building images with a Dockerfile reference
- Image tagging and meta-information
- Docker registries and repositories
- Securing images
- Managing images and other related objects
- Multistage building and image caches
- Templating images
- Image releases and updates

Let's get started!

Technical requirements

In this chapter, we will learn about Docker image building concepts. We'll provide some labs at the end of this chapter that will help you understand and learn about the concepts explained here. These labs can be run on your laptop or PC using the provided Vagrant standalone environment or any already deployed Docker host of your own. You can find additional information in this book's GitHub repository at `https://github.com/ PacktPublishing/Docker-Certified-Associate-DCA-Exam-Guide.git`.

Check out the following video to see the Code in Action:

`"https://bit.ly/31v3AJq"`

Building Docker images

Developers create their own images, along with their own code and runtime components, to run their application components. However, the building process usually starts with a previous image. All image build processes will start with a `FROM` statement. This indicates that the previous image (compound on layers) will be used to add new components, binaries, configurations, or actions for building our new image.

You may be asking yourself, *who is responsible for image creation?* Developers will probably create application images if they are not automatically generated using Continuous Integration platforms, but there will be teams who create images to be used by other users as base images. For example, database administrators would create database base images because they know what components should be included and how to ensure their security. Developers will take those base images for their components. In a big organization, there will be many teams creating images, or at least defining what components must be included, which users to use, ports to expose, and so on.

There is something else, however. Many applications these days come prepared for container environments, and software manufacturers will provide you with images to deploy their software. Enterprises will look for homogenization and architecture, while DevOps teams will provide their colleagues with standard base images. The container's infrastructure runtime would be common to all of them and monitoring applications, middleware, databases, and so on would be running on this environment alongside developed business application components.

There are three methods for creating images:

- Using a file with all the instructions to create this image (Dockerfile)
- Interacting with files in different container layers, executing one container, modifying its content, and then storing the changes made (commit)
- Using an empty layer and adding components by hand, file by file, also known as creating an image from scratch

Now, we will review each one, along with their pros and cons and use cases.

Creating images with Dockerfiles

A Dockerfile is a script file that describes all the steps required to create a new image. Each step will be interpreted and, in many cases, create a container to execute declared changes against previous layers. On this Dockerfile, we will have a guide to creating this image. This guide creates a reproducible process. We will ensure that every time we use this script, we will get the same results. Of course, this can depend on some variables, but with some key mechanisms, we can ensure the same results. In this chapter, we will cover the main primitives available for creating image Dockerfiles.

A Dockerfile looks similar to the following:

```
FROM ubuntu:18.04
RUN apt-get update -qq && apt-get install -qq package1 package2
COPY . /myapp
RUN make /myapp
CMD python /myapp/app.py
```

In this simple example, and as we mentioned previously, we have a FROM sentence at the beginning:

1. First, we used Ubuntu 18.04 as the base image. To use this image, we need it in our building environment. Therefore, if the image is not present in our environment, Docker daemon will download its layers for us to make it available locally for the next steps. This will happen automatically; Docker daemon will do this for us.

2. Using the downloaded Ubuntu 18.04 layers, Docker will automatically run a container using this image and execute the declared commands since we used the RUN primitive. In this simple case, the shell (because it is the default command on the Ubuntu 18.04 image) will execute apt-get update to update the container package cache. If everything goes well with this command, it will execute the installation of package1 and package2 using apt-get install.

3. After software installation, Docker will execute a `Docker container commit` command internally to persist these changes on a new layer in order to use them as a base for the next step. The third line will copy our current directory content into the application code directory on a new running container.

4. The next line will execute `make` (this is just an example; we haven't said anything about the programming language used for my application and so on). This line will run this action in a new container. As a result, a new image will be created automatically when the action has finished.

5. We learned that a container is always created using an image as a template. The last line of code defines the command line to be run each time we create a container using this image.

In summary, Dockerfiles provide a guide of all the steps required to create an image so that we can run our application. It is a reproducible process and therefore, every time we create a new image using this file, we should obtain the same results (for example, in this case, we have updated the package cache and installed the required software; perhaps these packages changed since last time we did a build, but if not, we will have the same image).

The built image has a unique identification in the `algorithm:hexadecimal_code_using_algorithm` format. This means that every time we build this image, we will get the same image identification unless there is some kind of change that's made during the process. This image ID, or digest ID, is calculated using an algorithm in relation to a layer's content, so we will get a new one with any layer change. This identification allows Docker Engine to verify whether the image described is the correct one to use. A Docker image contains information about all of its layers and informs Docker Engine of the layers' content that is required for the new container.

When we inspect the image information, we will get all the necessary layers to create this image, `RootFS`. Here is an example:

```
"RootFS": {
 "Type": "layers",
 "Layers": [
 "sha256:f1b5933fe4b5f49bbe8258745cf396afe07e625bdab3168e364daf7c956b6b81",
 "sha256:402522b96a27c1af04af5650819febc11f71db14152b1db8e5eab1ae581fdb2e",
 "sha256:cf2850b10a1aba79774a291266262f1af49fac3db11341a5ca1a396430f17507",
 "sha256:c1912ec50df66e3e013851f6deb80f41810b284509eebc909811115a97a1fe01"
 ]
 }
```

This output shows different layers being created using defined code in the Dockerfile. These layers will be interchangeable between images wherever possible. If we create an image using Dockerfile's first two lines, the layers that are created by those commands will be shared with the previous image. This ensures minimum disk space usage.

Creating images interactively

Images can be created interactively by running a container and making changes on the fly to `rootfs`. This is very useful when an application's installation cannot be automated but lacks reproducibility. Let's look at this process in action using an example:

1. Start an interactive container:

```
$ docker container run -ti debian
 Unable to find image 'debian:latest' locally
 latest: Pulling from library/debian
 4a56a430b2ba: Pull complete
 Digest:
sha256:e25b64a9cf82c72080074d6b1bba7329cdd752d51574971fd37731ed164f
3345
 Status: Downloaded newer image for debian:latest
 root@60265b7c8a61:/#
```

2. Once started, we will receive a command prompt because we launched the container by allocating a pseudo-terminal and did so interactively. We need to update the package's database and then install, for example, the `postfix` package, which needs some interactive configurations (please note that some of the output will be truncated and omitted):

```
root@60265b7c8a61:/# apt-get update -qq
 root@60265b7c8a61:/# apt-get install postfix
 Reading package lists... Done
 Building dependency tree
 Reading state information... Done
 The following additional packages will be installed:
 bzip2 cpio file libexpat1 libicu63 .....
 Suggested packages:
 bzip2-doc libarchive1 libsasl2-modules-gssapi-mit | libsasl2-
modules-gssapi-heimdal  .....
 The following NEW packages will be installed:
 bzip2 cpio file libexpat1 libicu63 libmagic-mgc libmagic1 l ....
 0 upgraded, 29 newly installed, 0 to remove and 5 not upgraded.
 Need to get 19.0 MB of archives.
 After this operation, 76.4 MB of additional disk space will be
used.
```

```
Do you want to continue? [Y/n] y
Get:1 http://cdn-fastly.deb.debian.org/debian buster/main amd64
libpython3.7-minimal amd64 3.7.3-2 [588 kB]
 .....
 .....
debconf: falling back to frontend: Teletype
Postfix Configuration
---------------------
Please select the mail server configuration type that best meets
your needs.
No configuration:
 Should be chosen to leave the current configuration unchanged.
 Internet site:
 Mail is sent and received directly using SMTP.
 Internet with smarthost:
 Mail is received directly using SMTP or by running a utility such
as fetchmail. Outgoing mail is sent using a smarthost.
 Satellite system:
 All mail is sent to another machine, called a 'smarthost', for
delivery.
 Local only:
 The only delivered mail is the mail for local users. There is no
network.

1. No configuration 2. Internet Site 3. Internet with smarthost 4.
Satellite system 5. Local only
 General type of mail configuration: 1
Unpacking postfix (3.4.5-1) ...
 ......
 ......
 Adding group `postfix' (GID 102) ...
 Done.
 Adding system user `postfix' (UID 101) ...
 Adding new user `postfix' (UID 101) with group `postfix' ...
 Not creating home directory `/var/spool/postfix'.
 Creating /etc/postfix/dynamicmaps.cf
 Adding group `postdrop' (GID 103) ...
 Done.
 /etc/aliases does not exist, creating it.
Postfix (main.cf) was not set up. Start with
 cp /usr/share/postfix/main.cf.debian /etc/postfix/main.cf
 . If you need to make changes, edit /etc/postfix/main.cf (and
others) as
 needed. To view Postfix configuration values, see postconf(1).
After modifying main.cf, be sure to run 'service postfix reload'.
invoke-rc.d: could not determine current runlevel
 invoke-rc.d: policy-rc.d denied execution of start.
 Setting up libpython3-stdlib:amd64 (3.7.3-1) ...
```

```
Setting up python3.7 (3.7.3-2) ...
Setting up python3 (3.7.3-1) ...
......
......
Processing triggers for libc-bin (2.28-10) ...
```

3. The software was installed, and you were asked to confirm the installation of the `postfix` package and some default configuration. Now, we can exit the current container:

```
root@60265b7c8a61:/# exit
```

4. What we have done here is exit the current main process (which is a shell in a Debian image) and, as a result, returned to our host. We will look for the last container that was executed on our host and then save the container layer as a new image layer (which means that we have created a new image with a name or identification if we omit it):

```
$ docker container ls -1
CONTAINER ID IMAGE COMMAND LABELS
f11f8ad3b336 debian "bash"

$ docker container commit f11f8ad3b336 debian-with-postfix
sha256:a852d20d57c95bba38dc0bea942ccbe2c409d48685d8fc115827c1dcd501
0aa6
```

5. Finally, we review the newly created image on our host system (the IDs may change in your environment):

```
$ docker image ls
IMAGE ID REPOSITORY TAG CREATED AT
a852d20d57c9 debian-with-postfix latest 2019-10-05 13:18:45 +0200
CEST
c2c03a296d23 debian latest 2019-09-12 01:21:51 +0200 CEST
```

Using this method, we have created a new image interactively using a previously running Debian Docker container. As we can see, the new image has a different digest. If we inspect its meta-information, we can identify its preceding image layers:

```
"RootFS": {
  "Type": "layers",
  "Layers": [
"sha256:78c1b9419976227e05be9d243b7fa583bea44a5258e52018b2af4cdfe23d148d",
"sha256:998e883275f6192039dd6eff96ece024e259cf74dd362c44c5eb9db9f3830aa0"
    ]
  }
```

One key concept of images that are created using a Docker container commit is that they are not reproducible; you really don't know how they were created, so the necessary steps should be documented in relation to updates and management.

There is an image action that provides a detailed review of the steps to create an image. `docker image history` will provide a historic view of the steps that were taken to create that image. However, it will not work on images that are created using committed containers. We will just have a line with a bash, for example, indicating that all the actions that were taken were made on an active container and therefore, no additional information can be extracted. For example, using the previously created image, executing `docker image history debian-with-postfix` will provide the following output:

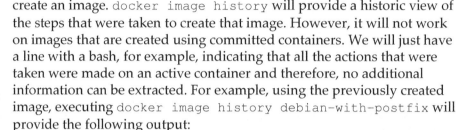

Creating images from scratch

Creating images from scratch is the most effective method. In this case, we will use a Dockerfile, as described in the first method, but the initial base image will be an empty reserved one known literally as `scratch`. A simple example definition will look as follows:

```
FROM scratch
ADD hello /
CMD ["/hello"]
```

The main difference in the Dockerfile definition is the `FROM` line because we use a defined empty image named `scratch`. `scratch` is not a real image; it only contains the root filesystem structure and its meta-information. Images built using this method must contain all binaries, libraries, and files required by our process (as should always be the case). However, we are not using a predefined image and its content; it will be empty and we have to add each required file. This procedure is not easy and requires much more practice, but images are way better because they will only contain the pieces required for our application. We will see a complete lab at the end of this chapter.

Understanding copy-on-write filesystems

In the previous chapter, we learned what a container is. The isolated process or processes running inside a container will have their own root filesystem among other namespaces. The container adds a thin layer on top of image layers and every change made during the execution of its processes will be stored only on this layer. In order to manage these changes, the Docker storage driver will use stackable layers and **copy-on-write** (sometimes referenced as **CoW**).

When a process inside a container needs to modify a file, the Docker daemon storage filesystem mechanism will make a copy of that file from the underlying layers to the top one. These are only available for container usage. The same happens when a new file is created; it will only be written to the top container storage layer. All the other processes running on other containers will manage their own version of the file. In fact, this will be the original file from the other layers if no changes were made. Each container uses its own top layer to write file changes.

We have seen how the image building process works using containers for each layer's creation. We learned that we can commit a container's layers to obtain a new image. The creation of images using Dockerfiles will run intermediate containers using previous images that will be committed in order to obtain an intermediate image with all file changes between their layers. This process will run sequentially, following the order defined in the Dockerfile's code. As a result, an image will be created that's a compendium of thin layers with the changes or differences between them.

Docker copy-on-write reduces the space needed to run containers and the time required to launch them because it is only required for the creation of this writable layer for each container:

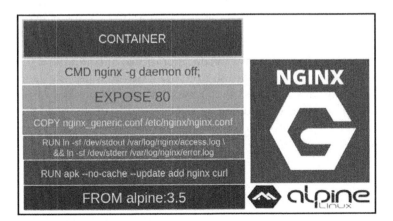

This image represents an NGINX process running as a container. The base image was created from a fresh `alpine` 3.5 image. We added some packages, performed some configurations, and copied our own `nginx.conf` file. Finally, we added some meta-information to be able to create containers using this image, declared which port we will use to expose NGINX, and declared the command line that will be used to run a container by default, starting NGINX in the foreground.

There are three strategies for CoW logic:

- On AUFS and overlay-based drivers, Docker uses union filesystems
- On BTFS and ZFS drivers, Docker uses filesystem snapshots
- On device-mapper (available on a Red Hat-like OS), Docker uses an LVM snapshot for blocks

Nowadays, almost all Docker host OSes use overlay-based drivers by default whenever possible. There are some old implementations that use block devices instead, but today, these are deprecated. Overhead added by the CoW process depends on the driver used.

 We can review how much space a container is using. Docker provides the `docker container ls -s/--size` option for this. It will return the current thin layer's used space and the read-only data used from the original image, defined as **virtual**. To understand how much space containers are really consuming, we will need to combine both sizes for each container to obtain the total amount of data used by all containers in our environment. This will not include volumes or a container's log files, among other small pieces that contribute to real used space.

CoW was prepared for maximum disk space efficiency, but it depends on how many layers are shared in your local images and how many containers will run using the same images. As you can imagine, containers that write a lot of data to their writable layer consume much more space than other containers.

CoW is a very fast process, but for heavy-write operations on containers, it is not enough. If we have a process that requires the creation of many small files, a very deep directory structure, or just very big files, we need to bypass CoW operations because performance will be impacted. This will lead us to using volumes to mitigate such situations. We will learn about volumes, which are the objects used for container persistent storage, in `Chapter 4`, *Container Persistency and Networking*.

Building images with a Dockerfile reference

As we mentioned previously, building images is easy, but building good images is not. This section will guide you through the basics and provide you with tips and tricks that you can use to improve the image building process using Dockerfiles.

Dockerfile quick reference

We have already learned which methods are available for building images. For production, it is recommended to use Dockerfiles because this method provides reproducibility and we can use a code versioning methodology. We will introduce the main Dockerfile instructions in their standard order of usage:

Instruction	Description and usage
FROM	This instruction sets the base image and initializes a new build (we will review this concept in the *Multistage building and image caches* section, later in this chapter). It is the only mandatory instruction that all Dockerfiles should start with. We can use any valid image as the base image for building or the reserved `scratch` word to start with an empty root filesystem, as we learned in the previous section. We can define a name for the build stage initialized using `AS name` in the same FROM instruction. We will use it in the *Multistage building* section at the end of this chapter. The base image can be defined using either its image name (repository) and a specific tag (version of that image) or its digest; for example, `FROM <image>[:tag]` or `FROM <image>[@digest]`.
ARG	The ARG instruction defines a variable that will be set to the value provided when building, passing its value as an argument using `--build-arg <variable>=<value>`. To avoid problems when building with missing values, we can use ARG to define a default value for a variable that will be overwritten if an argument is passed. ARG will take the value every time it is invoked. This is very important when creating Dockerfiles. ARG can be used, preceding the FROM instruction, to specify different base images using arguments.

LABEL	With LABEL, we can add meta-information to the image. This information should be in the key-value format and we can include many keys and values in the same LABEL sentence. Here, you have a number of brief examples:
	`LABEL version="1.0"`
	`LABEL description="This image has these \`
	`and these properties...."`
	`LABEL maintainer="Javier Ramirez" team="Docker Infrastructures"`
	`environment="preproduction"`

ENV	With the ENV instruction, we can set an environment variable for the next step and all subsequent steps thereafter. We can add more than one environment variable in the same sentence and values will be overwritten if we specify new values during Docker container creation: `ENV DATABASE_NAME=TEST`
WORKDIR	WORKDIR sets the working directory for the next sentences and subsequent ones thereafter. We can specify full paths or relative ones: `WORKDIR /myappcode`

RUN	RUN will probably be one of the most frequently used sentences in your Dockerfiles. It will execute all commands in the line in a new layer and will commit the results on a new one (as we described in the previous chapter). This new layer will be used in the next sentence as a base layer, with the changes made by the RUN sentence. This means that every RUN sentence will create a new layer. Therefore, RUN directly affects the resulting number of layers in our image. To avoid using more layers than needed, we usually add more than one command per RUN sentence:
	`RUN apt-get update -qq \`
	`&& apt-get install curl`

COPY	The COPY instruction copies new files and directories from the build context (set during build execution) into the specified directory of the container filesystem (remember that building images is based on execution on containers and committing results in images for subsequent stages). COPY admits the `--chown=<user>:<group>` argument for providing file ownership on Linux containers. The owner will be `root:root` if it is not used. COPY accepts `--from=<name or index>` in order to copy files or directories from other build stages (this is key when employing multistage building, as we will learn later in this chapter): `COPY mycode/* /myapp`
ADD	ADD is similar to COPY, but can be used with URLs and TAR package files as well. It accepts the same ownership arguments for changing destination files and directory permissions: `ADD http://example.com/bigpackagefile.tar.gz /myapp`

USER	The USER instruction is used to specify the user, along with the group to use in the following sentences. It is very important to understand the required permissions of our process and specify a user and its group with USER. If it is not present, the steps will use `root:root` and the process inside the container will run as root. It should be mandatory in production to use a specific non-root user for container processes and, if root is required, we should use user mappings (as described in the previous chapter): `USER www-data:www-data`
VOLUME	The VOLUME definition will create a mount point to bypass the CoW system. This means that this set directory's content will be out of the container's life cycle. As it is outside the container, any change in subsequent sentences affecting that directory will be discarded, so if we want to provide certain files during volume initialization, the VOLUME sentence should be after we've provisioned files inside the directory: `VOLUME /mydata`
EXPOSE	EXPOSE is used to inform Docker daemon about listening ports for containers created using this image. This does not mean that the defined ports listen at the Docker host level. They will just listen internally, inside the container's network. We can define which transport protocol to use – UDP or TCP (by default): `EXPOSE 80/tcp`

CMD	The CMD instruction defines the default process or argument when executing a container based on this image. This behavior will be applied irrespective of whether the ENTRYPOINT instruction is defined. By default, and depending on the format used, CMD will provide the default arguments for a shell, which is the default entry point (the main executor for processes inside a container):
	`CMD ["/usr/bin/curl","--help"]`
	`CMD /usr/bin/curl -I https://www.packtpub.com`

ENTRYPOINT	The ENTRYPOINT directive will set which command container will run as an executable. As we learned previously, CMD will be the argument for this command. The interaction between CMD and ENTRYPOINT defines the command that will be executed when running a container. They are not required, but it is a good practice to define at least CMD so as to have a default process to launch on execution.

HEALTHCHECK	HEALTHCHECK defines a command line that will run inside the container to verify the health of the process or processes. Without HEALTHCHECK, Docker daemon will only verify if the main process is alive, and if it isn't, the container will be exited. The HEALTHCHECK instruction allows us to improve the health of the application by defining a better script or binary-based process status monitoring.
	We can adjust the interval between checks, timeout, and the number of retries in case of failure before declaring a non-healthy state. And, if we have a process that takes time to start, we can set when to start monitoring the container processes' health:
	
	`HEALTHCHECK \`
	`--interval=DURATION (default: 30s) \`
	`--timeout=DURATION (default: 30s) \`
	`--start-period=DURATION (default: 0s) \`
	`--retries=N (default: 3) \`
	`CMD /bin/myverificationscript`
	
	It is very important to understand that, by default, the main process running inside a container that is not working as expected (the process is alive but the health check is failing) will not be set as unhealthy until there are three failed verifications, with 30 seconds between them by default. This means that, by default, a process could be failing for 90 seconds before the container is marked as unhealthy. This is too much in many cases, and you should take action to change this behavior.
	We can use our own scripts inside containers and we just have to manage two different exit statuses for the output (0 – verification is OK; 1 – verification is wrong).

 Be careful if you defined a primitive key multiple times in a Dockerfile. These files are read top to bottom and definition precedence matters because instruction values will be overwritten in some cases (ARG, ENV, CMD, ENTRYPOINT, LABEL, USER, WORKDIR, HEALTHCHECK, and so on) or added in others (VOLUME, EXPOSE, and so on).

There are some instructions that admit two different formats, shell and exec, that have different behaviors in each case:

- RUN: When using the shell form, all commands will be launched in a shell, as if we were using /bin/sh -c (on Linux by default) or cmd /S or cmd /C (on Windows by default). We can change which shell to use in this format by means of the SHELL directive:

```
RUN <command> <argument1> <argument2> <-- shell form
RUN ["executable", "argument1", "argument2"] <-- exec JSON form
```

We will need to use the `exec` format in Windows containers. This format is required in this case because the defined values for some keys, such as directory paths, will contain slashes (\) and must be avoided.

- `CMD`: This key will be used to define the command or arguments to pass to the main container process:

```
CMD <command> <argument1> <argument2> <-- shell form
CMD ["executable or argument0", "argument1", "argument2"] <-- exec
JSON form
```

As we learned previously, the shell form uses a shell to execute commands (this can be changed by setting a different shell using the `SHELL` key).

In order to execute CMD commands without a shell, we must use the `exec` form. If we want to use CMD values as arguments for a defined entrypoint, we will use the `exec` form too, but this must be used on both `ENTRYPOINT` and CMD definitions.

- `ENTRYPOINT`: This key will be used to define the main process to be executed inside the created container:

```
ENTRYPOINT <command> <argument1> <argument2> <-- shell form
ENTRYPOINT ["executable", "argument1", "argument2"] <-- exec JSON
form
```

The same behavior is expected here in shell form, but in this case, using this form will not allow the use of CMD values as arguments. Using the shell form for `ENTRYPOINT` is not recommended because it uses `/bin/sh -c` to launch the main process and, in this case, it will not have PID 1 and will not receive Unix signals directly (we will review how Unix signals interact with container processes in `Chapter 3`, *Running Docker Containers*.

Remember, in order to use CMD values as `ENTRYPOINT` arguments, `ENTRYPOINT` must be defined in `exec` form.

When we use a base image to create new ones, the base image's defined values are inherited by new images. This means that CMD and `ENTRYPOINT` definitions will be used unless we overwrite them, thereby setting new values on our image. However, there is an exception; if we set a new `ENTRYPOINT` on our new image, CMD will be reset to an empty value.

Building process actions

The Docker command line provides management actions for Docker objects, as we learned in the previous chapter. Images are Docker objects and the command line will provide tools for building and manipulating them.

I encourage the use of `docker image build` instead of the frequently used `docker build`. As you may have noticed, `docker image build` follows the `object action` schema, which is easier to remember.

We can review Docker image actions in different categories:

- **For management**: `ls`, `prune`, `rm`, and `tag`. These actions allow us to list, remove, and set identifications for images.
- **To get information**: `history` and `inspect`. These actions provide information about the steps that need to be followed to create that image and all its properties.
- **To share images between hosts:** `pull`, `push`, `load`, `import`, and `save`. These actions allow us to interact with the registry to download and upload image layers, and different ways to import and export images to and from different Docker hosts.
- **To create new images**: `build`. Using the `build` action, we will be able to create new images, using base images or starting from an empty root filesystem. Therefore, we will use the Docker image build to create new images. There are a few very important options that change the building behavior, and these must be reviewed for the Docker Certified Associate exam.

We will use `docker image build [options] <context>` with some additional options:

- `--add-host`: This option allows us to include host-to-IP entries with an image. It is very useful for adding non-DNS entries or for masking external resources, for example.
- `--build-arg`: Using arguments during the construction of new images is standard in Continuous Integration pipelines combined with templated Dockerfiles.

In cluster environments, we will need to specify which nodes should build the required image. To ensure that images are built on specific nodes, we will specify some of their labels as constraints by using them as arguments; for example, using `--build-arg constraint:ostype==linux` on a cluster with both Windows and Linux nodes will send the building process just to Linux ones.

- `--file` or `-f`: We can define which Dockerfile to use. We can have different files for each environment, architecture, and so on, but nowadays, there are other features, such as "target definition," that allow us to use a unique Dockerfile for different purposes and build each one as required.
- `--force-rm`: This option will keep your environment clean as it will remove all intermediate containers. By default, intermediate containers are only removed after a successful build.
- `--isolation`: This option is mandatory when building Windows images as we will choose which isolation to use.
- `--label`: This option allows us to add meta-information in key-value pairs format.
- `--no-cache`: By default, Docker daemon will use host cached layers when building a new image. There are some circumstances when we need to create a new fresh image, including, for example, new package updates. In these cases, we will avoid using previously built layers with this option. Take care of time and overheads when using this option since disabling caching will increase build times and we need to execute all the steps to produce a new image.
- `--tag` or `-t`: Tagging an image should be mandatory. By default, Docker will not "name" your images and we will just be able to reference the image using its IMAGE ID (we learned about this earlier in this chapter). It is very important to specify a repository name (we will learn what a repository is in the forthcoming sections; for now, just understand this concept as a simple name) and its version to help us with image management. We can apply more than one tag at build time using multiple `--tag` or `-t` arguments with image names and tags. We will learn that image names are also known as repository names and that we have to add our own registry (with a non-standard port), username, and team or organization that we belong to as a prefix when not using Docker Hub.

IMAGE IDs are unique. Each created image will have a unique ID that identifies this compound of layers on all systems. But we can add tags to this IMAGE ID for ease of management. An image will have just one unique identifier but can have many names and versions. This concept is very important and is key to ensuring the correct image is executed in production.

- `--target`: We can have multiple build stage definitions on the same Dockerfile. These definitions allow us to execute multistage builds using compiled binaries between different resulting images, for example, but they also allow us to have multiple architectures or environment definitions and choose which one to build, instead of using different Dockerfile files.

We can limit the resources used when building using options such as `--cpu-quota`, `--cpu-shares`, and `--memory`, which will limit the number of resources available on each container's execution during the build process.

The build context is a set of files located in a directory or URL (a Git URL or a tarball file) and we use it to refer to its files when building. These files are sent to Docker daemon, to either use them or not during the image build. Therefore, it's very important to know which files in the context directory, Git repository, or tarball are actually needed during compilation. If we have many small files inside our build context or very big files, Docker daemon will retrieve those files and will either incorporate them or not in the image, depending on the Dockerfile instruction. Therefore, the context directory should only contain those files required for the image. Files that should not be managed by Docker during image building should not be in the context path.

Irrespective of whether you use Git URLs or tarball files, the behavior will be similar. Docker daemon will retrieve the repository or `.tar` file and will unpackage or uncompress data to be able to treat the temporary directory as a build context.

We usually store Dockerfiles with our application code and, as a result, the build context is the location where the Dockerfile is located. Due to this, we use `.` to indicate the current directory if we launch the build from the same directory.

A simple command-line example of image building with a number of options is as follows:

```
$ docker image build [-t  MY_TAG] [--label MY_LABEL=VALUE] [--file
MY_DOCKERFILE] [BUILD_CONTEXT]
```

Docker daemon will try to find any file named Dockerfile to script the build. If you are not using this standard name, use `--file` or `-f`, along with the file location (we can use the full or relative path for Dockerfile, but take care of the build context location relative to it).

And, having substituted some real values, we will have something along the lines of the following (this line has been taken from one of the labs at the end of this chapter):

```
$ docker build --file Dockerfile.application -t templated:production --
build-arg ENVIRONMENT=production .
```

Here, we are using a non-standard Dockerfile name, creating an image named `templated:production` using the `ENVIRONMENT` variable with a `production` value inside the building process, and using the current location as the build context. Notice the . at the end of the command. This means that we are using the current directory as the build context to create the image. If we run this command from the previous directory, we will use the directory containing the required Dockerfile as the build context.

> Using the same Git repository philosophy, if there are some files that we want to be stored within our Docker build context (for example, files that come with our Git repository data), but that we do not want to be processed during the build, we can use the `.dockerignore` file to avoid them. Just write down unwanted filenames in `.gitignore` and Docker daemon will not treat them during the image build.

Image tagging and meta-information

Usually, you won't manage just a few images but probably hundreds or thousands, so having as much information as possible about them is very important.

Using labels, we will be able to search for specific images by environment, as follows:

```
$ docker image ls --filter label=environment
REPOSITORY     TAG        IMAGE ID         CREATED         SIZE
myapp          1.0        7dad160a2b02     4 seconds ago   5.6MB
myapp          latest     285c3d16e672     7 minutes ago   5.6MB

$ docker image ls --filter label=environment=test
REPOSITORY      TAG       IMAGE ID         CREATED         SIZE
myapp           latest    285c3d16e672     7 minutes ago   5.6MB
```

```
$ docker image ls --filter label=environment=production
  REPOSITORY        TAG          IMAGE ID        CREATED         SIZE
  myapp             1.0          7dad160a2b02    18 seconds ago  5.6MB

$ docker image inspect myapp:1.0 --format "{{ index .Config.Labels }}"
  map[environment:production]
```

Remember that an image can have multiple names and tags, but its digest is unique. Using different tags and names is very useful for interacting with different CI/CD workflow stages, using the same image content. For example, developers will create many images during development and testing, but only a few will make it to the quality and assurance or certification stages. We can automate these processes based on image names and tags on Docker Enterprise, as we will learn in Chapter 13, *Implementing an Enterprise-Grade Registry with DTR*.

We've already learned that we can have many names for the same image, so removing one image by its name will not really delete its content if it is still in use by other names. If we use its image ID to remove docker image rm <imageid>, Docker daemon will inform us about multiple images with different names using the same layers and will not delete the image unless we use --force, in which case it will remove that image, along with all its layers and referenced names.

 We can use docker rmi as a command alias for docker image rm. On the other hand, docker image prune will be used to remove dangling images.

There are special **untagged images** that will appear in our Docker build hosts as we create new images. These images are the result of making changes between different compilations. They are unreferenced and unused. In your host, when used as their layers, they are not used by any other image and therefore can be removed from our system (in fact, you should remove them because they are using precious disk space). These images are usually known as **dangling** images, and we will learn how to purge them later in this chapter.

To add a new tag to an image, we will use the Docker image tag, SOURCE_IMAGE[:TAG] TARGET_IMAGE[:TAG]. By default, if we omit tags, we are using the latest tag. Avoid using the latest tag for your images as this doesn't really indicate that this was the latest image built. The only way to ensure when the image was built is by reviewing its date of creation.

Docker registries and repositories

Images must be stored somewhere. Locally, each Docker host stores its own data under `/var/lib/docker/image` in Linux and `c:\programdata\docker\image` in Windows, by default. But these directories will work locally only, and we usually need to use images to build new ones and share them across multiple nodes.

We can use the Docker command line to export and import image layers on different hosts, but this is hard to maintain and this method does not scale. Docker Registry is a server application that will store and let us download and upload images as required. It provides an API for sharing information and image layers using a Docker client. As a result, we can define a registry as a store and content delivery system for container images. Images will be stored locally using the settings defined at the Docker daemon level. To use remote registries, we will set up different storage backends that can handle S3, Microsoft Azure, OpenStack Swift for cloud environments, and NFS for your local data center.

At the end of this chapter, we will have a lab in which we will create a local registry. Docker Registry is an open source solution and can be configured using the `/etc/docker/registry/config.yml` configuration file to change storage backends, ports, and other advanced settings.

Docker Hub is the cloud-based registry provided by Docker. We can use it to store public or private images and, as a software as a service solution, there are some features that require a paid subscription.

 Docker Registry will not provide any authentication method, nor TLS, to allow Docker clients to use encrypted connectivity. These security enhancements are only available in Docker Hub (Docker public/private image registry as a service) and Docker Trusted Registry (Registry deployed on the Docker Enterprise platform).

We usually describe three different image namespaces or naming conventions:

- **Root (docker.io hosted images)**: We reference these images using their names and tags; for example, `nginx:alpine` and `postgres:12.0`. They are public.
- **User or organization images under root (docker.io hosted images)**: In this case, images could be private or public, depending on user licensing. Image names will contain the username or an organization, where users are allowed to pull or push their images, for example, `frjaraur/simplest-demo:simplestapp` or `codegazers/colors:1.13`.

- **Full registry format (used for private registries on the cloud or on your own data center)**: We will use usernames, teams, or organizations, but we will need to use the fully qualified name of the registry; for example, `dtr.myorganization.com[:my_registry_port][/myteam or /myoraganization][/myusername]/<repository>[:tag]`.

 In fact, root registries and repository names can be completed using the full registry format; for example, we can pull the `docker.io/codegazers/colors:1.13` image using this full name convention.

You should have noticed that in this case, we added `my_registry_port` and `repository`. We added the first because, by default, Docker Hub and Docker Trusted Registry use HTTPS, and therefore the port is `443`, but we can deploy our own registries using custom ports. `repository` is a reference to a compound of same-named images, each one with a different `IMAGE` ID (unique) and tags (multiple). Consequently, when we talked about the `nginx:alpine` image, we were referring to the `docker.io` registry, the `nginx` repository, and the alpine tag, and the same rule should be applied to all other images used throughout the course of this chapter.

Securing images

As seen in the previous chapter, Docker containers are secure by default, but this is because they run inside namespaces and cgroups isolation. Images are different objects and their security is related to their content. With this idea, it is easy to understand that having less content will be more secure. So, the main rules for securing images are as follows:

- Images should only contain mandatory binaries, libraries, and configurations to run our containerized process. Don't add any non-required applications or debug tools to production images. Less attack surface is better, and having many binaries increases this surface.
- Always declare resources on your images. In this case, we use the term *resources* to describe users, exposed ports, and volumes. Always describe what is needed to run your image and avoid root usage inside a container.

- Update image content packages if there is some security bug fix, rebuild all derived images, and redeploy the containers. In fact, there are more steps to follow, but this statement is true. If you identify any exploit or bug that could result in any security issue, you must fix it as soon as possible using a Docker container's life cycle. To fix the base image with an updated build and rebuild all their derivatives, follow the CI/CD workflow and pass all the tests again before deploying these new image versions to production.

In the Docker Enterprise sections, we will learn about Docker image security scanning, which is an automated tool that verifies all of an image's content against the CVE database. We can mark images as insecure if a bug or exploit is found. This tool can trigger new events to implement a secure pipeline, scan all images before they go into the production stage, and provide information regarding any security risks found.

 We know that image layers are read-only for containers and that a new writable layer will be created for each container. In the next chapter, we will learn that we can improve this situation using the read-only root filesystem, allowing only write access to external volumes.

Managing images and other related objects

We have learned how to manage image containers throughout this chapter, so now, let's take a look at the most common image administration tasks.

Dangling images can be a nightmare if you do not take care of them from the very beginning. As we mentioned in the previous sections, *dangling images* are images that aren't referenced and therefore, are not used by any other image. In fact, they are the result of continuous builds as Docker uses them for caching and improving build performance. They are just layers used during image builds that are no longer used because, in a particular step, we changed a package, we updated our code, we changed a configuration file, and so on, and, as a result, it is not necessary. We should delete these images since they can consume a significant amount of disk space.

Since version 1.13, Docker provides the *Docker* image prune action, which, by default, will remove all dangling images. However, we can choose what images we want to remove, for example, by filtering by date or labels:

```
$ docker image prune --force --filter label=environment=test
Deleted Images:
deleted:
sha256:285c3d16e6721700724848024b9258b05a0c8cd75ab9bd4330d9d48f3313ff28
deleted:
```

```
sha256:62ee8a779b918d678f139941d19e33eeecc8e333a1c00d120c3b83b8545a6650
deleted:
sha256:fb077551608a1c7244c4ed5f88e6ba301b6be2b7db7dd2a4f7194e03db6e18dd
deleted:
sha256:9a704cd7c7c2a5233fad31df5f7186a9cf631b9b22bc89bc4d32d7ab0a1bc4a7

Total reclaimed space: 19.83kB
```

This command line has removed all dangling images with an environment label equal to `test`.

 The Docker image prune not only removes the dangling images but also the old images. However, you should manage this situation because it depends on what containers you have been running in your environment. Before removing non-dangling images in production, verify that there are no containers running using that image; for example, `docker container ls --filter ancestor=<image_to_be_removed>`.

Many containers are used in building operations. By default, Docker daemon will delete all the containers used during builds that exited correctly, so all the containers that were used during correct builds will be removed. However, containers that have been used on faulty builds should be removed by hand. It is easy to identify faulty containers related to image builds. We will usually set container names in all containers launched by hand in other situations. In *Section 2, Containers Orchestration*, dedicated to orchestration, we will learn about the naming patterns used by Kubernetes and Swarm orchestrators to create containers, thereby helping us identify their origin.

 It is always useful to take a look at Docker host filesystem usage, especially the space used by Docker daemon. We can use `docker system df --verbose` to obtain fine-grained information about the images, containers, and volume usage of each host.

Other common tasks involve inspecting images to understand the resources required in each case and sharing them.

Listing images

Listing images is a common task for reviewing host system content. We can modify the default `docker image ls` command's output using the `--format` modifier in the GoLang format structure:

```
$ docker image ls --format "table
{{.ID}}\\t{{.Repository}}:{{.Tag}}\\t{{.CreatedAt}}"
```

```
IMAGE ID                REPOSITORY:TAG              CREATED AT
  28b4509cdae8            debian-with-postfix:latest  2019-10-05 13:18:45 +0200
CEST
  c2c03a296d23            debian:latest               2019-09-12 01:21:51 +0200
CEST
  d87c83ec7a66            nginx:alpine                2019-08-28 00:20:07 +0200
CEST
```

As we learned in the previous examples, we can filter this output using labels, for example, to only show specific images.

Sharing images using registries

We learned that registries are servers where images can be stored using the HTTP REST API. The Docker client knows how to manage the required requests, thereby facilitating image management at these locations.

Images are always required to execute a container. Therefore, each time we run a new container, the image will be downloaded from a registry if it is not present on the Docker host.

We can download images manually using `docker image pull <IMAGE:TAG>`. This will download all image layers and we will be ready to launch a new container based on this image. This is very useful for warming hosts before launching containers; think of a 2 GB image that should be downloaded from the internet, for example.

 We can download all the images from a repository using `--all-tags`; for example, `docker image pull --all-tags --quiet codegazers/colors`. Using this command line, we are downloading all the images (all tags) that are available in the `codegazers/colors` repository without any output.

Consequently, we will use Docker `push` to upload images to registries. But remember to use the full name, including the registry's fully qualified domain name and port (if we are not using `docker.io` and the default `443` port). We will use the full path with custom registries – `myregistry.com[:non-default-port]/myusername/myrepository[:tag]`; for example, `$ docker push docker.io/codegazers/colors:test`.

Docker registries should require a login to access them, for both pulling and pushing. Usually, we will use TLS encryption to connect to registries and it is enabled by default on Docker Client. Docker Engine needs to trust registry certificates to permit login and image pulling or pushing. If you do not want to use this feature, you will need to add a registry as an insecure registry in /etc/docker/daemon.json and restart Docker Daemon.

There are other methods for sharing images. We can save an image, along with all its layers and meta-information, using docker image save. This command will stream content to standard output by default, so we usually use --output to store all the content in a file (or redirect its output to a file):

```
$ docker image save docker.io/codegazers/colors:test -o
/tmp/codegazers_colors_test.tar

$ file /tmp/codegazers_colors_test.tar
 /tmp/codegazers_colors_test.tar: POSIX tar archive

$ tar -tf /tmp/codegazers_colors_test.tar
.........
.........
d420450ab5b04122577e05172291941dcd735eaefd01ab61c64c056b148ebfde/layer.tar
 f99211cb5c4f5e30e2c5d6ce0f0f2ac42361aecbdcc77fd0e2eccf1650558a0c/
 f99211cb5c4f5e30e2c5d6ce0f0f2ac42361aecbdcc77fd0e2eccf1650558a0c/VERSION
 f99211cb5c4f5e30e2c5d6ce0f0f2ac42361aecbdcc77fd0e2eccf1650558a0c/json
 f99211cb5c4f5e30e2c5d6ce0f0f2ac42361aecbdcc77fd0e2eccf1650558a0c/layer.tar
 manifest.json
 repositories
```

As a result, docker image save will create a .tar file containing all the layers, along with all their files, and the manifest file (among other meta-information) required to recreate that image in your host. Notice that we choose the filename and its extension (.tar will not be added by default, but it does not affect content upload).

Uploading this image .tar file is easy. We have two options.

The first option will be to use docker image import. With this action, we will just import image layers, without any meta-information, and so we will not have a defined entry point, command arguments, exposed ports, volume definitions, and so on. It will just import the layers provided by the image into our host.

Consequently, we will not be able to run a container using this image as is (but we will be able to add Dockerfile-like instructions on import to avoid this situation):

```
$ docker import /tmp/codegazers_colors_test.tar
 sha256:5bd30fec31de659bbfb6e3a294e826ada0474817f4c4163dd8a62027b627c81d

$ docker image ls
 REPOSITORY                 TAG                    IMAGE ID            CREATED
SIZE
 <none>                     <none>                 5bd30fec31de        4 seconds
ago          77MB

$ docker inspect codegazers/colors:test --format '{{json
.Config.ExposedPorts }}'
 {"3000/tcp":{}}

$ docker inspect 5bd30fec31de --format '{{json .Config.ExposedPorts }}'
 null
```

We can use `docker image load` to upload a saved image, along with all its layers and information for launching containers. This is a direct step, without any modifications, and we can use this loaded image as is. This command uses standard input to read content by default, but we can use a `.tar` file by adding the `--input` argument or simply by using redirection:

```
$ docker image rm codegazers/colors:test
Untagged: codegazers/colors:test

$ docker image load </tmp/codegazers_colors_test.tar
 Loaded image: codegazers/colors:test

$ docker inspect codegazers/colors:test --format '{{json
.Config.ExposedPorts }}'
 {"3000/tcp":{}}
```

As you will have noticed, we haven't used any name because it takes it from the image `.tar` file's meta-information.

Using `docker image save` on the original host and Docker import/load on the destination host, we can avoid the use of external storage, but as the platform grows in terms of the number of images and hosts, this is not enough and you should use a registry to manage sharing images.

Multistage building and image caches

Multistage building is a feature that appeared with Docker 17.05. Prior to this version, if we wanted to ensure minimum image size and void compilers on final production images, we usually had to install the packages required for compiling, execute the binary's build, and then remove all non-required software, including used compilers, which are a real security problem in production.

Automating this kind of compilation was not easy, and sometimes, we needed to create our own scripts to reproduce those steps on every build, usually using third-party CI/CD orchestrations.

We can use many build definitions on a Dockerfile to create small and compiler-free images. These images will only include application libraries, executables, and configurations. All compilations steps will be done on another image and we will just include the resulting files in a new one. We could also use external images in this process. We will only copy the required files for our application to a new image. This is known as multistage building.

Let's look at an example that will help us understand this new process:

```
FROM alpine AS sdk
RUN apk update && \
apk add --update --no-cache alpine-sdk
RUN mkdir /myapp
WORKDIR /myapp
ADD hello.c /myapp
RUN mkdir bin
RUN gcc -Wall hello.c -o bin/hello

FROM alpine
COPY --from=sdk /myapp/bin/hello /myapp/hello
CMD /myapp/hello
```

In this example, we start a building stage named sdk. We add the name to be able to use it as a reference in the next stage. In the sdk stage, we compile our C code after installing the alpine-sdk package with the required tools for that task. As a result, we obtain a hello binary with our application, located in the /myapp/bin directory (check the WORKDIR instruction). In the next stage, we start again with a fresh alpine image and we just copy the compiled hello binary from the sdk build stage (from the previously compiled image container) to /myapp/hello on our new stage build container. And, as always in a building process, this container is committed as our new image.

Multistage building simplifies the creation of images and improves security. This way, the process will just add previously created binaries and libraries instead of compilers, which can cause a security breach.

Templating images

Using prepared Dockerfiles with a certain template format is common. It is certainly a very useful approach. Passing arguments and using environment variables during builds will create different images for different CI/CD stages, for example, using the same Dockerfile.

Templating is key when building using CI/CD orchestration, but there are a few rules:

- Don't use debugging tools in production images, so take care of these images and use slimmer ones (with fewer components) by default in templates.
- Don't use credentials as arguments when building. There are other mechanisms for managing users and passwords and the Docker `history` command will reveal this information.
- Proxy settings are prepared for use as arguments. Therefore, the `HTTP_PROXY`, `HTTPS_PROXY`, `FTP_PROXY`, and `NO_PROXY` environment variables can be used during build time. These variables will be excluded from the Docker history output and will not be cached, so we will need to use an ARG definition to allow changes in proxy settings between compilations using the same Dockerfile. In other words, before using the `HTTP_PROXY` variable, we should call the `ARG` instruction to retrieve its value from the Docker build arguments:

  ```
  FROM alpine:latest
  ARG HTTP_PROXY
  RUN apk update
  ```

The previous code shows an example that illustrates the behavior described since the proxy settings will get updated on every build if its value has changed.

 Operating systems and other applications would use `http_proxy`, `https_proxy`, `ftp_proxy`, and `no_proxy` instead of the capital strings described in this section. Review the application's requirements and use the appropriate format.

We will see a simple, but illustrative, lab at the end of this chapter that uses a templated Dockerfile that will build a different version for production and development, along with a different base image that includes some debugging tools for developers.

Image releases and updates

Earlier, we mentioned how we should manage image updates. In that instance, we were focused on security updates to avoid bugs and exploits in production. Similarly, we can apply this concept to application fixes and releases.

Base images should be updated in critical image components and these changes do not happen very frequently. Usually, the application releases are weekly or even daily (or hourly, depending on numerous factors, such as business requirements and critical fixes).

Depending on how many containers are running based on a specific image, a new image release can be a big change. These changes can be done in a couple of minutes or they can take you an hour. However, the procedure using containers is very quick; *let the orchestrator do its job*. Kubernetes and Swarm will provide automated image updates and rollback and we will be able to manage how this deployment should be done, how many containers will update their images in parallel, how much time we will wait between these updates, and more.

It is easy to understand that changes to base images (used for building the others) require special care. Those image updates must be managed in cascade to all derived images. We will usually automate this kind of cascade building. These changes will require all the derived images to be rebuilt and will involve much more effort. It is recommended to use a Continuous Integration orchestrator to automate these kinds of tasks.

On the other hand, when we create a code or binary update, the changes will be easier because we will only affect the containers that were created for a specific application. We can deploy these updates quickly after passing all the required tests in our organization.

Chapter labs

In this section, we will review the most important concepts for the Docker Certified Associate exam. For these labs, we will be using a CentOS Linux host with a Docker engine installed, which we covered in the previous chapter.

Deploy `environments/standalone-environment` from this book's GitHub repository (`https://github.com/PacktPublishing/Docker-Certified-Associate-DCA-Exam-Guide.git`) if you have not done so yet. You can use your own CentOS 7 server. Use `vagrant up` from the `environments/standalone-environment` folder to start your virtual environment.

If you are using `standalone-environment`, wait until it
status of our nodes using `vagrant status`. Connect to yo
`standalone`. `standalone` as the name of your node. You
with root privileges using `sudo`. You should get the followir

```
Docker-Certified-Associate-DCA-Exam-Guide/environ.
up
Bringing machine 'standalone' up with 'virtualbox'
...
Docker-Certified-Associate-DCA-Exam-Guide/environme
status
Current machine states:
standalone running (virtualbox)
...
Docker-Certified-Associate-DCA-Exam-Guide/environments/standalone$
```

We can now connect to the `standalone` node using `vagrant ssh standalone`. This
process may vary if you've already deployed a `standalone` virtual node before and you've
just started it using `vagrant up`:

```
Docker-Certified-Associate-DCA-Exam-Guide/environments/standalone$ vagrant
ssh standalone
[vagrant@standalone ~]$
```

Now, you are ready to start the labs.

Docker build caching

This lab will show us how caching works when building images. We will be able to speed
up the building process, but it will depend on how the image layers are sorted. Let's get
started:

1. First, create a directory named `chapter2` in your home directory on your
    Docker host. We will use this directory for these labs:

    ```
    [vagrant@standalone ~]$ cd $HOME
    [vagrant@standalone ~]$ mkdir chapter2
    [vagrant@standalone ~]$ cd chapter2
    ```

2. Create a file named `Dockerfile.cache` with the following simple content:

    ```
    FROM alpine:latest
    RUN echo "hello world"
    ```

build an image named `test1` while using this directory as an image
context:

```
[vagrant@standalone chapter2]$ docker image build \
--file Dockerfile.cache --no-cache --label lab=lab1 -t test1 .

Sending build context to Docker daemon 2.048kB
Step 1/2 : from alpine:latest
---> 961769676411
Step 2/2 : run echo "hello world"
---> Running in af16173c7af8
hello world
Removing intermediate container af16173c7af8
---> 9b3e0608971f
Successfully built 9b3e0608971f
Successfully tagged test1:latest
```

4. Since we have not used any specific tag, Docker adds `latest`. Now, rebuild the
   image without any changes:

```
[vagrant@standalone chapter2]$ docker image build \
--file Dockerfile.cache --no-cache --label lab=lab1 -t test2 .

Sending build context to Docker daemon 2.048kB
Step 1/2 : from alpine:latest
---> 961769676411
Step 2/2 : run echo "hello world"
---> Running in 308e47ddbf7a
hello world
Removing intermediate container 308e47ddbf7a
---> aa5ec1fe2ca6
Successfully built aa5ec1fe2ca6
Successfully tagged test2:latest
```

5. Now, we can list our images using the `lab` label we created during the build:

```
[vagrant@standalone chapter2]$ docker image ls --filter
label=lab=lab1
 REPOSITORY          TAG               IMAGE ID
CREATED             SIZE
 test2               latest            fefb30027241          About
a minute ago    5.58MB
 test1               latest            4fe733b3db42          About
a minute ago    5.58MB
```

Although we have not changed anything, the image ID is different. This is because we have avoided layer caches and we have always compiled each layer. Because we launched image buildings one after the other, only a few seconds passed between them. However, the meta-information has changed between them and they have different IDs, even though they contain the same content.

6. Now, we will use caching because it will improve the build time. In many situations, this can make a big difference. Let's add just a line for installing Python on our Dockerfile. Updating the package cache and the Python installation with its dependencies will take some time. When we use cached layers that have been created from previous builds, the building process will be quicker:

```
FROM alpine:latest
RUN echo "hello world"
RUN apk add --update -q python3
```

7. Now, we build again without caching, measuring how many seconds it took for the process to complete:

```
[vagrant@standalone chapter2]$ time docker image build \
--file Dockerfile.cache -q -t test3 --no-cache .
sha256:f2b524ac662682bdc13f77216ded929225d1b4253ebacb050f07d6d7e570
bc51

real    0m8.508s
user    0m0.021s
sys     0m0.042s
```

8. Now, add a new line for adding `httpie`, which needs Python (and the package cache) to be installed. Now, let's run the build with and without caching:

```
FROM alpine:latest
RUN echo "hello world"
RUN apk add --update -q python3
RUN apk add -q httpie
```

Without caching, it will take more than a minute:

```
[vagrant@standalone chapter2]$ time docker image build \
--file Dockerfile.cache -q -t test4 --no-cache .
sha256:b628f57340b34e7fd2cba0b50f71f4269cf8e8fb779535b211dd668d7c21
912f
real 1m28.745s
 user 0m0.023s
 sys 0m0.030s
```

Before launching a new build with caching, we removed the `test4` image using `docker image rm test4` because we just wanted to use the previous layers.

Using caching, it will just take a few seconds:

```
[vagrant@standalone chapter2]$ time docker image build --file
Dockerfile.cache -q -t test5 .
sha256:7bfc6574efa9e9600d896264955dcb93afd24cb0c91ee5f19a8e5d231e4c
31c7
real 0m15.038s
 user 0m0.025s
 sys 0m0.025s
```

Since this process used the previously cached layers, it only took 15 seconds (`test4`, without caching, took 1 minute and 28 seconds to build). We have just added one layer and, to install just one package, we got more than 1 minute of difference, even though the images are small (around 100 MB in size). It can take hours to compile 5 GB images (which is not recommended, even though it is a good approach for caching).

Where to use volumes in Dockerfiles

In this lab, we will review how the VOLUME key definition will be managed by Docker Daemon to specify persistent storage or to avoid container space when building. Let's get started:

1. Let's consider a small Dockerfile that's using a volume to persist data between layers when building. The volume definition will also inform Docker Daemon about bypassing the volume directory from the CoW mechanism. We will name this Dockerfile `Dockerfile.chapter2.lab2`:

    ```
    FROM alpine
    RUN mkdir /data
    RUN echo "hello world" > /data/helloworld
    VOLUME /data
    ```

2. Let's build this image:

    ```
    [vagrant@standalone ~]$ docker image build \
    -f Dockerfile.chapter2.lab2 -t ch2lab2 --label lab=lab2 .

     Sending build context to Docker daemon  3.072kB
     Step 1/5 : FROM alpine
    ```

```
---> 961769676411
Step 2/5 : RUN mkdir /data
---> Running in fc194efe122b
Removing intermediate container fc194efe122b
---> d2d208a0c39e
Step 3/5 : RUN echo "hello world" > /data/helloworld
---> Running in a390abafda32
Removing intermediate container a390abafda32
---> b934d9c51292
Step 4/5 : VOLUME /data
---> Running in 33df48627a75
Removing intermediate container 33df48627a75
---> 8f05e96b072b
Step 5/5 : LABEL lab=lab2
---> Running in 353a4ec552ef
Removing intermediate container 353a4ec552ef
---> 4a1ad6047fea
Successfully built 4a1ad6047fea
Successfully tagged ch21ab2:latest
```

3. Now, run a container using the `ch21ab2` image to retrieve the container's `/data` directory content:

```
[vagrant@standalone ~]$ docker container run ch21ab2 ls -lt /data
total 4
-rw-r--r--     1 root      root          12 Oct  7 19:30
helloworld
```

4. Now, we will change the VOLUME instruction order. We write the VOLUME definition before the execution of `echo`. We will use a new file named `Dockerfile.chapter2.lab2-2`:

```
FROM alpine
RUN mkdir /data
VOLUME /data
RUN echo "hello world" > /data/helloworld
```

5. Now, let's build a new image and review what happened with the `/data` content:

```
[vagrant@standalone ~]$ docker image build \
-f Dockerfile.chapter2.lab2-2 -t ch21ab2-2 --label lab=lab2 .

Sending build context to Docker daemon  4.096kB
Step 1/5 : FROM alpine
---> 961769676411
Step 2/5 : RUN mkdir /data
```

```
---> Using cache
---> d2d208a0c39e
Step 3/5 : VOLUME /data
---> Using cache
---> 18022eec6fd2
Step 4/5 : RUN echo "hello world" > /data/helloworld
---> Using cache
---> dbab99bb29a0
Step 5/5 : LABEL lab=lab2
---> Using cache
---> ac8ef5e1b61e
Successfully built ac8ef5e1b61e
Successfully tagged ch2lab2-2:latest
```

6. Let's review the /data content again:

```
[vagrant@standalone ~]$ docker container run ch2lab2-2 ls -lt /data
total 0
```

As we expected, the VOLUME directive allows containers to bypass the CoW filesystem. During builds, containers will not maintain volume content because the commit action will just transform container content into images, and volumes are not found inside containers.

Multistage building

In this lab, we will create a simple hello world binary in C and use an intermediate image to compile this code in the first stage and then copy the binary to a cleaner image. As a result, we will obtain a small image containing just the required components to run our compiled application. Let's get started:

1. Create a new directory named multistage inside the chapter2 directory:

```
[vagrant@standalone ~]$ cd $HOME/chapter2
[vagrant@standalone ~]$ mkdir multistage
[vagrant@standalone ~]$ cd multistage
```

2. Now, create a helloword.c file with the following content:

```
#include <stdio.h>
int main()
{
    printf("Hello, World!\n");
    return 0;
}
```

3. Prepare a multistage Dockerfile based on `alpine` called
   `Dockerfile.multistage`. The first stage will be named `compiler` and in it, we
   will install `alpine-sdk` to compile C code. We compile the C code in the first
   stage and we just use a `COPY` sentence to copy the binary from the previous stage.
   It will look like this:

```
FROM alpine AS compiler
RUN apk update && \
apk add --update -q --no-cache alpine-sdk
RUN mkdir /myapp
WORKDIR /myapp
ADD helloworld.c /myapp
RUN mkdir bin
RUN gcc -Wall helloworld.c -o bin/helloworld

FROM alpine
COPY --from=compiler /myapp/bin/helloworld /myapp/helloworld
CMD /myapp/helloworld
```

Using the previous code, we will build a new image:

```
[vagrant@standalone multistage]$ docker build \
--file Dockerfile.multistage --no-cache -t helloworld --label
lab=lab3 .

 Sending build context to Docker daemon  3.072kB
 Step 1/11 : FROM alpine AS compiler
 ---> 961769676411
 Step 2/11 : RUN apk update && apk add --update -q --no-cache
alpine-sdk
 ---> Running in f827f4a85626
 fetch
http://dl-cdn.alpinelinux.org/alpine/v3.10/main/x86_64/APKINDEX.tar
.gz
 fetch
http://dl-cdn.alpinelinux.org/alpine/v3.10/community/x86_64/APKINDE
X.tar.gz
 v3.10.2-102-ge3e3e39529
[http://dl-cdn.alpinelinux.org/alpine/v3.10/main]
 v3.10.2-103-g1b5ddad804
[http://dl-cdn.alpinelinux.org/alpine/v3.10/community]
 OK: 10336 distinct packages available
 Removing intermediate container f827f4a85626
 ---> f5c469c3ab61
 Step 3/11 : RUN mkdir /myapp
 ---> Running in 6eb27f4029b3
 Removing intermediate container 6eb27f4029b3
```

```
---> 19df6c9092ba
Step 4/11 : WORKDIR /myapp
---> Running in 5b7e7ef9504a
Removing intermediate container 5b7e7ef9504a
---> 759173258ccb
Step 5/11 : ADD helloworld.c /myapp
---> 08033f10200a
Step 6/11 : RUN mkdir bin
---> Running in eaaff98b5213
Removing intermediate container eaaff98b5213
---> 63b5d119a25e
Step 7/11 : RUN gcc -Wall helloworld.c -o bin/helloworld
---> Running in 247c18ccaf03
Removing intermediate container 247c18ccaf03
---> 612d15bf6d3c
Step 8/11 : FROM alpine
---> 961769676411
Step 9/11 : COPY --from=compiler /myapp/bin/helloworld
/myapp/helloworld
---> 18c68d924646
Step 10/11 : CMD /myapp/helloworld
---> Running in 7055927efe3e
Removing intermediate container 7055927efe3e
---> 08fd2f42bba9
Step 11/11 : LABEL lab=lab3
---> Running in 3a4f4a1ad6d8
Removing intermediate container 3a4f4a1ad6d8
---> 0a77589c8ecb
Successfully built 0a77589c8ecb
Successfully tagged helloworld:latest
```

4. We can now verify that helloworld:latest works as expected and that it will just contain the /myapp/helloworld binary on top of a clean alpine:latest image:

```
[vagrant@standalone multistage]$ docker container run
helloworld:latest
 Hello, World!
```

Now, we will list the images in order to review the image we created recently:

```
[vagrant@standalone multistage]$ docker image ls --filter
label=lab=lab3
 REPOSITORY          TAG                 IMAGE ID
CREATED             SIZE
 helloworld          latest              0a77589c8ecb        2
minutes ago         5.6MB
```

Deploying a local registry

In this lab, we will run a local registry and push/pull an image. Let's get started:

1. First, we'll deploy a registry using the official Docker Registry image. We will launch it on the standard registry port, `5000`:

   ```
   [vagrant@standalone ~]$ cd $HOME/chapter2

   [vagrant@standalone ~]$ docker container run -d \
   -p 5000:5000 --restart=always --name registry registry:2
   ....
   ....
   0d63bdad4017ce925b5c4456cf9f776551070b7780f306882708c77ce3dce78c
   ```

2. Then, we need to download a simple `alpine:latest` image (if you don't already have one):

   ```
   [vagrant@standalone ~]$ docker pull alpine
   Using default tag: latest
   latest: Pulling from library/alpine
   e6b0cf9c0882: Pull complete
   Digest:
   sha256:2171658620155679240babee0a7714f6509fae66898db422ad803b951257
   db78
   Status: Downloaded newer image for alpine:latest
   docker.io/library/alpine:latest
   ```

3. Then, we need to add a new tag to this image to be able to upload it to our local registry, which is running on port `5000`:

   ```
   [vagrant@standalone ~]$ docker tag alpine localhost:5000/my-alpine
   ```

   We will use `docker image tag <ORIGINAL_TAG> <NEW_TAG>` to add names and tags to images. This will add new names and tags; the old ones will stay until they are removed. We will use `docker image rm` to remove image names and tags. This will remove only the names and tags passed as arguments. Other images associated with the same ID will remain until they are specifically removed. If we create a new build, some layers will be un-referenced and even pushed out of any image construction chain.

We can remove all the images associated with a specific ID using `docker image rm --force <IMAGE_ID>`. All image names and tags associated with it will be removed.

Unreferenced images, also known as **dangling** images, should be removed, especially on image-building hosts. These are common in CI/CD environments where we assign some nodes to this process. We will use `docker image prune` to execute this image's housekeeping.

4. Then, we push the image to our local registry:

```
[vagrant@standalone ~]$ docker image push localhost:5000/my-alpine
The push refers to repository [localhost:5000/my-alpine]
6b27de954cca: Pushed
latest: digest:
sha256:3983cc12fb9dc20a009340149e382a18de6a8261b0ac0e8f5fcdf11f8dd5
937e size: 528
```

5. To ensure that no other alpine image is present, we remove it by its ID:

```
[vagrant@standalone ~]$ docker images --
filter=reference='alpine:latest'
REPOSITORY TAG IMAGE ID CREATED SIZE
alpine latest cc0abc535e36 42 hours ago 5.59MB
```

6. We remove this ID and all its children (the IDs may vary):

```
[vagrant@standalone ~]$ docker image rm cc0abc535e36 --force
Untagged: alpine:latest
Untagged:
alpine@sha256:2171658620155679240babee0a7714f6509fae66898db422ad803
b951257db78
Untagged: localhost:5000/my-alpine:latest
Untagged: localhost:5000/my-
alpine@sha256:3983cc12fb9dc20a009340149e382a18de6a8261b0ac0e8f5fcdf
11f8dd5937e
Deleted:
sha256:cc0abc535e36a7ede71978ba2bbd8159b8a5420b91f2fbc520cdf5f67364
0a34
```

7. Then, we run a container using the `localhost:5000/my-alpine:latest` image:

```
[vagrant@standalone ~]$ docker container run localhost:5000/my-
alpine:latest ls /tmp
Unable to find image 'localhost:5000/my-alpine:latest' locally
latest: Pulling from my-alpine
e6b0cf9c0882: Already exists
Digest:
sha256:3983cc12fb9dc20a009340149e382a18de6a8261b0ac0e8f5fcdf11f8dd5
937e
Status: Downloaded newer image for localhost:5000/my-alpine:latest
```

Here, we used the image we downloaded from our `localhost:5000` registry.

As we mentioned previously, Docker Registry is insecure by default. It is easy to deploy but we will need authentication and authorization in production. Authentication can be deployed using a frontend proxy with validation. NGINX can be deployed even with basic authentication and can also provide TLS certificate encryption. Authorization is not as easy, so Docker Trusted Registry is a better solution.

In this example, we published our registry on local port `5000`. The application container will restart if the main process dies and the image's data will be stored on the host under the `/var/lib/docker/volumes/REGISTRY_DATA/_data` directory. We have used the `REGISTRY_DATA` named volume, so the registry data will remain even if we remove the `registry` container.

Docker Registry can be configured to use different storage backends. We will learn about this feature regarding DTR in `Chapter 13`, *Implementing an Enterprise-Grade Registry with DTR*. Docker Registry can be configured using the `/etc/docker/registry/config.yml` file. To deploy a localhost configuration file under the current directory, we will use `$(pwd)/config.yml:/etc/docker/registry/config.yml`. This will integrate a custom file as a bind-mount volume.

8. Finally, we remove the registry we deployed:

```
[vagrant@standalone ~]$ docker container rm --force registry
registry
```

Image templating using Dockerfiles

This lab will show us how we can build images for different environments by adding some debugging tools, for example, to debug a container's processes.

Create a new directory named `templating` inside the `chapter2` directory:

```
[vagrant@standalone ~]$ cd $HOME/chapter2
[vagrant@standalone ~]$ mkdir templating
[vagrant@standalone ~]$ cd templating
```

We will have a couple of images: one for production and one for development. We will build each one with its own Dockerfile; in this case, we will use a simple `nginx:alpine` image as the basis for both:

- Development – `Dockerfile.nginx-dev`:

```
FROM nginx:alpine
RUN apk update -q
RUN apk add \
curl \
httpie
```

- Production – `Dockerfile.nginx`:

```
FROM nginx:alpine
RUN apk update -q
```

Let's build both images:

1. We build both images as `baseimage:development` and `baseimage:production`:

```
[vagrant@standalone templating]$ docker image build \
--quiet --file Dockerfile.nginx-dev -t baseimage:development --
label lab=lab4 .
sha256:72f13a610dfb1eee3332b87bfdbd77b17f38caf08d07d5772335e963377b
5f39

[vagrant@standalone templating]$ docker image build \
 --quiet --file Dockerfile.nginx -t baseimage:production --label
lab=lab4 .

sha256:1fc2505b3bc2ecf3f0b5580a6c5c0f018b03d309b6208220fc8b4b7a65be
2ec8
```

2. Now, we can review the image's sizes. These are pretty different because the debugging image has `curl` and `httpie` for testing (this is an example lab). We will use these images to launch debugging tools in order to review a container's processes or against other components:

```
[vagrant@standalone templating]$ docker image ls --filter
label=lab=lab4
 REPOSITORY        TAG          IMAGE ID        CREATED
SIZE
 baseimage       development    72f13a610dfb    13 seconds ago
83.4MB
 baseimage       production     1fc2505b3bc2    4 minutes ago
22.6MB
```

3. Now, we can build our application image for development and production environments using the ENVIRONMENT variable and a templated `Dockerfile.application` file:

```
ARG ENVIRONMENT=development
FROM baseimage:${ENVIRONMENT}
COPY html/* /usr/share/nginx/html
```

4. Now, we simply prepare a simple text file named `index.html` with some content inside the `html` directory:

```
[vagrant@standalone templating]$ mkdir html
[vagrant@standalone templating]$ echo "This is a simple test and of
course it is not an application!!!" > html/index.html
```

5. Finally, we just compile both images for the DEV and PROD environments. For development, we use the ENVIRONMENT argument, as follows:

```
[vagrant@standalone templating]$ docker image build \
--file Dockerfile.application \
-t templated:development \
--build-arg ENVIRONMENT=development \
--label lab=lab4 .
 Sending build context to Docker daemon  5.632kB
 Step 1/4 : ARG ENVIRONMENT=development
 Step 2/4 : FROM baseimage:${ENVIRONMENT}
 ---> 1fc2505b3bc2
 Step 3/4 : COPY html/* /usr/share/nginx/html
 ---> Using cache
 ---> e038e952a087
 Step 4/4 : LABEL lab=lab4
 ---> Running in bee7d26757da
 Removing intermediate container bee7d26757da
```

```
---> 06542624803f
Successfully built 06542624803f
Successfully tagged templated:development
```

For the production environment, we will do the same:

```
[vagrant@standalone templating]$ docker image build \
--file Dockerfile.application \
-t templated:production \
--build-arg ENVIRONMENT=production \
--label lab=lab4 .
 Sending build context to Docker daemon  5.632kB
 Step 1/4 : ARG ENVIRONMENT=development
 Step 2/4 : FROM baseimage:${ENVIRONMENT}
 ---> 1fc2505b3bc2
 Step 3/4 : COPY html/* /usr/share/nginx/html
 ---> Using cache
 ---> e038e952a087
 Step 4/4 : LABEL lab=lab4
 ---> Using cache
 ---> 06542624803f
 Successfully built 06542624803f
 Successfully tagged templated:production
```

With this lab, we built different images using just one Dockerfile. Arguments will change the building process.

Summary

This chapter guided us in terms of building container images. We learned about all the building steps and tips and tricks that will help us to ensure we have security in images. Building good and secure images is key for production and, as we learned, having good base images will help us build better application images. We will reuse many layers, so it is safer to ensure security from the bottom to the top. To ensure security, we just need to add the requisite software, expose the required processes, and avoid the root processes if they are not required.

We also learned how to store images and their meta-information using code versioning-like tags to ensure that the correct image is running in production.

Finally, we learned how to implement templates to create images for different environments or stages on CI/CD pipelines.

In the next chapter, we will learn how to run containers.

Questions

1. How can we uniquely identify an image?

   a) All images with their tags are unique
   b) The image ID is what really makes an image unique; we can have an image ID with many names and tags, but they will all reference the same layers and meta-information
   c) Only base images on the root registry namespace are unique because all other images are based on these
   d) All the preceding answers are correct

2. Which methods can be used to create container images?

   a) We can build images from containers, committing their read-write layers on top of read-only ones
   b) We can use a Dockerfile, starting with a base image
   c) We can start from an empty one, known as scratch
   d) All of the above.

3. Which image creation methods are reproducible?

   a) Committing containers to images is reproducible because we know which steps we followed
   b) Using Dockerfiles, we will ensure that the requisite steps are written and that the creation process is reproducible
   c) There is no reproducible method for creating images
   d) All of the above options are incorrect

4. Which Dockerfile instructions admit Shell and Exec formats?

   a) RUN
   b) Only CMD
   c) ENTRYPOINT and CMD
   d) All Dockerfile instructions admit both Exec and Shell formats

5. How can we avoid using command arguments when launching a container based on an image?

    a) We can avoid user modification of the main process arguments and parameters by using the shell format for ENTRYPOINT

    b) It is never possible to modify the container main process

    c) It is always possible to modify the main container process arguments, irrespective of the ENTRYPOINT format used

    d) None of the above options are correct

Further reading

You can refer to the following links for more information on topics covered in this chapter:

- Multi-architecture images using new builds: `https://www.docker.com/blog/multi-arch-images/`
- Dockerfile best practices: `https://www.docker.com/blog/intro-guide-to-dockerfile-best-practices/`
- Dockerfile reference: `https://docs.docker.com/engine/reference/builder/`

Running Docker Containers 3

This chapter is dedicated to the Docker command line. We have run some containers in the previous chapters, but we did not go into detail regarding the arguments and options used.

In this chapter, we will talk about different Docker objects, such as images, containers, and volumes, and their associated actions. Not all objects will have the same features and, consequently, they will not have the same actions and arguments.

 Remember that image building is based on container execution. Each layer is the result of executing commands on a container that is automatically "committed" in a Docker node's filesystem. All these layers, when grouped together, constitute an image.

In this chapter, we will cover the following topics:

- Reviewing the Docker command line in depth
- Learning about Docker objects
- Running containers
- Interacting with containers
- Limiting host resources
- Converting containers into images
- Formatting and filtering information
- Managing devices

Let's begin by looking at how to work with the Docker command line.

Technical requirements

In this chapter, we will learn about Docker container concepts. We'll provide some labs at the end of this chapter that will help you understand and learn about the concepts covered. These labs can be run on your laptop or PC using the provided Vagrant standalone environment or any Docker host of your own that you've deployed. Additional information can be found in this book's GitHub repository at `https://github.com/PacktPublishing/Docker-Certified-Associate-DCA-Exam-Guide.git`.

Check out the following video to see the Code in Action:

`"https://bit.ly/32AEGHU"`

Reviewing the Docker command line in depth

As we learned in the previous chapters, Docker is a client-server application. Previous versions of the software installed both components at the same time, but the newer versions allow us to just install the client for using remote servers.

We learned about the various Docker daemon options and arguments in `Chapter 1`, *Modern Infrastructures and Applications with Docker*. In this chapter, we are going to review the Docker client command line.

When we use the Docker command line on either Linux or Windows, we are always referencing the Docker client and, usually, the binary or executable program is `/usr/bin/docker` or `C:\ProgramData\Docker` on Linux and Windows, respectively.

Docker's command-line usage format is `docker [OPTIONS] COMMAND`. Various options are used to define the daemon we will connect to and how this communication will be created. Debugging and the level of logging are managed at this point too. Some of these options can be set using Docker client configuration in each user' s `config.json` file under their `home` directory.

> The Docker client configuration file, `config.json`, will manage filtering options, which we will learn about at the end of this chapter. It also stores login access to registries.

Environment variables can also be used to configure Docker client behavior. Here is a list of the most frequently used ones:

- `DOCKER_CONFIG`: This will set the Docker client's config file path.
- `DOCKER_CERT_PATH`: This sets the path for client-server certificates.
- `DOCKER_HOST`: We can use remote Docker engines. By default, we will use the local Docker daemon.
- `DOCKER_TLS`: This option enables TLS communication (requires certificates to work).
- `DOCKER_TLS_VERIFY`: This option will not validate remote daemon certificates.
- `DOCKER_CONTENT_TRUST`: We will use this option to use content trust features (image immutability and ownership).

Docker commands will always require a Docker daemon and they will be executed against **objects.** These are internal resources managed by Docker, distributed on categories with different features and properties. We'll look at this in more detail in the next section.

> All Docker objects have their own IDs. Names are tags associated with these IDs and therefore, in some cases, we will be able to have many names for an object. The object ID will uniquely identify each object and thus, Docker can show or manage information regarding that object without using its category. We recommend using categories that are always on the Docker command line.

The following table shows the commands that will be common to all objects:

`ls` or `list`	This will show a list of all objects in that category. The output may be different, depending on which objects are queried, but we will usually obtain object names and their IDs.We will use the `--all` or `-a` modifiers to show all the objects from a selected category because, in some cases, the output will only show a subset. For example, if we list container objects, by default, we will just get running containers. Dead (exited) containers will not be shown unless you use the `--all` command modifier. Filtering will allow us to retrieve only a subset of objects. We will use the `--filter` or `-f` arguments for this. Each object category will have its own keys for easy filtering. We will learn how to filter information later in this chapter. Formatting is also very important. We will use the `--format` option to format the output's information. The usual formats are `table` and `json` for obtaining table-like information and JSON formats, respectively. We can customize and sort obtained information. All filters should be constructed using the Go templates format. Formatting output is an art! We will see many options later in this chapter. A good starting point will always be to use `--format='{{json .}}'` to review which JSON keys can be used for formatting. We can avoid a full command's output using `--quiet` or `-q`. This parameter will show only listed object IDs in that category. This is very useful for concatenating or piping output to other commands.
`rm` or `remove`	This action will remove defined objects. We can remove them using their IDs or their names. Once deleted, they cannot be recovered. To avoid confirmation of object deletion, we will use the `--force` argument.
`create`	All objects can be created and removed, but each object will have its own arguments. Therefore, we will learn about each object's arguments in different chapters. We will start with container arguments in the next section.

`inspect`	To review object-defined properties, we will use the `inspect` action. By default, the object description will be shown in JSON format.
	We can also use `--format` to format its output. In this case, we can format the output of the object's description. This is very useful for getting just a few required values, as shown in the following example:
	`$ docker image inspect nginx:alpine --format "{{ json .Config.Cmd }}"`
	`["nginx","-g","daemon off;"]`

The Docker client was programmed in Go and it contains many Go template formatting and filtering options.

Every time we use `docker ps`, we are actually executing `docker container ls`.

In the next section, we will introduce the different resources or objects we have available in Docker.

Learning about Docker objects

Let's define the different categories of objects that are available for a standalone Docker daemon:

- **Images**: These are the basis for creating containers. In Chapter 2, *Building Docker Images*, we learned the concept of multi-layered templates for providing a root filesystem for the container's main process and all the meta-information required to execute it.
- **Containers**: As we learned in Chapter 1, *Modern Infrastructures and Applications with Docker*, a container is a compound of isolated namespaces, resources, and files for a process (or multiple processes). This process will run inside a wrapped environment as if it was alone in its own system, sharing the host kernel and its resources.
- **Volumes**: Volumes are used to bypass copy-on-write containers' filesystems. As a result, we will be able to store data out of containers, avoiding their life cycle. We will learn more about volumes in Chapter 4, *Container Persistency and Networking*.
- **Networks**: Containers run on their own network namespace, but they need to reach real infrastructure networks. They will use host physical interfaces in bridge mode, creating virtual interfaces for each container interface. We will learn more about this working model and many other options in Chapter 4, *Container Persistency and Networking*.
- **Plugins**: Docker plugins extend engine functionality using processes that will run alongside a Docker daemon. They will share information and configuration with the daemon to provide new features. There are three different kinds of plugins: authorization, volume, and network plugins. The Docker client command line provides the interface for installing and managing plugins. Their configurations will be deployed under the `/usr/lib/docker/plugins` or `/etc/docker/plugins` directories.

These objects are available in a standalone Docker Daemon, but there are other objects when the host participates in a distributed Docker Swarm cluster. We will talk about these in the orchestration chapters, but we will provide a brief synopsis here:

- **Swarm**: This object provides cluster properties. It allows us to create new clusters and join or leave previously created ones. It also maintains cluster security by managing certificate authority or locking access to cluster certificates.
- **Nodes**: Nodes are hosts that are part of the cluster. We can update node roles within the cluster and remove them when needed. We can also modify which nodes will run the defined workloads.
- **Services**: Docker Swarm will not manage containers. The minimum scheduling unit in Docker Swarm is the service. They will create tasks, and those will be represented by containers. In Docker Swarm, we deploy services by declaring their state and the number of tasks required to be healthy. We will be able to create services, update their properties (replicas, images used for containers, and so on), or remove them.
- **Stacks**: When we talk about deploying workloads on Swarm, we usually use stacks, which are multi-service applications. We will define all the components required by an application to run. These components will be services and all their volumes, networks, and so on, as well as their interactions.

Swarm objects have all the actions described previously. However, we can also use the update action to set and change object properties. This action is only available using Docker Swarm.

In the next section, we will learn how to run containers securely using the command line described.

Running containers

Containers are just processes that run in an isolated manner on the Docker host. All the features or properties required for the process to run may be tweaked on container creation.

Main container actions

Containers can be created, executed, and stopped when required. The following table will introduce the main container actions for this workflow:

create	Because containers are Docker objects, we can create them. When we create a container, we configure how this container will work, without starting it. This stage will prepare a container and we can review its static configuration using `inspect`. Any dynamic configuration will not be present because the container is not running yet.
start	Once the container has been created, it can be started using `start`. This means that the container-defined process will be executed with the configured isolation (memory, CPU, networking, and so on) and the external resources that are required. Once the container is started, we will be able to list it or review its state.
run	This action will create and then start a container. This is how we usually launch a container. There are some command aliases for many objects and actions; for example, `docker run`. We recommend using full sentences, including the object in which you are executing the action. A Docker container started with either `docker container run` or `docker run` will run in the foreground. Your Terminal, by default, will be attached to the container's output. To avoid this behavior, we must use `--detach` or `-d` to launch the container in the background, detached from the current Terminal.
pause/unpause	We can freeze the container's process using cgroups in Linux. The process will stay suspended until it is unfrozen.
stop	Stopping a container will follow the next workflow described. First, the main process will receive a `SIGTERM` signal. This will try to shut down and terminate the process normally. By default, the Docker daemon will wait 10 seconds before sending a second signal. Then, the daemon will send a `SIGKILL` signal to kill the process completely. Therefore, the daemon will first try to terminate the container's main process gracefully and will kill it if it was not stopped. We can configure what signal to send to stop a container using `--stop-signal`. It defaults to `SIGTERM`, as mentioned previously. Also, we can change the number of seconds to wait (10 seconds by default) before sending the second `SIGKILL` signal using the `--time` argument. This can be configured on container creation or execution using `--stop-timeout` when it is already running.

kill	As we mentioned earlier, when we run `docker container stop`, Docker daemon will first try to stop it gracefully. There are some cases where we want to kill the main process completely without waiting. In these cases, we can use `docker container kill` to stop the container immediately. A signal that's been sent can be changed using `-s` and, by default, a `SIGKILL` signal will be sent.
restart	The `restart` action will stop and start a container. This means that previously learned procedures will be taken and the Docker container's `stop` and `start` operations will be executed. Therefore, the previously described arguments will also be valid.
rm	Containers are not ephemeral, as we have learned in previous chapters. They will remain in our system until someone deletes them. We will use `docker container rm` to remove them. Running containers cannot be removed unless we use the `--force/-f` argument. It is recommended to stop containers in production before deleting them to avoid removing an important one by mistake.
prune	This command will remove all stopped containers. They can be forced using `--force`, and we can limit containers to be removed using filters with the `--filter` argument.
rename	With this action, we change the container name.
update	Using the `update` action, we can change the container's host resource limits and its restart policy.

 Only containers using Hyper-V isolation can be paused on Windows.

By default, all containers will be executed using non-limited resources. They will not run isolated unless we limit their access to host resources. To limit the number of resources available for a container, we must specify its thresholds during creation. We will use the same arguments for `docker container create` or `docker container run`. We will review how to manage container resources in the *Limiting host resources* section of this chapter.

We can use the `--rm` option to remove a container after its execution. It will also remove all unnamed volumes created during its lifetime. These volumes are defined ephemerally to override copy-on-write filesystems. We must remove them manually or use the `-v` argument with the `docker container rm` action.

Container network properties

Containers run in their own network namespace. They will get their own IP addresses and network resources. By default, a Docker daemon will use bridge networking, and containers will get their own name resolution configuration by copying the host values. We can change this behavior on container creation and execution. Let's review some options we can use to configure networking within containers:

`--name`	We can provide a name for each container. If we do not specify any container name, a random one will be generated. This way, we can manage containers using this defined name. It will be used as a hostname by default.
`--add-host`	Using this parameter, we are allowed to add hosts and their IP addresses. We will use `host:ip` formatted entries.
`--dns`	This option will allow us to avoid default DNS resolution. Every time a name cannot be resolved by the embedded DNS server, a query is forwarded to the defined external DNS servers (copied from hosts by default).
`--dns-option`	This will add container-related options to an embedded DNS server.

 Each bridge network will be provided with internal name resolution using the Docker-embedded DNS server, on `127.0.0.11`. There is only one exception: the default bridge interface. In this case, we will need to use `--link` to allow access to a deployed container from another one on a bridge interface according to its name.

`--dns-search`	This option sets the search domain names for name resolutions.
`--domainname`	This option sets the domain name for the container.
`--ip` and `--ip6`	Sometimes, we need to specify a container IP address, either for IPv4 or IPv6. We will just pass version 4 or version 6 addresses as arguments on container creation or execution. Internal IPAM will assign internal IP addresses from the bridged network interface range.
`--hostname`	We can set an internal container hostname. It defaults to the container ID.

--link	We can add internal name resolution to other containers using CONTAINER_NAME:DNS_ALIAS. These added linked names will be accessible to other containers using their names or IP addresses (this is the default option).
--mac-address	This option allows us to set a container MAC address.
--network	We can choose what type of network connectivity we will provide to containers. By default, all the containers will run on the default bridged network. In this chapter, we will just use the default networking mode, but there are other options as well, which we will learn about in the following chapters.
--network-alias	This option helps us specify an alias for the container on a network. We will have more name resolutions for a container IP.

We need to define a restart policy to manage the container's life. We require containers to stop/die and start fast. Resilience is the new key to an application's availability. We can manage this container's behavior with the --restart parameter. There are four options:

- no: This is the default option. The container will remain stopped if it died or it was stopped manually.
- on-failure: This option will restart the container only if it died because of the main process's failure.
- always: We don't care whether someone stopped the container or whether it died by itself. We require the container to be running; therefore, Docker daemon will always try to restart it.
- unless-stopped: This option will not restart the container if we have executed a Docker stop command.

These options are very important as they manage what a Docker daemon has to do with the containers when the Daemon is restarted; for example, when we have to reboot the host.

Container behavior definition

The following table shows some options that can be used to overwrite image predefined values:

--entrypoint	We can overwrite a defined entry point on container creation or execution. Don't rely on your security for this feature. Anyone can change your entry point for any other binary or script included in your image.

`--env` or `-e` or `--env-file`	We can overwrite variables defined within the base image or add new ones for new containers.
`--expose`	We can expose new ports for containers. These ports will be internally available. They are not published.

`--health-cmd,`
`--health-interval,`
`--health-retries,`
`--health-start-period,`
`--health-timeout`
	All these options will overwrite health check base image values.

`--no-healthcheck`	This option disables the image-defined health check.
`--label` or `-l` or `--label-file`	This option allows labels to be added upon container creation or execution. These labels will help us filter or find information pertaining to processes. There are some labels that are automatically added by the Docker daemon or orchestrators to identify grouped objects.
`--user` or `-u`	This option overwrites the image-defined user.
`--volume` or `-v`	This option uses a defined volume or host path mounted inside the container. This option is very important because ephemeral volumes (also referenced as unnamed volumes) that are used to bypass copy-on-write filesystems will be created under `/var/lib/docker/volumes` (or the equivalent path on MS Windows hosts). They are identified by a random ID. Volumes will not follow the container's life cycle and must be removed manually unless we use the `-v` argument with the `docker container rm` action.

Arguments passed on container creation will be added to the image-defined entry point as arguments. Therefore, image-defined CMD values will be overwritten with arguments passed upon container execution. Other arguments such as `--user`, `--env`, `--entrypoint`, or `--health-cmd`, `--health-timeout`, and so on will overwrite image-defined values, modifying the image's process behavior. Notice that the argument syntax is related to the image's defined keys.

Once a container has been created and executed, by default, the Terminal will be attached to its standard and error outputs. We will get all the main process errors and output. We can also launch containers interactively using the `--interactive` or `-i` options. We usually allocate a pseudo-Terminal using `--tty` or `-t` in order to have a fully functional Terminal attached to the main process.

Executing containers

A simple example will help us understand this behavior. We will launch a small web server using an `nginx:alpine` image. In this case, we are using the official `nginx` image from the `docker.io` registry tagged `alpine`, which is the smallest one based on Alpine Linux:

```
$ docker container run nginx:alpine
 Unable to find image 'nginx:alpine' locally
 alpine: Pulling from library/nginx
 9d48c3bd43c5: Already exists
 1ae95a11626f: Pull complete
 Digest:
 sha256:77f340700d08fd45026823f44fc0010a5bd2237c2d049178b473cd2ad977d071
 Status: Downloaded newer image for nginx:alpine
```

The output may vary if the image was already on your Docker host. All the object IDs will be different on your system as they are created automatically for you.

> We can exit from running the container's standard output by executing either the `exit` command or the *Ctrl + C* keyboard combination.

We are stuck on this Terminal because we started a container with Nginx as the main process. What happened? Well, we are attached to the container's main process. If we issue a *Ctrl + C* sequence, since we are attached to that process, we will send an interruption to the container's main process and `nginx` will die. However, if we open another Terminal and list the running containers, it will be listed as expected:

```
$ docker container ls
 CONTAINER ID IMAGE COMMAND CREATED STATUS PORTS NAMES
 f84f6733537c nginx:alpine "nginx -g 'daemon of..." 11 seconds ago Up 10
 seconds 80/tcp gallant_lederberg
```

Since we have not set a name for our container, we get a random one; in this case, `gallant_lederberg`.

> All names will be created using random combinations of names and adjectives.

We can also inspect this running container to get its current IP address. To access its information, we can use either its ID or name. We will obtain all object information managed by the Docker daemon. We will now take a look at the NetworkSettings section from the docker container inspect command's output:

```
$ docker container inspect gallant_lederberg
[
 {
 "Id": "f84f6733537c3733bda67387b394cabce3f35cf7ee50a46937cb1f59f2a7a680",
 "Created": "2019-10-20T09:34:46.179017074Z",
 "Path": "nginx",
 . . . . . .
 . . . . . .
 . . . . . .
 "NetworkSettings": {
 "Bridge": "",
 "SandboxID":
 "7bb519745e9b7becc806f36bc16b141317448388f7c19a3bd86e1bc392bea469",
 "HairpinMode": false,
 . . . . . .
 . . . . . .
 "Gateway": "172.17.0.1",
 "IPAddress": "172.17.0.2",
 . . . . . .
 . . . . . .
```

This output shows that the container was created and that it is running on our system with an IP of 172.17.0.2. We have not exposed its service to the world, although we did notice its port and protocol (80/tcp) on the docker container ls output earlier. The people who created the nginx:alpine image declared this port to access the container's main process. We are not going to continue reviewing the networking aspects of this container here as we have a complete chapter on networking, that is, Chapter 4, *Container Persistency and Networking*. Just be aware that we have a running nginx process in our system that is not accessible for users:

```
$ ps -fea |grep -v grep |egrep -e nginx -e f84f67
 zero 1524 5881 0 11:34 pts/0 00:00:00 docker container run nginx:alpine
 root 1562 1693 0 11:34 ? 00:00:00 containerd-shim -namespace moby -workdir
/var/lib/containerd/io.containerd.runtime.v1.linux/moby/f84f6733537c3733bda
67387b394cabce3f35cf7ee50a46937cb1f59f2a7a680 -address
/run/containerd/containerd.sock -containerd-binary /usr/bin/containerd -
runtime-root /var/run/docker/runtime-runc
 root 1594 1562 0 11:34 ? 00:00:00 nginx: master process nginx -g daemon
off;
 systemd+ 1644 1594 0 11:34 ? 00:00:00 nginx: worker process
 systemd+ 1646 1594 0 11:34 ? 00:00:00 nginx: worker process
```

```
systemd+ 1647 1594 0 11:34 ? 00:00:00 nginx: worker process
systemd+ 1648 1594 0 11:34 ? 00:00:00 nginx: worker process
```

We have not changed any of the parameters from the original image, so we are using image creator options and declared values. For example, nginx is running as root inside the container. Container port 80 is not accessible from outside the bridged network.

We have already learned that there are some parameters that allow container interaction, so let's start a simple busybox to access the previous container's service:

```
$ docker run -ti busybox
 Unable to find image 'busybox:latest' locally
 latest: Pulling from library/busybox
 7c9d20b9b6cd: Pull complete
 Digest:
sha256:fe301db49df08c384001ed752dff6d52b4305a73a7f608f21528048e8a08b51e
 Status: Downloaded newer image for busybox:latest
# wget http://172.17.0.2 -q -O -
 <!DOCTYPE html>
 <html>
 <head>
 <title>Welcome to nginx!</title>
 <style>
 body {
 width: 35em;
 margin: 0 auto;
 font-family: Tahoma, Verdana, Arial, sans-serif;
 }
 </style>
 </head>
 <body>
 <h1>Welcome to nginx!</h1>
 <p>If you see this page, the nginx web server is successfully installed
and
 working. Further configuration is required.</p>

 <p>For online documentation and support please refer to
 <a href="http://nginx.org/">nginx.org</a>.<br/>
 Commercial support is available at
 <a href="http://nginx.com/">nginx.com</a>.</p>

 <p><em>Thank you for using nginx.</em></p>
 </body>
 </html>
/ # exit
```

In the running `nginx` container's output, we will read a few lines. These are `nginx` logfile lines because the main `nginx` process is redirected to standard output. In fact, both error and access logs are redirected to the container's output. If we go back to the first Terminal, this is what we get from running the `nginx` container's standard output and error:

```
$ docker container run nginx:alpine
 172.17.0.3 - - [20/Oct/2019:10:26:56 +0000] "GET / HTTP/1.1" 200 612 "-"
"Wget" "-"
 172.17.0.3 - - [20/Oct/2019:10:27:09 +0000] "GET / HTTP/1.1" 200 612 "-"
"Wget" "-"
```

Notice that the `busybox` container's IP (running from the second Terminal) is shown on `nginx` requests.

We have learned that running two containers together on the same network subnet will have unlimited access. This happens because we don't have any rules to disallow this interaction. Both containers use the default bridge network, which is why they run in the same network.

If we exit the `busybox` container using a simple `exit` command line on the container's shell, we will exit the main process (shell) and consequently, the container will die.

We can list non-running containers by using `--all` or `-a` because, by default, `docker container ls` will only show running containers:

```
$ docker container ls --all
 CONTAINER ID IMAGE COMMAND CREATED STATUS PORTS NAMES
 4848ed569f61 busybox "sh" 34 minutes ago Exited (0) 31 minutes ago
interesting_yalow
 f84f6733537c nginx:alpine "nginx -g 'daemon of..." About an hour ago Up
About an hour 80/tcp gallant_lederberg
```

Here, we can see that we can review running and stopped containers. We will stop the `gallant_lederberg` container (ID: `f84f6733537c`). Remember that executing `docker container stop` will first try to issue a graceful stop before killing the main process:

```
$ docker stop gallant_lederberg
 gallant_lederberg
```

The container is stopped immediately. Now, let's run another container that is not so easy to stop. We can run a `busybox` image executing an infinite ping to `www.google.com`, for example, and review what happens when we try to stop it:

```
$ docker container run --name ping busybox ping www.google.com
 PING www.google.com (172.217.16.228): 56 data bytes
 64 bytes from 172.217.16.228: seq=0 ttl=56 time=694.384 ms
```

```
64 bytes from 172.217.16.228: seq=1 ttl=56 time=291.257 ms
64 bytes from 172.217.16.228: seq=2 ttl=56 time=365.674 ms
64 bytes from 172.217.16.228: seq=3 ttl=56 time=433.928 ms
64 bytes from 172.217.16.228: seq=4 ttl=56 time=718.424 ms
```

We have changed the `busybox` image-defined CMD with the passed argument, `ping www.google.com`. As a result, we will get an infinite ping output. To stop this container and review how much time it takes to die, we can send a `stop` command from another Terminal:

```
$ time docker container stop ping
ping
real 0m10,721s
user 0m0,019s
sys 0m0,032s
```

We added `time` before the Docker command to review how many seconds the container took to stop. As we expected, the ping had to be killed and, as a result, the `stop` command took more than the default 10 seconds.

We launched a named container using the `--name` argument. To ensure the uniqueness of containers, once a container is created with a name, it is not possible to create another one with the same name. When we get into the orchestration chapters of this book, we will learn how orchestrators manage the naming of containers. To deploy another ping container, in this case, we will need to remove the first ping container using `docker container rm ping`.

We have seen how to launch a container using the `docker container run` command and how to stop it. Let's now review container creation to understand the container's life cycle:

```
$ docker container create --name webserver nginx:alpine
6121184dd136781ceb87a210049b25334ce140968dd110ea7d6945ced3ca6668
```

We obtained the container's identification, but it is not running. We can verify this situation by executing `docker container ls --filter name=webserver`.

If we filter using all containers, including those that are not running, we can see that the container was created:

```
$ docker container ls --all --filter name=webserver
  CONTAINER ID          IMAGE               COMMAND                   CREATED
  STATUS                PORTS               NAMES
  6121184dd136          nginx:alpine        "nginx -g 'daemon of..."  2 minutes
ago         Created                                 webserver
```

Now that the container has been created, we can start it using `docker container start`:

```
$ docker container start webserver
webserver
```

The container was started, but we are not attached to its main process's input/output. Container creation is different from running a container. As we will learn, Docker Swarm services and Kubernetes pods will create container configurations and they will also start a defined number of replicas. This is different from starting a single container.

The STATUS column shows that the container is now running:

```
$ docker container ls --filter name=webserver
  CONTAINER       ID        IMAGE       COMMAND         CREATED        STATUS
PORTS NAMES
  6121184dd136 nginx:alpine "nginx -g 'daemon of..." 10 minutes ago   Up        3
minutes 80/tcp webserver
```

 We can add attachments to the container's input/output by adding the `--attach` argument to the `docker container run` action. This way, we will run the container interactively. Remember that your interaction with the container's main process will depend on the parameters that are passed when it was created. We can also use `--interactive` as the `start` parameter.

Container security options

There are a number of options for container creation and execution related to its security. Let's review the most important ones with some examples:

`--cap-add or --cap-drop`	Remember that not all system calls are available inside containers. We can add or drop default ones using this option. For example, if a container needs some special networking features for creating interfaces or allowing ports under 1024, we will add NET_ADMIN capability.
`--disable-content-trust`	We use this option to disable any content trust verification (check image origin or ownership, for example). This is not recommended in production environments.
`--isolation`	This option is only used on MS Windows containers. Allowed values are `process` or `hyper-v`. We will choose which isolation will be used in our container. Remember that they have different features, as we learned in Chapter 1, *Modern Infrastructures and Applications with Docker*.

--privileged	Privileged containers will run with all capabilities and without any resource limitations. Be careful with these kinds of containers and always try to establish what capabilities are required by your application instead of using the privileged mode.
--read-only	We can run containers using a read-only root filesystem. This is a very good practice in general but we must ensure that all the required container storage will use volumes.
--security-opt	We will be able to change container options when changing default security behavior; for example, using a different seccomp profile or specifying that the container will run unconfined. Custom SELinux policies will also use this parameter to inform SELinux of non-default values.

All the security options described here must be used with care. It is very important to understand what capabilities or requirements the applications have instead of using default or insecure configurations.

It is very important to understand that executing containers using privileged mode will bypass all resource restrictions. Be sure that the --privileged option is only used in specific situations where you really understand the implications of running a container with all capabilities and without any resource limits. Users allowed to execute privileged containers can run processes without CPU or memory limits and can modify important system files.

Take your time to review the application requirements before executing the privileged containers. Only use them under very clear circumstances and watch out for any suspicious behavior on those containers.

Executing containers in read-only mode is very useful. We can ensure that the applications will not change during their lifetime. Of course, using read-only mode depends on your application, but it is good to take some time to analyze the process and try to make it work with a read-only filesystem. We will separate writable directories into ephemeral volumes to store process data. This is a very good practice for improving security easily.

Using host namespaces

The following options are not directly related to security, but they are very important. These are related to container isolation and must be managed with care because any misuse may cause significant security problems:

`--ipc`
`--pid`
`--uts`
	We can share host namespaces if needed. For example, if we are executing a monitoring application inside a container and we need to be able to watch for host processes, we will include a host `pid` namespace using `--pid host`. Take care of these options as this container will be able to manage host processes if we also use extra capabilities or privileged mode.

`--network`	We have mentioned this option before, but not in this context. We can use a host network. In this case, we will use the host's network inside a container. Therefore, all host interfaces will be available inside the container. Other containers' interfaces will also be included.
`--userns`	In the first chapter, we talked about user namespaces inside containers. We learned about process isolation when we introduced the main container's concepts. This option will allow us to implement an isolated user namespace inside a container. We must first prepare user mappings and then we will set which one to use on container creation or execution.

We can easily verify some of the options mentioned in our Docker host. For example, we can run a container using the host network mode and retrieve the container's interface:

```
$ docker container run busybox ip add
 1: lo: <LOOPBACK,UP,LOWER_UP> mtu 65536 qdisc noqueue qlen 1000
 link/loopback 00:00:00:00:00:00 brd 00:00:00:00:00:00
 inet 127.0.0.1/8 scope host lo
 valid_lft forever preferred_lft forever
 37: eth0@if38: <BROADCAST,MULTICAST,UP,LOWER_UP,M-DOWN> mtu 1500 qdisc
noqueue
 link/ether 02:42:ac:11:00:03 brd ff:ff:ff:ff:ff:ff
 inet 172.17.0.3/16 brd 172.17.255.255 scope global eth0
 valid_lft forever preferred_lft forever
```

Now, we can launch another container using the same image but with a host network:

```
$ docker container run --network=host busybox ip add
 1: lo: <LOOPBACK,UP,LOWER_UP> mtu 65536 qdisc noqueue qlen 1000
 link/loopback 00:00:00:00:00:00 brd 00:00:00:00:00:00
 inet 127.0.0.1/8 scope host lo
 valid_lft forever preferred_lft forever
 inet6 ::1/128 scope host
 valid_lft forever preferred_lft forever
```

```
 2: enp0s25: <NO-CARRIER,BROADCAST,MULTICAST,UP> mtu 1500 qdisc fq_codel
qlen 1000
 link/ether 68:f7:28:c1:bc:13 brd ff:ff:ff:ff:ff:ff
 3: wlp3s0: <BROADCAST,MULTICAST,UP,LOWER_UP> mtu 1500 qdisc mq qlen 1000
 link/ether 34:02:86:e3:f6:25 brd ff:ff:ff:ff:ff:ff
 inet 192.168.200.161/24 brd 192.168.200.255 scope global dynamic wlp3s0
 valid_lft 49sec preferred_lft 49sec
 inet6 fe80::ee87:e44f:9189:f720/64 scope link
 valid_lft forever preferred_lft forever
 6: virbr1: <NO-CARRIER,BROADCAST,MULTICAST,UP> mtu 1500 qdisc noqueue qlen
1000
 link/ether 52:54:00:f7:57:34 brd ff:ff:ff:ff:ff:ff
 inet 192.168.39.1/24 brd 192.168.39.255 scope global virbr1
 valid_lft forever preferred_lft forever
 ......
```

All host interfaces are available inside this small busybox container. This is very useful for monitoring host resources. This can help us solve host network problems without installing any software, especially in a production environment.

In the next section, we will learn how to interact with running containers, execute new processes inside them, and copy content to or from them.

Interacting with containers

We can interact with running or stopped containers. We need to interact with containers to run some processes within them, review some of their files, or retrieve the main process output. These are the main actions we will use to interact with containers:

attach	Using `attach`, we will be able to connect to the main process's STDIN/STDOUT/STDERR. In other terms, we will be attached to this process to interact with it. Be careful because sending a signal with your keyboard may interrupt the process and container's life (we can omit this behavior using `--sig-proxy false`). We can only attach to running containers.
cp	This action will allow us to send /receive content to/from the container's filesystem. It acts as a normal copy but we can maintain file ownership using `--archive`. We will just use the source path and destination and we will use the `<container>:</path_to_file>` notation to reference files inside containers. Containers can be stopped when we copy files to/from the Docker host.

exec	Using `exec`, we will be able to execute a command inside the container's isolation. This new command inherits all main process namespaces. As a result, the new command seems to be running inside the container because they share namespaces.
logs	We can review all the container's output by accessing the container's `STDERR` and `STDOUT`. Logging can be improved using logging drivers to extend its functionality; for example, sending these logs to an external host or logging backend. Logging is fundamental when we execute background containers or services. The only way to know what is happening inside a container is by supervising its log.

> Once attached to a container, we can detach using the *Ctrl + P + Q* keyboard sequence, but we can change this keyboard combination using the `--detach-keys` option while attaching, and when creating or starting a container.

We will now take a quick look at our running containers (if you do not have any, run one container, as described in the previous section):

```
$ docker container ls
 CONTAINER ID IMAGE COMMAND CREATED STATUS PORTS NAMES
 4b2806790a4f nginx:alpine "nginx -g 'daemon of..." 2 hours ago Up 40 minutes
80/tcp webserver
```

Now, we execute `ps -ef` inside the container using `docker exec`:

```
$ docker container exec webserver ps -ef
 PID USER TIME COMMAND
 1 root 0:00 nginx: master process nginx -g daemon off;
 6 nginx 0:00 nginx: worker process
 7 nginx 0:00 nginx: worker process
 8 nginx 0:00 nginx: worker process
 9 nginx 0:00 nginx: worker process
 10 root 0:00 ps -ef
```

We executed the command inside the container's isolation using the main process declared user (`root`, in this example).

If we want to execute an interactive command – a shell, for example – we can do so by specifying `--interactive` (or `-i`) and allocating a pseudo-tty using `--tty` (or `-t`). We can set environment variables for this new process with `--env` or change the execution user using `--user`. If we need to execute the new command with special privileges inside a container, we can also use `--privileged`. This can be very useful in debugging on test environments:

```
$ docker exec -ti --user nginx --env ENVIRONMENT=test webserver /bin/sh
/ $ id
uid=101(nginx) gid=101(nginx) groups=101(nginx)
/ $ env|grep ENVIRON
ENVIRONMENT=test
```

We can copy a file located in the host `/tmp` directory, for example, inside our container using `docker container cp`:

```
$ docker container cp /tmp/TEST webserver:/tmp/TEST
```

As we mentioned previously, logging is an important aspect of managing containers. We can use `docker container logs` on running or stopped containers. These are very useful options to improve the manner in which logs are shown:

`--follow` or `-f`	With this option, we can obtain the online output of a running container. The output will be updated with every new entry.
`--tail`	With this option, we can specify how many previous lines we want to show. By default, all the lines will be shown.
`--since` or `--until`	Both of these options are very useful for showing logging only from or before a timestamp or relative period of time (30 minutes or 30 m, for example).

Now, let's review some of the `docker container logs` arguments in the previously executed web server container. In the following example, we will retrieve all the lines from the `webserver` container's output:

```
$ docker container logs --tail all webserver
172.17.0.3 - - [20/Oct/2019:18:39:52 +0000] "GET / HTTP/1.1" 200 612 "-"
"Wget" "-"
172.17.0.3 - - [20/Oct/2019:18:39:55 +0000] "GET / HTTP/1.1" 200 612 "-"
"Wget" "-"
172.17.0.3 - - [20/Oct/2019:18:39:57 +0000] "GET / HTTP/1.1" 200 612 "-"
"Wget" "-"
```

In the next section, we will review how to avoid host problems by limiting container access to host resources.

Limiting host resources

We have seen some options for limiting the container's resource consumption. We will be able to limit access to CPU, memory, and block devices. There are two types of limits when we focus on memory resources: soft and hard limits.

Soft limits will represent a reservation of resources. This means that a container could consume more memory than declared, but this value will be reserved.

On the other hand, a hard limit will ensure that no more than the declared value will be consumed. In fact, the container will die if this limit is surpassed. An **out-of-memory** (also known as **OOM**) killer will kill the main process to prevent host problems.

 Remember that, by default, if you do not specify any limits, containers will be able to consume all your host resources.

There are many options available to ensure limited access to resources. We can modify default cgroups settings automatically with these parameters:

`--cpu-period` and `--cpu-quota`	CFS is the Linux kernel CPU scheduler and, with these parameters, we modify the scheduler period. Both must be configured in microseconds and will modify the CPU limits.
`--cpu-shares`	This parameter manages the weights for the container's main process. By default, it will start with a value of 1024 and we can set the proportion of CPU cycles by increasing or decreasing this value. This is a soft limit, which means that the Docker daemon will not prevent container scheduling on Docker Swarm.
`--cpus` or `-c`	This option helps us set the amount of available CPU resources that will be provided to a container process. It is related to the number of CPUs available in the host. For example, in a host with three CPUs, using a value of `--cpus=1.5` will guarantee half of the CPU resources for this container.
`--cpuset-cpus`	This CPU setting is simpler than CPU shares or setting how many CPUs to use. We will just specify a comma-separated list of host CPUs where the container can run (we will start at 0 when writing a CPU range).

`--memory` or `-m`	This will set the maximum amount of memory available for a container's process. This is a threshold and the Docker daemon will not allow the container to surpass this limit. Whenever this limit is surpassed, the kernel will kill the container's main process. We will obtain an out-of-memory error. This procedure is known as `oom-killer`. We can disable `oom-killer` using `--oom-kill-disable`. This can be dangerous and you must be careful with this option as containers could take all the host memory resources.
`--memory-reservation`	With this parameter, we will configure a reservation of memory for our processes. It should be set to a lower value than the previously mentioned `--memory` threshold value.

`--blkio-weight`
and
`--blkio-weight-device`
	The first argument will manage how much total block direct I/O bandwidth will be available for a container, while the second one will manage how much bandwidth will be available for a specific block device. By default, all containers run with the same bandwidth. This value is 500, and we can increase or decrease this value so that it's between 10 and 1,000.

 Many of the features we will use to isolate access to resources require that the host kernel supports Linux capabilities. We can review all disabled capabilities using `docker system info`, looking for any `WARNING` messages.

Whenever we need to update the container limits, we can use the `docker container update` action, which allows us to change memory, CPU, and block device usage limits on containers.

There are a few actions that will help us in reviewing the container's resource usage.

We will use `docker container stats` to retrieve container usage metrics. By default, only CPU usage percentage, memory usage and its limit, network and block I/O, and the number of processes inside containers will be shown. We can format its output using the `--format` parameter, with common Go language format patterns. We will usually use a table format:

```
$ docker stats --all --format "table [{{.Container}}]
{{.Name}}\t{{.CPUPerc}}\t{{.MemUsage}}"
 [CONTAINER] NAME CPU % MEM USAGE / LIMIT
 [8ab15ccdc42f] stress 0.00% 0B / 0B
 [ed19e4376cdc] intelligent_easley 0.00% 0B / 0B
 [0ca76903840f] vigilant_mendeleev 0.00% 0B / 0B
 [afa67a5a2162] inspiring_mclaren 0.00% 0B / 0B
 [49229db83166] mystifying_maxwell 0.00% 0B / 0B
 [4cef73c07691] naughty_diffie 0.00% 0B / 0B
```

```
[5dcc40de271e] adoring_wright 0.00% 0B / 0B
[07aeb6f9c6df] focused_fermi 0.00% 0B / 0B
[bbe4cb0d9cac] magical_chaplygin 0.00% 0B / 0B
[4b2806790a4f] webserver 0.00% 4.676MiB / 11.6GiB
```

We can specify a container's name or ID to only show its statistics. It is important to know that `docker stats` is a stream-like command. This means that it will be continuously refreshing content with new data unless we use the `--no-stream` argument to obtain static output on a single page.

 Depending on the amount of data shown, sometimes, values are truncated. This can happen in many other objects' actions. To avoid the truncation of important data, we can use `--no-trunc` any time we need to retrieve all column data.

On the other hand, `docker container top` will show us information in a top-like format regarding all the container's internal processes. Using our web server from the previous examples, we can execute `docker container top webserver` to obtain the `nginx` main process and its child's states:

```
$ docker container top webserver
 UID PID PPID C STIME TTY TIME CMD
 root 17878 17848 0 19:06 ? 00:00:00 nginx: master process nginx -g daemon
off;
 systemd+ 17924 17878 0 19:06 ? 00:00:00 nginx: worker process
 systemd+ 17925 17878 0 19:06 ? 00:00:00 nginx: worker process
 systemd+ 17927 17878 0 19:06 ? 00:00:00 nginx: worker process
 systemd+ 17928 17878 0 19:06 ? 00:00:00 nginx: worker process
```

We can add swap access using `--memory-swap` and `--memory-swappiness` but this is not recommended. Swapping could decrease application performance and it really breaks the logic of distributed microservices. Orchestration will allow us to run different components on different nodes, depending on their requirements.

In the next section, we will review actions related to images. With these, we will be able to create an image from a container, as we learned in `Chapter 2`, *Building Docker Images*.

Converting containers into images

We have learned about three different methods for building images, and all of them use containers in some shape or form. Let's review the container actions that can be used to create images:

commit	docker commit will allow us to create an image from a container. We will add a container's layer as a new image layer. As a result, we obtain a new image. We will set a new image name (although we learned that we can change image names whenever we need to) with its tag. The container will be paused during the commit to avoid file changes during its execution.
export	This action will create a .tar file containing the container's filesystem (including data from all of its layers). By default, this command will stream binary content to STDOUT, but we can use --output or -o to define a file for this content.

When we need to know about the changes we made to the original image layers, we can use docker container diff. This will show a list of all the files that have been modified or created on the container's layer.

Using the container web server from the previous examples, we can observe all the changes that were made during its execution:

```
$ docker container diff webserver
 C /var
 C /var/cache
 C /var/cache/nginx
 A /var/cache/nginx/client_temp
 A /var/cache/nginx/fastcgi_temp
 A /var/cache/nginx/proxy_temp
 A /var/cache/nginx/scgi_temp
 A /var/cache/nginx/uwsgi_temp
 C /root
 A /root/.ash_history
 C /run
 A /run/nginx.pid
 C /tmp
 A /tmp/TEST
```

This list shows added files, marked as A, as well as changed files and directories, marked with C. Notice that every time we add a file to a directory, the directory is also changed.

We will usually deploy tens, hundreds, or even thousands of containers within Docker hosts. It is important to be able to retrieve information about them in order to manage their properties and states. In the next section, we will review some of the options available to format and filter information in container environments.

Formatting and filtering information

Formatting and filtering the output of any command is always useful. In Docker commands with long lists or outputs, it is really necessary. Let's begin with formatting some command output.

Almost all actions that represent or show any kind of information can be formatted. Docker uses Go templates to modify the output format. It is very useful to be able to format output for our specific needs. We will use the table format here. Each column will represent a specified key.

We will consider a brief example output listing all the deployed containers in a host using `docker container ls` with the table format:

```
$ docker container ls --all --format "table {{.Names}}: {{.Image}}
{{.Command}}" --no-trunc
NAMES: IMAGE COMMAND
loving_diffie: alpine "/bin/sh"
recursing_fermi: alpine "/bin/sh"
silly_payne: centos "/bin/bash"
wonderful_visvesvaraya: centos "/bin/bash"
optimistic_lamarr: centos "/bin/bash"
focused_shtern: centos "/bin/bash"
stress: frjaraur/stress-ng:alpine "stress-ng stress-ng --vm 2 --vm-bytes 1G
--timeout 60s"
vibrant_faraday: baseimage:development "curl"
lucid_wright: baseimage:production "curl"
elastic_cori: baseimage:production "env"
```

We have used `--no-trunc` to disable the truncation of printed values. Without using this option, all long strings will be truncated and will only show a few characters. Usually, they will be enough to identify a value, but sometimes, we need the entire string; for example, to review the container's main executed command.

It is very useful to know what keys can be queried for formatting. To obtain all allowed keys for formatting, we will use `--format='{{json .}}'`. This will show all the columns or keys for a specified action (for example, try `docker container ls --all --format='{{json .}}'`). The output will be shown in unformatted JSON.

> The unformatted JSON output is not easy to read. We can use **jq** (`https://stedolan.github.io/jq/`), which is a command-line JSON processor for better reading. Using jq, we will obtain more prettily formatted JSON.

There are a number of customized options for formatting:

`json`	As we have seen, this option will format the output as a single-line JSON string. For example, we can use `--format='{{json .Config}}'` with `docker inspect` output for a container to obtain all its configuration keys and values.
`table`	The table format option is not available in all outputs, but it will work pretty well on lists.
`join/split`	With these options, we will be able to join or split key outputs; for example, `'{{json .Mounts}}'` or `'{{split .Image ":"}}'`.
`lower/upper/title`	These options allow us to change strings to lowercase, uppercase, or just capitalize the first character; for example, `'{{title .Name}}'` will show all names with a capitalized first character.
`range`	This option will help us format list/array values. You have to use `'{{range <JSON keys> }}{{end}}'` to correctly manage the listed values.
`println`	This option will print each queried value in a new line. It is very interesting for formatting range values.

> The `--pretty` option is available for inspecting some objects. It is very useful but, as we mentioned previously, it is not available for all objects. For example, you can use it to inspect services, which we will learn about in `Chapter 8`, *Orchestration Using Docker Swarm*.

Formatting will help us to obtain only required pieces of information, but it will not be easy when we have to manage a lot of items. We will filter the information using the `--filter` option to retrieve only specific objects matching some keys and values. Not all keys will be available for filtering. We will use keys with their values for filters and we can use as many filter options as required. If we add more than one filter with the same key, they will be used as OR. But if we use different keys, this will be an AND filter. We will use "equal" (using =) or "different" (using <>) to compare key values.

Container objects can be filtered by means of the following:

- **ID or name**: With these options, we can find containers by their IDs or names.
- **Label**: This case is special as we can express the query using a key to match all the containers with that label or key-value format, in order to find a specific value for that key.
- **Exited**: We will use this option with an exited integer when using `--all` to filter containers stopped with errors, for example.
- **Status**: We use this option to filter by container state (`created`, `restarting`, `running`, `removing`, `paused`, `exited` or `dead`).
- **Ancestor**: This is very important because it will allow us to filter by image name and tags.
- **Before/since**: This filter allows us to specify dates, for example, to find a container running for a long time or filter by its creation date.
- **Volume/network**: This option allows us to filter which containers are using a volume or network. It is useful for removing old resources.
- **Publish or expose**: These options filter which containers are publishing or exposing specified ports. We can use a range of ports and protocols (`<startport-endport>/[<proto>]`).
- **Health**: This filter allows us to search containers by their health check status (healthy, unhealthy, starting, or none).
- **Is-task**: This option is very interesting because it allows us to filter containers created by tasks when using Docker Swarm orchestration.

> Notice that `--format` is used for filtering on the `docker <object> inspect` command. We can only query specific object keys and subkeys. For example, using `--format='{{json .Config}}'` will just show keys and values under the `Config` key.

In the next section, we will review how to use host attached devices as if they were inside containers.

Managing devices

We can provide access to host devices inside containers. We use the `--device` argument with `docker container create` or `docker container run` for this. We will be able to use hardware devices connected directly to a host, such as serial controllers, block storage, or audio devices.

By default, devices will have read and write permissions. To be able to manipulate special devices, the mknod permission is also added by default. We can override these default settings using r, w, and m in the command line as modifiers of the --device option.

As an example, we can mount our lvm mapped block device to a defined directory; notice that the mounting capability must be added. In this example, we added SYS_ADMIN capabilities:

```
$ docker run -ti --cap-add SYS_ADMIN --device /dev/mapper/centos-
root:/dev/sdx centos
 [root@5ccb0ef8ce84 /]# mkdir /data
 [root@5ccb0ef8ce84 /]# mount /dev/sdx /data
 [root@5ccb0ef8ce84 /]# cd /data
 [root@5ccb0ef8ce84 data]# ls
 bin  boot  dev  etc  home  lib  lib64  media  mnt  opt  proc  root  run
sbin  srv  sys  tmp  usr  vagrant  var
```

In the following example, we are using our host sound device inside a container. Adding these devices to containers will allow us to run some applications with sound:

```
$ docker container run -ti --device /dev/snd alpine
/ # apk add --update -q alsa-utils
/ # speaker-test -t wav -c 6 -11

speaker-test 1.1.9

Playback device is default
Stream parameters are 48000Hz, S16_LE, 6 channels
WAV file(s)
Rate set to 48000Hz (requested 48000Hz)
Buffer size range from 2048 to 16384
Period size range from 1024 to 1024
Using max buffer size 16384
Periods = 4
was set period_size = 1024
was set buffer_size = 16384
 0 - Front Left
 1 - Front Right
 2 - Unused
 3 - Unused
 4 - Unused
 5 - Unused
Time per period = 8.298695
```

Here, we have learned that not just files or directories can be accessed inside containers. We can use special devices as if they were directly attached to containers.

Chapter labs

In the labs in this chapter, we will run containers and interact with them. We will also review some examples, limiting their resources and formatting and filtering the command output.

To run these labs, deploy `environments/standalone-environment` from this book's GitHub repository (`https://github.com/PacktPublishing/Docker-Certified-Associate-DCA-Exam-Guide.git`) if you have not done so yet. You can use your own CentOS 7 server. Use `vagrant up` from the `environments/standalone-environment` folder to start your virtual environment.

If you are using `standalone-environment`, wait until it is running. We can check the statuses of our nodes using `vagrant status`. Connect to your lab node using `vagrant ssh standalone`. `standalone` is the name of your node. You will be using the `vagrant` user with root privileges using `sudo`. You should get the following output:

```
Docker-Certified-Associate-DCA-Exam-Guide/environments/standalone$ vagrant
up
Bringing machine 'standalone' up with 'virtualbox' provider...
...
Docker-Certified-Associate-DCA-Exam-Guide/environments/standalone$ vagrant
status
Current machine states:
standalone running (virtualbox)
...
Docker-Certified-Associate-DCA-Exam-Guide/environments/standalone$
```

We can now connect to the `standalone` node using `vagrant ssh standalone`. This process may vary if you've already deployed a `standalone` virtual node before and you just started it using `vagrant up`:

```
Docker-Certified-Associate-DCA-Exam-Guide/environments/standalone$ vagrant
ssh standalone
[vagrant@standalone ~]$
```

If you are reusing your `standalone-environment`, this means Docker Engine is installed. If you started a new instance, please execute the `/vagrant/install_requirements.sh` script so that you have all the required tools (Docker Engine and docker-compose):

```
[vagrant@standalone ~]$ /vagrant/install_requirements.sh
```

Now, you are ready to start the labs.

Reviewing Docker command-line object options

The Docker command line will allow us to interact with Docker daemons. We will use Docker objects or resources with their allowed actions. In the following screenshot, we can easily review this behavior in the Docker `help` command's output:

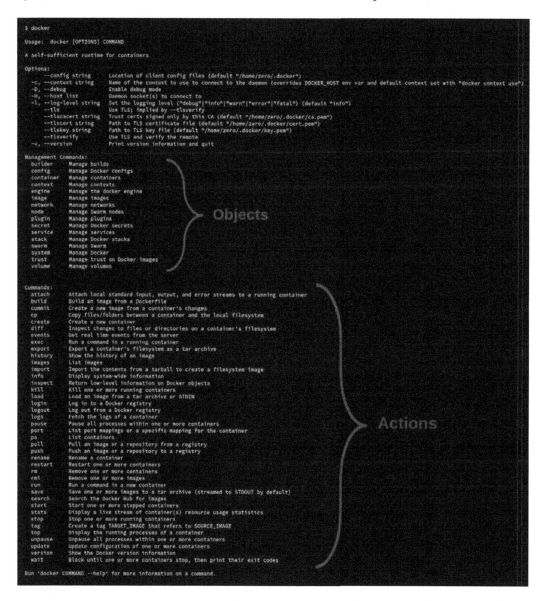

Objects will appear in the first part, after common options. At the bottom, we will have all the options allowed. As we mentioned in this chapter, not all objects have the same actions. This chapter is dedicated to containers. So, let's review what actions are allowed with containers (the output is truncated):

```
[vagrant@standalone ~]$ docker container --help
Usage: docker container COMMAND
Manage containers
Commands:
  attach Attach local standard input, output, and error streams to a running
container
  commit Create a new image from a container's changes
. . . . .
. . . . .
. . . . .
  unpause Unpause all processes within one or more containers
  update Update configuration of one or more containers
  wait Block until one or more containers stop, then print their exit codes
Run 'docker container COMMAND --help' for more information on a command.
```

We should use `--help` with each kind of object to review what actions are available for them. If we have not set any `DOCKER_HOST` variable (nor using `-H`), we will interact with the local Docker daemon. We will use these arguments in the command line to connect to remote daemons.

Actually, there are many well-known Docker command-line aliases:

- `docker run`: `docker container run`
- `docker ps`: `docker container ls`
- `docker rm`: `docker container rm`
- `docker start/stop`: `docker container start/stop`
- `docker port`: `docker container port`
- `docker rmi`: `docker image rm`

It is recommended to use long command-line terms as they actually indicate an object and action. This will avoid confusion or the misspelling of commands.

Executing containers

This is a long lab in which we are going to review many actions and options available to containers. Let's get started:

1. Execute an interactive container based on an Alpine image in the background:

   ```
   [vagrant@standalone ~]$ docker container run -ti -d alpine
   aa73504ba37299aa7686a1c5d8023933b09a0ff13845a66be0aa69203eea8de7
   ```

2. Now, we will review and rename the container `myalpineshell`:

   ```
   [vagrant@standalone ~]$ docker container ls -l
   CONTAINER ID IMAGE COMMAND CREATED STATUS PORTS NAMES
   aa73504ba372 alpine "/bin/sh" About a minute ago Up About a minute
   elastic_curran
   ```

    We use `-l` or `--last` to obtain the latest container that was executed on our Docker host. Notice that we will use `-q` in the following code to obtain the container's ID.

   Now, we rename the previously launched container using its ID:

   ```
   [vagrant@standalone ~]$ docker container rename $(docker container
   ls -ql) myalpineshell
   ```

   If we review the latest container again, we will see that we have a different name. Notice that the container is running (the output will show different dates for you):

   ```
   [vagrant@standalone ~]$ docker container ls -l
   CONTAINER ID IMAGE COMMAND CREATED STATUS PORTS NAMES
   aa73504ba372 alpine "/bin/sh" 11 minutes ago Up 11 minutes
   myalpineshell
   ```

3. We attach our Terminal to the running `myalpineshell` container and we create an empty file named `TESTFILE` under the `/tmp` directory. Then, we `exit` from the container:

   ```
   [vagrant@standalone ~]$ docker container attach myalpineshell
   / # touch /tmp/TESTFILE
   / # exit
   ```

4. If we review the container's status again, we will find that it has stopped, but that it exited correctly:

```
[vagrant@standalone ~]$ docker container ls -1
CONTAINER ID IMAGE COMMAND CREATED STATUS PORTS NAMES
aa73504ba372 alpine "/bin/sh" 14 minutes ago Exited (0) 46 seconds
ago myalpineshell
```

The container now shows an Exited (0) status. The Alpine image's main process is a shell. Its CMD is /bin/sh. We exited by issuing the exit command. Therefore, the exit status was 0. No problem was identified during execution.

5. Now, we are going to force a failure status by executing, for example, a command that doesn't exist in the image. We will execute the curl command on a new container:

```
[vagrant@standalone ~]$ docker container run alpine curl
www.google.com
docker: Error response from daemon: OCI runtime create failed:
container_linux.go:345: starting container process caused "exec:
\"curl\": executable file not found in $PATH": unknown.
ERRO[0001] error waiting for container: context canceled
```

As the curl binary does not exist, we cannot even execute the desired command. As a result, the container was created but not executed:

```
[vagrant@standalone ~]$ docker container ls -1
CONTAINER ID IMAGE COMMAND CREATED STATUS PORTS NAMES
466cc346e5d3 alpine "curl www.google.com" 17 seconds ago Created
fervent_tharp
```

6. Now, we will execute ls -1 /tmp/TESTFILE on a new container:

```
[vagrant@standalone ~]$ docker container run alpine ls -1
/tmp/TESTFILE
ls: /tmp/TESTFILE: No such file or directory

[vagrant@standalone ~]$ docker container ls -1
CONTAINER ID IMAGE COMMAND CREATED STATUS PORTS NAMES
7c328b9a0609 alpine "ls -1 /tmp/TESTFILE" 8 seconds ago Exited (1)
6 seconds ago priceless_austin
```

As expected, the /tmp/TESTFILE file does not exist in this new container. We only created it in the myalpineshell container. In fact, the file is still there. Notice that this time, the container was executed and that the exit status shows an error code. This is the exit code of the execution of the ls command against a non-existent file.

7. Let's rename the last executed container again:

```
[vagrant@standalone ~]$ docker container rename $(docker container
ls -ql) secondshell
```

8. Now, we will create the /tmp/TESTFILE file on our own host filesystem and copy it to the secondshell container:

```
[vagrant@standalone ~]$ touch /tmp/TESTFILE

[vagrant@standalone ~]$ docker container cp /tmp/TESTFILE
secondshell:/tmp/TESTFILE
```

 It is not possible to copy files from one container to another using docker container cp.

9. Now, let's start the secondshell container again and observe the new results:

```
[vagrant@standalone ~]$ docker container start secondshell
secondshell

[vagrant@standalone ~]$ docker container ls -l
CONTAINER ID IMAGE COMMAND CREATED STATUS PORTS NAMES
7c328b9a0609 alpine "ls -l /tmp/TESTFILE" 32 minutes ago Exited (0)
4 seconds ago secondshell
```

The file now exists inside the secondshell container and, as a result, the execution exited correctly. We can notice this new result in the STATUS column (Exited (0)). We have manipulated a dead container by copying a file inside it. Therefore, containers are still present in our host system until we remove them.

10. Now, we will remove the secondshell container and try to filter the container list's output. We will search for the secondshell and myalpineshell containers:

```
[vagrant@standalone ~]$ docker container rm secondshell
secondshell
```

```
[vagrant@standalone ~]$ docker container ls --all --filter
name=myalpineshell --filter name=secondshell
CONTAINER ID IMAGE COMMAND CREATED STATUS PORTS NAMES
aa73504ba372 alpine "/bin/sh" 59 minutes ago Exited (0) 45 minutes
ago myalpineshell
```

As expected, we only get the `myalpineshell` container.

11. To finish this lab, we will start the `myalpineshell` container once more using
`docker container start -a -i` to attach our Terminal to the started
container. Then, we will send the container to the background using the *Ctrl + P +
Q* escape sequence. Finally, we will attach a second shell to the container using
the `docker container exec` command:

```
[vagrant@standalone ~]$ docker container start -a -i myalpineshell
<PRESS Ctrl+p+q>
/ # read escape sequence

[vagrant@standalone ~]$ docker container exec -ti myalpineshell sh
/ # ps -ef
PID USER TIME COMMAND
  1 root 0:00 /bin/sh
  6 root 0:00 sh
 11 root 0:00 ps -ef
/ # exit
```

We can observe that exiting from the newly executed shell process does not kill
the `myalpineshell` container. Both processes share the same namespaces:

```
[vagrant@standalone ~]$ docker container ls --all --filter
name=myalpineshell
CONTAINER ID IMAGE COMMAND CREATED STATUS PORTS NAMES
aa73504ba372 alpine "/bin/sh" About an hour ago Up 4 minutes
myalpineshell
```

Limiting container resources

In this lab, we are going to use the `frjaraur/stress-ng:alpine` image from Docker
Hub. This image is based on Alpine Linux with the `stress-ng` packages installed. It is
small and will help us stress our containers.

We will start with testing memory limits. In this lab, we will use two Terminals on the same host. On the first Terminal, we will launch `docker container stats`. Keep this running during all these labs because, in this Terminal, we are going to observe different behaviors.

In the second Terminal, we will launch two containers that will try to consume 2 GB of memory. We will use `--vm 2 --vm-bytes 1024M` to create two processes with 1,024 MB of memory in each:

1. We are going to launch a container with a memory reservation. This means that the Docker daemon will reserve at least that amount of memory for this container. Remember that this is not a limit; it is a reservation:

   ```
   [vagrant@standalone ~]$ docker container run --memory-
   reservation=250m --name 2GBreserved -d frjaraur/stress-ng:alpine --
   vm 2 --vm-bytes 1024M
   b07f6319b4f9da3149d41bbe9a4b1440782c8203e125bd08fd433df8bac91ba7
   ```

2. Now, we will launch a limited container. Only 250 MB of memory will be allowed, although the container will try to consume 2 GB:

   ```
   [vagrant@standalone ~]$ docker container run --memory=250m --name
   2GBlimited -d frjaraur/stress-ng:alpine --vm 2 --vm-bytes 1024M
   e98fbdd5896d1d182608ea35df39a7a768c0c4b843cc3b425892bee3e394eb81
   ```

3. In the first Terminal, we have `docker container stats` running to review our container's resource consumption. We will have something like this (IDs and usage will vary):

   ```
   CONTAINER ID NAME CPU % MEM USAGE / LIMIT MEM % NET I/O BLOCK I/O
   PIDS
   b07f6319b4f9 2GBreserved 203.05% 1.004GiB / 11.6GiB 8.65% 6.94kB /
   0B 0B / 0B 5
   e98fbdd5896d 2GBlimited 42.31% 249.8MiB / 250MiB 99.94% 4.13kB / 0B
   1.22GB / 2.85GB 5
   ```

   If you obtain a warning message about limiting resources, this is normal. The `WARNING: Your kernel does not support swap limit capabilities or the cgroup is not mounted. Memory limited without swap.` message indicates that your operating system will not limit `swap` for containers. It comes disabled by default on Debian/Ubuntu.

We can observe that the non-limited container is taking more than the specified memory. In the second case, the container was limited to 250 MB, although the process could consume more, it was limited and it will not get more than this memory. It is confined to 250 MB, as we can observe in the MEM USAGE/LIMIT MEM column. It could reach 100% of its confined memory, but it cannot surpass that limit.

4. Remove the 2GBreserved and 2GBlimited containers:

```
[vagrant@standalone ~]$ docker container rm -f 2GBlimited
2GBreserved
2GBlimited
2GBreserved
```

Now, we will limit the CPU consumption.

5. We will launch three containers with different CPU limitations and process requirements. The first container is limited to one CPU, but with two CPU requirements. This is not a genuine requirement, but the process will try to use two CPUs if they are present in this system:

```
[vagrant@standalone ~]$ docker container run -d --cpus=1 --name
CPU2vs1 frjaraur/stress-ng:alpine --cpu 2 --timeout 120
```

The second container is limited to two CPUs with a requirement of two CPUs. It will try to use both during execution:

```
[vagrant@standalone ~]$ docker container run -d --cpus=2 --name
CPU2vs2 frjaraur/stress-ng:alpine --cpu 2 --timeout 120
```

The third container is limited to four CPUs with two CPUs required. In this case, the processes could consume four CPUs, but as they will just use two CPUs, they will not have a real limitation unless we try to use more than four CPUs:

```
[vagrant@standalone ~]$ docker container run -d --cpus=4 --name
CPU2vs4 frjaraur/stress-ng:alpine --cpu 2 --timeout 120
```

6. If we observe the Docker container's stats output, we can confirm the expected results:

```
CONTAINER ID          NAME              CPU %              MEM
USAGE / LIMIT    MEM %              NET I/O            BLOCK I/O
PIDS
0dc652ed28b0          CPU2vs4           132.47%
7.379MiB / 11.6GiB   0.06%              4.46kB / 0B        0B /
0B               3
```

```
ec62ee9ed812          CPU2vs2              135.41%
7.391MiB / 11.6GiB    0.06%                5.71kB / 0B          0B /
0B            3
bb1034c8b588          CPU2vs1              98.90%
7.301MiB / 11.6GiB    0.06%                7.98kB / 0B          262kB
/ 0B          3
```

With that, we have reviewed how we can limit the container's resources. We tested CPU and memory usage with `docker container stats`, pushing them to their defined limits.

Now, let's review formatting and filtering with some labs.

Formatting and filtering container list output

In this lab, we will review the `docker container ls` output. Let's get started:

1. Launch a number of containers. For this example, we will run three `nginx:alpine` instances with sequence names:

   ```
   [vagrant@standalone ~]$ docker run -d --name web1 --label
   stage=production nginx:alpine
   bb5c63ec7427b6cdae19f9172f5b0770f763847c699ff2dc9076e60623771da3

   [vagrant@standalone ~]$ docker run -d --name web2 --label
   stage=development nginx:alpine
   4e7607f3264c52c9c14b38412c95dfc8c286835fd1ffab1d7898c5cfab47c9b8

   [vagrant@standalone ~]$ docker run -d --name web3 --label
   stage=development nginx:alpine
   fcef82c80ed0b049705609885bc9c518bf062a39bbe2b6d68b7017bcc6dcaa14
   ```

2. Let's list the running containers using the `docker container ls` default output:

   ```
   [vagrant@standalone ~]$ docker container ls
   CONTAINER ID IMAGE COMMAND CREATED STATUS PORTS NAMES
   fcef82c80ed0 nginx:alpine "nginx -g 'daemon of..." About a minute
   ago Up 59 seconds 80/tcp web3
   4e7607f3264c nginx:alpine "nginx -g 'daemon of..." About a minute
   ago Up About a minute 80/tcp web2
   bb5c63ec7427 nginx:alpine "nginx -g 'daemon of..." About a minute
   ago Up About a minute 80/tcp web1
   ```

3. Since we want to be able to review the current status of the containers, we can format the output so that it includes label information:

```
[vagrant@standalone ~]$ docker container ls \
--format "table {{.Names}} {{.Command}}\\t{{.Labels}}"

NAMES COMMAND                    LABELS
web3 "nginx -g 'daemon of..."    maintainer=NGINX Docker Maintainers
<docker-maint@nginx.com>,stage=development
web2 "nginx -g 'daemon of..."    stage=development,maintainer=NGINX
Docker Maintainers <docker-maint@nginx.com>
web1 "nginx -g 'daemon of..."    stage=production,maintainer=NGINX
Docker Maintainers <docker-maint@nginx.com>
```

4. Now, let's filter just the development containers (stage=development):

```
[vagrant@standalone ~]$ docker container ls --format "table
{{.Names}} {{.Command}}\\t{{.Labels}}" --filter
label=stage=development
NAMES COMMAND LABELS
web3 "nginx -g 'daemon of..." maintainer=NGINX Docker Maintainers
<docker-maint@nginx.com>,stage=development
web2 "nginx -g 'daemon of..." maintainer=NGINX Docker Maintainers
<docker-maint@nginx.com>,stage=development
```

5. Now, let's kill just those development containers using the list output:

```
[vagrant@standalone ~]$ docker container kill $(docker container ls
--format "{{.ID}}" --filter label=stage=development)

[vagrant@standalone ~]$ docker container ls --format "table
{{.Names}}\\t{{.Labels}}"
NAMES                   LABELS
web1                    maintainer=NGINX Docker Maintainers <docker-
maint@nginx.com>,stage=production
```

Only web1, labeled as production, is still running as expected.

Filtering and formatting are very useful. Practice these methods because they are important for the Docker Certified Associate exam.

Summary

This chapter was dedicated to the Docker command line and running containers. We found a powerful command line that allowed us to create containers from image artifacts, share them between hosts, and execute the already built application components.

We learned how to interact with different Docker objects, as well as what kind of objects are available in standalone Docker host environments and what objects are available in orchestrated environments.

We then reviewed how containers can be created, executed, paused/unpaused, and stopped or killed. They will stay in our Docker host until they are removed from the system. We also learned how to manipulate the container's execution behavior and how they exist within the network. To improve security, we introduced a number of options and we also learned how executing containers in read-only mode can be very useful.

Limiting the container's resources is necessary for production. By default, they will be able to consume all the host's resources, which can be very dangerous. We learned how to avoid this situation using soft and hard limits to ensure that our applications will run on a host with enough resources and does not disturb others.

Formatting and filtering specific information is needed while deploying applications on dynamic environments. We learned how format and filter actions will help us retrieve specific information.

We concluded this chapter by learning how to use a host's devices as if they were attached directly to containers.

In the next chapter, we will look at container persistency and their networking features.

Questions

1. Which of the following options is not available for containers?

   a) `build`
   b) `update`
   c) `destroy`
   d) `create`

2. Which of the following sentences is false?

    a) A container's life is managed using `start` and `stop` commands
    b) Containers always stop after 10 seconds
    c) Containers can be created and then started
    d) Volumes created during the container's lifetime must be deleted by hand unless we use the `-v` option when deleting the container

3. Which of the following sentences is true in relation to `docker kill`?

    a) It will kill all container processes
    b) It will send a `SIGKILL` signal to the container's main process
    c) It will remove the container once it is killed
    d) It will wait 10 seconds by default before really killing the container

4. We executed a container named `webserver`. Which of the following sentences is false?

    a) It can be removed using `docker container rm --force`
    b) We can update its image using `docker container update`
    c) We can rename the `webserver` container to `websrv` using `docker container rename`
    d) We can view the container's output using `docker container logs`

5. We have executed the `docker container run --name app1 --user 1000 --memory 100m --privileged alpine touch /testfile` command. Which of the following sentences are true?

    a) `/testfile` was created as root because the container was executed with all capabilities.
    b) The container will not be able to consume more than 100 m of host memory.
    c) `/testfile` was not created because we used a user with an ID of `1000` and it will not be able to write on `/`, the root directory.
    d) We used `--privileged`. This option will disable all root capabilities inside the container and, as a result, the file can't be created.

Further reading

Refer to the following links to find out more about the topics that were covered in this chapter:

- Docker command-line reference: `https://docs.docker.com/engine/reference/commandline/docker/`
- Memory limits behavior: `https://medium.com/faun/understanding-docker-container-memory-limit-behavior-41add155236c`

4
Container Persistency and Networking

Containers are processes that run on a host. This seems very simple, but how will this work on a pool of nodes? If we are looking for high availability, being able to run our containers on any host from a pool will ensure execution everywhere. But this approach requires some special logic in our applications. Our applications must be completely portable and avoid friction and dependencies on any host. Applications with many dependencies are always less portable. We need to find a way to manage status data for containers. We will review different persistence strategies in this chapter.

On the other hand, the aforementioned pool of hosts must be able to communicate with all containers. In this chapter, we will learn about basic standalone host networking and introduce advanced cluster-orchestrated networking concepts.

In this chapter, we will cover the differences between stateless and stateful applications, how volumes work and how can we use them, and how the Docker daemon provides networking on standalone environments. We'll also consider interactions between containers and how to publish services provided by processes running within containers.

The following topics will be covered in this chapter:

- Understanding stateless and stateful containers
- Learning about different persistence strategies
- Networking in containers
- Learning about container interactions
- Publishing applications

Let's get started!

Technical requirements

In this chapter, we will learn about Docker volumes and networking concepts. We'll provide some labs at the end of this chapter that will help you understand and learn about the concepts shown. These labs can be run on your laptop or PC using the provided Vagrant standalone environment or any already deployed Docker host of your own. You can find additional information in this book's GitHub repository: `https://github.com/PacktPublishing/Docker-Certified-Associate-DCA-Exam-Guide.git`

Check out the following video to see the Code in Action:

"`https://bit.ly/34DJ3V4`"

Understanding stateless and stateful containers

Portability is key in modern applications because they should run in every environment (on-premises or the cloud). Containers are prepared for these situations. We will also seek the high availability of applications in production, and containers will help us here too.

Not all applications are ready for containers by default. Processes' states and their data are difficult to manage inside containers.

In `Chapter 1`, *Modern Infrastructures and Applications with Docker*, we learned that containers are not ephemeral. They live in our hosts. Containers are created, executed, and stopped or killed, but they will remain in our host until they are deleted. We can restart a previously stopped container. But this is only true in standalone environments because all information resides under the host data path-defined directory (`/var/lib/docker` and `C:\ProgramData\docker` by default on Linux and Windows, respectively). If we move our workloads (that is, our application components running as containers) to another host, we will not have their data and state there. What happens if we need to upgrade their image versions? In that case, we could run a new container and everything will be recreated again. We can launch a new container, but we need to maintain all application data.

Previously, we introduced volumes as a method used to bypass the internal filesystem of containers and their life cycles. Everything inside a volume is, in fact, outside of the container's filesystem. This will help us with application performance using direct access to a host's devices' but it will also keep data. Volumes will persist even when containers are removed (unless we use `--volumes` or `-v` on removal). Therefore, volumes will help us maintain application data locally, but how about execution on other Docker hosts? We can share images, but a container's associated data will not be there unless we can also share volumes between them.

Under these circumstances, stateless processes – those that do not require any kind of persistent data to work – are easier to manage. These processes are always candidates to run within containers.

And what about stateful processes – those using persistent data between executions? We have to take care in this case. We should provide external volumes or databases to store the process's state and its required data. These concepts are very important when we design microservice-based application architectures.

Let's deep dive into how volumes work.

Learning how volumes work

Previously, we learned how to define volumes in images to simply bypass a container's filesystem. Here is a simple Dockerfile definition showing a defined volume (this is an excerpt from the PostgreSQL database official image):

```
FROM alpine:3.10
RUN set -ex; \
 postgresHome="$(getent passwd postgres)"; \
 postgresHome="$(echo "$postgresHome" | cut -d: -f6)"; \
 [ "$postgresHome" = '/var/lib/postgresql' ]; \
 mkdir -p "$postgresHome"; \
 chown -R postgres:postgres "$postgresHome"
...
...
RUN mkdir -p /var/run/postgresql && chown -R postgres:postgres
/var/run/postgresql && chmod 2777 /var/run/postgresql
ENV PGDATA /var/lib/postgresql/data
RUN mkdir -p "$PGDATA" && chown -R postgres:postgres "$PGDATA" && chmod 777
"$PGDATA"

VOLUME /var/lib/postgresql/data

COPY docker-entrypoint.sh /usr/local/bin/
```

```
ENTRYPOINT ["docker-entrypoint.sh"]
EXPOSE 5432
CMD ["postgres"]
```

We have omitted many lines because we just want to review the VOLUME definition. In this case, all data stored under the /var/lib/postgresql/data directory will be outside of the container's filesystem. This is an **unnamed volume** definition and it will be identified in our system by a random ID when we run a container using this image. It was defined for bypassing copy-on-write filesystems. Every time we create or run a new container, a new random identifier volume will be created. These volumes should be removed manually or by using the --volume or -v options when we remove their associated containers.

Now, it is time to define the different volumes types we can have on Docker:

- **Unnamed volumes**: These are the volumes that are defined on images and therefore created using random identifiers. It is hard to track them on local filesystems because they are unnamed. As volumes can grow very fast, depending on your application, it is very important to check for volume definitions before running any image on your local system. Remember that unnamed volumes will grow under your Docker data root path, wherever it is.

- **Named volumes**: These are the volumes we create manually. As we learned in *Chapter 1*, *Modern Infrastructures and Applications with Docker*, volumes are Docker objects and we have some actions to control them. In this chapter, we will learn about their associated actions and how to use them. These volumes will be located under the data root path also, but we can use different plugins or drivers to create them. Drivers will allow local or remote volumes, via NFS for example. In these cases, what we will have under the data root path is a link to the real mounted remote filesystem. Consequently, these volumes will not consume local storage if they are remote.

- **Localhost directories or files**: In this case, we will use host directories and files inside containers. We usually refer to these volumes as **bind mounts**. We must take care of file and directory permissions because we can also use any special file inside containers (including devices). Adding permissions that are too open will give users access to your host's devices. They will require appropriate process capabilities and permissions. It is important to understand that Docker does not care about how block devices, directories, and filesystems are mounted on the Docker host. They will be used always as if they were locally available. Bind mounts will not be listed as volumes.

- **tmpfs volumes**: This kind of volume is temporal. They will only persist in the host memory. When the container stops, the volume will be removed. Files inside them will not persist.

 All kinds of volumes can be mounted in read-only mode inside containers. This is very important and useful when volume data shouldn't be modified by running processes, for example, when serving static web content. We can have containers that should be able to modify data and others that will only read and serve this modified data using read-only mode.

Named volumes or bind mounts will retain data. Unnamed volumes will be created with new containers. Keep this in mind. If we need to provide some data to an unnamed volume, it should be done when the container starts. We can also define a procedure in the image definition. This concept is very important as the position of the VOLUME definition in Dockerfiles matters. As we learned in Chapter 2, *Building Docker Images*, image creation is based on a sequence of container executions. If we add a volume for a specific path, all subsequent executions will not retain data in that directory. The building process will create a new unnamed volume on each new container and content will not be used between executions.

Learning about volume object actions

Volumes can be created, used, and removed. We will also be able to inspect all their properties. The following table shows the actions that are allowed for volume objects:

Objects	Actions
create	We are able to create named volumes. We can add labels for filtering the listing output, as we learned in previous chapters. We can specify the driver to be used for creating a new volume. By default, volumes will use a local driver. This driver will create directories under the volumes directory. Each new volume will have its own directory containing the required meta-information and a _data subdirectory. This directory contains all files added to the volume. As we mentioned previously, some drivers will provide host external storage resources. Linked directories will provide connection information instead of their data. We will use --driver to specify a driver other than local. The --opt or -o arguments allow us to add required options for the specified driver. Each driver will have its own special options.

inspect	All objects can be inspected. In this case, the `inspect` action will provide information about the object's location, the driver used, and the labels provided.
ls	We can list all volumes using the `ls` action. Almost all filtering and formatting options learned throughout this book can be applied. Formatting will also depend on a given volume's properties.
prune	The `prune` option will help us with volume housekeeping. It will remove all created volumes not used by any container. It will not delete any bind mount because they are not really treated as volumes.
rm	We can remove volumes using the `rm` action. It is important to note that volumes attached to existing containers cannot be removed. Containers should be removed before volumes. Alternatively, you can use the `--volumes` option on container removal.

Now, let's introduce how containers use volumes.

Using volumes in containers

First, we will start with unnamed volumes. These are volumes defined in a container's images. As we mentioned previously, always review images before execution. If we run an application that stores a huge amount of data on a predefined unnamed volume, our Docker host can run out of disk space. It is very important to review what image will run and what resources will be required. If we take a quick view of the `postgres:alpine` image (the PostgreSQL database image based on Alpine Linux), for example, we will find a volume definition (we first pull the `postgres:alpine` image from Docker Hub):

```
$ docker image pull --quiet postgres:alpine
docker.io/library/postgres:alpine

$ docker image inspect postgres:alpine --format "{{ .Config.Volumes }} "
map[/var/lib/postgresql/data:{}]
```

As we can see, `postgres:alpine` will define an unnamed volume to bypass the copy-on-write container filesystem to allow a process to write or modify any content under the `/var/lib/postgresql/data` directory.

Let's create a container named `mydb` using the `postgres:alpine` image:

```
$ docker container run -d --name mydb postgres:alpine
e1eb5e5df725541d6a3b31ee86746ab009251c5292b1af95b22b166c9d0922de
```

Now, we can inspect the `mydb` container, looking for its mount points (identifiers will be different in your system):

```
$ docker container inspect mydb --format "{{ .Mounts }} "
[{volume c888a831d6819aea6c6b4474f53b7d6c60e085efaa30d17db60334522281d76f
/var/lib/docker/volumes/c888a831d6819aea6c6b4474f53b7d6c60e085efaa30d17db60
334522281d76f/_data /var/lib/postgresql/data local true }]
```

Using the obtained volume identifier, we can review its properties:

```
$ docker volume inspect
c888a831d6819aea6c6b4474f53b7d6c60e085efaa30d17db60334522281d76f
[
  {
  "CreatedAt": "2019-11-03T19:20:59+01:00",
  "Driver": "local",
  "Labels": null,
  "Mountpoint":
"/var/lib/docker/volumes/c888a831d6819aea6c6b4474f53b7d6c60e085efaa30d17db6
0334522281d76f/_data",
  "Name":
"c888a831d6819aea6c6b4474f53b7d6c60e085efaa30d17db60334522281d76f",
  "Options": null,
  "Scope": "local"
  }
]
```

The output shows where this volume is mounted on our host (`/var/lib/docker/volumes/c888a831d6819aea6c6b4474f53b7d6c60e085efaa30d1 7db60334522281d76f/_data`) and what container is using it that it's mounted on (`/var/lib/postgresql/data`).

If we take a look at the `/var/lib/docker/volumes/c888a831d6819aea6c6b4474f53b7d6c60e085efaa30 d17db60334522281d76f/_data` directory, we can list all PostgreSQL database data files (notice in the following log that the directory is owned by root, so root access will be required):

```
$ sudo ls -lart
/var/lib/docker/volumes/c888a831d6819aea6c6b4474f53b7d6c60e085efaa30d17db60
334522281d76f/_data
total 64
drwxr-xr-x 3 root root 19 nov 3 19:20 ..
-rw------- 1 70 70 3 nov 3 19:20 PG_VERSION
drwx------ 2 70 70 6 nov 3 19:20 pg_twophase
...
...
```

```
-rw------- 1 70 70 94 nov 3 19:20 postmaster.pid
drwx------ 2 70 70 25 nov 3 19:42 pg_stat_tmp
```

Notice that files and directories are owned by userid (70) and groupid (70). This is because the container's main process is not running under the root user and, as a result, all files created by the PostgreSQL process will be owned by an internal postgres:postgres user, whose ID may be different or even may not exist on our host. This is the ID used within the container.

Let's stop the mydb container and check our volume. You will see that the volume is still in our system:

```
$ docker container stop mydb
mydb
```

```
$ docker volume ls --filter
name=c888a831d6819aea6c6b4474f53b7d6c60e085efaa30d17db60334522281d76f
 DRIVER VOLUME NAME
 local c888a831d6819aea6c6b4474f53b7d6c60e085efaa30d17db60334522281d76f
```

Again, we can start our mydb container and it will reuse its volume data. If we had added data to this database, we would still be able to access it, because the volume persists our data.

Now, let's remove the mydb container:

```
$ docker container rm mydb
mydb
```

We can verify that the volume is still under /var/lib/docker/volumes:

```
$ docker volume ls --filter
name=c888a831d6819aea6c6b4474f53b7d6c60e085efaa30d17db60334522281d76f
DRIVER VOLUME NAME
local c888a831d6819aea6c6b4474f53b7d6c60e085efaa30d17db60334522281d76f
```

Volumes survive containers unless we use --volume to remove them with its associated container. We can also reuse volume content with other containers. But unnamed containers are not easy to manage because they are identified only by a digest. We will remove this volume:

```
$ docker volume rm
c888a831d6819aea6c6b4474f53b7d6c60e085efaa30d17db60334522281d76f
c888a831d6819aea6c6b4474f53b7d6c60e085efaa30d17db60334522281d76f
```

Now, let's create a volume named `mydata`:

```
$ docker volume create mydata
mydbdata
```

In this case, we can create a new container using this volume and its content will be available for our new process.

 It is important to understand that the VOLUME definition in an image is not required to use volumes on containers. But they will help us understand what directories should be managed out of the container filesystem. Good container images will define the directories where persistent data should be stored.

Docker containers can mount volumes using two different options in terms of container creation or execution:

`--volume` or `-v`	We will use this option with three arguments, separated by `:`. We will use the last argument to declare what type of access will be provided (read-only or read-write). The second argument will indicate the container's directory or file where the volume will be mounted within the container. The first argument will be different, depending on what type of resource we are using. If we are using bind mounts, we will use them as a file or directory in the host. If we are using named volumes, this argument will declare which volume will be mounted inside the container.

 There are other options for the third argument when using the `--volume` option. In addition to read or write access, we can specify `z` or `Z` when we use SELinux. If the volume is going to be shared between multiple containers, we will use these options to declare the volume content as private and unshareable.

`--mount`	This notation allows more arguments than `--volume`. We will use the key/value format to declare multiple options. The available keys are as follows: - **type**: Values available are `bind`, `volume`, or `tmpfs`. - **source (or src)**: This will describe the volume or host path. - **destination (or dst or target)**: This describes the path where the volume content will be mounted. - **readonly**: This identifies the access type for the volume content.

There is only one difference between using the `--volume` and `--mount` options. Using `--volume` will create the endpoint if we specify a path that does not exist in the Docker host when using bind mounts, while `--mount` will raise an error in this instance and it will not be created.

Now, we'll start an `alpine` container using the defined volume mounted in `/data`. We named it `c1` here. We will just touch a file under its `/data` directory:

```
$ docker container run --name c1 -v mydata:/data -ti alpine
/ # touch /data/persistent-file-test
/ # exit
```

After exiting the container, we can list the files under the `mydata` volume filesystem:

```
$ sudo ls -lart /var/lib/docker/volumes/mydata/_data
total 0
drwxr-xr-x 3 root root 19 nov 3 20:34 ..
-rw-r--r-- 1 root root 0 nov 3 20:44 persistent-file-test
drwxr-xr-x 2 root root 34 nov 3 20:44 .
```

Now, we can create a new container and reuse our previously created named volume, `mydata`. In this example, we will mount it under `/tmp`:

```
$ docker container run --name c2 -v mydata:/tmp -ti alpine ls -lart /tmp
total 0
-rw-r--r-- 1 root root 0 Nov 3 19:44 persistent-file-test
drwxr-xr-x 2 root root 34 Nov 3 19:44 .
drwxr-xr-x 1 root root 6 Nov 3 19:48 ..
```

Now, both containers, `c1` and `c2`, have mounted the `mydata` volume. Consequently, we can't remove the `mydata` volume unless both are removed from the local system (even if we use `--force` for removal):

```
$ docker volume rm mydata
Error response from daemon: remove mydata: volume is in use -
[a40f15ab8977eba1c321d577214dc4aca0f58c6aef0eefd50d6989331a8dc723,
472b37cc19571960163cdbcd902e83020706a46f06fbb6c7f9f1679c2beeed0e]
```

We will only be able to remove the `mydata` volume when both containers have been removed:

```
$ docker container rm c1 c2
c1
c2

$ docker volume rm mydata
mydata
```

Now, let's learn about some strategies and use cases for storing persistent data in containerized environments.

Learning about different persistence strategies

As we've already learned, there are different approaches to persistence in containers. Choosing the right solution will depend on the use case or requirements of the environment and our applications.

Local persistence

We will use local directories or files whenever we are deploying applications on isolated and standalone Docker daemons. In this approach, you should take care of filesystem permissions and secure module configurations. This strategy is quite interesting for developers as they can run multi-container applications on their laptops using local source code files inside containers. Therefore, all changes made on their local files will be synced within the containers (in fact, they will not quite be synced; rather, they are the same files that are mounted inside the container filesystem as a bind mount volume). We will review some examples of this in the *Chapter labs* section. This solution will not provide high availability.

Distributed or remote volumes

These are the preferred solutions for orchestrated environments. We should provide a pool of distributed or remote storage endpoints to allow applications to run everywhere within the cluster. Depending on your applications, volume speed could be key for deciding which driver to use. We will also have different choices regarding cloud providers. But for common use cases with static content, **Network File System** (**NFS**) will be fine. While it would not be enough for databases or high I/O application requirements, locking filesystem files is needed when we scale instances using shared resources. The Docker daemon will not manage these situations as they are out of Docker's scope. Volume I/O and file locking will really depend on the application logic and its architecture. Neither distributed nor remote volume solutions will provide high availability. In fact, Docker doesn't really know anything about storage. It just cares about volumes, no matter how storage was implemented on your host.

Volume drivers provide extensions to extend Docker's out-of-the-box features. The Docker plugin system changed in version 1.12 of Docker. Therefore, we refer to old plugins as *legacy plugins*, which are not managed using `docker plugin` actions. We can find a list of legacy volume plugins at `https://docs.docker.com/engine/extend/legacy_plugins/` `#volume-plugins`. New plugins are always managed using `docker plugin` command-line actions. These plugins may require special capabilities because they should be able to execute privileged actions at the host system level. We will review a quick lab at the end of this chapter, where we'll use the `sshfs` plugin.

These described use cases are closer to data management. But what about the application state? This is usually managed using volumes, but it really depends on your application architecture. One recommendation for new application development projects is to track the application state out of containers or even volumes. This makes it easier to manage instance replication when we need to scale up or down some components. But remember, it should be managed at the application level. Docker will just manage how your containerized application components run; it will not manage their application states or dependencies.

Now that we know how to manage container data and their states using persistent volumes, let's get into networking features.

Networking in containers

We have already learned that containers are processes that run isolated on top of host operating systems. This isolation is provided using different namespaces for users, processes trees, inter-process communications, and a set of complete network resources for each containerized process. Therefore, each container will have its own network interfaces. To be able to communicate with the world, by default, the Docker daemon will create a bridged interface called `docker0`. The Docker network plane has not changed too much in the latest releases. It can be extended using external tools and plugins and is based on bridged and virtual network interfaces that connect hosts and container resources.

By default, a fresh Docker installation will show three network objects:

```
$ docker network ls
 NETWORK ID NAME DRIVER SCOPE
 033e4c3f3608 bridge bridge local
 82faac964567 host host local
 2fb14f721dc3 none null local
```

As we have already learned, all objects are identified by their unique ID. The Docker network listing shows the network NAME (we can set our own network name), DRIVER (the network type), and SCOPE columns (indicating where this network will be available). There are different types of networks, according to which network driver containers will be used to attach to that network.

Besides all common object actions such as create, list (using ls), inspect, and remove (using rm or prune), networks also have connect and disconnect actions in order to attach or detach containers to/from them.

Let's review some of the creation options before deep diving on each network type:

Option	Description
--attachable	This option enables manual container attachment. It is not required for locally scoped networks.
--aux-address	Using --aux-address, we can add a host and its addresses to this network. For example, we can use --aux-address="mygateway=192.168.1.10" to set a specific host-to-IP mapping on the declared network. It is usually used on macvlan networks.
--config-from and --config-only	We can create (or reuse previously created) network configurations. This is very useful for building configurations using automation tools, for example, on different hosts and being able to use them when needed.
--driver or -d and --opt	This option allows us to specify which driver to use. By default, we can only use macvlan, none, host, and bridge. But we can extend Docker's networking capabilities using other external plugins. We will use --opt to customize the applied driver.
--gateway	We can overwrite the default gateway (the lower IP address of the defined subnet, by default) and specify another IP address for this purpose.
--ingress	This option will be used in cases where we want to create a special Swarm vxLan network for internal service management.
--internal	This option is only available on overlay networks. We will only use it to define internal networks because, by default, all overlay networks will be attached to the docker_gwbridge bridge network (created automatically when operating on a Swarm) to provide external connectivity.
--ip-range	Once we have configured a subnet, we can specify a range of IP addresses to be used for containers.

`--ipam-driver` and `--ipam-opt`	With these options, we can use an external IP address management driver.
`--ipv6`	We will use this option to enable IPv6 on this network.
`--label`	With this, we can add metadata information to networks for better filtering.
`--scope`	With this option, we declare the scope where the network will be created for local or Swarm usage.
`--subnet`	This specifies a subnet in CIDR format that represents a network segment.

Once created, network objects will exist until they are removed. But removal is only possible when no containers are attached to them. It is important to understand that dead containers will still have endpoints configured for existing networks and must, as a result, be deleted before network removal. On the other hand, the `prune` action will remove all unused networks.

Docker manipulates the `iptables` rules for you every time a network is created or some connection or container process publication must be implemented. You can avoid this feature, but we strongly recommend allowing the Docker daemon to manage these rules for you. It is not easy to track unexpected behaviors and there will be many rules to manage.

Now that we have the basic `create` command options under our belts, let's look at the different standard networks we can create.

Using the default bridge network

Bridge is the default network type for all containers. Any other network types must be declared on container creation or execution using the `--network` optional parameter.

In operating system terms, we use bridged interfaces to allow forwarded traffic from other virtual interfaces. All those virtual interfaces will use a physical interface, associated with the bridge, to talk to other network devices or connected hosts. In the world of containers, all container interfaces are virtual and they will be attached to these bridge interfaces at the host level. Therefore, all containers attached to the same bridge interface will see each other.

Let's look at a quick example of using a bridge network:

1. We just run two containers, `c1` and `c2`, attached to the default network (notice that we have not defined any network at all):

```
zero@sirius:~$ docker container run -ti -d --name c1 alpine ping
8.8.8.8
c44fbefb96b9321ef1a0e866fa6aaeb26408fc2ef484bbc9ecf904546f60ada7

zero@sirius:~$ docker container run -ti -d --name c2 alpine ping
8.8.8.8
cee980d7f9e587357375e21dafcb406688ac1004d8d7984ec39e4f97533492ef
```

2. We find their IP addresses:

```
$ docker container inspect c1 --format "{{
.NetworkSettings.Networks.bridge.IPAddress }}"
172.17.0.2

$ docker container inspect c2 --format "{{
.NetworkSettings.Networks.bridge.IPAddress }}"
172.17.0.3
```

3. Consequently, we can ping each of them:

```
$ docker exec c1 ping -c 2 172.17.0.3
PING 172.17.0.3 (172.17.0.3): 56 data bytes
64 bytes from 172.17.0.3: seq=0 ttl=64 time=0.113 ms
64 bytes from 172.17.0.3: seq=1 ttl=64 time=0.210 ms
--- 172.17.0.3 ping statistics ---
2 packets transmitted, 2 packets received, 0% packet loss
round-trip min/avg/max = 0.113/0.161/0.210 ms
```

4. Let's quickly review some of the `c1` container properties:

```
$ docker container inspect c1 --format "{{json
.NetworkSettings.Networks }}"
{"bridge":{"IPAMConfig":null,"Links":null,"Aliases":null,"NetworkID
":"033e4c3f360841b0826f3b850fe9f5544d145bea644ee1955717e67d02df92ce
","EndpointID":"390d2cf0b933ddd3b11fdebdbf6293c97f2a8568315c80794fa
d6f5b8eef3207","Gateway":"172.17.0.1","IPAddress":"172.17.0.2","IPP
refixLen":16,"IPv6Gateway":"","GlobalIPv6Address":"","GlobalIPv6Pre
fixLen":0,"MacAddress":"02:42:ac:11:00:02","DriverOpts":null}}
```

5. Each container will have its own IP address and `EndpointID`. Let's inspect the bridge network's configuration (created by Docker by default):

```
$ docker network inspect bridge
[
    {
        "Name": "bridge",
        "Id":
"033e4c3f360841b0826f3b850fe9f5544d145bea644ee1955717e67d02df92ce",
        ...
        "IPAM": {
            ...
            "Config": [
                {
                    "Subnet": "172.17.0.0/16",
                    "Gateway": "172.17.0.1"
                }
            ]
        },
        ...
        "Containers": {
"c44fbefb96b9321ef1a0e866fa6aaeb26408fc2ef484bbc9ecf904546f60ada7":
{
                "Name": "c1",
                "EndpointID":
"390d2cf0b933ddd3b11fdebdbf6293c97f2a8568315c80794fad6f5b8eef3207",
                "MacAddress": "02:42:ac:11:00:02",
                "IPv4Address": "172.17.0.2/16",
                "IPv6Address": ""
            },
"cee980d7f9e587357375e21dafcb406688ac1004d8d7984ec39e4f97533492ef":
{
                "Name": "c2",
                "EndpointID":
"cb49b93bc0bdd3eb887ad3b6fcd43155eb4ca7688c788719a27acc9e2f2e2a9d",
                "MacAddress": "02:42:ac:11:00:03",
                "IPv4Address": "172.17.0.3/16",
                "IPv6Address": ""
            }
        },
        "Options": {
            "com.docker.network.bridge.default_bridge": "true",
            "com.docker.network.bridge.enable_icc": "true",
            "com.docker.network.bridge.enable_ip_masquerade":
"true",
            "com.docker.network.bridge.host_binding_ipv4":
"0.0.0.0",
            "com.docker.network.bridge.name": "docker0",
```

```
            "com.docker.network.driver.mtu": "1500"
          },
          "Labels": {}
        }
    ]
```

Let's talk about some of the most important sections in this output:

- This network is not using IPv6. It's called `bridge`, was created using the `bridge` driver, and will only be available locally on this host.
- It was created using the `172.17.0.0/16` subnet and consequently, all containers on this network will get an IP address on this segment range.
- The bridge interface has the IP address `172.17.0.1` and will be the default gateway for all containers.
- We have two running containers on this network. They are both listed under the `Containers` section with their virtual MAC addresses, IP addresses, and associated endpoints.
- There are a number of options that can be used during network creation that are of interest:
    - `com.docker.network.bridge.default_bridge: true`: This means that this is the default bridge when no network is defined.
    - `com.docker.network.bridge.enable_icc: true`: This parameter indicates that containers connected to this network can talk to each other. We can disable this feature on custom bridges, allowing just North-South traffic.
    - `com.docker.network.bridge.name: docker0`: This is the name of the associated host interface.

 When we refer to *North-South traffic*, we mean the type of communication that goes out of the Docker host to the containers and vice versa. On the other hand, *East-West traffic* is the traffic between different containers. These are references to well-known network terms that are applied to describe network traffic.

Understanding null networks

Null or none networks are used when we need to deploy a container that should run without any network interface. Although it might sound useless, there are many situations where we may need to launch a task for executing a mathematical operation, compression, or many other examples that don't require networking capabilities. In these cases, we just need to use volumes and we really do not need any network operation. Using a null network ensures that the task will only have access to its required resources. If it does not require network access, do not provide it. By default, the container will use a `bridge` network unless we specify `none`:

```
$ docker run -ti --network none alpine
/ # ip add
1: lo: <LOOPBACK,UP,LOWER_UP> mtu 65536 qdisc noqueue state UNKNOWN qlen
1000
 link/loopback 00:00:00:00:00:00 brd 00:00:00:00:00:00
 inet 127.0.0.1/8 scope host lo
 valid_lft forever preferred_lft forever
/ #
```

Now that we understand that containers can have a null interface to avoid networking, we can look at the host's network namespace.

Understanding the host network

Host networking is only available on Linux hosts. This is important because it is an important difference in Windows containers.

Using host networking, the container shares the `host` networking namespace. Therefore, the container will get all host IP addresses, and every port that's used at the container level will be set on the host. Consequently, no more than one container using a specific given port will be allowed to run at a time. But, on the other hand, network performance is better because container services are directly attached to host ports. There isn't any NAT or firewall rule adaptation:

```
$ docker run -ti --network host alpine
/ # ip add
1: lo: <LOOPBACK,UP,LOWER_UP> mtu 65536 qdisc noqueue state UNKNOWN qlen
1000
 link/loopback 00:00:00:00:00:00 brd 00:00:00:00:00:00
 inet 127.0.0.1/8 scope host lo
 valid_lft forever preferred_lft forever
 inet6 ::1/128 scope host
 valid_lft forever preferred_lft forever
```

```
2: enp0s25: <NO-CARRIER,BROADCAST,MULTICAST,UP> mtu 1500 qdisc fq_codel
state DOWN qlen 1000
 link/ether 68:f7:28:c1:bc:13 brd ff:ff:ff:ff:ff:ff
3: wlp3s0: <BROADCAST,MULTICAST,UP,LOWER_UP> mtu 1500 qdisc mq state UP
qlen 1000
 link/ether 34:02:86:e3:f6:25 brd ff:ff:ff:ff:ff:ff
 inet 192.168.200.165/24 brd 192.168.200.255 scope global dynamic wlp3s0
 valid_lft 51sec preferred_lft 51sec
 inet6 fe80::ee87:e44f:9189:f720/64 scope link
 valid_lft forever preferred_lft forever
...
...
10: docker0: <BROADCAST,MULTICAST,UP,LOWER_UP> mtu 1500 qdisc noqueue state
UP
 link/ether 02:42:11:73:cc:2b brd ff:ff:ff:ff:ff:ff
 inet 172.17.0.1/16 brd 172.17.255.255 scope global docker0
 valid_lft forever preferred_lft forever
 inet6 fe80::42:11ff:fe73:cc2b/64 scope link
 valid_lft forever preferred_lft forever
...
...
18: docker_gwbridge: <BROADCAST,MULTICAST,UP,LOWER_UP> mtu 1500 qdisc
noqueue state UP
 link/ether 02:42:4b:21:09:6d brd ff:ff:ff:ff:ff:ff
 inet 172.18.0.1/16 brd 172.18.255.255 scope global docker_gwbridge
 valid_lft forever preferred_lft forever
 inet6 fe80::42:4bff:fe21:96d/64 scope link
 valid_lft forever preferred_lft forever
20: veth82a8134@if19: <BROADCAST,MULTICAST,UP,LOWER_UP,M-DOWN> mtu 1500
qdisc noqueue master docker_gwbridge state UP
 link/ether a6:5d:02:ed:79:0a brd ff:ff:ff:ff:ff:ff
 inet6 fe80::a45d:2ff:feed:790a/64 scope link
 valid_lft forever preferred_lft forever
22: veth4b1102e@if21: <BROADCAST,MULTICAST,UP,LOWER_UP,M-DOWN> mtu 1500
qdisc noqueue master docker0 state UP
 link/ether fa:08:70:aa:b1:4b brd ff:ff:ff:ff:ff:ff
 inet6 fe80::f808:70ff:feaa:b14b/64 scope link
 valid_lft forever preferred_lft forever
27: wwp0s20u4: <BROADCAST,MULTICAST,NOARP> mtu 1428 qdisc noop state DOWN
qlen 1000
 link/ether 06:1b:05:d6:e9:12 brd ff:ff:ff:ff:ff:ff
/ #
```

Here, you can see that all host interfaces are listed because the container is using its network namespace.

This networking mode is risky because we are allowing any kind of communication on the containers. This should be used with care in **privileged mode**. It is very common in monitoring tools or when we run applications that require high levels of network interface performance.

We can define our own network interfaces. We'll create custom bridge networks in the next section.

Creating custom bridge networks

As we discussed in the default bridge network example, this networking type will be associated with host `bridge` interfaces. By default, it is attached to `docker0`, but every time we create a new bridge network, a new `bridge` interface will be created for us and all attached containers will have a virtual interface linked to this one.

There are a few very important differences between a default bridge network and custom created ones:

- **Custom bridge isolation**: Each new custom bridge network created will have its own associated bridge with its own subnet and host `iptables`. This feature provides a higher level of isolation as only attached containers can talk to each other. All other containers running on the same host will not *see* these containers running on custom bridge networks.
- **Internal DNS**: The Docker daemon provides a custom DNS for each custom bridge network. This means that all containers running on the same network will know each other by name. This is a very important feature because your service discovery will not need any external source of knowledge. But remember that this is valid only for internal usage within the network.

We can provide this kind of DNS resolution on default bridge networks using the legacy `--link` functionality. This was the way of interconnecting containers on old Docker releases. Nowadays, using custom bridge networks is considered as providing better isolation.

- **On-the-fly container attachment**: In default bridge networks, we must provide connectivity in terms of container creation or execution. Imagine that we used a null or none network for a container and we want to attach it to a default bridge network later – this is not possible. Once a container is created, it can't be attached to a default bridge network later. It must be recreated from the beginning with that network attachment. On the other hand, custom bridge networks are attachable, which means that we can consider a situation where our container was created without a specific attachment and can add it later. We can also run a container with multiple interfaces on different custom networks, with its name resolution.

Let's review a quick example. We will provide more detailed examples in the *Chapter labs* section of this chapter:

```
$ docker network create --driver bridge --internal --subnet 192.168.30.0/24
--label internal-only internal-only
c275cdd25b422b35d3f2b4fbbb153e7cd09c8721133667cfbeb9c297af89364a
```

We review the created network properties (notice the defined subnet) and internal settings:

```
$ docker network inspect internal-only
[
    {
        "Name": "internal-only",
        "Id":
"c275cdd25b422b35d3f2b4fbbb153e7cd09c8721133667cfbeb9c297af89364a",
        "Created": "2019-11-10T11:03:20.490907017+01:00",
        "Scope": "local",
        "Driver": "bridge",
        "EnableIPv6": false,
        "IPAM": {
            "Driver": "default",
            "Options": {},
            "Config": [
                {
                    "Subnet": "192.168.30.0/24"
                }
            ]
        },
        "Internal": true,
        "Attachable": false,
        "Ingress": false,
        "ConfigFrom": {
            "Network": ""
        },
        "ConfigOnly": false,
```

```
        "Containers": {},
        "Options": {},
        "Labels": {
            "internal-only": ""
        }
    }
]
```

Now, we create a container and test internet access:

```
$ docker container run --network internal-only -ti --name intc1 alpine sh
/ # ping 8.8.8.8 -c 2
PING 8.8.8.8 (8.8.8.8): 56 data bytes
--- 8.8.8.8 ping statistics ---
2 packets transmitted, 0 packets received, 100% packet loss
/ #
```

> Remember to use the *Ctrl* + *P* + *Q* shortcut to leave the `intc1` container running in the background.

You may have noticed that we do not have any egress connectivity. Let's review the internal connectivity with another container:

```
$ docker container run --network internal-only -ti --name intc2 alpine sh
/ # ping intc1 -c2
PING intc1 (192.168.30.2): 56 data bytes
64 bytes from 192.168.30.2: seq=0 ttl=64 time=0.185 ms
64 bytes from 192.168.30.2: seq=1 ttl=64 time=0.157 ms
--- intc1 ping statistics ---
2 packets transmitted, 2 packets received, 0% packet loss
round-trip min/avg/max = 0.157/0.171/0.185 ms
/ #
```

As shown in the preceding output, we have internal communication and DNS resolution, but we are unable to talk to any other external IP address.

If we take a look at `iptables`, we can see that the creation of the internal network added some very interesting rules to our local firewall. Executing `iptables -L` and avoiding all non-Docker related rules, we can observe these rules:

```
Chain DOCKER (4 references)
target prot opt source destination
Chain DOCKER-ISOLATION-STAGE-1 (1 references)
target prot opt source destination
DOCKER-ISOLATION-STAGE-2 all -- anywhere anywhere
```

```
DOCKER-ISOLATION-STAGE-2 all -- anywhere anywhere
DROP all -- !192.168.30.0/24 anywhere
DROP all -- anywhere !192.168.30.0/24
DOCKER-ISOLATION-STAGE-2 all -- anywhere anywhere
DOCKER-ISOLATION-STAGE-2 all -- anywhere anywhere
RETURN all -- anywhere anywhere

Chain DOCKER-ISOLATION-STAGE-2 (4 references)
target prot opt source destination
DROP all -- anywhere anywhere
DROP all -- anywhere anywhere
DROP all -- anywhere anywhere
DROP all -- anywhere anywhere
RETURN all -- anywhere anywhere

Chain DOCKER-USER (1 references)
target prot opt source destination
RETURN all -- anywhere anywhere
```

These are the rules that manage the internal network isolation we created previously.

We will examine some multi-interface examples toward the end of this chapter in the *Chapter labs* section.

The MacVLAN network – macvlan

The MacVLAN driver assigns a virtual MAC address to each container interface. Consequently, a container will be able to manage its own IP address on the real network. To manage this type of network interface, we need to declare a host physical interface. As containers will get their own MACs, we can use VLANs on these interfaces to provide containers with access only to the defined VLAN. But note that in these cases, we will need to assign all required VLANs to the macvlan assigned host interface.

 The macvlan driver will only work on Linux hosts (with a kernel version above 3.9; 4.0 is recommended). This kind of interface is usually blocked on cloud providers.

As a result, we have described two different modes for macvlan:

- **Bridge mode**: In this case (the default one), traffic will go through the defined host physical interface.
- **802.1q trunk bridge mode**: Traffic will go through an 802.1q VLAN interface, created by the Docker daemon on network creation.

In these networks, we usually use `--aux-address` to add existing nodes or network devices to this newly created Docker network.

We have been reviewing different interfaces that are provided by Docker out of the box. Now, let's continue our journey and understand how these communications happen at the host level.

Learning about container interactions

There are two different types of communication in container environments:

- Communication with the external world
- Inter-container communications

We'll take a look at both of these in this section.

Communication with the external world

There are two features at the host level that are required to allow containers to talk to the external world:

- IP forwarding is required to allow packets from container IP addresses to go outside the containerized environment. This is done at the kernel level and the Docker daemon will manage the required parameters (the `ip_forward` kernel parameter will be set to 1) to allow this strategy. We can change this default behavior setting with `--ip-forward=false` in the daemon configuration. This forwarding is required for all kinds of communications between containers in general.
- `iptables` will manage the required rules to strictly allow only required communications once forwarding is enabled. We can manually set `iptables` rules, instead of allowing the Docker daemon to take care of these settings, using the `--iptables=false` option in the daemon configuration. It is recommended to allow the Docker daemon to manage these rules unless you are sure of what changes to implement. Docker will only manage DOCKER and DOCKER-ISOLATION filter chains and we are able to manage custom rules in the DOCKER-USER chain.

By default, Docker forwards all packets and permits all external source IP addresses. If we need to allow only required IP addresses, we can add custom rules to `DROP` all non-permitted communications.

Inter-container communications

We can also manage inter-container communications with IP forwarding and `iptables`. As we've already learned, we can use `--internal` on network creation to only allow internal communications. Any other communication out of this defined subnet will be dropped.

On the other hand, we can disallow any inter-container communication by applying `--icc=false`. This option manages the internal interaction within containers linked to the same bridge. If we set this parameter to `false`, no inter-container communication will be allowed, even if they are running on the same subnet. This is the most secure network configuration because we can still allow specific communications using the `--link` option. Container links will create special `iptables` rules to allow these specific communications.

DNS on custom bridge networks

We've already learned that custom bridge networks own an internal DNS. This means that any container interaction can be managed using container names. This internal DNS will always run on `127.0.0.11`. We can modify some of its features, such as adding new hosts, for example.

Let's review some of the common features that can easily be manipulated to improve application discovery and interactions:

Features	Description
`--network-alias=ALIAS`	This option allows us to add another internal DNS name to a container.
`--link=CONTAINER_NAME:ALIAS`	We have been talking about the link option for legacy environments. It is also a way to allow specific communications when no container interaction is allowed by default. This option will also add an entry to the internal DNS to allow the resolution of `CONTAINER_NAME` as a defined `ALIAS`. This use case is different to `--network-alias` because it is used on different containers.

`--dns,`
`--dns-search,`
and `--dns-option`
	These options will manage forwarded DNS resolution in cases where an internal DNS cannot resolve a defined name. We can add a forwarder DNS, with its specific options to allow or disallow external searches for some containers. This will help us use different name resolutions to access internal or external applications.

Now that we have learned about the different interfaces that are available and how communications work at the host system level, let's go ahead and learn how applications will be accessed from the client side. We have just introduced `iptables` as a mechanism to gain that access automatically when deploying containers on different networks. In the next section, we will deep dive into publishing application methods for standalone Docker hosts.

Publishing applications

By default, all container processes are isolated from outside access. This means that although we had defined a port for the process service (using `EXPOSE` on images), it will not be accessible unless we declare it publicly available. This is a great security measure. No external communication will be allowed until it is specifically declared. Only containers attached to the same bridged network or host, using its host internal IP (attached to the bridge), will be able to use the process service.

Let's review a quick example using the `nginx:alpine` base image. We know that `nginx:alpine` exposes port `80`:

```
$ docker container run -d --name webserver nginx:alpine
4a37b49721b4fe6ffc57aee07c3fb42e5c08d4bcc0932e07eb7ce75fe696442d

$ docker container inspect webserver --format "{{json
.NetworkSettings.Networks.bridge.IPAddress }}"
"172.17.0.4"

$ curl http://172.17.0.4
<!DOCTYPE html>
<html>
<head>
<title>Welcome to nginx!</title>
<style>
    body {
        width: 35em;
```

```
        margin: 0 auto;
        font-family: Tahoma, Verdana, Arial, sans-serif;
    }
</style>
</head>
<body>
<h1>Welcome to nginx!</h1>
<p>If you see this page, the nginx web server is successfully installed and
working. Further configuration is required.</p>

<p>For online documentation and support please refer to
<a href="http://nginx.org/">nginx.org</a>.<br/>
Commercial support is available at
<a href="http://nginx.com/">nginx.com</a>.</p>

<p><em>Thank you for using nginx.</em></p>
</body>
```

Our host IP on the default bridge network is `172.17.0.1` in this case, and we can reach container port `80`, but no other host will be able to reach this port. It is exposed internally by a `webserver` container.

To publish a port exposed internally, we need to declare it during container creation or execution using the `--publish` or `-p` parameters.

We will use `--publish [HOST_IP:][HOST_PORT:]CONTAINER_PORT[/PROTOCOL]` for this. This means that the only required argument is the container port. By default, the TCP protocol and a random port between `32768` and `65000` will be used, and the port will be publicly published on all host IP addresses (`0.0.0.0`). We can also use `-P` to publish all ports exposed in a given container's image definition.

If we need to declare a UDP application publication, we need to specify this protocol.

 Host mode networking does not require any publication of ports because any exposed container process will be accessible from outside.

We can declare a range of ports in the form `--publish StartPort-EndPort[/PROTOCOL]` to publish more than one port.

For security reasons, it is important to use a specific IP address on multi-homed hosts in order to only allow access to specified IP addresses:

```
$ docker container run -d --name public-webserver --publish 80 nginx:alpine
562bfebccd728fdc3dff649fe6ac578d52e77c409e84eed8040db3cfc5589e40

$ docker container ls --filter name=public-webserver
CONTAINER ID IMAGE COMMAND CREATED STATUS PORTS NAMES
562bfebccd72 nginx:alpine "nginx -g 'daemon of..." About a minute ago Up
About a minute 0.0.0.0:32768->80/tcp public-webserver

$ curl http://0.0.0.0:32768
<!DOCTYPE html>
<html>
<head>
<title>Welcome to nginx!</title>
<style>
    body {
        width: 35em;
        margin: 0 auto;
        font-family: Tahoma, Verdana, Arial, sans-serif;
    }
</style>
</head>
<body>
<h1>Welcome to nginx!</h1>
<p>If you see this page, the nginx web server is successfully installed and
working. Further configuration is required.</p>

<p>For online documentation and support please refer to
<a href="http://nginx.org/">nginx.org</a>.<br/>
Commercial support is available at
<a href="http://nginx.com/">nginx.com</a>.</p>

<p><em>Thank you for using nginx.</em></p>
</body>
</html>
```

We will see more examples of this in the next section.

Chapter labs

This chapter was dedicated to learning how to manage stateful environments and the magic behind container networking. Now, let's complete some labs to review what we've learned. For these labs, we will use a CentOS Linux host with a Docker engine installed.

Deploy `environments/standalone-environment` from this book's GitHub repository (`https://github.com/PacktPublishing/Docker-Certified-Associate-DCA-Exam-Guide.git`) if you have not done so yet. You can use your own CentOS 7 server. Use `vagrant up` from the `environments/standalone-environment` folder to start your virtual environment.

If you are using a standalone environment, wait until it is running. We can check the statuses of our nodes using `vagrant status`. Connect to your lab node using `vagrant ssh standalone`. `standalone` is the name of your node. You will be using the `vagrant` user with root privileges using `sudo`. You should have the following output:

```
Docker-Certified-Associate-DCA-Exam-Guide/environments/standalone$ vagrant
up
Bringing machine 'standalone' up with 'virtualbox' provider...
...
Docker-Certified-Associate-DCA-Exam-Guide/environments/standalone$ vagrant
status
Current machine states:
standalone running (virtualbox)
...
Docker-Certified-Associate-DCA-Exam-Guide/environments/standalone$
```

We can now connect to the standalone node using `vagrant ssh standalone`. This process may vary if you deployed a standalone virtual node previously and you just started it using `vagrant up`:

```
Docker-Certified-Associate-DCA-Exam-Guide/environments/standalone$ vagrant
ssh standalone
[vagrant@standalone ~]$
```

If you are reusing your standalone environment, this means Docker Engine is installed. If you started a new instance, please execute the `/vagrant/install_requirements.sh` script so that you have all the required tools (Docker Engine and `docker-compose`):

```
[vagrant@standalone ~]$ /vagrant/install_requirements.sh
```

Now, you are ready to start the labs.

Using volumes to code on your laptop

In this lab, we will run a container with our application code inside. As the application is created using an interpreted language, any change or code modification will be refreshed (we added debugging to reload the application on each change using `debug=True`):

1. We've created a simple Python Flask application for you. The following is the content of the `app.py` file:

```
from flask import Flask, render_template

app = Flask(__name__)

@app.route('/')

def just_run():
    return render_template('index.html')

if __name__ == '__main__':
    app.run(debug=True, host='0.0.0.0')
```

2. We only require the `Flask` Python module, so we will only have one line in our `requirements.txt` file:

```
Flask
```

3. We will use a simple template HTML file under `templates/index.html` with this content:

```
<!DOCTYPE html>
<html lang="en">
<head>
    <meta charset="UTF-8">
    <title>Simple Flask Application</title>
</head>
<body>
    <h1>Simple Flask Application</h1>
    <h1>Version 1</h1>
</body>
</html>
```

4. We will run this application inside a container. We will create a Dockerfile and build an image called `simpleapp`, with a tag of `v1.0`. This is the content of the Dockerfile:

```
FROM python:alpine
WORKDIR /app
COPY ./requirements.txt requirements.txt
RUN pip install -r requirements.txt
COPY app.py .
COPY templates templates
EXPOSE 5000
CMD ["python", "app.py"]
```

5. Let's build our application image (`simpleapp:v1.0`):

```
[vagrant@standalone ~]$ docker image build -q -t simpleapp:v1.0 .
sha256:1cf398d39b51eb7644f98671493767267be108b60c3142b3ca9e0991b4d3
e45b
```

6. We can run this simple application by executing a detached container exposing port `5000`:

```
[vagrant@standalone ~]$ docker container run -d --name v1.0
simpleapp:v1.0
1e775843a42927c25ee350af052f3d8e34c0d26f2510fb2d85697094937f574f
```

7. Now, we can review the container's IP address. We are running this container in a host, which means we can access the process port and defined IP address:

```
[vagrant@standalone ~]$ docker container ls --filter name=v1.0
CONTAINER ID IMAGE COMMAND CREATED STATUS PORTS NAMES
1e775843a429 simpleapp:v1.0 "python app.py" 35 seconds ago Up 33
seconds 5000/tcp v1.0
 "python app.py" 35 seconds ago Up 33 seconds 5000/tcp v1.0

[vagrant@standalone ~]$ docker container inspect v1.0 \
 --format "{{ .NetworkSettings.Networks.bridge.IPAddress }}"

172.17.0.6
```

8. We can access our application as expected using the container's defined IP and port:

```
[vagrant@standalone ~]$ curl http://172.17.0.6:5000
<!DOCTYPE html>
<html lang="en">
<head>
```

```
        <meta charset="UTF-8">
        <title>Simple Flask Application</title>
    </head>
    <body>
        <h1>Simple Flask Application</h1>
        <h1>Version 1</h1>
    </body>
    </html>
```

9. It is simple to change index.html if we get into the container. The problem is that when we run a new container, changes will not be stored and index.html will be lost. Every time, we will get index.html defined in the base image. As a result, if we want changes to persist, we need to use volumes. Let's use a bind mount to change the index.html file while the container is running:

```
[vagrant@standalone ~]$ docker container run -d \
--name v1.0-bindmount -v $(pwd)/templates:/app/templates
simpleapp:v1.0

fbf3c35c2f11121ed4a0eedc2f47b42a5ecdc6c6ff4939eb4658ed19999f87d4

[vagrant@standalone ~]$ docker container inspect v1.0-bindmount --
format "{{ .NetworkSettings.Networks.bridge.IPAddress }}"
172.17.0.6

[vagrant@standalone ~]$ curl http://172.17.0.6:5000
<!DOCTYPE html>
<html lang="en">
<head>
    <meta charset="UTF-8">
    <title>Simple Flask Application</title>
</head>
<body>
    <h1>Simple Flask Application</h1>
    <h1>Version 1</h1>
</body>
</html>
```

10. We can now change templates/index.html because we have used -v $(pwd)/templates:/app/templates, assuming the current directory. Using the vi editor, we can modify the content of the templates/index.html file:

```
<!DOCTYPE html>
<html lang="en">
<head>
    <meta charset="UTF-8">
```

```
        <title>Simple Flask Application</title>
</head>
<body>
        <h1>Simple Flask Application</h1>
        <h1>Version 2</h1>
</body>
</html>
~
~
```

11. We change the line containing the `Version` key and we access it again using `curl`:

```
[vagrant@standalone ~]$ curl http://172.17.0.6:5000
<!DOCTYPE html>
<html lang="en">
<head>
        <meta charset="UTF-8">
        <title>Simple Flask Application</title>
</head>
<body>
        <h1>Simple Flask Application</h1>
        <h1>Version 2</h1>
</body>
</html>
```

The changes are reflected because we did them on our host filesystem and it is mounted inside our container. We can also change our application code by mounting `app.py`. Depending on what programming language we are using, we can change the application code on the fly. If changes must be persistent, we need to follow a versioning strategy. We will build a new image with the required changes.

Mounting SSHFS

In this lab, we will install and use the `sshfs` volume plugin:

1. First, we need to install the `sshfs` plugin:

```
[vagrant@standalone ~]$ docker plugin install vieux/sshfs
Plugin "vieux/sshfs" is requesting the following privileges:
 - network: [host]
 - mount: [/var/lib/docker/plugins/]
 - mount: []
 - device: [/dev/fuse]
 - capabilities: [CAP_SYS_ADMIN]
```

```
Do you grant the above permissions? [y/N] y
latest: Pulling from vieux/sshfs
52d435ada6a4: Download complete
Digest:
sha256:1d3c3e42c12138da5ef7873b97f7f32cf99fb6edde75fa4f0bcf9ed27785
5811
Status: Downloaded newer image for vieux/sshfs:latest
Installed plugin vieux/sshfs
```

2. Let's review our host IP address and start the `sshd` or `ssh` daemons (depending on your system and whether it is already running):

```
[vagrant@standalone ~]$ sudo systemctl status ssh
● ssh.service - OpenBSD Secure Shell server
   Loaded: loaded (/lib/systemd/system/ssh.service; enabled; vendor
preset: enabled)
   Active: active (running) since Mon 2019-11-11 23:59:38 CET; 6s
ago
 Main PID: 13711 (sshd)
    Tasks: 1 (limit: 4915)
   CGroup: /system.slice/ssh.service
           └─13711 /usr/sbin/sshd -D

nov 11 23:59:38 sirius systemd[1]: Starting OpenBSD Secure Shell
server...
nov 11 23:59:38 sirius sshd[13711]: Server listening on 0.0.0.0
port 22.
nov 11 23:59:38 sirius sshd[13711]: Server listening on :: port 22.
nov 11 23:59:38 sirius systemd[1]: Started OpenBSD Secure Shell
server.
```

3. Let's review the installed plugin:

```
[vagrant@standalone ~]$ docker plugin ls
ID NAME DESCRIPTION ENABLED
eb37e5a2e676 vieux/sshfs:latest sshFS plugin for Docker true
```

Since plugins are objects, we can inspect installed plugins. We can review important aspects such as version, debug mode, or the type of mount points that will be managed with this plugin:

```
[vagrant@standalone ~]$ docker plugin inspect eb37e5a2e676
[
    {
        "Config": {
        ..
            "Description": "sshFS plugin for Docker",
            "DockerVersion": "18.05.0-ce-rc1",
```

```
                "Documentation":
"https://docs.docker.com/engine/extend/plugins/",
                "Entrypoint": [
                    "/docker-volume-sshfs"
                ],
    . . .
    . . .

                    "Source": "/var/lib/docker/plugins/",
                    "Type": "bind"
                },
    . . .
    . . .

            "Enabled": true,
            "Id":
"eb37e5a2e676138b6560bd91715477155f669cd3c0e39ea054fd2220b70838f1",
            "Name": "vieux/sshfs:latest",
            "PluginReference": "docker.io/vieux/sshfs:latest",
            "Settings": {
                "Args": [],
                "Devices": [
    . . .
    . . .
    ]
```

4. Now, we will create a new volume named `sshvolume` (we assume that you have a valid SSH username and password here). Notice that we're using `127.0.0.1` and the `/tmp` directory or filesystem for demo purposes:

```
[vagrant@standalone ~]$ docker volume create -d vieux/sshfs \
-o sshcmd=ssh_user@127.0.0.1:/tmp \
-o password=ssh_userpasswd \
sshvolume
```

5. Now, we can easily run an `alpine` container by mounting previously created `sshvolume`:

```
[vagrant@standalone ~]$ docker container run --rm -it -v
sshvolume:/data alpine sh
/ # ls -lart /data
total 92
drwx------ 1 root root 17 Nov 9 08:27 systemd-
private-809bb564862047608c79c2cc81f67f24-systemd-timesyncd.service-
gQ5tZx
drwx------ 1 root root 17 Nov 9 08:27 systemd-
private-809bb564862047608c79c2cc81f67f24-systemd-resolved.service-
QhsXg9
drwxrwxrwt 1 root root 6 Nov 9 08:27 .font-unix
```

```
drwxrwxrwt 1 root root    6 Nov  9 08:27 .XIM-unix
drwxr-xr-x 1 root root   30 Nov 11 23:13 ..
drwxrwxrwt 1 root root 4096 Nov 11 23:13 .
/ #
```

Let's continue with some network labs.

Multi-homed containers

We will now look at a quick lab on attaching containers to multiple networks. Let's get started:

1. First, we'll create two different zones, `zone-a` and `zone-b`:

    ```
    [vagrant@standalone ~]$ docker network create zone-a
    bb7cb5d22c03bffdd1ef52a7469636fe2e635b031b7528a687a85ff9c7ee4141

    [vagrant@standalone ~]$ docker network create zone-b
    818ba644512a2ebb44c5fd4da43c2b1165f630d4d0429073c465f0fe4baff2c7
    ```

2. Now, we can start a container named `cont1` on `zone-a`:

    ```
    [vagrant@standalone ~]$ docker container run -d --name cont1 --
    network zone-a alpine sleep 3000
    ef3dfd6a354b5310a9c97fa9247739ac320da1b4f51f6a2b8da2ca465b12f95e
    ```

3. Next, we connect the `cont1` container to `zone-b` and review its IP addresses:

    ```
    [vagrant@standalone ~]$ docker network connect zone-b cont1

    $ docker exec cont1 ip add
    1: lo: <LOOPBACK,UP,LOWER_UP> mtu 65536 qdisc noqueue state UNKNOWN
    qlen 1000
     link/loopback 00:00:00:00:00:00 brd 00:00:00:00:00:00
     inet 127.0.0.1/8 scope host lo
     valid_lft forever preferred_lft forever
    92: eth0@if93: <BROADCAST,MULTICAST,UP,LOWER_UP,M-DOWN> mtu 1500
    qdisc noqueue state UP
     link/ether 02:42:ac:13:00:02 brd ff:ff:ff:ff:ff:ff
     inet 172.19.0.2/16 brd 172.19.255.255 scope global eth0
     valid_lft forever preferred_lft forever
    94: eth1@if95: <BROADCAST,MULTICAST,UP,LOWER_UP,M-DOWN> mtu 1500
    qdisc noqueue state UP
     link/ether 02:42:ac:14:00:02 brd ff:ff:ff:ff:ff:ff
     inet 172.20.0.2/16 brd 172.20.255.255 scope global eth1
     valid_lft forever preferred_lft forever
    ```

4. Now, we can run two containers with just one interface. One of them will run attached to `zone-a`, while the other one will just be attached to `zone-b`:

```
[vagrant@standalone ~]$ docker container run -d --name cont2 --
network zone-b --cap-add NET_ADMIN alpine sleep 3000
048e362ea27b06f5077306a71cf8adc95ea9844907aec84ec09c0b991d912a33

[vagrant@standalone ~]$ docker container run -d --name cont3 --
network zone-a --cap-add NET_ADMIN alpine sleep 3000
20c7699c54786700c65a0bbe002c750672ffb3986f41d106728b3d598065ecb5
```

5. Let's review the IP addresses and routes on both containers:

```
[vagrant@standalone ~]$ docker exec cont2 ip route
default via 172.20.0.1 dev eth0
172.20.0.0/16 dev eth0 scope link src 172.20.0.3

[vagrant@standalone ~]$ docker exec cont3 ip route
default via 172.19.0.1 dev eth0
172.19.0.0/16 dev eth0 scope link src 172.19.0.3
```

6. If we want the `cont3` container to contact the `cont2` container, we should add a route through the `cont1` container, which contains both networks. In the `cont2` container, enter the following command:

```
[vagrant@standalone ~]$ docker exec cont2 route add -net 172.19.0.0
netmask 255.255.255.0 gw 172.20.0.2

[vagrant@standalone ~]$ docker exec cont2 ip route
default via 172.20.0.1 dev eth0
172.19.0.0/24 via 172.20.0.2 dev eth0
172.20.0.0/16 dev eth0 scope link  src 172.20.0.3
```

In the `cont3` container, enter the following:

```
[vagrant@standalone ~]$ docker exec cont3 route add -net 172.20.0.0
netmask 255.255.255.0 gw 172.19.0.2

[vagrant@standalone ~]$ docker exec cont3 ip route
default via 172.19.0.1 dev eth0
172.19.0.0/16 dev eth0 scope link  src 172.19.0.3
172.20.0.0/24 via 172.19.0.2 dev eth0
```

7. Remember that we don't have name resolution between different networks. Therefore, we cannot reach `cont2` using its name:

```
[vagrant@standalone ~]$ docker exec cont3 ping -c 3 cont2
ping: bad address 'cont2'

[vagrant@standalone ~]$ docker exec cont3 ping -c 3 cont1
PING cont1 (172.19.0.2): 56 data bytes
64 bytes from 172.19.0.2: seq=0 ttl=64 time=0.063 ms
64 bytes from 172.19.0.2: seq=1 ttl=64 time=0.226 ms
64 bytes from 172.19.0.2: seq=2 ttl=64 time=0.239 ms

--- cont1 ping statistics ---
3 packets transmitted, 3 packets received, 0% packet loss
round-trip min/avg/max = 0.063/0.176/0.239 ms
```

As we expected, name resolution within the `zone-a` network works fine. Any other container on another network will not be able to resolve containers by their names.

8. We should be able to ping from `cont3` to `cont2` using its IP address:

```
[vagrant@standalone ~]$ docker exec cont3 ping -c 3 172.20.0.3
PING 172.20.0.3 (172.20.0.3): 56 data bytes
64 bytes from 172.20.0.3: seq=0 ttl=63 time=0.151 ms
64 bytes from 172.20.0.3: seq=1 ttl=63 time=0.229 ms
64 bytes from 172.20.0.3: seq=2 ttl=63 time=0.201 ms

--- 172.20.0.3 ping statistics ---
3 packets transmitted, 3 packets received, 0% packet loss
round-trip min/avg/max = 0.151/0.193/0.229 ms
```

So, although we do not have name resolution, we can reach containers on other networks using a container gateway that has interfaces on all networks. For this to work, we added a route to each network container to route all other network traffic to the gateway container. We could have added aliases to reach other network containers by name. Try it yourself – it's easy!

Publishing applications

In this lab, we are going to deploy a simple three-layer application. In fact, it's a two-layer application with the addition of a load balancer for our lab purposes:

1. First, we'll create a bridge network named `simplenet`, where we will attach all application components:

   ```
   [vagrant@standalone ~]$ docker network create simplenet
   b5ff93985be84095e70711dd3c403274c5ab9e8c53994a09e4fa8adda97f37f7
   ```

2. We will deploy a PostgreSQL database with `changeme` as the password for the root user. We created a simple database named `demo` with a `demo` user and a password of `d3m0` for this lab:

   ```
   [vagrant@standalone ~]$ docker container run -d \
   --name simpledb \
   --network simplenet \
   --env "POSTGRES_PASSWORD=changeme" \
   codegazers/simplestlab:simpledb
   ```

   Notice that we have not published any port for the database.

    Never use environment variables for secure content. There are other mechanisms to manage this kind of data. Use the secrets functionality of Docker Swarm or Kubernetes to provide security for these keys.

3. Now, we need to launch the backend application component, named `simpleapp`. Notice that in this case, we used many environment variables to configure the application side. We set the database host, database name, and the required credentials, as follows:

   ```
   [vagrant@standalone ~]$ docker container run -d \
    --name simpleapp \
   --network simplenet \
   --env dbhost=simpledb \
   --env dbname=demo \
   --env dbuser=demo \
   --env dbpasswd=d3m0 \
   codegazers/simplestlab:simpleapp
   556d6301740c1f3de20c9ff2f30095cf4a49b099190ac03189cff3db5b6e02ce
   ```

   We have not published the application. Therefore, it is only accessible locally.

4. Let's review the application component IP addresses deployed. We will inspect the containers attached to `simplenet`:

```
[vagrant@standalone ~]$ docker network inspect simplenet --format
"{{range .Containers}} {{.IPv4Address }} {{.Name}} {{end}}"
 172.22.0.4/16 simpleapp 172.22.0.3/16 simpledb
```

5. If we take a look at the exposed (not published) ports on each image definition, we will observe the following in the database component:

```
[vagrant@standalone ~]$ docker inspect
codegazers/simplestlab:simpledb \
--format "{{json .Config.ExposedPorts }}"

{"5432/tcp":{}}
```

In the application backend, we will observe the following:

```
[vagrant@standalone ~]$ docker inspect
codegazers/simplestlab:simpleapp \
--format "{{json .Config.ExposedPorts }}"

{"3000/tcp":{}}
```

6. Now, we have all the required information to test the connections to both components. We can even use the `curl` command to test whether the server is a database server. Let's try the database with an IP address of `172.22.0.3` on port `5432`. We will use `curl -I` because we don't really care about the response content. We just want to be able to connect to the exposed port:

```
[vagrant@standalone ~]$ curl -I 172.22.0.3:5432
curl: (52) Empty reply from server
```

In this case, `Empty reply from server` is `OK` (it does not use the HTTP protocol). The database is listening on that IP-port combination. The same will happen on the application backend on IP address `172.22.0.4` and port `3000`:

```
[vagrant@standalone ~]$ curl -I 172.22.0.4:3000
HTTP/1.1 200 OK
Content-Type: text/html; charset=UTF-8
Date: Sat, 16 Nov 2019 11:38:22 GMT
Connection: keep-alive
```

In this situation, we will be able to open `http://172.22.0.4:3000` in the browser. The application will be visible, but it can only be consumed locally. It hasn't been published yet.

7. Let's deploy the load balancer component. This component will publish a port on our host. Notice that we added two environment variables to allow the load balancer to connect to the backend application (we configured the load balancer on the fly with these variables because this image is modified for this behavior):

```
[vagrant@standalone ~]$ docker container run -d \
--name simplelb \
--env APPLICATION_ALIAS=simpleapp \
--env APPLICATION_PORT=3000 \
--network simplenet \
--publish 8080:80 \
codegazers/simplestlab:simplelb
35882fb4648098f7c1a1d29a0a12f4668f46213492e269b6b8262efd3191582b
```

8. Let's take a look at our local `iptables`. The Docker daemon has added a NAT rule to guide traffic from port `8080` to port `80` on the load balancer component:

```
[vagrant@standalone ~]$ sudo iptables -L DOCKER -t nat --line-
numbers --numeric
Chain DOCKER (2 references)
num target prot opt source destination
1 RETURN all -- 0.0.0.0/0 0.0.0.0/0
2 RETURN all -- 0.0.0.0/0 0.0.0.0/0
3 RETURN all -- 0.0.0.0/0 0.0.0.0/0
4 RETURN all -- 0.0.0.0/0 0.0.0.0/0
5 RETURN all -- 0.0.0.0/0 0.0.0.0/0
6 DNAT tcp -- 0.0.0.0/0 0.0.0.0/0 tcp dpt:8080 to:172.22.0.2:80
```

Notice that the load balancer will be available on all host IP addresses because we have not set any specific IP in the publish option.

9. Now, open `http://localhost:8080` in your web browser. You will be able to consume the deployed application. You will see the following GUI in your browser:

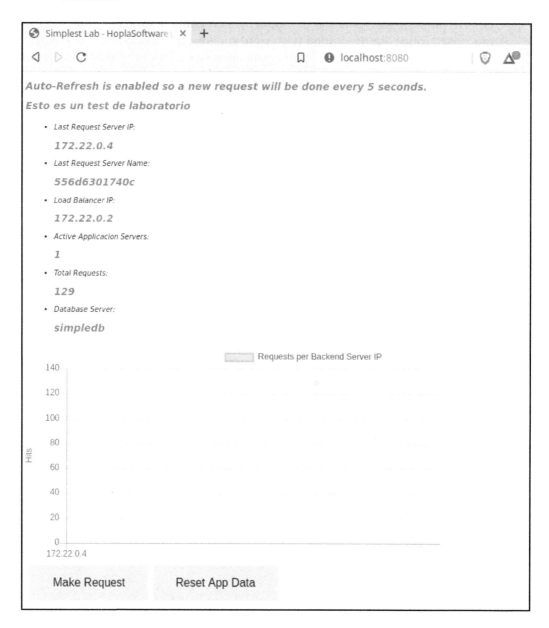

This GUI is, in fact, the application backend's front page. As we mentioned previously, it is not a real three-layer application. We added a load balancer as a frontend just to be able to publish it and add some rules there.

To ensure that the application only listens on the required interfaces, we can specify them to avoid unsecured ones. Always use a specific IP address with the `--publish` option (for example, `--listen MY_PUBLIC_IP_ONLY:8080:80`) to publish your application on a defined IP address.

In this lab, we published a simple application and ensured that only specific components are visible externally. Remember that it is possible to use container gateways and internal-only networks. These features will improve application security.

Summary

Throughout this chapter, we have reviewed how to manage data associated with containers. We took a look at different strategies to manage the data of processes and their statuses. We used host filesystems and unnamed and named volumes, and we learned how to extend the available Docker daemon volume management functionality by using plugins. We noticed that the Docker daemon will not take care of any application lock or even determine how storage resources are defined at the host level.

There are two different options for mounting volumes or bind mounts on containers using `--volume` or `--mount`. We also reviewed all the parameters required and the differences between them.

We talked about how to manage data and process states in high-availability environments. We haven't introduced any orchestration concepts yet, but it is important to understand that high availability or multiple instances of a process will require special application logic. Docker will not manage that logic and this is something you must be aware of.

We also introduced some basic networking concepts. We explained the different types of networks we can use out of the box on the Docker daemon and the special features of each one. We then reviewed the interactions between containers and how they can talk to external networks. Lastly, we finished this chapter by learning how to publish application processes running inside containers.

The next chapter will introduce you to how to run applications on multiple containers. We will learn how an application's components run and interact.

Questions

In this chapter, we reviewed container persistency and networking in non-cluster environments. Let's verify our understanding of these topics with some questions:

1. Which of the following statements is not true?

    a) Containers are not ephemeral – once created, they will stay in the host unless they are removed.
    b) We can run more than one container at a time using the same image.
    c) Containers created from the same image share their filesystems.
    d) All of these statements are false.

2. Which methods are allowed when creating a volume?

    a) We can manually create a volume using the `docker volume create` command for volume objects.
    b) We can declare a `VOLUME` sentence in a Dockerfile to use a volume on containers created from a built image.
    c) We can use Docker host filesystems inside containers as if they were Docker volumes.
    d) Volume creation is only allowed in terms of container creation or execution.

3. When we remove a container, all associated volumes will be removed. Is this true?

    a) This is false. You need to use the `--force` or `-f` option on container removal.
    b) This is false. You need to use the `--volumes` or `-v` options on container removal.
    c) This is false. You need to use the `--volumes` or `-v` options on container removal, and only unnamed volumes are removed.
    d) This is false. Volumes can only be removed manually using `docker volume rm` or `docker volume purge`.

4. Which of the following statements is not true regarding container networking?

   a) By default, all exposed container ports are accessible from the Docker host`

   b) `docker network prune` will remove all unused networks`

   c) By default, all bridge networks are attachable on the fly`

   d) Docker provides an internal DNS for each custom bridge network`

5. Which of the following statements is true regarding a container publishing an Nginx web server with port 80 exposed?

   a) If we use the host driver, we need to run this container with `NET_ADMIN` capabilities.

   b) If we use the `--publish-all` or `-P` options, a random port between `32768` and `65535` will be associated at the host level with each container port exposed. You need to add a NAT rule in `iptables` to allow requests to reach the container's internal port `80`.

   c) Using `--publish 192.168.2.100:1080:80`, we will ensure that only requests to the host IP address `192.168.2.100` on port `1080` will be redirected to the internal web server container port. (We are assuming that IP address `192.168.2.100` is a host interface.)

   d) If we use `--publish 80` or `-p 80`, a random port between `32768` and `65535` will be associated at the host level with port `80`, and a NAT rule will be added to `iptables`.

Further reading

The following links will help you learn more about volumes and networking concepts:

- Using storage volumes: `https://docs.docker.com/storage/volumes/`
- Volume plugins: `https://docs.docker.com/engine/extend/legacy_plugins/`
- Networking overview: `https://docs.docker.com/network/`

5
Deploying Multi-Container Applications

In this chapter, we will learn about the Docker Compose tool, a key component of any Docker environment. Using Docker Compose, we can manage multi-container applications, and all the actions and functionalities we usually use to manage a container-based application will be made available in multi-container environments by Docker Compose. We are able to build all the required images for a project at once. There is no need to build, pull/push, and execute containers one by one. We can declare all the pieces, along with their interconnections, storage, environments, and so on, in a single file. We are also able to debug multi-container applications from a single endpoint, which is vital when you have many separate elements running on production environments.

But this is not just a tool. Docker Compose declares a new type of file, `docker-compose.yaml`. This file provides all the requirements for multi-container applications and can be used with other Docker tools. The introduction of this kind of file is very important because it was the basis for Swarm-orchestrated deployments and the newest CNAB-based applications. We will not cover **Cloud-Native Application Bundles** (**CNABs**) in this book, but if you are interested, take a look at `https://cnab.io`. Docker has its own CNAB implementation, but it is in the experimental stage at the time of writing this book and is not part of the DCA exam.

In this chapter, we will review Docker Compose. We will learn how to install this tool with different methods, along with its keys and how we should use them. We will discover some of the actions provided by the tool and their use cases. We will finish with some tips that will help us to use `docker-compose` with variables. This allows us to provision dynamic content for different environments using the same deployment files.

We will cover the following topics in this chapter:

- Installing and using Docker Compose
- Understanding the docker-compose.yaml file
- Using docker-compose
- Customizing images with docker-compose
- Automating your desktop and CI/CD with docker-compose

Let's get started!

Technical requirements

In this chapter, we will learn about Dockerized multi-container applications. We'll provide some labs at the end of this chapter that will help you understand and learn the concepts covered. These labs can be run on your laptop or PC using the provided Vagrant standalone environment or any already deployed Docker host of your own. Check the additional information in this book's GitHub code repository at `https://github.com/ PacktPublishing/Docker-Certified-Associate-DCA-Exam-Guide.git`.

Check out the following video to see the Code in Action:

`"https://bit.ly/3hz0IB0"`

Installing and using Docker Compose

Before deep-diving into the Docker Compose tool, let's learn about the differences between multi-container applications and multi-service applications:

- Multi-container applications are applications based on multiple containers. These containers will run together on the same host. Therefore, we can deploy multi-container applications on our laptop or on any other Docker daemon. All application components will run together on a host. As a result, possible network performance issues will be mitigated because all the pieces will run together. Take into account that this deployment will not provide high availability if the host goes down. We will be able to configure the automatic restart of all components, but that is not enough for production.

- Multi-service applications are applications based on multiple services. These applications will run using Swarm orchestration and containers will run distributed on different hosts. We will learn about Docker Swarm orchestration in `Chapter 8`, *Orchestrating with Docker Swarm*. But you should understand that services are the smallest unit of scheduling on Docker Swarm environments. We will not schedule containers; we will schedule a service, based on the execution of a number of tasks. Those tasks are associated with containers; in fact, one container per task. Therefore, a service is represented by a number of tasks (known as replicas) that run containers. We schedule a service in Docker Swarm, setting the number of replicas required to be healthy. Docker Swarm will take care of the container's status. As we mentioned previously, services will run distributed on different hosts. Multi-service application components will usually run distributed cluster-wide. Components' interconnections will rely on internal and external networking, while Swarm provides out-of-the-box high availability based on resilience for all services' tasks. Keep these features in mind. We will learn about the great features behind Swarm and Kubernetes orchestrations in the *Container orchestration* section.

In summary, we deploy multi-container applications on one node while multi-service applications run distributed in different nodes.

 `docker-compose` does not come with Docker packages when you install it. It is a different product. On Docker Desktop for macOS and Windows, Docker Compose is included and ready to use.

The first thing we have to learn about Docker Compose is that it is a Python-based application. Therefore, we can install it as we would any other Python module or download it as a binary file. We can also run `docker-compose` within a container. We can find easy instructions at `https://docs.docker.com/compose/install`. Notice that at the time of writing, the latest `docker-compose` release was 1.24.1. We will use this version for all of the following installation methods.

Installing docker-compose as a Python module

Installation using `pip` (the Python module installer) is easy on Linux systems. We will review this method and we will also download the Docker Compose binary. First, we need to have `pip` installed on our system. It is a package that's available on almost all Linux systems and, consequently, whether it's already installed or not will depend on the Linux flavor used (the package name can be `py-pip`, `python3-pip`, or `pip-python`; it really depends on your operating system and the Python version used).

We will not cover this package installation and will assume you have pip installed on your system. We will install the docker-compose module as the root user to allow all host users to use it.

 There is a version of pip for Python 2.x and another for Python 3.x. Remember that Python 2.x is obsolete nowadays, so it might be time to move to Python 3.x. We will cover Python 3 installation only, for this reason.

We use sudo as root with -H to use our logged-in user's home path:

```
$ sudo -sH pip install -q docker-compose
```

After execution, we will have docker-compose installed at /usr/local/bin/docker-compose.

Installing docker-compose using downloaded binaries

Here, we just need curl or wget to download the defined version binaries from this project's GitHub page (https://github.com/docker/compose/releases). Make sure to choose the right binary and version for your architecture processor and system. We will review the installation for the CentOS 7 Linux system, which is used for all our labs:

```
$ curl -sL
"https://github.com/docker/compose/releases/download/1.24.1/docker-compose-
$(uname -s)-$(uname -m)" -o /tmp/docker-compose

$ sudo chmod +x /tmp/docker-compose

$ sudo mv /tmp/docker-compose /usr/local/bin/docker-compose
```

We can also use a container to execute docker-compose, as we will learn in the next section.

Executing docker-compose using a container

This is quite interesting because, as we have learned, executing applications as containers just requires a Docker daemon running on our system. It is a great way to execute applications! In this case, run.sh is a script that will prepare all the required volumes and parameters (curl -L will follow redirections and the -o argument will allow us to choose the destination filename):

```
$ sudo curl -L --fail
https://github.com/docker/compose/releases/download/1.24.1/run.sh -o
/usr/local/bin/docker-compose

$ sudo chmod +x /usr/local/bin/docker-compose
```

Docker Compose can also be installed on Windows nodes, as we will learn in the next section.

Installing docker-compose on Windows servers

On Windows servers, we will use an elevated PowerShell (that is, run it as administrator).

Since GitHub now requires TLS1.2, it is required to run the following on our administrator PowerShell before executing the installation:

```
[Net.ServicePointManager]::SecurityProtocol =
[Net.SecurityProtocolType]::Tls12
```

Once in the administrator's PowerShell, we need to run the following command:

```
Invoke-WebRequest
"https://github.com/docker/compose/releases/download/1.24.1/docker-compose-
Windows-x86_64.exe" -UseBasicParsing -OutFile
$Env:ProgramFiles\Docker\docker-compose.exe
```

In the next section, we will learn about Docker Compose files.

Understanding the docker-compose.yaml file

Docker Compose introduces the concept of multi-container applications using an all-in-one application components' definition file. This file is known as `docker-compose.yaml`. Usually, we will manage a `docker-compose.yaml` file. Notice that this is a YAML file; therefore, indentation is fundamental. The file will contain all of the application components and their properties.

This is how a simple `docker-compose.yaml` file looks (we can use either the `.yaml` or `.yml` extension for YAML files):

```
version: "3.7"
services:
  lb:
    build: simplestlb
    image: myregistry/simplest-lab:simplestlb
    environment:
      - APPLICATION_ALIAS=simplestapp
      - APPLICATION_PORT=3000
    networks:
      simplestlab:
          aliases:
          - simplestlb
    ports:
      - "8080:80"
  db:
    build: simplestdb
    image: myregistry/simplest-lab:simplestdb
    environment:
        - "POSTGRES_PASSWORD=changeme"
    networks:
      simplestlab:
        aliases:
          - simplestdb
    volumes:
      - pgdata:/var/lib/postgresql/data
  app:
    build: simplestapp
    image: myregistry/simplest-lab:simplestapp
    environment:
      - dbhost=simplestdb
      - dbname=demo
      - dbuser=demo
      - dbpasswd=d3m0
```

```
    networks:
       simplestlab:
        aliases:
          - simplestapp
    depends_on:
      - lb
      - db
volumes:
  pgdata:
networks:
  simplestlab:
    ipam:
      driver: default
      config:
        - subnet: 172.16.0.0/16
```

The `docker-compose.yaml` file will contain definitions for all Docker-based application components (services, networks, and volumes). In this file, we first declare the file definition version. This definition manages how Docker Compose should interpret some of the directives written. We will use version 3.x for our file definition because it is the most up to date and is recommended at the time of writing. There are a few differences between versions, although `docker-compose` provides backward compatibility, so you should check the Docker documentation for more information. It is important to know that keys and definition structures may vary between versions, and you should use specific versions with older Docker engines. We will use version 3.7 (the current version at the time of writing).

Let's learn a bit about the file contents.

 We are using environment variables to provide credentials and access to some services. This is just for demo purposes – never use environment variables for your passwords, credentials, or connection strings. In Docker Swarm, we use secrets and configuration objects. In Docker Compose, we do not have this kind of object, so it's preferred to use external configuration tools or secure key-value stores to manage these values.

We have a section for `services` and another one for `networks`. We can also have a `volumes` section. The `volumes` and `networks` sections will define their properties for the application. In these sections, we will declare special features and the drivers used for them. In the example file, we have declared a special subnet to use on the `simplestlab` network with the default bridge driver. This is the network that will be created and used for all the components, as we can see in all of our service definitions.

> In Docker Swarm, we can also define `Configs` and `Secrets`, which are cluster objects. We will declare objects in one section of the file and then we will use these objects inside each service definition.

Each service represents one component. Let's take a closer look at the definitions of the `app` service, for example.

Each service definition has some key configurations to explain how this application component will run. In the `app` service, we have a `build` definition, which indicates how this component will be created. The value of the `build` key indicates the context path for building an image for these components (the `simplestapp` directory). Therefore, we can build this component with this `docker-compose.yaml` file and the `simplestapp` directory content. We've learned that to build an image, we need a Dockerfile; consequently, a Dockerfile is mandatory inside the `simplestapp` directory. All the files required to compile the `myregistry/simplest-lab:simplestapp` image should be in this directory.

> When we talk about multi-container applications with Docker Compose, services definitions are different from Swarm Services, which are managed by Swarm orchestration. In non-Swam environments, we refer to services as application components.

The next line, which contains the `image` key, defines the name of the image. If the image does not exist in your host, it will be built with this name. If we do not have a `build` definition, the Docker daemon will try to download the defined image from the registry.

The next key defines a list of variables and their values to be used as environment variables during container execution. We can override the image-defined ENVIRONMENT, CMD, ENTRYPOINT, and VOLUME values, among others, as we usually do within containers. We will take a look at the Docker Compose definitions later, but keep in mind that almost every option we use on the `docker container run` or `docker container create` actions is available as a key on `docker-compose.yaml`.

Then, we define the networks to be used in this component. We also defined an alias name to use in this network. This component will be known as `app`, which is its service name, and also by its defined alias, which is `simplestapp`.

It is important to note that Docker Compose allows us to define an order of execution, as we can see in the last few lines. We used the `depends_on` key to wait until all the components in the list were available (that is, all the containers were marked as healthy).

With that, we have reviewed the `services` section of the preceding code file. In this example, we also have `volumes` and `networks` sections.

In the `volumes` section, we have the simplest definition. It is empty and just defines a volume with the default parameters (the local driver). In the `services` section, we define where and how these volumes should be attached.

Now that we know the basics, we can take a look at some of the most used key definitions:

Key	Definitions
build	This key will define the options used to build the application images. These are some of the most used options: • context: This option defines the path to the build context, the directory that contains the Dockerfile, and all the other files required for the image. • dockerfile: This defines an alternative Dockerfile name. • args: We can set Dockerfile arguments here. • labels: This option allows us to set image labels.
image	This is the name of the image to be used. If the image does not exist, it will be pulled from the registry. If the image must be built, it will use this value for its name.

environment	We are able to set environment variables within containers. This will overwrite any image-defined values. We can also use `env_file` to define a file with many values.
command	This will set or overwrite the image's `command` definition.
entrypoint	This will set or overwrite the image's `entrypoint` definition.
ports	These are the ports to be exposed by the services to be reachable at the host level.
expose	This option defines which service ports will be available for other services.
privileged cap_add/cap_drop read_only	These options will set the same features we learned about when we talked about container execution in Chapter 3, *Running Docker Containers*.
user	This will set or overwrite the image's `user` definition.
labels	This will set or overwrite image labels.
restart	With `restart`, we can set how associated containers should be managed. If they die, should Docker restart them or leave them stopped? Remember the options defined for our containers – we will use the same values here.
container_name	We are able to set the container name using this variable. If not defined, the container name will be generated using the service project name as a prefix, followed by the service name and the instance number, starting from 1. Take care with this parameter; as you've already learned, there can only be one container with a defined name per host.
hostname domainname	These options will allow us to change the container hostname and its domain name. Under the `network` definition, we are able to add as many DNS aliases as required.
extra_hosts	With this option, we can add external hosts to be discovered via internal DNS. This will help us reach external services as if they were running within containers.
depends_on	This key allows us to set components' dependencies. It is deprecated now in version 3 but is included here to explain to you that it did not provide real dependency. This option will just control the boot order.

networks	We can set which network drivers to use, their options and subnet ranges, and how they will be accessible (internal and/or attachable). Let's review a simple example:
	
	``yaml
	networks:
	  mynet:
	    driver: bridge
	    ipam:
	      driver: default
	      config:
	        - subnet: 172.28.0.0/16
	``
	In the preceding code, we have defined `mynet` as a bridge network with a defined subnet for all our containers. We can use this defined network on each service section:
	
	``yaml
	  myservice:
	build:
	context: .
	dockerfile: ./src/myapp/Dockerfile
	networks:
	- mynet
	``

volumes	Volumes are defined in the `volumes` section. We will be able to set their drivers and special options. The following is an example of a simple local definition that we can use in the `services` section:
	
	``yaml
	...
	
	...
	  myservice:
	    image: myregistry/myimage:tag
	    volumes:
	      - data:/appdata/
	...
	
	...
	volumes:
	  config-data:
	    driver: local
	``

tmpfs	We can use an in-memory filesystem with `tmpfs`. This option is very useful for bypassing the overlay filesystem to improve I/O performance or for security reasons. The in-memory filesystem will disappear when the container dies:
	
	``yaml
	- type: tmpfs
	    target: /app
	    tmpfs:
	      size: 1000
	``

healthcheck	This will set or overwrite the image's `healthcheck` definitions.

These keys are the most commonly used ones. Consult the Docker Compose documentation for more information, which is available on the Docker website at `https://docs.docker.com/compose/compose-file/`.

 There are many keys that are only allowed on Docker Swarm environments. We didn't include them in the preceding information table because the Swarm options will be shown in `Chapter 8`, *Orchestration Using Docker Swarm*. Defining container resource limits in `docker-compose.yaml` files is only allowed either using Docker Swarm mode or using Docker Compose version 2.

Once we have created our `docker-compose.yaml` file, we will be able to use the Docker Compose command-line definitions written in this file.

Using the Docker Compose command-line interface

We installed the `docker-compose` binary in the previous section, which means we can now review the actions available to us. `docker-compose` will provide most of the actions available for Docker because we will execute them on multiple containers at once. Let's review the available `docker-compose` actions in the following table:

Command	Definition
build	As expected, this action will build or rebuild all `docker-compose.yaml` file components, or just the selected ones. This action will look for any `build` keys in our `docker-compose.yaml` file and launch a build or rebuild. If we set a project name using `--project`, all images will be created as `<project_name>_<service_name>` if no image name is defined. If so, this is the name that will be used if we push them to a registry.
pull/push	We will be able to push or pull all images at once because we manage all the application components with `docker-compose`.
images	This action will list all application images.
create	Remember that we can create containers. In this case, we will create all containers required by the application, but they will not be launched until a `start` action is executed.
rm	This action will remove all stopped containers. Remember to use the project name, or leave it empty to use the current directory as the application name.

up (-d or --detach)	We will create and start all components with this simple action. All the components will run at once. We will use --detach to run the application in the background, as we learned with containers.
down	To remove all application components, we will use the down action. This will end all application containers or just the specified ones. Take care as externally defined resources will not be deleted and must be removed manually.
start/stop/restart	These options will allow us to manage components, applying either to all components at once or only those specified.
run	With this option, we can execute one component to run a specified command, such as to initialize a database or create a required file.
pause/unpause	As we learned with containers, we can pause and unpause application components.
ps	docker-compose will show all application containers (processes) and their ports.
top	This option will show the processes running on each container deployed for the application.
exec	We will be able to run a process within any application container namespace. Remember what we learned in Chapter 3, *Running Docker Containers*.
logs	It is very useful to be able to retrieve all application container' logs using a single command. We can use the logs action to retrieve all application logs at once. Logs will appear together, along with their service names, to help us identify each component.
config	We can verify a Docker Compose definition using the config action. We can also list the defined services using services as the argument.

With this information, we can quickly see how the usual container workflow can be achieved in multi-container environments with Docker Compose, which gives us a new command-line interface to build, share, and run all our application components at once.

We can define external resources such as volume or networks. We will use the external: true option in these cases and you'll have to create these resources manually.

Each application that's deployed using `docker-compose` will have its own project definition. Each project will run in isolation alongside others in the same host. By default, `docker-compose` will use the current directory name as the project's name. We can override this behavior using `--project-name` or `-p` to set a more descriptive name.

In `Chapter 1`, *Modern Infrastructures and Applications with Docker*, we learned that object names are unique (we can have objects with many names, but each is unique, and we cannot have repeated names); therefore, `docker-compose` adds the project's name as a prefix to each created object. This way, we identify all application components and ensure that they have unique names. Of course, we can use the same `docker-compose` file to deploy the same application twice, but we should choose a different project name each time.

> We can use the `docker-compose.yaml` file to launch the same application multiple times, but we cannot share unique resources such as ports, volumes, and IP addresses between volumes. Sharing a volume between components depends on application behavior, but IP addresses or ports will be unique to a given Docker host.

Let's review the complete application deployment workflow with the previous `docker-compose.yaml` file (seen in the *Understanding the docker-compose file* section).

First, we need to build the application images. You can download all the application code from this book's GitHub repository at `https://github.com/PacktPublishing/Docker-Certified-Associate-DCA-Exam-Guide.git`.

Let's clone the repository to get all the source code directories and configuration files. Your output may vary from the following:

```
$ git clone
https://github.com/PacktPublishing/Docker-Certified-Associate-DCA-Exam-Guid
e.git
Cloning into 'dca-book-code'...
remote: Enumerating objects: 26, done.
remote: Counting objects: 100% (26/26), done.
remote: Compressing objects: 100% (22/22), done.
remote: Total 26 (delta 0), reused 26 (delta 0), pack-reused 0
Unpacking objects: 100% (26/26), done.
```

We will have a directory for the `simplest-lab` project with a `docker-compose.yaml` file and different directories for each application component:

```
$ cd chapter5/simplest-lab/

$ ls -lRt
.:
total 4
-rw-rw-r-- 1 zero zero 982 nov 24 11:06 docker-compose.yaml
drwxrwxr-x 2 zero zero 146 nov 24 11:06 simplestapp
drwxrwxr-x 3 zero zero 112 nov 24 11:06 simplestdb
drwxrwxr-x 2 zero zero 80 nov 24 11:06 simplestlb
./simplestapp:
total 32
-rw-rw-r-- 1 zero zero 91 nov 24 11:06 dbconfig.json
-rw-rw-r-- 1 zero zero 466 nov 24 11:06 Dockerfile
-rw-rw-r-- 1 zero zero 354 nov 24 11:06 package.json
-rw-rw-r-- 1 zero zero 191 nov 24 11:06 README.md
-rw-rw-r-- 1 zero zero 1244 nov 24 11:06 reset.html
-rw-rw-r-- 1 zero zero 3837 nov 24 11:06 simplestapp.html
-rw-rw-r-- 1 zero zero 6556 nov 24 11:06 simplestapp.js
./simplestdb:
total 12
drwxrwxr-x 2 zero zero 26 nov 24 11:06 docker-entrypoint-initdb.d
-rwxrwxr-x 1 zero zero 2587 nov 24 11:06 docker-entrypoint.sh
-rw-rw-r-- 1 zero zero 152 nov 24 11:06 Dockerfile
-rw-rw-r-- 1 zero zero 2568 nov 24 11:06 Dockerfile.scratch
./simplestdb/docker-entrypoint-initdb.d:
total 4
-rw-rw-r-- 1 zero zero 484 nov 24 11:06 init-demo.sh
./simplestlb:
total 16
-rw-rw-r-- 1 zero zero 467 nov 24 11:06 Dockerfile
-rwxrwxr-x 1 zero zero 213 nov 24 11:06 entrypoint.sh
-rw-rw-r-- 1 zero zero 837 nov 24 11:06 nginx.conf
-rw-rw-r-- 1 zero zero 24 nov 24 11:06 README.md
```

In each project directory, there is a Dockerfile we can use to build that specific component. So, let's build all the components at once.

> **TIP**
>
> We have the same options for removing the intermediate containers (used for building and disallowing image caching) as we had with the `docker image build` command. We will use `--force-rm` and `--no-cache`, respectively.

To ensure that the defined `docker-compose.yaml` file is valid, we can use `docker-compose config --quiet`. If there is an issue, it will be reported. We can also list the names of the services or volumes that have been defined:

```
$ docker-compose config --services
db
lb
app

$ docker-compose config --volumes
pgdata
```

We will use these service name definitions later on in this section.

We will execute `docker-compose build` to build all the component images defined in our `docker-compose.yaml` file. This command will take some time because we are not just building an image, but all the images required. The following output is truncated:

```
$ docker-compose build
Building db
Step 1/2 : FROM postgres:alpine
alpine: Pulling from library/postgres
....
Successfully built 336fb84e7fbf
Successfully tagged myregistry/simplest-lab:simplestdb
Building lb
Step 1/10 : FROM alpine:latest
latest: Pulling from library/alpine
....
Successfully built 4a5308d90123
Successfully tagged myregistry/simplest-lab:simplestlb
Building app
Step 1/15 : FROM alpine
 ---> 965ea09ff2eb
Step 2/15 : RUN apk --update --no-progress --no-cache add nodejs npm
....
Successfully built ffa49ee4228e
Successfully tagged myregistry/simplest-lab:simplestapp
```

After a few minutes (or seconds, depending on your internet connection and processor speed), all three images will be created. As we have not set a project name, docker-compose has created one for you. As we mentioned previously, by default, all the components will be created with the directory name prefixed. In this case, we have an image key on our docker-compose.yaml file, so that image naming syntax will be used instead of a local directory reference.

Notice that we have used a dummy registry name (myregistry). This means that we cannot push images to this dummy registry, but it is important to understand the logic behind image names. If we list current images on our Docker daemon, we should have all the images created for this project:

```
$ docker images --filter=reference='myregistry/*:*'
REPOSITORY TAG IMAGE ID CREATED SIZE
myregistry/simplest-lab simplestapp ffa49ee4228e About an hour ago 56.5MB
myregistry/simplest-lab simplestlb 4a5308d90123 About an hour ago 7MB
myregistry/simplest-lab simplestdb 336fb84e7fbf About an hour ago 72.8MB
```

Now that we have our images, we can share them. We can now execute the docker-compose push command to push them to myregistry (in our example file). This will upload the images one by one with defined tags.

We are ready to run all the application components together using docker-compose up. To launch it in the background, we will use the --detach option. If we do not use this option, we will be attached to all our container's standard and error outputs. We learned how to attach to container output in Chapter 3, *Running Docker Containers*. Remember that this behavior is expected on docker container run without the --detach or -d option:

```
$ docker-compose up --detach
Creating network "simplest-lab_simplestlab" with the default driver
Creating simplest-lab_db_1 ... done
Creating simplest-lab_lb_1 ... done
Creating simplest-lab_app_1 ... done
```

With this line, we have just started our application. It is important to understand that docker-compose up does more than merely execute all the components. In this case, we built our components first, but the docker-compose up instruction will verify that component images are present on the Docker host. If not, it will build or pull them. If the images are not present, they should be downloaded, and that is what the Docker daemon will do.

The application should be running. Let's verify the execution of all components. We will use `docker-compose ps` to obtain the application component status:

```
$ docker-compose ps
 Name Command State Ports
------------------------------------------------------------------------
-------
simplest-lab_app_1 node simplestapp.js 3000 Up 3000/tcp
simplest-lab_db_1 docker-entrypoint.sh postgres Up 5432/tcp
simplest-lab_lb_1 /entrypoint.sh /bin/sh -c ... Up 0.0.0.0:8080->80/tcp
```

Take a look at the application component names. They are all created with the `simplest-lab` prefix, followed by _ and the name used in the service definition. This is what we expected because we have not defined a project name. The directory name was used as the project name by default.

We can also see that component names end with _, followed by a number (in this case, 1). This indicates the number of replicas we have for this component. We use more than one replica for some application components. Keep in mind that Docker Compose does not know anything about our application logic. Therefore, it is up to us to code this component to make it scalable. In our example, we have a three-layer application with three components: a simple load balancer, `lb`, an application's backend, `app`, and a database component, `db`. We will not be able to scale up our database component because this will corrupt the database data. No more than one `postgres` process can use a specific set of data files, and this applies to our case. On the other hand, our `app` sample application component is prepared to run multiple times.

Let's take a look at our application environment. By reviewing the output of `docker-compose ps`, we can see that only one component is exposing its service. We have only published the `lb` component. This is our application frontend (in fact, it is a load balancer component that will route traffic to different `app` component backends). If we open a web browser on `http://0.0.0.0:8080`, we will have a web application similar to the one shown in the following screenshot:

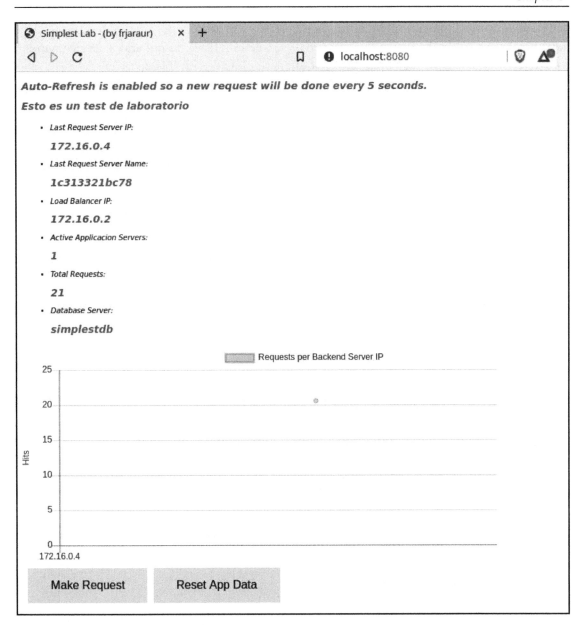

At this point, the application is already deployed. We can review the component logs using the service name with the docker-compose logs action. If we do not add a service name, we will be reviewing the logs of all the containers deployed with this docker-compose.yaml file. This is very useful because we will be able to review all their outputs from a single endpoint. Each component's log will appear in a different color to help us distinguish between them.

For example, to review the database component log, we will use the following command:

```
$ docker-compose logs db
Attaching to simplest-lab_db_1
db_1 |
db_1 | PostgreSQL Database directory appears to contain a database;
Skipping initialization
db_1 |
db_1 | 2019-11-24 11:57:14.011 UTC [1] LOG: starting PostgreSQL 12.1 on
x86_64-pc-linux-musl, compiled by gcc (Alpine 8.3.0) 8.3.0, 64-bit
db_1 | 2019-11-24 11:57:14.011 UTC [1] LOG: listening on IPv4 address
"0.0.0.0", port 5432
db_1 | 2019-11-24 11:57:14.011 UTC [1] LOG: listening on IPv6 address "::",
port 5432
db_1 | 2019-11-24 11:57:14.025 UTC [1] LOG: listening on Unix socket
"/var/run/postgresql/.s.PGSQL.5432"
```

It is important to notice that the service name is the name defined in our docker-compose.yaml file. It is not the name of the service running.

All docker-compose commands need a docker-compose.yaml file (or any other filename using the --file or -f options) and a project name (defined using the --project or -p options, or the current directory by default). These two parameters define the instances where all the docker-compose commands will be applied.

As we did with containers in Chapter 3, *Running Docker Containers*, we can run a new process within the container's process namespaces using docker-compose exec:

```
$ docker-compose exec app sh
/APP $ ls -lart
total 344
-rwxr-xr-x 1 root root 314658 May 24 2017 Chart.js
-rw-rw-r-- 1 root root 6556 Nov 24 10:06 simplestapp.js
-rw-rw-r-- 1 root root 1244 Nov 24 10:06 reset.html
-rw-rw-r-- 1 root root 354 Nov 24 10:06 package.json
-rw-rw-r-- 1 root root 91 Nov 24 10:06 dbconfig.json
-rw-rw-r-- 1 root root 3826 Nov 24 14:38 simplestapp.html
-rw-r--r-- 1 root root 7654 Nov 24 14:38 package-lock.json
```

```
drwxr-xr-x 31 root root 4096 Nov 24 14:38 node_modules
drwxr-xr-x 1 root root 22 Nov 24 14:38 .
drwxr-xr-x 1 root root 6 Nov 24 14:38 ..
```

Notice that it allocates a Terminal by default. Therefore, it is not necessary to use the `-t` and `-i` options.

Using `docker-compose top`, we will obtain the consumption of each process on each container:

```
$ docker-compose top
simplest-lab_app_1
UID PID PPID C STIME TTY TIME CMD
------------------------------------------------------------------------------
zero 9594 9564 0 15:38 ? 00:00:05 node simplestapp.js 3000

simplest-lab_db_1
UID PID PPID C STIME TTY TIME CMD
------------------------------------------------------------------------------
-------------------
70 9374 9304 0 15:38 ? 00:00:00 postgres
70 9558 9374 0 15:38 ? 00:00:00 postgres: checkpointer
70 9559 9374 0 15:38 ? 00:00:00 postgres: background writer
70 9560 9374 0 15:38 ? 00:00:00 postgres: walwriter
70 9561 9374 0 15:38 ? 00:00:00 postgres: autovacuum launcher
70 9562 9374 0 15:38 ? 00:00:00 postgres: stats collector
70 9563 9374 0 15:38 ? 00:00:00 postgres: logical replication launcher
70 9702 9374 0 15:38 ? 00:00:00 postgres: demo demo 172.16.0.4(37134) idle

simplest-lab_lb_1
 UID PID PPID C STIME TTY TIME CMD
------------------------------------------------------------------------------
-------------------------------------------
root 9360 9295 0 15:38 ? 00:00:00 nginx: master process nginx -g pid
/run/nginx.pid; daemon off;
systemd+ 9467 9360 0 15:38 ? 00:00:01 nginx: worker process
systemd+ 9468 9360 0 15:38 ? 00:00:00 nginx: worker process
```

Let's review some of the objects created by this multi-container deployment. We have a new network, with the name defined following the format we learned about previously; that is, `<project or directory name>_ <defined_network_name>`. We have not specified a special network type, so, by default, it is a bridge network, as expected. The output may vary in your environment, but the name for the newly deployed network will exist:

```
$ docker network ls
NETWORK ID NAME DRIVER SCOPE
0950a6281629 bridge bridge local
82faac964567 host host local
2fb14f721dc3 none null local
a913507af228 simplest-lab_simplestlab bridge local
```

Remember that all custom bridge networks manage their own internal DNS resolution. As a result, all services (application components) deployed on the same network can be reached using their service names.

The same occurs with our defined volumes. If we list our local volume, we will get a new volume following the same naming convention. The output may vary in your environment, but the name for the newly deployed volume will exist:

```
$ docker volume ls
DRIVER VOLUME NAME
local 3f93b55b105f64dd03a9088405484909d2f8cad83dacc5fb5a53ea27af1f33e6
local mydbdata
local simplest-lab_pgdata
vieux/sshfs:latest sshvolume
```

We can stop and start (or restart) any service defined in the `docker-compose.yaml` file using their names. The following action will restart all the instances of a defined service:

```
$ docker-compose restart lb
Restarting simplest-lab_lb_1 ... done
```

Let's go back to the concept of instances. We can have more than one instance of a defined process for a service. This is the reason we have numbered all our instances. As we mentioned previously, the ability of a process to be scaled up or down is not defined in Docker. It is related to your application logic. In this example, we can scale up the number of instances of the app component. We can use `docker-compose scale` to change the number of instances (containers) for a defined application component:

```
$ docker-compose scale app=5
WARNING: The scale command is deprecated. Use the up command with the --
scale flag instead.
Starting simplest-lab_app_1 ... done
Creating simplest-lab_app_2 ... done
Creating simplest-lab_app_3 ... done
Creating simplest-lab_app_4 ... done
Creating simplest-lab_app_5 ... done
```

Note that the `scale` action is deprecated, so nowadays, we should use `docker-compose up --scale <service=number_of_instances>`.

As a result, we now have five instances of the app application component. All the instances' IP addresses are added to the internal DNS resolution. Therefore, we can resolve the service name to all the instances' IP addresses in a round-robin sequence:

```
$ docker-compose ps
 Name Command State Ports
---------------------------------------------------------------------------
-------
simplest-lab_app_1 node simplestapp.js 3000 Up 3000/tcp
simplest-lab_app_2 node simplestapp.js 3000 Up 3000/tcp
simplest-lab_app_3 node simplestapp.js 3000 Up 3000/tcp
simplest-lab_app_4 node simplestapp.js 3000 Up 3000/tcp
simplest-lab_app_5 node simplestapp.js 3000 Up 3000/tcp
simplest-lab_db_1 docker-entrypoint.sh postgres Up 5432/tcp
simplest-lab_lb_1 /entrypoint.sh /bin/sh -c ... Up 0.0.0.0:8080->80/tcp
```

If we go back to the application GUI at `http://localhost:8080/`, we'll notice that the chart has changed because the requests are now distributed across five different backends:

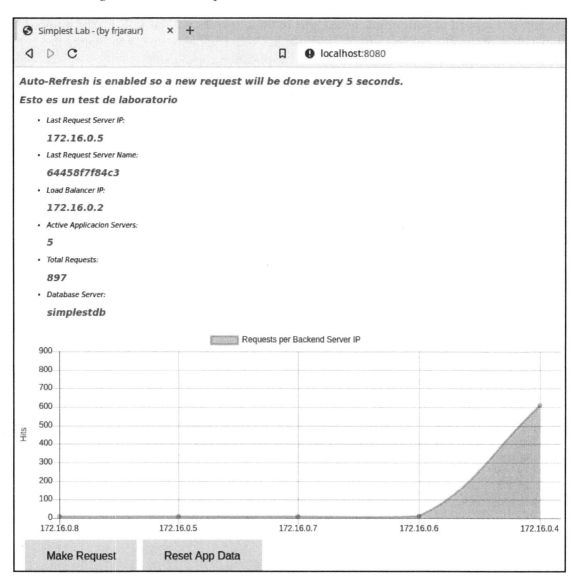

In this chart, we can see that we now have five different IP addresses and that requests are distributed between them. Because we have been running the application for a long time (and automated requests are executed during this period), we have more requests for the first IP address (the first instance launched).

We can remove previous data from the database using the **Reset App Data** button. Let's click this button and review the requests count. You can either wait for more requests (a new request is made every 5 seconds) or simply click the **Make Request** button a few times. You should now have something similar to the following chart:

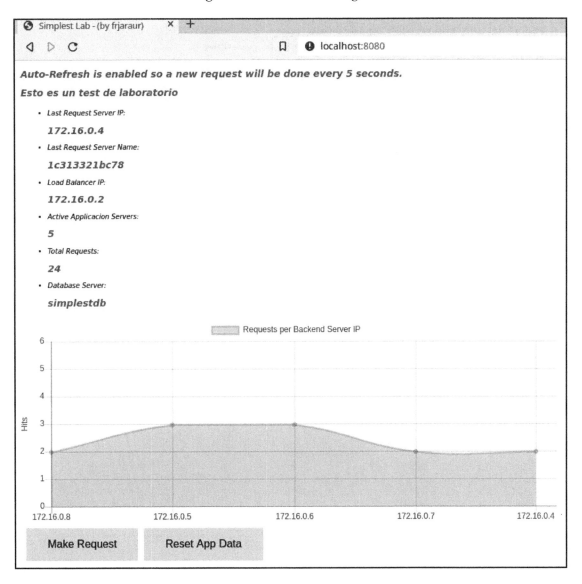

This chart shows the request distribution of the five defined instances of the app component. Now, let's scale down to three instances, as follows:

```
$ docker-compose up -d --scale app=3
simplest-lab_db_1 is up-to-date
simplest-lab_lb_1 is up-to-date
Stopping and removing simplest-lab_app_4 ... done
Stopping and removing simplest-lab_app_5 ... done
Starting simplest-lab_app_1 ... done
Starting simplest-lab_app_2 ... done
Starting simplest-lab_app_3 ... done
```

Now, we can review the app instances:

```
$ docker-compose ps app
 Name Command State Ports
-----------------------------------------------------------------
simplest-lab_app_1 node simplestapp.js 3000 Up 3000/tcp
simplest-lab_app_2 node simplestapp.js 3000 Up 3000/tcp
simplest-lab_app_3 node simplestapp.js 3000 Up 3000/tcp
```

The chart will change again and only three backends will receive requests (there are only three running). Once again, we will use the **Reset App Data** button and get a chart similar to the following one:

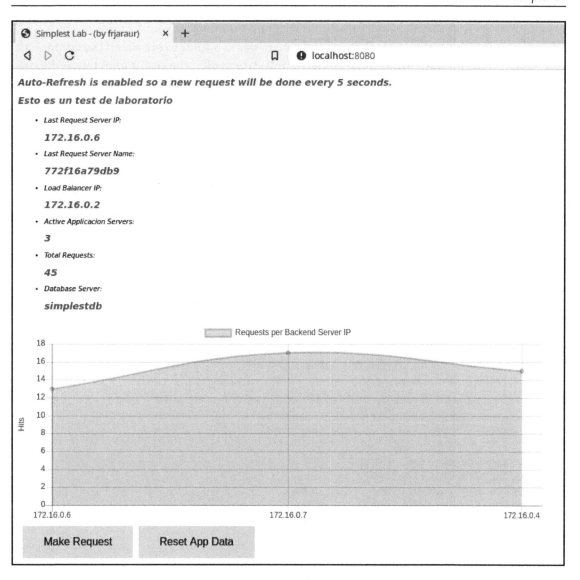

Take a quick look at the running containers associated with the deployed `docker-compose.yaml` application file. In this case, we are using a filter to obtain all the containers with names starting with the `simplest` pattern. We formatted the result to obtain only their names and labels:

```
$ docker container ls --filter name="/simplest*" --format "table {{ .Names }}\t {{.Labels}}\n\n"
NAMES           LABELS

simplest-lab_app_3    com.docker.compose.version=1.24.0,com.docker.compose.config-hash=9ea63f358f0d5376566073c929b0d487d8c1c3d7dccc83506c8d9b042f9007fa,com.do
cker.compose.container-number=3,com.docker.compose.oneoff=False,com.docker.compose.project=simplest-lab,com.docker.compose.service=app

simplest-lab_app_2    com.docker.compose.container-number=2,com.docker.compose.oneoff=False,com.docker.compose.project=simplest-lab,com.docker.compose.service
=app,com.docker.compose.version=1.24.0,com.docker.compose.config-hash=9ea63f358f0d5376566073c929b0d487d8c1c3d7dccc83506c8d9b042f9007fa

simplest-lab_app_1    com.docker.compose.oneoff=False,com.docker.compose.project=simplest-lab,com.docker.compose.service=app,com.docker.compose.version=1.24.0
,com.docker.compose.config-hash=9ea63f358f0d5376566073c929b0d487d8c1c3d7dccc83506c8d9b042f9007fa,com.docker.compose.container-number=1

simplest-lab_lb_1    com.docker.compose.container-number=1,com.docker.compose.oneoff=False,com.docker.compose.project=simplest-lab,com.docker.compose.service=
lb,com.docker.compose.version=1.24.0,com.docker.compose.config-hash=fc6feb3cf80fac4d71a389bcB187fce64045ac3ed6c7da4413c9a7043c2088f8

simplest-lab_db_1    com.docker.compose.version=1.24.0,com.docker.compose.config-hash=827c1a6becc9b2b4337d04dcfe2b01115da440ece3a6a2a974db41c5d2d25ad5,com.doc
ker.compose.container-number=1,com.docker.compose.oneoff=False,com.docker.compose.project=simplest-lab,com.docker.compose.service=db
```

Notice that `docker-compose` has added labels for each application component, indicating the name of the project, the container name, and the associated service name.

We can easily stop or kill a single component or all of them at once. We can also remove all the components using the `down` or `rm` options. Usually, we use `docker-compose down` because it is easier to remember. We can also define a timeout for components to stop using `stop_grace_period`, which defaults to 10 seconds (review the `docker-compose` file reference for available options at `https://docs.docker.com/compose/compose-file/`). Using `docker-compose down`, components will be removed once they are stopped:

```
$ docker-compose down
Stopping simplest-lab_app_3 ... done
Stopping simplest-lab_app_2 ... done
Stopping simplest-lab_app_1 ... done
Stopping simplest-lab_lb_1 ... done
Stopping simplest-lab_db_1 ... done
Removing simplest-lab_app_3 ... done
Removing simplest-lab_app_2 ... done
Removing simplest-lab_app_1 ... done
Removing simplest-lab_lb_1 ... done
Removing simplest-lab_db_1 ... done
Removing network simplest-lab_simplestlab
```

Let's take a look at all the application-related objects. Here, we can see that `network` was removed but `volume` persists. This is because Docker does not know what to do with the volume. Are we going to use it later? Consequently, it is preferred not to delete the volume unless we use the `docker-compose down --volumes` (or `-v`) option to remove all the volumes associated with the application:

```
$ docker volume ls
DRIVER VOLUME NAME
local 3f93b55b105f64dd03a9088405484909d2f8cad83dacc5fb5a53ea27af1f33e6
local mydbdata
local simplest-lab_pgdata
vieux/sshfs:latest sshvolume

$ docker network ls
NETWORK ID NAME DRIVER SCOPE
0950a6281629 bridge bridge local
82faac964567 host host local
2fb14f721dc3 none null local
```

In this section, we have learned about all of the main `docker-compose` actions associated with the usual Docker workflow. In the next section, we will review some specific options for building images.

Customizing images with docker-compose

Building applications using `docker-compose` is very useful because we can use it for creating all the images in Docker Swarm or Kubernetes environments. We just need a `docker-compose` file definition and the application components' code.

We have been using a static `docker-compose` file definition, but in many cases, we will use some variables to fulfill their values for specific needs. In fact, we could use variables in Dockerfiles as well, to complete the dynamic configurations at all levels.

Let's introduce some variables to our application's `docker-compose.yaml` file (we do this to allow different behaviors):

```
version: "3.7"

services:
  lb:
    build:
      context: ./simplestlb
      args:
        alpineversion: "latest"
```

```
    dockerfile: Dockerfile.custom
    labels:
      org.codegazers.dscription: "Test image"
  image: ${dockerhubid}/simplest-lab:simplestlb
environment:
  - APPLICATION_ALIAS=simplestapp
  - APPLICATION_PORT=3000
networks:
  simplestlab:
      aliases:
      - simplestlb
ports:
  - "${LB_PORT}:80"


...
...
```

You will find this file in `https://github.com/PacktPublishing/Docker-Certified-Associate-DCA-Exam-Guide.git` as `docker-compose.dev.yaml`, along with all the other code files that were used in the previous section.

First, we'll review the definition configuration using the `docker-compose config` action:

```
$ docker-compose --file docker-compose.dev.yaml config
WARNING: The dockerhubid variable is not set. Defaulting to a blank string.
WARNING: The LB_PORT variable is not set. Defaulting to a blank string.
ERROR: The Compose file './docker-compose.dev.yaml' is invalid because:
services.lb.ports contains an invalid type, it should be a number, or an
object
```

These warnings and errors indicate that the following variables must be set:

- `dockerhubid`: By default, this will be empty.
- `LB_PORT`: This must be set to a port number because it is the one we will publish to consume the application.

We need to have values for these variables. We can also use variables on Dockerfiles to add even more granularity. However, this is not the point here and we will not deep dive into Dockerfile variable usage again. For the Docker Certified Associate exam, it is important to know how to use variables to provide values to `docker-compose` deployments. We can use dynamic configurations with variables to deploy different projects using just one `docker-compose.yaml` file. This is very useful for building debugging images with developer tools, for example.

Let's set the `LB_PORT` and `dockerhubid` variables and review our project configuration once more:

```
$ LB_PORT=8081 docker-compose --file docker-compose.dev.yaml config
WARNING: The dockerhubid variable is not set. Defaulting to a blank string.
networks:
  simplestlab:
    ipam:
      config:
      - subnet: 172.16.0.0/16
      driver: default
services:
  app:
    build:
      context: <..>/Docker-Certified-Associate-DCA-Exam-Guide/simplest-
lab/simplestapp
    depends_on:
    - db
    - lb
    environment:
      dbhost: simplestdb
      dbname: demo
      dbpasswd: d3m0
      dbuser: demo
    image: myregistry/simplest-lab:simplestapp
    networks:
      simplestlab:
        aliases:
        - simplestapp
  db:
    build:
      context: <..>/Docker-Certified-Associate-DCA-Exam-Guide/simplest-
lab/simplestdb
    environment:
      POSTGRES_PASSWORD: changeme
    image: myregistry/simplest-lab:simplestdb
    networks:
      simplestlab:
        aliases:
        - simplestdb
    volumes:
    - pgdata:/var/lib/postgresql/data:rw
  lb:
    build:
      args:
        alpineversion: latest
      context: <..>/Docker-Certified-Associate-DCA-Exam-Guide/simplest-
lab/simplestlb
```

```
        dockerfile: Dockerfile.custom
        labels:
          org.codegazers.description: Test image
      environment:
        APPLICATION_ALIAS: simplestapp
        APPLICATION_PORT: '3000'
      image: /simplest-lab:simplestlb
      networks:
        simplestlab:
          aliases:
          - simplestlb
      ports:
      - published: 8081
        target: 80
  version: '3.7'
  volumes:
    pgdata: {}
```

The other variables have been left empty. We defined different configurations to provide some features for production, for example, using specific credentials:

```
$ LB_PORT=8081 dockerhubid=frjaraur docker-compose --project-name test --
file docker-compose.dev.yaml build --build-arg alpineversion="3.6"
Building db
Step 1/2 : FROM postgres:alpine
...
...
[Warning] One or more build-args [alpineversion] were not consumed
Successfully built 336fb84e7fbf
Successfully tagged myregistry/simplest-lab:simplestdb
Building lb
Step 1/12 : ARG alpineversion=latest
...
...
Step 12/12 : LABEL org.codegazers.dscription=Test image
 ---> Using cache
 ---> ea4739af8eb5
Successfully built ea4739af8eb5
Successfully tagged frjaraur/simplest-lab:simplestlb
Building app
Step 1/15 : FROM alpine
...
...
[Warning] One or more build-args [alpineversion] were not consumed
Successfully built ff419f0998ae
Successfully tagged myregistry/simplest-lab:simplestapp
```

If we review the new build image, we will notice that it now has a new label and was created using `alpine:3.6` instead of the latest version:

```
"Labels": {
  "org.codegazers.dscription": "Test image"
  }
```

With that, we have learned how we can prepare different environments using variables. With variables, we can use one `docker-compose.yaml` file for any stage in our environment. We have learned how to prepare a deployment for the following:

- Development, using images with compilers or debugging utilities
- Tests, thereby adding tools to verify connectivity with third-party applications, for example
- Pre-production or integration, with libraries to execute load and performance tests before passing the application to production
- The production stage, with only well-tested application components within images being tagged as `release`, for example

Docker Compose allows us to keep track of all configurations required for each stage with a YAML file. This file will be stored in our infrastructure as a code repository. Versioning will help us keep control of deployed applications in production.

Automating your desktop and CI/CD with Docker Compose

Docker Compose allows us to easily develop on our own laptops. DevOps teams will provide complete application stack files, `docker-compose.yaml` files, along with all the required components and configurations. Developers do not have to learn how all the components work. They can focus on the component they are developing because the rest of the components will run automatically thanks to `docker-compose`.

We can use Docker Compose on a **Continuous Integration/Continuous Deployment (CI/CD)** pipeline, building all the components at once.

Docker Compose helps us build all the application components at the development stage, but we can also use this tool to run all the components together. CI/CD orchestrators will execute `docker-compose` files at different stages.

With the described steps and variables, it is easy to imagine how to implement a pipeline starting at the development stages and ending with the application in production. We would use different image tags in production, which are created by applying different variable values between environments.

It is very important to understand that `docker-compose.yaml` files are key in **Infrastructure-as-Code** (**IaC**) environments. We need to store them and use version control systems. These files describe what application components will run and what resources they will use. We can add variables for an application's published ports, for example, to avoid port conflicts if we deploy a couple of applications using the same `docker-compose` files in the same host. We can also use the same `docker-compose` file for development and testing, as well as deploying applications to these environments. To avoid environment conflicts, we can use variables to define an application's component endpoints, such as databases or any connection chain that should be different between environments.

Developers will use these files to launch the required application components on their laptops while they are developing new features or fixing code errors. They can focus on coding because they do not need to create complex infrastructures to test what they are coding. In fact, they do not need development infrastructures at all, as they can use their own computers.

We will continue this chapter by reviewing some labs to help us understand and build on the concepts we've learned so far.

Chapter labs

We will deploy a simple lab to review the different steps described during this chapter. First, we will build the images required and will continue executing and scaling up components. We will use a CentOS Linux host with Docker Engine installed.

Deploy `environments/standalone-environment` from this book's GitHub repository (`https://github.com/PacktPublishing/Docker-Certified-Associate-DCA-Exam-Guide.git`) if you have not done so yet. You can use your own CentOS 7 server. Use `vagrant up` from the `environments/standalone-environment` folder to start your virtual environment.

If you are using `standalone-environment`, wait until it is running. We can check the node's status using `vagrant status`. Connect to your lab node using `vagrant ssh standalone`. Now, `standalone` is the name of your node. You will be using the `vagrant` user with root privileges using `sudo`. You should get the following output:

```
Docker-Certified-Associate-DCA-Exam-Guide/environments/standalone$ vagrant
up
Bringing machine 'standalone' up with 'virtualbox' provider...
...
Docker-Certified-Associate-DCA-Exam-Guide/environments/standalone$ vagrant
status
Current machine states:
standalone running (virtualbox)
...
Docker-Certified-Associate-DCA-Exam-Guide/environments/standalone$
```

We can now connect to the `standalone` node using `vagrant ssh standalone`. This process may vary if you deployed the `standalone` virtual node previously and you started it using `vagrant up`:

```
Docker-Certified-Associate-DCA-Exam-Guide/environments/standalone$ vagrant
ssh standalone
[vagrant@standalone ~]$
```

If you are reusing your `standalone-environment` instance, this means that Docker Engine is already installed. If you started a new instance, please execute the `/vagrant/install_requirements.sh` script to get access to all the required tools (Docker Engine and `docker-compose`):

```
[vagrant@standalone ~]$ /vagrant/install_requirements.sh
```

Now, you are ready to start the labs.

Colors application lab

We will start these labs by deploying a simple application that will run a small Python process. This process is a web server that was developed using Flask that will show a colored page (a random color, by default) with some information about the container name, its IP address, and the application version.

All the files required for this lab can be found in the `Docker-Certified-Associate-DCA-Exam-Guide/chapter5` folder in this book's GitHub repository at `https://github.com/PacktPublishing/Docker-Certified-Associate-DCA-Exam-Guide.git`. Let's get started:

1. Let's begin by cloning our repository, navigating to our folder, and listing the files present inside the folder:

```
[vagrant@standalone ~]$ git clone
https://github.com/PacktPublishing/Docker-Certified-Associate-DCA-E
xam-Guide.git
[vagrant@standalone ~]$ cd Docker-Certified-Associate-DCA-Exam-
Guide/chapter5
[vagrant@standalone chapter5]$ ls -1
app
docker-compose.loadbalancer.yaml
docker-compose.multicolor.yaml
docker-compose.random.yaml
docker-compose.red.yaml
lb
Readme.md
```

2. Let's quickly review the `docker-compose.random.yaml` file's content:

```
version: "3.7"
services:
    red:
        build: app
        environment:
            COLOR: "red"
        labels:
            role: backend
        ports:
        - 3000
        networks:
        - lab
networks:
    lab:
```

It is very simple. We defined a `random` service using the code contained in the `app` directory. We will expose container port `3000` to a random host one.

3. We will now build images using `lab1` as the project name. Notice that we defined the `lab` network. The Docker daemon will create a `lab1_random` image and the `lab1_lab` network:

```
[vagrant@standalone chapter5]$ docker-compose -p lab1 -f docker-compose.random.yaml build
Building random
Step 1/9 : FROM node:alpine
alpine: Pulling from library/node
89d9c30c1d48: Already exists
5320ee7fe9ff: Pull complete
 . . .
 . . .
Step 9/9 : EXPOSE 3000
 ---> Running in 51379c5e7630
Removing intermediate container 51379c5e7630
 ---> c0dce423a972

Successfully built c0dce423a972
Successfully tagged lab1_random:latest
```

4. Now, we execute our multi-container application (in this case, we just have one service definition):

```
[vagrant@standalone chapter5]$ docker-compose -p lab1 -f docker-compose.random.yaml up -d
Creating network "lab1_lab" with the default driver
Creating lab1_random_1 ... done
```

Let's review the `docker-compose` project's `lab1` execution:

```
[vagrant@standalone chapter5]$ docker-compose -p lab1 -f docker-compose.random.yaml ps
    Name Command State Ports
--------------------------------------------------------------------
------
lab1_random_1 docker-entrypoint.sh node ... Up
0.0.0.0:32780->3000/tcp
```

Notice that the application's port, `3000`, is linked to the Docker host port `32780` (using NAT).

5. We can access the application via that random port; that is, `32780`:

```
[vagrant@standalone chapter5]$ curl 0.0.0.0:32780/text
APP_VERSION: 1.0
COLOR: blue
CONTAINER_NAME: 17bc24f60799
CONTAINER_IP: 172.27.0.2
CLIENT_IP: ::ffff:172.27.0.1
CONTAINER_ARCH: linux
```

We can use a web browser to access the running application. We can also use `curl` because the application is prepared to show a text response using the `/text` URI:

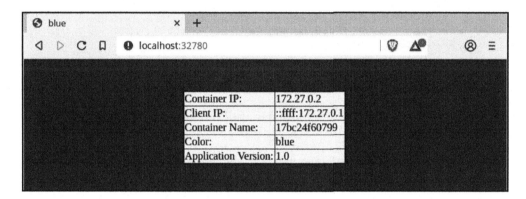

A random color will be used. In this case, we get a blue page. It may vary in your environment because a random color will be chosen if the COLOR variable is not set.

If you deployed the `random color` application using the provided `vagrant` standalone environment, you should use `192.168.56.11:<PUBLISHED_PORT>` in your browser because you are using a virtual machine. However, we prepared a host-to-virtual node interface (the `192.168.56.11` IP address).

6. We can now remove the application and continue to the next lab using `docker-compose down`:

```
[vagrant@standalone chapter5]$ docker-compose -p lab1 -f docker-compose.random.yaml down
Stopping lab1_random_1 ... done
Removing lab1_random_1 ... done
Removing network lab1_lab
```

Now, we will create a `red` application, defining a simple variable to change the application's behavior.

Executing a red application

In this lab, we will change the application's behavior by setting the `COLOR` environment variable. In this case, we will execute our `red` application. This new application can be deployed with just a few changes, which will help us integrate more components in the following labs.

Now, let's execute a `red` application. In this case, we just change the service name and add an environment variable to define the backend color (a `COLOR` key and a `red` value). The following is the content of the `docker-compose.red.yaml` file:

```
version: "3.7"

services:
  red:
    build: app
    environment:
      COLOR: "red"
    labels:
      role: backend
    ports:
    - 3000
    networks:
    - lab

networks:
  lab:
```

We can reuse the `lab1` project name or create a new one. If we use `lab2` as the new project name, new tags will be added. Building it will not create new layers because we haven't changed any code. We will simply use `docker-compose up -d`, as follows:

```
[vagrant@standalone ~]$ docker-compose -p lab2 -f docker-compose.red.yaml
up -d
Creating network "lab2_lab" with the default driver
Building red
Step 1/9 : FROM node:alpine
 ---> fac3d6a8e034
Step 2/9 : ENV APPDIR /APP
 ---> Using cache
 ---> 61bbe191216e
Step 3/9 : WORKDIR ${APPDIR}
```

```
  ---> Using cache
...
...
 ---> Using cache
 ---> df0f6838dfca
Step 9/9 : EXPOSE 3000
 ---> Using cache
 ---> 24ae28db3e15

Successfully built 24ae28db3e15
Successfully tagged lab2_red:latest
WARNING: Image for service red was built because it did not already exist.
To rebuild this image you must use `docker-compose build` or `docker-
compose up --build`.
Creating lab2_red_1 ... done
```

We can review the deployment status using `docker-compose ps`:

```
[vagrant@standalone ~]$ docker-compose -p lab2 -f docker-compose.red.yaml
ps
    Name Command State Ports
-------------------------------------------------------------------------
--
lab2_red_1 docker-entrypoint.sh node ... Up 0.0.0.0:32781->3000/tcp
```

We can easily access `0.0.0.0:32781` to access the `red` application using `curl`:

```
[vagrant@standalone ~]$ curl 0.0.0.0:32781/text
APP_VERSION: 1.0
COLOR: red
CONTAINER_NAME: fc05e400d02a
CONTAINER_IP: 172.29.0.2
CLIENT_IP: ::ffff:172.29.0.1
CONTAINER_ARCH: linux
```

Now, let's try to scale up the number of application instances.

Scaling the red application's backends

In this lab, we will increase the number of application backends by scaling one of its components up using `docker-compose`.

Let's set the new number of instances required for the application using `docker-compose scale`:

```
[vagrant@standalone ~]$ docker-compose -p lab2 -f docker-compose.red.yaml
scale red=5
WARNING: The scale command is deprecated. Use the up command with the --
scale flag instead.
Starting lab2_red_1 ... done
Creating lab2_red_2 ... done
Creating lab2_red_3 ... done
Creating lab2_red_4 ... done
Creating lab2_red_5 ... done
```

Notice that in this case, we are deploying a stateless application, without any persistence. There is something else to take note of in this case – we left the host-linked port unset. Therefore, a random one is always used for each container instance. Let's review the new instance port number with `docker-compose ps`:

```
[vagrant@standalone ~]$ docker-compose -p lab2 -f docker-compose.red.yaml
ps
    Name Command State Ports
----------------------------------------------------------------------------
--
lab2_red_1 docker-entrypoint.sh node ... Up 0.0.0.0:32781->3000/tcp
lab2_red_2 docker-entrypoint.sh node ... Up 0.0.0.0:32784->3000/tcp
lab2_red_3 docker-entrypoint.sh node ... Up 0.0.0.0:32785->3000/tcp
lab2_red_4 docker-entrypoint.sh node ... Up 0.0.0.0:32783->3000/tcp
lab2_red_5 docker-entrypoint.sh node ... Up 0.0.0.0:32782->3000/tcp
```

Now, we can access all the instances. Each one is using its own NAT port, all of which are available in the Docker host. We can check this again using `curl`:

```
[vagrant@standalone ~]$ curl 0.0.0.0:32781/text
APP_VERSION: 1.0
COLOR: red
CONTAINER_NAME: fc05e400d02a
CONTAINER_IP: 172.29.0.2
CLIENT_IP: ::ffff:172.29.0.1
CONTAINER_ARCH: linux

[vagrant@standalone ~]$ curl 0.0.0.0:32782/text
APP_VERSION: 1.0
COLOR: red
CONTAINER_NAME: f5de33465357
CONTAINER_IP: 172.29.0.3
CLIENT_IP: ::ffff:172.29.0.1
CONTAINER_ARCH: linux
```

```
[vagrant@standalone ~]$ curl 0.0.0.0:32783/text
APP_VERSION: 1.0
COLOR: red
CONTAINER_NAME: 5be016aadadb
CONTAINER_IP: 172.29.0.4
CLIENT_IP: ::ffff:172.29.0.1
CONTAINER_ARCH: linux

[vagrant@standalone ~]$ curl 0.0.0.0:32784/text
APP_VERSION: 1.0
COLOR: red
CONTAINER_NAME: 413c9d605bd5
CONTAINER_IP: 172.29.0.5
CLIENT_IP: ::ffff:172.29.0.1
CONTAINER_ARCH: linux

[vagrant@standalone ~]$ curl 0.0.0.0:32785/text
APP_VERSION: 1.0
COLOR: red
CONTAINER_NAME: fe879a59c3aa
CONTAINER_IP: 172.29.0.6
CLIENT_IP: ::ffff:172.29.0.1
CONTAINER_ARCH: linux
```

All the IP addresses are different because we are accessing different containers. However, all of them are red, as expected.

Let's remove all the application instances:

```
[vagrant@standalone ~]$ docker-compose -p lab2 -f docker-compose.red.yaml
down
Stopping lab2_red_2 ... done
Stopping lab2_red_3 ... done
Stopping lab2_red_4 ... done
Stopping lab2_red_5 ... done
Stopping lab2_red_1 ... done
Removing lab2_red_2 ... done
Removing lab2_red_3 ... done
Removing lab2_red_4 ... done
Removing lab2_red_5 ... done
Removing lab2_red_1 ... done
Removing network lab2_lab
```

In the next lab, we will add more colors using a single file.

Adding more colors

We will now increase our application's components by adding more colors.

Let's add more color applications. In the `docker-compose.multicolor.yaml` file, we'll add a couple of services, along with their own `COLOR` variables:

```yaml
version: "3.7"

services:
  red:
    build: app
    environment:
      COLOR: "red"
    labels:
      role: backend
    ports:
    - 3000
    networks:
    - lab
  green:
    build: app
    environment:
      COLOR: "green"
    labels:
      role: backend
    ports:
    - 3000
    networks:
    - lab
  white:
    build: app
    environment:
      COLOR: "white"
    labels:
      role: backend
    ports:
    - 3000
    networks:
    - lab

networks:
  lab:
```

We will launch our red, green, and white applications using docker-compose up:

```
[vagrant@standalone ~]$ docker-compose -p lab3 -f docker-
compose.multicolor.yaml up -d
Creating network "lab3_lab" with the default driver
Building white
Step 1/9 : FROM node:alpine
 ---> fac3d6a8e034
...
Successfully built 24ae28db3e15
Successfully tagged lab3_white:latest
...
Building green
...
Successfully tagged lab3_green:latest
...
Building red
...
Successfully tagged lab3_red:latest
WARNING: Image for service red was built because it did not already exist.
To rebuild this image you must use `docker-compose build` or `docker-
compose up --build`.
Creating lab3_green_1 ... done
Creating lab3_white_1 ... done
Creating lab3_red_1 ... done
```

We will be able to access different applications. Let's review their processes and ports using docker-compose ps and then access each instance using curl:

```
[vagrant@standalone ~]$ docker-compose -p lab3 -f docker-
compose.multicolor.yaml ps
 Name Command State Ports
--------------------------------------------------------------------------------
----
lab3_green_1 docker-entrypoint.sh node ... Up 0.0.0.0:32789->3000/tcp
lab3_red_1 docker-entrypoint.sh node ... Up 0.0.0.0:32791->3000/tcp
lab3_white_1 docker-entrypoint.sh node ... Up 0.0.0.0:32790->3000/tcp

$ curl 0.0.0.0:32789/text
APP_VERSION: 1.0
COLOR: green
CONTAINER_NAME: a25a4cc36232
CONTAINER_IP: 172.31.0.2
CLIENT_IP: ::ffff:172.31.0.1
CONTAINER_ARCH: linux

$ curl 0.0.0.0:32791/text
APP_VERSION: 1.0
```

```
COLOR: red
CONTAINER_NAME: 5e12b0de196c
CONTAINER_IP: 172.31.0.4
CLIENT_IP: ::ffff:172.31.0.1
CONTAINER_ARCH: linux

$ curl 0.0.0.0:32790/text
APP_VERSION: 1.0
COLOR: white
CONTAINER_NAME: b67b09c8c836
CONTAINER_IP: 172.31.0.3
CLIENT_IP: ::ffff:172.31.0.1
CONTAINER_ARCH: linux
```

In this situation, all application components are accessible using random published ports. We can use fixed ports to route users' requests to external load balancers, for example. We would not use random ports in production.

 Note that the backend ports are dynamically associated with random ports. This allows us to run this application more than once without any `docker-compose` file changes. We will just need to use another project name to ensure the created objects' uniqueness.

Now, let's add a simple load balancer to see some other deployment features. We will publish this load balancer, and other services will only be accessible through this component.

Adding a simple load balancer

In this lab, we will add a simple `nginx` load balancer to route traffic to different color backends.

Let's take a look at the new deployment file:

```
version: "3.7"

services:
  loadbalancer:
    build: lb
    environment:
      APPLICATION_PORT: 3000
    ports:
    - 8080:80
    networks:
    - lab
```

```
  red:
    build: app
    environment:
      COLOR: "red"
    labels:
      role: backend
    networks:
    - lab
  green:
    build: app
    environment:
      COLOR: "green"
    labels:
      role: backend
    networks:
    - lab
  white:
    build: app
    environment:
      COLOR: "white"
    labels:
      role: backend
    networks:
    - lab

networks:
  lab:
```

Notice that we have removed all the color's service backends' ports. Now, we are just exposing port 8080, which is linked to the internal nginx component's port; that is, port 80.

Let's launch the application deployment and review the results using docker-compose up -d:

```
[vagrant@standalone ~]$ docker-compose -p lab5 -f docker-
compose.loadbalancer.yaml up -d
Creating network "lab5_lab" with the default driver
Building white
...
Successfully tagged lab5_white:latest
WARNING: Image for service white was built because it did not already
exist. To rebuild this image you must use `docker-compose build` or
`docker-compose up --build`.
Building green
...
Successfully tagged lab5_green:latest
```

```
WARNING: Image for service green was built because it did not already
exist. To rebuild this image you must use `docker-compose build` or
`docker-compose up --build`.
Building red
...
Successfully tagged lab5_red:latest
WARNING: Image for service red was built because it did not already exist.
To rebuild this image you must use `docker-compose build` or `docker-
compose up --build`.
Building loadbalancer
...Successfully tagged lab5_loadbalancer:latest
WARNING: Image for service loadbalancer was built because it did not
already exist. To rebuild this image you must use `docker-compose build` or
`docker-compose up --build`.
Creating lab5_loadbalancer_1 ... done
Creating lab5_white_1 ... done
Creating lab5_red_1 ... done
Creating lab5_green_1 ... done
```

Once all our components are ready, we can test all the color backends using different host headers to reach each backend. We prepared a simple nginx load balancing configuration for this (we've provided a quick review of the load balancer configuration file in lb/nginx.conf). Every time we ask for a specific host header using each color, we will be routed to the right backend:

```
[vagrant@standalone ~]$ cat lb/nginx.conf
...
...
 server {
 listen 80;
 set $port "__APPLICATION_PORT__";
...
...
 location / {
 proxy_pass http://$host:$port;
 }
...
...
```

Using curl, we can test all the backends:

```
[vagrant@standalone ~]$ curl -H "Host: white" 0.0.0.0:8080/text
APP_VERSION: 1.0
COLOR: white
CONTAINER_NAME: 86871cba5a71
CONTAINER_IP: 192.168.208.5
CLIENT_IP: ::ffff:192.168.208.4
CONTAINER_ARCH: linux
```

```
[vagrant@standalone ~]$ curl -H "Host: green" 0.0.0.0:8080/text
APP_VERSION: 1.0
COLOR: green
CONTAINER_NAME: f7d90dc89255
CONTAINER_IP: 192.168.208.2
CLIENT_IP: ::ffff:192.168.208.4
CONTAINER_ARCH: linux

[vagrant@standalone ~]$ curl -H "Host: red" 0.0.0.0:8080/text
APP_VERSION: 1.0
COLOR: red
CONTAINER_NAME: 25bb1b66bab8
CONTAINER_IP: 192.168.208.3
CLIENT_IP: ::ffff:192.168.208.4
CONTAINER_ARCH: linux
```

Remember, none of the services are accessible except `loadbalancer`. Let's review the published ports using `docker-compose ps`:

```
[vagrant@standalone ~]$ docker-compose -p lab5 -f docker-
compose.loadbalancer.yaml ps
        Name Command State Ports
-----------------------------------------------------------------------
--------
lab5_green_1 docker-entrypoint.sh node ... Up 3000/tcp
lab5_loadbalancer_1 /entrypoint.sh /bin/sh -c ... Up 0.0.0.0:8080->80/tcp
lab5_red_1 docker-entrypoint.sh node ... Up 3000/tcp
lab5_white_1 docker-entrypoint.sh node ... Up 3000/tcp
```

What will happen if we scale up the `green` service to four instances? We expect to reach all the instances because the service instances will be added to the internal DNS. Let's scale up this service using `docker-compose up -d`:

```
[vagrant@standalone ~]$ docker-compose -p lab5 -f docker-
compose.loadbalancer.yaml up -d --scale green=4
Starting lab5_green_1 ...
lab5_white_1 is up-to-date
lab5_red_1 is up-to-date
Starting lab5_green_1 ... done
Creating lab5_green_2 ... done
Creating lab5_green_3 ... done
Creating lab5_green_4 ... done
```

Let's ask for the `green` service again using `curl`:

```
[vagrant@standalone ~]$ curl -H "Host: green" 0.0.0.0:8080/text
APP_VERSION: 1.0
COLOR: green
```

```
CONTAINER_NAME: ba90c57914f9
CONTAINER_IP: 192.168.208.7
CLIENT_IP: ::ffff:192.168.208.4
CONTAINER_ARCH: linux

[vagrant@standalone ~]$ curl -H "Host: green" 0.0.0.0:8080/text
APP_VERSION: 1.0
COLOR: green
CONTAINER_NAME: c1a9ebcf82ac
CONTAINER_IP: 192.168.208.6
CLIENT_IP: ::ffff:192.168.208.4
CONTAINER_ARCH: linux

[vagrant@standalone ~]$ curl -H "Host: green" 0.0.0.0:8080/text
APP_VERSION: 1.0
COLOR: green
CONTAINER_NAME: d5436822ca8f
CONTAINER_IP: 192.168.208.8
CLIENT_IP: ::ffff:192.168.208.4
CONTAINER_ARCH: linux

[vagrant@standalone ~]$ curl -H "Host: green" 0.0.0.0:8080/text
APP_VERSION: 1.0
COLOR: green
CONTAINER_NAME: f7d90dc89255
CONTAINER_IP: 192.168.208.2
CLIENT_IP: ::ffff:192.168.208.4
CONTAINER_ARCH: linux
```

As we expected, we get different backends on each request because the DNS gave the load balancer a different backend IP address.

To finish this lab, let's install the `bind-tools` package on the `loadbalancer` container to query the internal DNS using the `host` tool. We will query the `red` and `green` services to verify the internal DNS resolution. This is key in application deployment when using components' names. We will use `docker-compose exec` to install the `bind-tools` package in the `loadbalancer` container. Once the package is installed, we will use `docker-compose exec` again with the `host` command to query the DNS:

```
[vagrant@standalone ~]$ docker-compose -p lab5 \
-f docker-compose.loadbalancer.yaml exec loadbalancer apk add -q --update
bind-tools

[vagrant@standalone ~]$ docker-compose -p lab5 -f docker-
compose.loadbalancer.yaml \
exec loadbalancer host red
red has address 192.168.208.3
```

```
[vagrant@standalone ~]$ docker-compose -p lab5 \
-f docker-compose.loadbalancer.yaml exec loadbalancer host green
green has address 192.168.208.8
green has address 192.168.208.2
green has address 192.168.208.7
green has address 192.168.208.6
```

The internal DNS gave us all the IP addresses associated with the `green` and `red` services. Those are the associated containers' IP addresses. Therefore, our defined `green` service is load-balanced to all running `green` backends.

Remove all the labs using `docker-compose down` with the appropriate `docker-compose` file and project name.

Summary

This chapter covered how to deploy multi-container applications on Docker hosts. We learned that the `docker-compose` command does not just deploy applications, but allows us to build and share all application components. Reviewing all the components' statuses is also easier because `docker-compose` provides a command-line interface for retrieving all the application container's standard and error outputs. We can start and stop all the components at once. But we can go even further than this: we are also able to scale the number of instances of each component up and down. This feature depends on our application logic because the Docker daemon does not know anything about our application processes.

All application components are defined in a YAML-formatted file that can be customized using variables. We learned about the most important keys and their default values in this instance. The `docker-compose` file is key as it describes all the application components and its resources, as well as their interactions. Each component has its own version because we use images with their tags and arguments. We can also code versioning systems to be able to track `docker-compose` changes because this provides IaC information. We need to know exactly what application components are running in production, and Docker Compose allows us to apply release numbers to the files used for application deployments. This will ensure that the right application components are running. Introducing variables in these files allows us to use them at different development and deployment stages with only minor changes.

In the following section, there are some questions that you can have a go at to consolidate your understanding of the topics that we've learned about in this chapter. The next chapter will teach us how to manage image ownership and content using Docker Content Trust.

Questions

1. Which of these statements is not true?

   a) Docker Compose can run multi-service applications distributed on different services.

   b) Docker Compose can run multi-container applications on a Docker host.

   c) Docker Compose is a software application that is not installed with standard Docker packages.

   d) All of the above are true.

2. What can we do with `docker-compose`?

   a) We can build all application images.

   b) We can pull and push application component images.

   c) We can run all application components at once.

   d) All of the above.

3. What will happen if we execute `docker-compose up` with a `docker-compose` file in which we have defined the frontend, backend, and database services? (Choose all of the correct statements out of the following options.)

   a) Docker Compose will look for all the services' defined images and will pull them if they are not present in the current host.

   b) Docker Compose will execute only images with the `start` key defined.

   c) Docker Compose will run all containers at once and your terminal will be attached to their standard and error outputs.

   d) All of the above are false.

4. How can we use a `docker-compose` file to launch application services more than once?

   a) In actual fact, we cannot do that, but we can launch service process instances using the `scale` action. This service name will resolve to all replica IP addresses.

   b) Docker Compose will only execute images with the `start` key defined.

   c) Docker Compose will run all the containers at once, without any precedence.

   d) All of the above are false.

5. What does the execution of `docker-compose down` do?

    a) It will stop all running containers associated with an application.
    b) It will try to stop all running containers associated with an application.
    c) It will try to stop all running containers associated with an application.
    Once they're all stopped, it will remove them.
    d) It will try to stop all running containers associated with an application.
    Once they're all stopped, it will remove them, along with all of their
    associated resources, unless they were defined externally.

Further reading

You can refer to the following links for more information regarding the topics that were covered in this chapter:

- The Docker Compose file reference: https://docs.docker.com/compose/compose-file/
- Docker Compose's GitHub repository: https://github.com/docker/compose.git
- Docker Compose with Visual Studio Code: https://code.visualstudio.com/docs/containers/docker-compose
- Docker Compose samples: https://github.com/dockersamples/example-voting-app
- Docker Compose releases: https://github.com/docker/compose/releases

6

Introduction to Docker Content Trust

In this chapter, we will learn about the Docker Content Trust concept and its related tools. To provide trusted content in Docker environments, we will use Docker Content Trust to encrypt metadata information applied to Docker objects. Therefore, any unauthorized changes or object manipulation will be reported. We will be able to ensure that all the objects in our environment are trusted if none of these issues are found.

First, we will introduce The Update Framework, and then we will learn how to sign images. After that, we will learn how to verify signatures to ensure their precedence and ownership. Finally, we will apply those concepts to run a trusted environment in production.

We will cover the following topics in this chapter:

- The Update Framework
- Signing images
- Reviewing signatures
- Creating and running applications in trusted environments

Let's get started!

Technical requirements

In this chapter, we will learn about various Docker Content Trust concepts. We'll provide some labs at the end of this chapter that will help you understand and learn about the shown concepts. These labs can be run on your laptop or PC using the provided Vagrant standalone environment or any already-deployed Docker host deployed by yourself. You can find additional information in this book's GitHub code repository: https://github. com/PacktPublishing/Docker-Certified-Associate-DCA-Exam-Guide.git.

Check out the following video to see the Code in Action:

`"https://bit.ly/3b0qviR"`

The Update Framework

Before learning about **The Update Framework**, also known as **TUF**, we will introduce a number of concepts. The following concepts will help us understand why we need tools to manage application updates:

- **Software update system**: A software update system is an application that looks for new updates continuously. When they are found, it triggers processes to get these updates and installs these changes. A good example is the Google Chrome web browser update system. It continuously looks for its components' updates and, once they are found, it will show us a **There is a new release, do you want to update now?** message.
- **Library package managers**: The library package managers will manage and update programming language libraries and their dependencies. Python's **Package Installer for Python (PIP)** and Node.js's **Node Package Manager (NPM)** are good examples. These applications look for library updates and install them with their requisite dependencies.
- **Operating system component updates**: In this case, different package managers will manage all software updates and their dependencies, triggering, in some cases, some of the aforementioned solutions (software update systems or library package managers).

An application update usually takes three logical steps:

1. It looks for any update or change.
2. It downloads updates.
3. It applies changes to our system.

What would happen if those updates were malicious because the code was intercepted and modified by an attacker?

TUF was created to prevent these situations. It will handle the steps described for application updates to ensure that downloaded changes are trusted. No manipulated changes will be allowed. TUF metadata includes information related to trusted keys, cryptographic hashes and files, component versions, creation and expiration dates, and signatures. An application that requires a number of updates does not have to manage this verification process. It will ask TUF to manage these processes. To summarize, we can say, in a way, that TUF provides a secure method of obtaining trusted files.

TUF is currently hosted by the Linux Foundation as part of the **Cloud Native Computing Foundation** (**CNCF**). It is open source and can be used in production environments. It is recommended to use this in conjunction with some vendor tools because it will be easier to manage and use.

TUF metadata provides information about the truthfulness of the update to the software update system. This component will then make the right decision (install or reject the update). This metadata information will be presented in JSON format. We will talk about four levels of signing. We will refer to them as roles:

- **Root metadata (**`root.json`**) and role**: This role is related to the owner of the change. It is the top role; others will be related to this one.
- **Targets metadata (**`targets.json`**) and role**: This role is related to the files included in the package.
- **Snapshot metadata (**`snapshot.json`**) and role**: All files apart from `timestamp.json` will be listed on this role to ensure the consistency of updates.
- **Timestamp metadata (**`timestamp.json`**) and role**: This sign will ensure the exact date of the update and that it is the only one required when checking for updates, for example.

The update application uses TUF to interact with the repositories and sources of files while managing their updates. Roles, trusted keys, and target files should not be included in those repositories because they will be used to manage them.

There should be a client side on this framework so that we can include the roles described in its normal usage. Therefore, a client side must manage the following:

- Trusted root keys, from all possible owners that must be trusted
- Target delegation, when there is a target with many owners
- Checking for updates using timestamp role dates
- All signing processes

Now that we know the benefits of using TUF to manage repository updates, let's review how this is implemented in Docker.

Docker Content Trust is the Docker implementation of TUF. It is integrated using Notary, which is an open source tool for publishing and managing trusted content. The Docker client provides an interface that allows us to sign and verify content publishers.

Notary is a separate piece of software; it can be downloaded and used to inspect keys included in a Docker registry. Docker integrates Notary using its library. Therefore, every time we pull an image when Docker Content Trust is enabled (disabled by default), the Docker daemon will validate its signatures. Image pulling is done by its digest. Image names and tags will not be used. This ensures that only the right image will be downloaded.

 Notary usage is beyond the scope of this book. At the time of writing, it is not required in order to pass the DCA certification exam. It is recommended, however, to read about some of the Notary features provided at the following link: `https://docs.docker.com/notary/getting_started`.

When we use Docker Content Trust and we push an image, the Docker client will ask us to sign at all the levels described (root, target, snapshot, and timestamp).

In summary, Docker Content Trust (Docker's TUF implementation) will do the following:

- Ensure image provenance
- Sign content prior to distribution
- Ensure that everything running on a host is trusted.

In the next section, we will learn how to sign and use signed images that have been validated by Docker Engine.

Signing images

So far, we have learned about the different roles and the metadata information that will be used to validate and trust image content. Let's look at a quick summary before getting into the Docker signing action:

- The root key will validate other keys. It signs the `root.json` file, which contains the list of IDs of the root, targets, snapshot, and timestamp public keys. To verify content signatures, the Docker client will use these public keys. The root key is offline and must be kept safe. The owner of a collection of images should maintain this key. Don't lose this key. You can recreate it, but all your signed images will be invalid.

- The target key signs the `targets.json` file, which contains a list of your content filenames, along with their sizes and hashes. This file is used to delegate trust to other users in a team so that others can sign the same repository. This key is held by administrators and owners of a collection (repository).

- The delegation key is used to sign delegation metadata files. This key is held by administrators and everyone who can contribute to the specified collection.

- The snapshot key signs the `snapshot.json` metadata file. This file also contains filenames, as well as the sizes and hashes of root, targets, and delegation files in the collection. This key will be held by administrators and the collection owner. If we use the Notary service, this key can also be held by this service to allow signing by collection collaborators. This key represents the current package signature.

- The timestamp key ensures the freshness of the collection. It is used to verify the integrity of the `snapshot.json` file. Because this key is only valid for a period of time, it is better to be held in Notary. In this case, it will not be necessary that owners recreate the key each time it expires. Notary will regenerate this key as needed.

Now, let's sign an image using the Docker client.

First, we will enable Docker Content Trust. By default, it is not enabled. We can enable it for all Docker commands or add an argument each time we want to enable it. To enable Docker Content Trust for all subsequent Docker commands, we need to define the `DOCKER_CONTENT_TRUST` variable:

```
$ export DOCKER_CONTENT_TRUST=1
```

Alternatively, we can enable Docker Content Trust for only specified commands:

```
$ docker pull --disable-content-trust=false busybox:latest
```

We used `--disable-content-trust=false` here because, by default, Docker Content Trust is disabled.

Now that we have enabled Docker Content Trust for all commands in this session by setting DOCKER_CONTENT_TRUST= 1, we can pull an image using `docker image pull`:

```
$ export DOCKER_CONTENT_TRUST=1

$ docker image pull busybox
Using default tag: latest
Pull (1 of 1):
busybox:latest@sha256:1303dbf110c57f3edf68d9f5a16c082ec06c4cf7604831669faf2
c712260b5a0
sha256:1303dbf110c57f3edf68d9f5a16c082ec06c4cf7604831669faf2c712260b5a0:
Pulling from library/busybox
0f8c40e1270f: Pull complete
Digest:
sha256:1303dbf110c57f3edf68d9f5a16c082ec06c4cf7604831669faf2c712260b5a0
Status: Downloaded newer image for
busybox@sha256:1303dbf110c57f3edf68d9f5a16c082ec06c4cf7604831669faf2c712260
b5a0
Tagging
busybox@sha256:1303dbf110c57f3edf68d9f5a16c082ec06c4cf7604831669faf2c712260
b5a0 as busybox:latest
docker.io/library/busybox:latest
```

Notice that the `docker image pull` command's output changed. In fact, the downloaded image was managed by its hash; in this case, `busybox@sha256:1303dbf110c57f3edf68d9f5a16c082ec06c4cf7604831669fa f2c712260b5a`.

> Docker's official images and certified images are always signed. Official images are managed and built by Docker, and they are located under `docker.io/<REPOSITORY>:<TAG>`.

Let's run this image using `docker container run` and see what happens:

```
$ docker container run -ti busybox sh
/ # ls
bin dev etc home proc root sys tmp usr var
/ # touch NEW_FILE
/ # exit
```

It worked, as expected. We added a file because we wanted to modify a container before committing its content to create a new, untrusted image. For this process, we will run `docker container commit`, setting `DOCKER_CONTENT_TRUST=0` for the command. We do this because Content Trust was previously enabled in our current session:

```
$ DOCKER_CONTENT_TRUST=0 docker container commit 3da3b341e904
busybox:untrusted
sha256:67a6ce66451aa10011d379e4628205889f459c06a3d7793beca10ecd6c21b68a
```

Now, we have an untrusted `busybox` image. What will happen if we try to execute this image?

```
$ docker container run -ti busybox:untrusted sh
docker: No valid trust data for untrusted.
See 'docker run --help'.
```

We cannot run this image because it is not trusted; it does not have any content trust metadata. Therefore, it cannot be validated and will not be allowed to run. If Docker Content Trust is enabled, unsigned images will not be allowed.

Let's sign this image. In this case, we will change the image name and create a new `trusted` tag. The signing process requires two passphrases, as described here:

1. First, we will be asked to set a `root` passphrase. You will be asked twice to validate the password that's entered as it is not shown.
2. Then, you will be asked to set a `repository` passphrase. You will be asked twice again to validate the password that's entered as it is not shown.

We have been asked for the passphrase twice because we are setting their values for the first time. Next time we use these keys to push or pull to this repository, we will be asked just once (or more if it was typed in incorrectly). Let's execute `docker image push`:

```
$ docker image push frjaraur/mybusybox:trusted
The push refers to repository [docker.io/frjaraur/mybusybox]
0736ae522762: Pushed
1da8e4c8d307: Mounted from library/busybox
trusted: digest:
sha256:e58e349eee38baa38f8398510c44e63a1f331dc1d80d4ed6010fe34960b9945f
size: 734
Signing and pushing trust metadata
You are about to create a new root signing key passphrase. This passphrase
will be used to protect the most sensitive key in your signing system.
Please
choose a long, complex passphrase and be careful to keep the password and
the
key file itself secure and backed up. It is highly recommended that you use
```

```
a
password manager to generate the passphrase and keep it safe. There will be
no
way to recover this key. You can find the key in your config directory.
Enter passphrase for new root key with ID 6e03824:
Repeat passphrase for new root key with ID 6e03824:
Enter passphrase for new repository key with ID b302395:
Repeat passphrase for new repository key with ID b302395:
Finished initializing "docker.io/frjaraur/mybusybox"
Successfully signed docker.io/frjaraur/mybusybox:trusted
```

The root passphrase is very important. Keep it safe because if you lose it, you will need to start again. If this happens, your already-signed images will be untrusted and you will need to update them. If you lose a key, you will need to contact Docker Support (support@docker.com) to reset the repository state.

 The passphrases you choose for both the root key and your repository should be strong. It is recommended to use randomly generated ones.

Now, we have a signed image. It is owned by us (in this example, I am the owner of frjaraur/mybusybox:trusted).

Now, we can execute this newly signed (and hence trusted) image using docker container run:

```
$ docker container run -ti frjaraur/mybusybox:trusted
/ # touch OTHERFILE
/ # exit
```

To manage Docker Content Trust, we can use docker trust with its available actions. We will be able to manage keys (load and revoke) and sign images (this process is similar to the one previously described). We can review these signatures using docker trust inspect:

```
$ docker trust inspect --pretty docker.io/frjaraur/mybusybox:trusted

Signatures for docker.io/frjaraur/mybusybox:trusted

SIGNED TAG DIGEST SIGNERS
trusted e58e349eee38baa38f8398510c44e63a1f331dc1d80d4ed6010fe34960b9945f
(Repo Admin)

Administrative keys for docker.io/frjaraur/mybusybox:trusted

  Repository Key:
```

```
b3023954026f59cdc9be0b7ba093039353ce6e2d1a06c1338e4387689663abc0
  Root Key:
e9120faa839a565838dbad7d45edd3c329893ae1f2085f225dc039272dec98ed
```

 Notice that we have used `docker.io/frjaraur/mybusybox:trusted` instead of `frjaraur/mybusybox:trusted`. This is because if we do not use the registry's **fully qualified domain name (FQDN)** and the image exists locally, it will be used to retrieve all signature information and you will receive a `WARN[0006] Error while downloading remote metadata, using cached timestamp – this might not be the latest version available remotely` message because you will be using the cached timestamp instead of the real one.

Now that we have learned how to sign content – in this case, images – let's move on and learn how to verify signatures.

Reviewing signatures

The Docker client stores content trust-related files under the `.docker/trust` directory, inside the user's home directory.

If we navigate to the trusted directory, we will find different registry files under `.docker/trust/tuf`. We used Docker Hub in this chapter's examples. Therefore, we will find the `docker.io` registry and different repositories. This may vary in your environment; you may have more registries or repositories. It will depend on when you started to use Docker Content Trust in your Docker host. Using the examples from the previous sections, we will find a tree-like directory structure under the `.docker` directory:

```
trust/tuf/docker.io/frjaraur/mybusybox/metadata:
total 16
-rw------- 1 zero zero  494 nov 30 17:29 timestamp.json
-rw------- 1 zero zero  531 nov 30 17:28 targets.json
-rw------- 1 zero zero  682 nov 30 17:28 snapshot.json
-rw------- 1 zero zero 2417 nov 30 17:03 root.json
...
...
trust/tuf/docker.io/library/busybox/metadata:
total 28
-rw------- 1 zero zero  498 nov 30 17:17 timestamp.json
-rw------- 1 zero zero 13335 nov 30 16:41 targets.json
-rw------- 1 zero zero  688 nov 30 16:41 snapshot.json
-rw------- 1 zero zero 2405 nov 30 16:41 root.json
```

Remember the JSON files described in the previous section. All these files are located under each registry and repository's structure.

> The Docker client will store your keys under your `.docker/trust/private` directory. It is very important to keep them safe. To back up these keys, use the `$ umask 077; tar -zcvf private_keys_backup.tar.gz ~/.docker/trust/private; umask 022` command.

Notary will assist us in managing signatures. It is an open source server and client application and can be downloaded from its GitHub project page (`https://github.com/theupdateframework/notary`).

> Notary can be installed either on Linux or Windows hosts.

We will simply download the latest release using the `curl` command and modify its permissions and path:

```
$ curl -o /tmp/notary -sL
https://github.com/theupdateframework/notary/releases/download/v0.6.1/notar
y-Linux-amd64

$ sudo mv /tmp/notary /usr/local/bin/notary

$ sudo chmod 755 /usr/local/bin/notary
```

In this section, we will use Docker's own Notary server that's been published on the internet (`https://notary.docker.io`) and that is associated with Docker Hub.

> Docker Enterprise will run its own Docker Notary server implementation in your environment.

Let's verify, for example, all the signatures associated with a Docker Hub repository. In this example, we are reviewing the `busybox` repository. We use `notary list` with the appropriate server and directory arguments:

```
$ notary -s https://notary.docker.io -d ~/.docker/trust list
docker.io/library/busybox
NAME DIGEST SIZE (BYTES) ROLE
```

```
____ _____ _____ ____
1 1303dbf110c57f3edf68d9f5a16c082ec06c4cf7604831669faf2c712260b5a0 1864
targets
...
...
1.31.1-uclibc
817e459ca73c567e9132406bad78845aaf72d2e0c0965ff68861b318591e949a 1210
targets
buildroot-2013.08.1
c0a08c5e4c15c53f03323bae8e82fdfd9f4fccb7fd01b97579b19e3e3205915c 5074
targets
buildroot-2014.02
ced99ae82473e7dea723e6c467f409ed8f051bda04760e07fd5f476638c33507 5071
targets
glibc 0ec061426ef36bb28e3dbcd005f9655b6bfa0345f0d219c8eb330e2954f192ac 1638
targets
latest 1303dbf110c57f3edf68d9f5a16c082ec06c4cf7604831669faf2c712260b5a0
1864 targets
...
...
uclibc 817e459ca73c567e9132406bad78845aaf72d2e0c0965ff68861b318591e949a
1210 targets
```

We listed all the targets on a remote trusted collection – in this case, the `busybox` collection on Docker Hub (`docker.io/library/busybox`).

Now, let's learn how to automate these processes and ensure security to build a trusted environment in our organization.

Creating and running applications in trusted environments

In this section, we will consider a trusted environment where `CONTENT_TRUST_ENABLED` is used for all actions. This will ensure that images built in that environment will always be signed. All images that have been pushed and pulled will be signed, and we will only run containers based on trusted images.

It is interesting to add CI/CD orchestration tools to these processes. It is not easy to disallow non-trusted content without some system or even higher security policies. If we set the DOCKER_CONTENT_TRUST value to only allow Docker Content Trust, but users are allowed to interact with the Docker host directly, they can disable this feature at the command line.

Automation is key in production environments, although it is true that Docker Enterprise provides other methods, which we will discuss later on in Chapter 12, *Universal Control Plane*. Kubernetes also provides features to force security for trusted content, but this topic is beyond the scope of this book.

Using an external CI/CD, we can automate the building, sharing, or deployment of Docker content. Let's look at a brief example of building and pushing an image:

```
$ export
DOCKER_CONTENT_TRUST_ROOT_PASSPHRASE="MyVerySecureRootPassphraseForAutomati
on"
$ export
DOCKER_CONTENT_TRUST_REPOSITORY_PASSPHRASE="MyVerySecureRepositoryPassphras
eForAutomation"

$ docker build -t docker/trusttest:testing .
Using default tag: latest
latest: Pulling from docker/trusttest
b3dbab3810fc: Pull complete
a9539b34a6ab: Pull complete
Digest: sha256:d149ab53f871

$ docker push docker/trusttest:latest
The push refers to a repository [docker.io/docker/trusttest] (len: 1)
a9539b34a6ab: Image already exists
b3dbab3810fc: Image already exists
latest: digest: sha256:d149ab53f871 size: 3355
Signing and pushing trust metadata
```

We can write a script for a CI/CD orchestration job using the root and repository passphrases to ensure that content trust is applied during building and pushing to our registry. We can follow the same method to deploy on production, disallowing any user interaction with this secure environment. Take care of environment variables for passphrases on scripts because they will be visible. CI/CD orchestrators will provide secure methods to manage this. This will give you an idea of how you should implement a secure chain with your own management configuration tools.

Now, let's review a lab to better understand the topics we've learned in this chapter.

Chapter labs

We will now complete a lab that will help us improve on the concepts we've learned about.

Deploy `environments/standalone-environment` from this book's GitHub repository (`https://github.com/PacktPublishing/Docker-Certified-Associate-DCA-Exam-Guide.git`) if you have not done so yet. You can use your own CentOS 7 server. Use `vagrant up` from the `environments/standalone-environment` folder to start your virtual environment.

If you are using a standalone environment, wait until it is running. We can check the statuses of our nodes using `vagrant status`. Connect to your lab node using `vagrant ssh standalone`. `standalone` is the name of your node. You will be using the `vagrant` user with root privileges using `sudo`. You should get the following output:

```
Docker-Certified-Associate-DCA-Exam-Guide/environments/standalone$ vagrant
up
Bringing machine 'standalone' up with 'virtualbox' provider...
...
Docker-Certified-Associate-DCA-Exam-Guide/environments/standalone$ vagrant
status
Current machine states:
standalone running (virtualbox)
...
Docker-Certified-Associate-DCA-Exam-Guide/environments/standalone$
```

We can now connect to a standalone node using `vagrant ssh standalone`. This process may vary if you've already deployed a standalone virtual node before and you've just started it using `vagrant up`:

```
Docker-Certified-Associate-DCA-Exam-Guide/environments/standalone$ vagrant
ssh standalone
[vagrant@standalone ~]$
```

If you are reusing your standalone environment, this means Docker Engine is installed. If you started a new instance, please execute the `/vagrant/install_requirements.sh` script so that you have all the required tools (Docker Engine and `docker-compose`):

```
[vagrant@standalone ~]$ /vagrant/install_requirements.sh
```

Now, you are ready to start the labs.

Signing images for Docker Hub

First, sign in to `https://hub.docker.com/signup` to create your own account at Docker Hub if you do not already have one. You can use your own registry, but you should have a Notary server running. Let's get started:

 This lab will use the `frjaraur/pingo` repository in Docker Hub. You must substitute `frjaraur` with your username.

1. In this lab, we will start from the very beginning. This is a lab, so don't remove your own `.docker/trust` directory if you have been signing images beforehand. In that case, back up your trust directory somewhere safe so that you can recover it later or just create a dummy user in your Docker host system. To create this backup, we will just execute `cp -pR ~/.docker/trust ~/.docker/trust.BKP`. After these labs, you can recover it:

   [vagrant@standalone ~]$ rm -rf ~/.docker/trust/

2. Now, enable Docker Content Trust and create a directory for this lab:

   [vagrant@standalone ~]$ export DOCKER_CONTENT_TRUST=1

   [vagrant@standalone ~]$ cd $HOME
   [vagrant@standalone ~]$ mkdir chapter6
   [vagrant@standalone ~]$ cd chapter6

3. We have prepared a quite-simple Dockerfile, executing `ping` to `8.8.8.8` for `300` times. These lab files can be found in the `chapter6` directory if you have downloaded the book samples from this book's GitHub repository. Create a `Dockerfile` file with the following content using your file editor:

   ```
   FROM alpine:3.8
   RUN apk add --update curl
   CMD ping 8.8.8.8 -c 300
   ```

4. Now, we can build the image. Remember that Docker Content Trust was enabled. We will use `docker image build` in the directory where you wrote your Dockerfile:

   [vagrant@standalone chapter6]$ docker image build -t frjaraur/pingo:trusted .

   Sending build context to Docker daemon 2.048kB

```
Step 1/3 : FROM
alpine@sha256:04696b491e0cc3c58a75bace8941c14c924b9f313b03ce5029ebb
c040ed9dcd9
sha256:04696b491e0cc3c58a75bace8941c14c924b9f313b03ce5029ebbc040ed9
dcd9: Pulling from library/alpine
c87736221ed0: Pull complete
Digest:
sha256:04696b491e0cc3c58a75bace8941c14c924b9f313b03ce5029ebbc040ed9
dcd9
Status: Downloaded newer image for
alpine@sha256:04696b491e0cc3c58a75bace8941c14c924b9f313b03ce5029ebb
c040ed9dcd9
 ---> dac705114996
Step 2/3 : RUN apk add --update curl
. . .
. . .
Successfully built b3aba563b2ff
Successfully tagged frjaraur/pingo:trusted
Tagging
alpine@sha256:04696b491e0cc3c58a75bace8941c14c924b9f313b03ce5029ebb
c040ed9dcd9 as alpine:3.8
```

You may have noticed new messages from the Docker daemon. The daemon used the `alpine:3.8` image hash, `sha256:04696b491e0cc3c58a75bace8941c14c924b9f313b03ce5029ebbc04 0ed9dcd9`, instead of the image name and tag. If we had an image locally with the same `image:tag` values, it would have been verified. If the hash did not match, it would have been avoided and the real image would have been downloaded from Docker Hub. This will ensure that the trusted `alpine:3.8` image will be downloaded.

5. Now, we will sign this image using `docker trust sign`. This process will ask us to create a `root` passphrase, a `repository` passphrase, and a `user` passphrase (this is new in this chapter because we did not use Docker Content Trust in previous chapters). This will create a new `trust` directory under `.docker`. When the image is pushed, you will be asked about your registry user passphrase again. This is not your Docker Hub password. This is the passphrase you created so that you can perform signing. We will use `docker trust sign`:

```
[vagrant@standalone chapter6]$ docker trust sign
frjaraur/pingo:trusted
You are about to create a new root signing key passphrase. This
passphrase
will be used to protect the most sensitive key in your signing
```

```
system. Please
choose a long, complex passphrase and be careful to keep the
password and the
key file itself secure and backed up. It is highly recommended that
you use a
password manager to generate the passphrase and keep it safe. There
will be no
way to recover this key. You can find the key in your config
directory.
Enter passphrase for new root key with ID 9e788ed:
Repeat passphrase for new root key with ID 9e788ed:
Enter passphrase for new repository key with ID fb7b8fd:
Repeat passphrase for new repository key with ID fb7b8fd:
Enter passphrase for new frjaraur key with ID f1916d7:
Repeat passphrase for new frjaraur key with ID f1916d7:
Created signer: frjaraur
Finished initializing signed repository for frjaraur/pingo:trusted
Signing and pushing trust data for local image
frjaraur/pingo:trusted, may overwrite remote trust data
The push refers to repository [docker.io/frjaraur/pingo]
6f02cc23eebe: Pushed
d9ff549177a9: Mounted from library/alpine
trusted: digest:
sha256:478cd976c78306bbffd51a4b5055e28873697d01504e70ef85bddd9cc348
450b size: 739
Signing and pushing trust metadata
Enter passphrase for frjaraur key with ID f1916d7:
Successfully signed docker.io/frjaraur/pingo:trusted
```

6. With that, the image was signed and pushed to Docker Hub. We can verify that
   the image was uploaded by using `curl`:

```
[vagrant@standalone chapter6]$ curl -s
https://hub.docker.com/v2/repositories/frjaraur/pingo/tags|jq
{
  "count": 1,
  "next": null,
  "previous": null,
  "results": [
    {
      "name": "trusted",
      "full_size": 4306493,
      "images": [
        {
          "size": 4306493,
          "digest":
"sha256:478cd976c78306bbffd51a4b5055e28873697d01504e70ef85bddd9cc34
8450b",
```

```
            "architecture": "amd64",
            "os": "linux",
            "os_version": null,
            "os_features": "",
            "variant": null,
            "features": ""
          }
        ],
        "id": 78277337,
        "repository": 8106864,
        "creator": 380101,
        "last_updater": 380101,
        "last_updater_username": "frjaraur",
        "image_id": null,
        "v2": true,
        "last_updated": "2019-11-30T22:03:28.820429Z"
      }
    ]
  }
```

7. Finally, we will review the image signatures using `docker trust inspect`:

```
[vagrant@standalone chapter6]$ docker trust inspect --pretty
frjaraur/pingo:trusted
Signatures for frjaraur/pingo:trusted
SIGNED TAG DIGEST SIGNERS
trusted
478cd976c78306bbffd51a4b5055e28873697d01504e70ef85bddd9cc348450b
frjaraur
List of signers and their keys for frjaraur/pingo:trusted
SIGNER KEYS
frjaraur f1916d7ad60b
Administrative keys for frjaraur/pingo:trusted
Repository Key:
fb7b8fdaa22738c44b927110c377aaa7c56a6a15e2fa0ebc554fe92a57b5eb0b
 Root Key:
4a739a076032b94a79c6d376721649c79917f4b5f8c8035ca11e36a0ed0696b4
```

Now, let's look at a brief summary of the topics that were covered in this chapter before we look at some questions.

Summary

Docker Content Trust helps us guarantee content security in container environments and ensure image provenance and trusted content. In production environments, it is critical to be able to ensure that any running container was generated from trusted content. If image security cannot be validated, no container should be allowed to run based on that image.

We have learned that Content Trust improves Docker repository security by means of four fundamental keys. The root key ensures ownership and the targets key will allow content to be verified in specific collections or repositories. These keys will be protected by passphrases and we will be asked for them when signing. The snapshot and timestamp keys will not require any user interaction and will be generated automatically to guarantee the content key files and the dates and expiration of the signed image.

In the next chapter, we will introduce the concept of orchestration. We will review all the features required to manage container-based applications in distributed environments.

Questions

1. Which of these sentences is not true?

    a) Docker Content Trust is based on TUF.
    b) TUF was developed to ensure software updating processes.
    c) It is not possible to validate new software releases.
    d) All of the preceding statements are false.

2. Which of the following names represent Docker Content Trust keys used to validate image content?

    a) Targets
    b) Users
    c) Groups
    d) Timestamp

3. How can we ensure that the `busybox:latest` release is, in fact, the latest one?

   a) We cannot ensure the freshness of images.
   b) `busybox:latest` indicates that this image is the latest one created.
   c) Content Trust will validate the freshness of images; therefore, we can ensure that the host really executes the `busybox:latest` image, although we cannot ensure that it is the latest one.
   d) All of the preceding statements are false.

4. Why will we obtain a `denied: requested access to the resource is denied` error when trying to sign `busybox:trusted`?

   a) This image does not exist.
   b) We are not allowed to modify that repository.
   c) Docker Content Trust was probably not enabled.
   d) All of the preceding.

5. We lost our root key because we changed our laptop. Which of the following statements is true?

   a) If we don't have a key under `.docker/trust/private`, a new one will be generated when signing.
   b) We can recover the private root key if we perform a backup.
   c) If we generate a new key, our old images will become untrusted and we will need to resign them.
   d) All of the preceding statements are true.

Further reading

You can refer to the following links for more information on the topics that were covered in this chapter:

- TUF: `https://theupdateframework.io/`
- TUF specification: `https://github.com/theupdateframework/specification`
- Notary: `https://github.com/theupdateframework/notary`
- Docker Content Trust: `https://docs.docker.com/engine/security/trust/content_trust/`

2
Section 2 - Container Orchestration

In this section, we will cover the orchestration of containers on cluster-wide environments. We will learn how to deploy applications based on cluster-wide distributed components. You will also learn how orchestrators manage applications' processes and their interactions, and how to publish them for users.

This section comprises the following chapters:

- Chapter 7, *Introduction to Orchestration*
- Chapter 8, *Orchestration Using Docker Swarm*
- Chapter 9, *Orchestration Using Kubernetes*

Introduction to Orchestration

7

In this chapter, we will talk about orchestration concepts that can be applied to container environments. We will learn why we need orchestration to deploy applications based on container components on a pool of nodes. Orchestrators provide new features to an environment but they also introduce new management challenges. We will also look at new definitions so that we can provide Docker Engine features in a distributed orchestrated environment. This chapter will introduce important concepts that will help you understand the Swarm and Kubernetes orchestrators.

We will learn about orchestration as a concept and we will also introduce some interesting topics, such as the importance of orchestration in distributed and dynamic environments, and the fact that it allows us to easily scale up and down and update application components. We will also learn how to manage stateless and stateful components and provide data persistency on distributed deployments.

By the end of this chapter, you will know what an orchestrator is and how it applies to container-based application environments.

We will cover the following topics in this chapter:

- Introducing orchestration concepts
- Learning about container orchestration
- Scheduling applications cluster-wide
- Managing data and persistency
- Scaling and updating application components

 This chapter does not include any labs as it is an introductory chapter with theoretical and general concepts.

Let's start by introducing orchestration as a key concept for managing distributed applications.

Introducing orchestration concepts

Understanding orchestration concepts is key in this chapter so that we can learn more about Docker Swarm or Kubernetes. Let's imagine an orchestra: there are violinists, pianists, percussionists, and so on; every player has studied for many years to become a professional musician. They can play alone perfectly, but things get difficult when we add more instruments. Players can read the musical score and each one will play their part. But even the best musicians need someone to guide them when they're playing together. The orchestra director is key to making all the instruments work together.

When we divide our applications into small pieces – microservices – orchestration is required. An application requires a lot of components to work together. Remember that splitting a monolithic application into different functionalities also creates a new development workflow. We can have different groups of developers working who are focused on just one functionality. Each application component is an atomic piece.

Deploying an application requires the execution and management of all its components at the same time. An orchestrator will manage these components and the application life cycle.

Orchestration will also manage components' dependencies, or will at least provide some tools to allow us to implement application logic.

Orchestration is even more necessary when applications run their components distributed in a pool of computation nodes. We can even distribute these components on different cloud providers or mix on-premises and cloud infrastructures.

 Time synchronization is critical on distributed environments and it is even more important when we are securing connections using **Secure Sockets Layer/Transport Layer Security (SSL/TLS)** or other certificate-based solutions.

To summarize, we can say that orchestration provides the tools that we need to manage an application's components in a seamless way across distributed environments.

Now that we know what an orchestrator should do on distributed applications, let's deep dive into container environments.

Learning about container orchestration

Orchestration helps us manage applications running multiple components. In our case, these components or microservices will run on containers. Therefore, let's summarize what features are required in a container environment:

- **Deployment**: All application components must run in a coordinated manner. An orchestrator should help us deploy application components as they are required and they should run in the right order.

- **Configuration**: It is not easy to manage configuration in distributed environments. An orchestrator should manage this configuration and the configuration should be available anywhere a container needs it.

- **Resilience**: If one application component fails, the orchestrator should keep the application healthy, if possible.

- **Scaling up/down**: The microservices concept allows application components to be replicated to increase application performance if needed. If no extra power is required, we should be able to decommission these replicas to save resources.

- **Node distribution**: To ensure high availability, we will provide a pool of orchestrated compute nodes. This way, we will distribute all application components on different nodes. If some of these nodes die, the orchestrator should ensure that the components running on those nodes run automatically on other healthy ones.

- **Networking**: Because we distribute applications within different hosts, the orchestrator will need to provide the required application component interactions. Networking is key in this situation.

- **Publishing**: The orchestrator should also ensure a way to interact with running application components since our application's purpose is to provide a service to customers.

- **State**: An application component's state is hard to manage. Therefore, it is easier to orchestrate stateless components. This is why people think of containers as ephemeral artifacts. We learned that containers have their own life cycles and that they are not really ephemeral. They exist on hosts until someone deletes them, but orchestration should schedule these components wherever it is permitted. This means that a container's state should be managed in a coordinated way and that components should run with the same properties everywhere. Application components have to maintain their status when they are moved to another host. In most cases, we will run a new, fresh container if a component dies, instead of trying to restart an unhealthy one.

- **Storage**: If some application components require storage, such as for persistence data, the orchestrator should provide an interface to interact with the host's available storage providers.

As you can see, orchestration helps us to maintain application logic, but it cannot do magic. In fact, an orchestrator does not know anything about your application logic. We must provide that logic in some kind of configuration.

In this chapter, we are introducing concepts that can be applied to well-known container orchestrators. Kubernetes and Swarm are the most commonly used, although there are others.

Orchestration will not run containers. Containers are packaged into other orchestration structures. These atomic structures will be scheduled cluster-wide, depending on certain properties or key values. The orchestrator should decide on the best place to launch these atomic components. All orchestrators need a database-like component to store orchestration objects, their properties, and their state.

In Kubernetes, we deploy Pods, which are multiple containers running together. In Swarm, we deploy services, which are based on tasks – which, in the end, are containers. Therefore, we never launch containers. We have other units of deployment. If we deploy a container on a host as-is, it will not be managed by the orchestrator.

In the API era, orchestrators are managed using their exposed API. In fact, we will use the `kubectl` and `docker` commands to interact with orchestration processes via their APIs. This will be transparent for us. Client applications will do the job with different arguments and actions applied.

Orchestrators are also based on microservices architectures. They have many distributed components. At least a database is required, as we mentioned previously, and an API server and a scheduler to decide where to run the defined application workloads. We will think about applications as groups of logical components, defined using scheduling units.

In the next section, we will cover how orchestration decides where to run application components in cluster-wide environments.

Scheduling applications cluster-wide

So far, we have learned what to expect from an orchestrator and the basic components required to make it work. We mentioned distributing application components on different hosts. To be able to distribute application components, we will need to deploy a cluster. A cluster is a set of nodes working together. Deploying an application to a host should be similar to deploying the same application to a cluster. The orchestrator will manage the entire workflow, and this process should be transparent for us.

Orchestrators usually manage nodes with different roles. Depending on the kind of processes those nodes run, we will define manager and worker nodes. The names may differ for each orchestrator implementation, but the logic will be the same. Manager nodes execute the orchestration control plane, while workers execute the application deployments. Worker nodes, therefore, are compute nodes.

Control plane nodes manage all the actions required for an orchestration framework to work. The aforementioned database, which is required for storing all object definitions and states, will run on these nodes. The scheduler logic will also run on these nodes. Depending on the database used, for the orchestration to work, it may require a number of odd nodes. Many orchestrators rely on key-value databases (very fast databases accessible via HTTP/HTTPS protocols).

In these cases, databases use the Raft consensus protocol. This means that a defined number of nodes have to vote for every change in the environment before they are stored in the database by just one of them. Once all the required votes are correctly received, database values are synced to other nodes. This ensures that all the nodes have the same information and that the database is safe if some of them go down. This is a very important feature in these environments. And this is the reason why Swarm and Kubernetes, among others, require a specific number of manager nodes to work correctly.

All orchestrated objects have labels. Some of them are automatically added by the orchestrator, for example, to set cluster node architectures. Other labels can be manually configured to define some special behaviors or characteristics, such as to define the application tier or layer for a component. Layers are key to managing cluster object interactions.

The orchestrator will also manage all node resources (CPU, memory, and the ports that are available, among other things) and review whether there are enough resources to run a defined workload before it is deployed.

The orchestrator will review all the node resources, labels, and other application requirements before deciding where to execute workloads. We will be able to set some affinity and anti-affinity features to specify some special requirements and, of course, we will be able to use labels to help the orchestrator choose the right place for them. We will use these labels to associate application components with faster nodes, closer to some required components, or distributed on each node in the cluster.

Remember that application components can be deployed cluster-wide. The orchestrator should manage their network interactions and provide access to these deployments.

These are the basic components for orchestration and the logic behind orchestration scheduling. In the next section, we will take a quick look at how data and application states are managed. Remember that this chapter is just a quick introduction to some orchestration concepts that Docker Swarm and Kubernetes will implement on their workflows, with different architectures and more complexity.

Managing data and persistency

In many cases, application components need to store some data. This can be very complicated in distributed environments. That is why we usually talk about containers as ephemeral components. Stateless components are easy to implement, but in stateful components, we try to decouple persistent data from a container's filesystems. Remember that data in containers can be lost. In fact, orchestration does not care about data and therefore, if a container dies, it will just run a new one. In these cases, we need to persist data out of a container's environment. We can use what we learned about volume objects in Chapter 4, *Container Persistency and Networking*, to do this. We defined volumes to bypass a container's filesystem to improve performance and to store data out of the container's life cycle.

In distributed environments, using the host's local storage will leave application components in inconsistent states when they are moved from one host to another. To avoid these situations, we will use the host's external volumes. In fact, we will choose a storage driver that will allow us to run our application components everywhere, alongside their required storage. All orchestrators can provide NFS storage to containers as required, but in some cases, this is not enough and specialized drivers are required. Cloud providers and many on-premises **software-defined storage** (**SDS**) manufacturers provide REST API interfaces. Storage drivers use these definitions to allow an orchestrator to find the right node to run our application components.

An orchestrator does not know anything about our application logic. It is our responsibility to implement application logic in its code. Some orchestrators, for example, will not manage any kind of dependencies between components. We will also need to implement component health checks, rules, and procedures to follow in case any dependent component dies. We should implement retry procedures if a required component is not accessible.

Docker Swarm and Kubernetes provide objects to ensure configuration files and secrets (authentication files or credentials) are distributed cluster-wide. As we mentioned previously, orchestration will not manage data, just these kinds of configuration objects.

In the next section, we will learn how orchestrators allow us to implement replicated components and how application upgrades are easier in these environments.

Scaling and updating application components

Orchestrators provide another great feature. If my application is prepared to run more than one instance of some components, the orchestrator will help us easily manage this replication. This is easy because components are based on containers, so if we need to run more than one replica of a component, we can ask the orchestrator to execute more containers. In fact, this feature is key because, in orchestration, we define an application component with the number of required healthy replicas. If all required replicas are alive, that application component will be healthy. If one replica dies, a new one will be executed to ensure that the required number is accomplished.

The management of replicas is one of the features provided by orchestrators. If application performance is compromised and application logic allows replication, we will be able to scale up or down the number of replicas or instances of a component.

On the other hand, we learned that the microservices application model is better for components' life cycles. Developers can focus on each component, and fixing errors and upgrades is easier. Each component is treated as an isolated piece of functionality. This allows us to manage each piece separately from others. We are able to upgrade this component without impacting others. The orchestrator also manages these procedures. We set a new definition or property, such as a new image for an application component or a different port, and the orchestrator deploys these changes for us. We are able to set how this process has to be done. For example, we decide how many instances will be updated at a time or the interval between updates, among other interesting settings.

We will review all these features in depth in each orchestrator chapter. We will learn about Docker Swarm and Kubernetes in Chapter 8, *Orchestration Using Docker Swarm*, and Chapter 9, *Orchestration Using Kubernetes*.

Summary

In this short chapter, we learned about some important concepts that will help us understand Docker Swarm and Kubernetes. We reviewed the orchestration concept in general before taking a look at the features that orchestration provides. Thanks to orchestration, we are able to distribute application components cluster-wide on different nodes to provide better performance and availability. Application stability is also improved because we are able to execute many instances of one component. We can define an application component with the number of replicas required to be considered healthy. The orchestrator will manage the application's health and will deploy new instances if some of them die. We are also able to scale up and down components as required in our environment if the application permits this behavior.

Orchestration uses new cluster objects. They are stored in a distributed database for high availability. A component's status and other orchestration data will be also stored in this database. The application's components' data and the necessary logic are not managed by the orchestrator. We use external components to share information and the orchestrator interacts with them to ensure the required data is available whenever a component is deployed on a different host.

In the next chapter, we will deep dive into Docker Swarm and learn how Docker implements the orchestration features we have reviewed.

Questions

In this chapter, we learned about orchestration in general. We will review some of the topics presented here with some questions:

1. Which of these sentences is true?

    a) Kubernetes and Swarm are orchestrators that run distributed applications.
    b) Orchestration replicates application logic into container-based objects.
    c) It is not possible to manage application data in distributed environments.
    d) All of the preceding sentences are false.

2. What do orchestrators manage?

> a) Application components' data.
> b) Application components' logic.
> c) Application components' resilience.
> d) All of the preceding options are incorrect.

3. What challenges do we have when we deploy applications with multiple components in distributed environments?

> a) Application component networking.
> b) Application component logic.
> c) Application component resilience.
> d) None of the preceding options are correct.

4. What features does orchestration provide to application deployments?

> a) We deploy application components by setting the number of replicas required to be considered healthy.
> b) Application components can be scaled up or down as required in your environment and the orchestrator will launch the required instances.
> c) Application components are updated all at once.
> d) None of the preceding options are correct.

5. How does an orchestrator choose where to run application components?

> a) Nodes with enough resources can receive workloads.
> b) We can label nodes to fix some components on specific nodes.
> c) The orchestrator will review the defined rules to choose where to run each component
> d) All of the preceding sentences are correct.

Further reading

- Raft consensus algorithm: https://raft.github.io/
- Docker Swarm features: https://docs.docker.com/engine/swarm/
- Kubernetes introduction and features: https://kubernetes.io/docs/concepts/overview/what-is-kubernetes/

Orchestration Using Docker Swarm

8

In the previous chapter, we learned about orchestration features. In this chapter, we will build on this by learning about Docker Swarm. It comes with Docker Engine (Docker installation packages) out of the box, so we don't need to install any other software. It is simpler to master the basics of Docker Swarm compared to the other orchestrators available, and it is powerful enough for production deployments.

In summary, in this chapter, we will learn how to deploy Docker Swarm in production. We will also review the new objects introduced by Docker Swarm and the steps required to deploy a complete application based on containers with orchestration. Networking is key for node-distributed applications, so we will examine how Docker Swarm provides solutions for internal networking, service discovery, and publishing deployed applications. At the end of the chapter, we will review how Docker Swarm can help us upgrade our application's components without service interruption.

We will cover the following topics in this chapter:

- Deploying Docker Swarm
- Creating a Docker Swarm cluster
- Scheduling workloads in the cluster – tasks and services
- Deploying applications using Stacks and other Docker Swarm resources
- Networking in Docker Swarm

Let's get started!

Technical requirements

In this chapter, we will learn about Docker Swarm's orchestrator features. We'll provide some labs at the end of this chapter that you can use to test your understanding and demonstrate the concepts you've learned. These labs can be run on your laptop or PC using the provided Vagrant "Docker Swarm" environment, or any already deployed Docker Swarm cluster of your own. Check out this book's GitHub code repository for the code we're going to be using in this chapter, along with additional information, at `https://github.com/PacktPublishing/Docker-Certified-Associate-DCA-Exam-Guide.git`.

Check out the following video to see the Code in Action:

`"https://bit.ly/31wfqmu"`

Deploying Docker Swarm

Docker Swarm is the built-in orchestrator that comes with Docker Engine out of the box. It was introduced in Docker Engine release 1.12 (the release numbers changed after 1.13 to four-digit numbers) as *swarm mode*. There was a previous swarm approach currently known as Legacy Swarm, which was closer in architecture to Kubernetes. It required an external key-value store database, among other components. Swarm mode is different from this because it includes everything needed for the orchestrator to work out of the box.

The Swarm architecture is quite simple as it provides secure communications between components by default. Before deploying a Docker Swarm cluster, let's review its main features:

- **Container orchestration for multiple nodes is included on each Docker Engine**: This means that we can deploy a cluster without any other software. Docker Engine provides all the required components to deploy and manage the cluster out of the box.
- **Node roles can be changed at runtime**: Orchestration is based on different node roles. While the control plane is managed by managers or master nodes, computation or application deployment will be done on slave, worker, or minion nodes. Each orchestrator uses different names for these different roles, but they are essentially the same. Swarm allows us to change nodes from one role to another when one of them is unhealthy or when we need to do some maintenance tasks.

- **Workloads will be declared as services, defining a number of instances to be healthy**: The Docker orchestrator will keep the required number of replicas alive. If some of them die, the orchestrator will run new tasks to keep the required number alive. The orchestrator will manage this reconciliation process. If a node dies, the orchestrator will move all containers to a new, healthy node.

- **As workloads are based on the number of instances required, the orchestrator will allow us to change this number any time we require**: As a result, we can scale up or down the number of instances of a service (application component) to respond to a high demand for requests, for example.

- **We will deploy applications based on multiple service components, with all their requirements and connectivity between them**: As components may run on any cluster node, Docker Swarm will provide an internal overlay network to interconnect all application components.

- **Swarm will provide service discovery and internal load balancing**: In the *Service discovery and load balancing* section, we will learn how Docker Swarm can provide internal application DNS resolution so that all the components will easily be able to discover each other, along with load balancing between service replicas using a virtual IP.

- **Orchestration will allow us to update application components automatically**: In fact, all we need to decide is how these updates will be managed; orchestration will do the rest. This way, we can update application components without impacting users.

- **We can ensure that our cluster runs securely by default**: Docker Swarm will deploy **Transport Layer Security** (**TLS**) to interconnect control plane components. It will manage certificates for all of our nodes, creating an internal CA and verifying all node certificates itself.

It is important to know that only the control plane is secure by default. Users' access to features such as application publishing will require additional configuration.

As we learned in the previous chapter, orchestrators require databases to store and manage workloads and any other cluster resource information. Docker Swarm has a built-in key-value store under the `/var/lib/docker/swarm` path (this is on Linux; it can be found in its equivalent directory on Windows, under `C:\ProgramData\docker`).

It is important to understand that the `/var/lib/docker/swarm` directory is essential, should we need to restore an unhealthy cluster. Take care of this directory and keep a backup of it.

We can lock users' access to the `/var/lib/docker/swarm` path using a key. This improves security. If it is unlocked, someone with enough system privileges can obtain Docker Swarm certificates.

Docker Swarm overall architecture

As we mentioned previously, Docker Swarm deploys its own secure control plane. There are two kinds of node roles:

- **Managers**: These manage the overall Swarm cluster environment. They share an internal key-value database. More specifically, one of the managers has a different role. This is the manager's leader. There is only one leader per cluster and it makes all the necessary updates to the database. All other manager nodes will follow and sync their databases with the leader's one. Managers maintain cluster health, serve the Swarm HTTP API, and schedule workloads on available compute nodes.
- **Workers**: Workloads will run on worker nodes. It is important to know that managers have worker roles too. This means that workloads can also run on managers if we do not specify any special scheduling location. Workers will never participate in scheduling decisions; they will just run assigned workloads.

We manage workload locations either by using location constraints on each workload or by disabling container execution on some nodes.

On nodes with multiple interfaces, we will be able to choose which interface we will use for the control plane. Manager nodes will implement the Raft consensus algorithm to manage the Swarm cluster state. This algorithm requires multiple servers coming to an agreement on data and status. Once they reach a decision on a value, that decision is written to disk. This will ensure information distribution with consistency across multiple managers.

As we mentioned previously, there is a leader node that modifies and store changes on its database; all other nodes will sync their databases with it. To maintain this consistency, Swarm implements Raft. This algorithm will manage all changes in the database, as well as the election of a new leader when it is unhealthy. When the leader needs to make a change (such as to the application's component status, and its data), it will query all the other nodes for their opinions. If they all agree with the change, the leader will commit it, and the change will be synced to all the nodes. If the leader fails (as in, the node goes down, the server process dies, and so on), a new election is triggered. In this case, all the remaining manager nodes will vote for a new leader.

This process requires reaching a consensus, with the majority of nodes agreeing on the result of the election. If there is no majority, a new election process will be triggered until a new leader is elected. After that, the cluster will be healthy again. Keep these concepts in mind because they are key in Docker Swarm and other orchestrators.

The following diagram represents the basic architecture of a Swarm orchestrator:

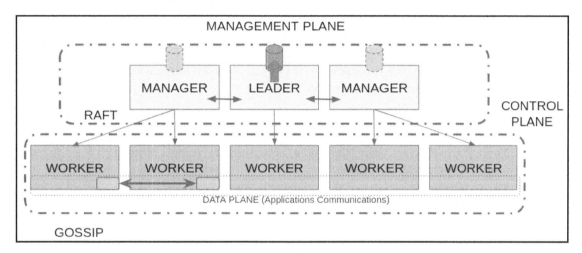

Let's review each plane in detail.

Management plane

The management plane is the layer where all management tasks run. All cluster management traffic and workload maintenance will take place on this plane. The management plane provides high availability based on an odd number of manager nodes.

All communication in this plane is mutually encrypted using TLS (mutual TLS) by default. This is where the Raft protocol operates.

Control plane

This plane manages the state of the cluster. The gossip protocol will periodically inform all nodes about the cluster state, reducing the amount of information required by nodes to simply having an overview of the health of the cluster. This protocol manages host-to-host communications and is called the *control plane* because each host communicates only with its closest companions, and information flows through this to reach all the nodes within the control plane.

Data plane

The data plane manages all the service's internal communications. It is based on VXLAN tunneling, encapsulating layer-2 packets within layer-3 headers. It will use UDP transport but VXLAN guarantees no dropped packets. We will be able to isolate the data plane from the control and management planes using the appropriate flags upon Docker Swarm creation (or joining).

When we initialize a new Docker Swarm cluster, it generates a self-signed **Certificate Authority (CA)** and issues self-signed certificates to every node. This ensures mutual TLS communication. The following is a summary of the steps taken to ensure secure communications when a new node joins the cluster:

1. When a node joins, it sends the manager its join token, along with a certificate request.
2. Then, if the token is valid, the manager accepts the node's request and sends back a self-signed node certificate.
3. The manager then registers the new node in the cluster and it will appear as part of the Docker Swarm cluster.
4. Once the node is included in the cluster, it is ready (by default) to accept any new workload scheduled by the manager.

In the next section, we will learn how to easily deploy a Docker Swarm cluster using common Docker command-line actions.

Deploying a Docker Swarm cluster using the command line

We can use the Docker `swarm` object to initialize a new cluster, join or leave a previously created one, and manage all Docker Swarm properties. Let's take a look at the `docker swarm` actions:

- `init`: We will use `docker swarm init` to initialize a new cluster or recreate an existing one (we will describe this situation in more detail in the *High availability with Swarm* section). We will set many cluster options during cluster creation, but there are a few that can be changed later. The most important options are `--data-path-addr` and `--data-path-port` because they are used to set which node interface will be dedicated to the control plane on multi-homed nodes.

These are the most commonly used arguments for creating the cluster:

- `--advertise-addr`: This option allows us to set which interface will be used to announce the cluster. All other nodes will use this interface's IP address to join the cluster.
- `--data-path-addr`/`--data-path-port`: These options configure the interface and port used for the control plane. All traffic in this interface will be encrypted using TLS, and certificates will be managed internally by Swarm. We can use the IP address/port or host interface notation. The default port is `4789`.
- `--external-ca`/`--cert-expiry`: Although Swarm will manage TLS for us, we can deploy our own CA for all certificates using this parameter. We can also specify how often certificates will be rotated. By default, they will be automatically recreated every 90 days (2,160 hours).
- `--listen-addr`: This option allows us to specify which host interface will be used to serve the cluster API. We can use IP address/port or host interface notation, with the default of `0.0.0.0:2377`.
- `--autolock`: As we mentioned previously, we can lock access to internal Docker Swarm data. This is important because `/var/lib/docker/swarm` contains the CA and other certificates. If you are not sure about node access, it is better to lock this directory from users. Take care with this option because any system or Docker daemon restart will require the unlock key in order to enable this node in the cluster again.
- `--dispatcher-heartbeat`: This option will manage how often nodes will report their health. It defaults to 5 seconds, but you can change it if your cluster has high latency.
- `--max-snapshots`/`--snapshot-interval`: Swarm will take database snapshots for manager synchronization. We can set the number of snapshots to keep. By default, none will be kept (just one for synchronization), but these can be useful for debugging or disaster recovery. We can also set the interval between snapshots. Take care when changing this option because having many snapshots will trigger a lot of sync operations to other nodes and can incur high-performance costs. But on the other hand, syncing less frequently can guide the cluster to non-synced states. This parameter defaults to 10,000 ms.

- `join`: After cluster initialization, all the other nodes will join the previously created cluster, regardless of whether they are managers or workers. Joining Docker nodes to a cluster requires a cluster-specific token, with different tokens for the manager and worker nodes. We will always require a token and the leader IP address to join the cluster. Remember that the leader can change from time to time. We will also be able to set the control plane's IP and port, the IP address to be announced to the other nodes, and the listen IP address for the API. We will execute this command on the joining node using the following format: `docker swarm join --token <MANAGER_OR_WORKER_TOKEN> <LEADER_IP:PORT>`.

- `leave`: Once a node is part of the cluster, it can leave it whenever we need it to. It is important to understand what it means to *leave* the cluster. The `leave` command will be executed on the node leaving the cluster. Manager nodes are not able to leave the cluster because this would force the cluster into an unhealthy state. We can use `--force` to make a node leave the cluster, even if it is a manager node, but this comes with risks that you need to understand before proceeding. Leaving the cluster will not remove the node from the internal Docker Swarm database. Rather, we need to inform the managers of this change by issuing `docker node rm <NODE_NAME_OR_ID>`.

- `update`: With this action, we can change some of the Docker Swarm cluster's described properties, such as the external CA, certificate expiration settings, and snapshot behavior.

- `ca`: As we mentioned previously, all internal control plane communication is based on TLS certificates. The `ca` option allows us to customize the CA and other certificate behavior. We can rotate them or choose our own CA.

- `join-token`: With this action, we can review the current tokens for managers and workers. In fact, we can execute `join-token`, followed by the required role, to retrieve their values. We do not need to keep them safe since we can retrieve them as needed. These tokens are only used when joining the cluster. We can change them whenever we want, using `docker swarm join-token --rotate` to create a new one. This will not affect already joined nodes. We usually execute `docker swarm join-token worker` to retrieve the command line and token required to join the node to the cluster. We can use `--quiet` to retrieve only the token, which is useful for automating the joining process.

- `unlock/unlock-key`: We mentioned previously that it is unsafe to allow users to access the `/var/lib/docker` directory. Access is only allowed to root by default, but it is even more secure to lock Docker Swarm information. For example, all cluster certificates will be stored under the `/var/lib/docker/swarm/certificates` directory. Locking Swarm information is a good practice, but be aware of losing your unlock key. Every time the cluster node starts (such as a Docker Engine or node restart, for example), the unlock key will be required. This leaves the cluster in a non-automatic, high-availability environment in some situations. The `unlock` option unlocks the Docker Swarm cluster information, while `unlock-key` allows us to manage the defined key used for this behavior.

Docker Swarm will also create new objects:

- `swarm`: This is the cluster itself, along with its own properties, as described earlier.
- `node`: These are the nodes that are part of the cluster. We will add labels to them and manage their roles as part of the cluster.
- `service`: We deploy services on our Docker Swarm cluster. We won't deploy a standalone container. We will learn more about services in the *Scheduling workloads in the cluster – tasks and services* section.
- `secret` and `config`: Both objects allow us to share service configurations in the cluster. Remember, it is not easy to manage information on different hosts, even if the application is completely stateless.
- `stack`: We will use stacks to deploy applications. We will use a Docker Compose-like file format containing all application components and their interactions.

All these objects will have common actions associated with them, including listing, deploying/creating, removing, and inspecting their properties. Services and stacks will have containers associated with them, so we will be able to list their processes' distributions cluster-wide.

 We can run a single node cluster on our laptop. It is not a problem running a single node cluster for testing or developing services or stacks.

In the next section, we will learn how to deploy a Docker Swarm environment with high availability.

Deploying Docker Swarm with high availability

So far, we have learned about the different roles in Docker Swarm clusters. However, in order to provide high availability, we will need to deploy more than one manager and worker.

The Raft consensus algorithm requires an odd number of healthy nodes to work because a majority of the nodes must agree on all the changes and resources states. This means that we will need at least *N/2+1* healthy nodes to agree before committing a change or resource state. In other words, we will not grant Docker Swarm availability if fewer than *N/2+1* manager nodes are healthy. Let's review the options in the following table to get a better understanding:

Number of managers	Required for consensus (N/2+1)	Allowed failures	Provides high availability?
1	1	0	No.
2	2	0	No.
3	2	1	Yes.
4	3	1	Yes, but this is not better than the three-manager option and can lead to election problems if the leader fails.
5	3	2	Yes.
6	4	2	Yes, but this is not better than the five-manager option and can lead to election problems if the leader fails.
7	4	3	Yes.

When a manager fails in the 3-manager configuration, two nodes can agree and changes will be updated without problems. But if one of those fails, only one will be left and changes can't be committed. There is no consensus and no cluster operations can be deployed. This means that any service deployed in the cluster will stay running. Users will not be affected unless one service loses some replicas and Docker Swarm should have started new ones to achieve the required number. No automatic actions will be allowed because these have to update the database data, and this is not permitted. We will not be able to add or remove any nodes in that situation, so the cluster will be inconsistent.

Consequently, Swarm requires an odd number of managers to provide high availability. Although there is no limit regarding the number of manager nodes, more than seven is not recommended. Increasing the number of managers will reduce write performance because the leader will require more acknowledged responses from more nodes to update cluster changes. This will result in more round-trip network traffic.

It is key to understand these behaviors. Even if we have deployed a three-node cluster, we can still lose quorum if a sufficient number of nodes become unhealthy. It is important to attend to node failures as soon as possible.

We will usually deploy three-node clusters because they allow for the failure of 1 node. It is enough for production, but in some critical environments, we will deploy five-node clusters to allow for two node failures.

> In cases where a Swarm cluster needs to be distributed between different locations, the recommended number of managers is seven. It will allow distribution across multiple data centers. We will deploy three nodes in the first data center, two in the second data center, and a final two in the third data center (3+2+2). This distribution will allow us to handle a full data center failure with services being redistributed if worker nodes have sufficient resources.

What happens when a manager node fails? The leader will start to store committed changes in order to sync the unhealthy manager node when it is ready again. This will increase Docker Swarm's directory size. If you did not set your node disk space sufficiently to allow for these situations, your nodes will probably consume your entire filesystem if the failure doesn't recover soon. And then, you will get a second unhealthy node and your cluster will be inconsistent. This situation we've described is not a horror movie – it happens all too often on new installations where administrators think that the cluster will be alright with some unhealthy nodes for weeks at a time.

We mentioned one important option in the `docker swarm` command-line table when we talked about Docker Swarm cluster initialization. We will use `docker swarm init --force-new-cluster` in situations where the cluster is unhealthy, but at least one manager is working. If the cluster isn't quorate and no operations can be performed with cluster resources (that is, nodes can't be added/removed and services won't be repaired if they fail), we can force a new cluster. This is an extreme situation.

Take care of your environment before recreating the cluster. Forcing a new cluster will set the node where the command was executed as the leader. All other nodes in the cluster (including those managers that were insufficient for a quorum) will be set as workers. It is like a **cluster quorum reset**. Services and other resources will retain their states and configurations (as they were committed or retrieved from nodes). Therefore, we will end up with a one-manager node cluster with all the other nodes as workers. Services and other stuff should not be affected. In these situations, it is a good practice to review the manager node's logs because some containers can be left unmanaged if some cluster changes were not committed.

Although managers can act as workers, it is safer in production to run workloads on worker-role nodes only. A manager's processes may impact the application and vice versa.

We will always deploy more than one worker in production environments. This will ensure the health of our services if one of the workers goes offline unexpectedly or if we need to perform any maintenance tasks, such as updating Docker Engine. We should usually deploy worker nodes according to our application's resource requirements. Adding workers will increase the total cluster workload capacity.

In the next section, we will learn how to deploy a Docker Swarm cluster.

Creating a Docker Swarm cluster

Now that we have reviewed the Docker Swarm architecture and the command-line actions required to initialize the cluster, we can create a cluster. By the end of this chapter, we will have a fully functional cluster with high availability. Let's start by reviewing the Docker Swarm cluster creation process:

1. First, we initialize a Swarm cluster on a manager node. This node automatically becomes the cluster leader because no other manager is available. If we have a node with multiple interfaces, we will choose which interface will be associated with the control plane and which ones will be announced for other nodes and the Swarm API. The output will vary from the following in your environment. Let's execute docker swarm init:

   ```
   $ docker swarm init
   Swarm initialized: current node (ev4ocuzk6l1j0375z80mkba5f) is now
   a manager.
   To add a worker to this swarm, run the following command:
   docker swarm join --token
   SWMTKN-1-4dtk2ieh3rwjd0se5rzwyf2hbk7zlyxh27pbh4plg2sn0qtitx-50zsub5
   f0s4kchwjcfcbyuzn5  192.168.200.18:2377
   To add a manager to this swarm, run 'docker swarm join-token
   manager' and follow the instructions.
   ```

2. Once the cluster has been created, we can review the cluster nodes and their properties by using docker node ls:

   ```
   $ docker node ls
   ID                              HOSTNAME      STATUS AVAILABILITY
   MANAGER STATUS ENGINE VERSION
   ```

```
ev4ocuzk611j0375z80mkba5f   * sirius     Ready     Active
Leader               19.03.2
```

The first column shows the node object identifier. As we mentioned previously, new objects have been created with Docker Swarm. The second column shows its name from the internal host resolution service (this may contain a **Fully Qualified Domain Name (FQDN)**). Notice the asterisk near the hostname. This means that we are working on this node right now. All the commands are executed on that node, regardless of whether it is a leader.

On Docker Swarm, cluster commands related to cluster-wide objects are only available on manager nodes. We won't need to execute commands on the leader node, but we won't be able to execute any cluster commands on a worker node. We can't list nodes or deploy a service.

The last column shows each node's Docker Engine version. Let's take a look at the STATUS, AVAILABILITY, and MANAGER STATUS columns:

- STATUS, as its name suggests, shows the status of the node within the cluster. If it is not healthy, it will be shown here.
- MANAGER STATUS shows the current role of the node (in this case, the node is the leader). We have three different states:
    - Leader, when the node is the cluster leader.
    - Manager, which means that the node is one of the cluster managers.
    - An empty value will mean that the node has a worker role, and is therefore not part of the control plane.
- AVAILABILITY represents a node's availability to receive workloads. Here, we can see that managers can receive workloads too. We can set this node property. In fact, there are three different states:
    - active, which means that the node will be able to receive any workload.
    - passive, which means that the node will not run any other additional workload. Those already running will maintain their state, but no additional workloads will be allowed.
    - drain is the state that we get when we disable any workload on this node. When this happens, all running workloads on the node will be moved to any other healthy and available node.

We can enforce the behavior of any node when joining the cluster, or even when we create the cluster, using the `--availability` flag with `docker swarm init` or `docker swarm join`. We will set the node availability for new workloads (`active` | `pause` | `drain`). By default, all the nodes will be active and ready to receive workloads.

3. We will join another node as a worker to demonstrate this, using the previously shown cluster initialization output with `docker swarm join`:

```
$ docker swarm join --token
SWMTKN-1-4dtk2ieh3rwjd0se5rzwyf2hbk7z1yxh27pbh4p1g2sn0qtitx-50zsub5
f0s4kchwjcfcbyuzn5 192.168.200.18:2377
```

4. Now, we can review the cluster node status (remember, this command will only be available on manager nodes) once more by executing `docker node ls`:

```
$ docker node ls
ID                              HOSTNAME       STATUS    AVAILABILITY
MANAGER STATUS   ENGINE VERSION
glc1ovbcqubmfw6vgzh5ocjgs      antares        Ready     Active
19.03.5
ev4ocuzk611j0375z80mkba5f * sirius           Ready     Active
Leader           19.03.2
```

In this example, we are executing commands on the `sirius` node (marked with *), which is a leader and hence a manager. Notice that `antares` is a worker node because it has an empty value in the `MANAGER STATUS` column.

We can review node information by executing the `docker node inspect` action (the following output is truncated):

```
$ docker node inspect antares
[
    {
        "ID": "glc1ovbcqubmfw6vgzh5ocjgs",
...
        "Spec": {
            "Labels": {},
            "Role": "worker",
            "Availability": "active"
        },
        "Description": {
            "Hostname": "antares",
            "Platform": {
                "Architecture": "x86_64",
                "OS": "linux"
```

```
        },
        "Resources": {
            "NanoCPUs": 16000000000,
            "MemoryBytes": 33736785920
        },
        "Engine": {
            "EngineVersion": "19.03.5",
            ...
            ...
        },
        "TLSInfo": {
            "TrustRoot": "-----BEGIN CERTIFICATE-----
\nMIIBaTCCARCgAwIBAgIUUB8yKqt3uUh2wmF/z450dyg9EDAwCgYIKoZIzj0EAwIw\
nEzERMA8GA1UEAxMIc3dhcm0tY2EwHhcNMTkxMjI5MTA1NTAwWhcNMzkxMjI0MTA1\n
NTAwWjATMREwDwYDVQQDEwhzd2FybS1jYTBZMBMGByqGSM49AgEGCCqGSM49AwEH\nA
0IABACDe6KWpqXiEMyWB9Qn6y2O2+wH8HLoikR+48xqnjeU0SkW/+rPQkW9PilB\ntI
YGwaviLPXpuL4EpVBWxHtMDQCjQjBAMA4GA1UdDwEB/wQEAwIBBjAPBgNVHRMB\nAf8
EBTADAQH/MB0GA1UdDgQWBBTbL48HmUp/1YB1Zqu3GL7q5oMrwTAKBggqhkjO\nPQQD
AgNHADBEAiAh1TVNulaIHf2vh6zM9v6raer5WgTcGu8xQYBcDViPnwIgU4sl\ntK70b
gSfEzLx6WpOv4yjr+c0tlJt/6Gj3waQl10=\n-----END CERTIFICATE-----\n",
            "CertIssuerSubject":
"MBMxETAPBgNVBAMTCHN3YXJtLWNh",
            "CertIssuerPublicKey":
"MFkwEwYHKoZIzj0CAQYIKoZIzj0DAQcDQgAEAIN7opampeIQzJYH1CfrLY7b7Afwcu
iKRH7jzGqeN5TRKRb/6s9CRb0+KUG0hgbBq+Is9em4vgSlUFbEe0wNAA=="
        }
    },
    "Status": {
        "State": "ready",
        "Addr": "192.168.200.15"
    }
}
]
```

When we inspect a node, information regarding its status, node IP address, and TLS information will be shown in JSON format.

We can use labels on nodes to help Docker Swarm choose the best location for specific workloads. It uses node architectures to deploy workloads in the right place, but if we want a workload to run on a specific node, we can add a unique label and add a constraint to deploy the workload. We will learn more about service locations and labels in the *Chapter labs* section.

Under the `Spec` key, we can review the node role in the `docker node inspect` output. We can change the node role whenever necessary. This is a big improvement over other orchestrators, where roles are static. Keep in mind that role changes will affect your Docker Swarm architecture because it will change the number of managers and worker nodes. Keep high availability in mind, its requirement of an odd number of managers, and the consequences of this in case of node failures.

5. A role is just a node property, which means we can change it just like any other object property. Remember that changes can only be deployed from manager nodes. We change a node's role by executing `docker node update`:

```
$ docker node update --role manager antares
antares
```

Once again, let's list all the nodes in the cluster by executing `docker node ls`, this time with a filter to retrieve only managers:

```
$ docker node ls --filter role=manager
ID HOSTNAME STATUS AVAILABILITY MANAGER STATUS ENGINE VERSION
glc1ovbcqubmfw6vgzh5ocjgs antares Ready Active Reachable 19.03.5
ev4ocuzk611j0375z80mkba5f * sirius Ready Active Leader 19.03.2
```

We can now use `docker node inspect` to retrieve the `ManagerStatus` key:

```
$ docker node inspect antares --format "{{.ManagerStatus}}"
{false reachable 192.168.200.15:2377}
```

Nodes can be removed from the cluster by using `docker node rm`, just as we did with other Docker objects. We will only remove worker nodes. The usual sequence for removing a manager node from a Docker Swarm cluster will require a previous step to change its role to a worker. Once a node role has changed to a worker, we can remove the node. If we need to remove a failed manager, we can force node removal using `--force`. However, this is not recommended as you can leave the cluster in an inconsistent state. The manager's database should be updated before you remove any node, which is why the removal sequence we've described here is so important.

 Remember to make sure that you have an odd number of manager nodes if you demote or remove any manager. If you have problems with the leader when you do not have an odd number of managers, you can reach an inconsistent state when other managers have to elect a new leader.

As we mentioned previously, labels are node properties. We can add and remove them at runtime. This is a big difference compared to the labels learned about in `Chapter 1`, *Modern Infrastructures and Applications with Docker*. Those labels were set at the Docker daemon level and are static. We needed to add them to the `daemon.json` file, so we were required to restart the node's Docker Engine to make them effective. In this case, however, node labels are managed by Docker Swarm and can be changed with the common node object's `update` action (`docker node update`).

 The Docker command line provides some shortcuts, as we have observed in previous chapters. In this case, we can change node roles by demoting a manager to a worker role, or by promoting a worker to a manager role. We use `docker node <promote|demote> <NODENAME_OR_ID>` to change between node roles.

We can also change a node's workload availability. This allows a node to receive (or not) cluster-deployed workloads. As with any other node property, we will use `docker node update --availability <available|drain|pause> <NODENAME_OR_ID>` to drain or pause a node when it was active. Both drain and pause will prevent us from scheduling any new workload on the node, while drain on its own will remove any currently running one from the affected node.

 Remember that when we drain a node, the scheduler will reassign any tasks running on the affected node to another available worker. Keep in mind that the other nodes should have enough resources before draining the given node.

In the next section, we will review how to back up and recover a faulty Docker Swarm cluster.

Recovering a faulty Docker Swarm cluster

We will review a few steps to back up and restore Docker Swarm clusters. Losing your cluster quorum is not a big problem. As we have learned, we can recover the cluster by forcing the initialization of a new one, even with just one healthy manager. However, losing your cluster data will completely destroy your environment if you don't have any manager nodes that are operational and working correctly. In these situations, we can recover the cluster by restoring a copy containing healthy data that was taken when the cluster was running correctly. Let's learn how to take backups of our clusters now.

Backing up your Swarm

As we learned in this chapter, `/var/lib/docker/swarm` (and its Microsoft Windows equivalent directory) contains the key-value store data, the certificates, and the encrypted Raft logs. Without them, we can't recover a faulty cluster, so let's back up this directory on any manager.

Having a consistent backup requires static files. If files are opened or some process is writing them, they will not be consistent. Therefore, we need to stop Docker Engine on the given node. Do not launch the backup procedure on the leader node.

Keep in mind that while the backup operation is running, if the Docker daemon is stopped, the number of managers will be affected. The leader will continue managing changes and generating new sync points to recover synchronization with the lost manager. Your cluster will be vulnerable to losing quorum if other managers fail. If you plan to do daily backups, consider using five managers.

Recovering your Swarm

In case we need to recover a completely failed cluster (where no managers can't achieve quorum and we can't force a new cluster), we will stop Docker Engine on one manager. Remove all `/var/lib/docker/swarm` directory content (or its Microsoft Windows equivalent) and restore the backed-up content to this directory. Then, start Docker Engine again and reinitialize the cluster with `docker swarm init --force-new-cluster`.

When the single-manager cluster is healthy, start to add the other old Swarm cluster managers. Before adding those managers, ensure that they've left the old Swarm cluster.

 If we set up Swarm auto-lock, we will need the key that was stored with the restored backup. Even if you changed it after the backup was issued, you will still need the old one.

In the next section, we will learn how workloads are deployed on the cluster and how Docker Swarm tracks the health of application components to ensure that services are not impacted when something goes wrong.

Scheduling workloads in the cluster – tasks and services

We don't run containers on a Swarm cluster; rather, we deploy services. These are atomic workloads that can be deployed in a Docker Swarm cluster. Services are defined by tasks, and each task is represented by a container in the Docker Swarm model. Swarm is based on SwarmKit and its logic is inherited. SwarmKit was created as a response to clustering any kind of task (such as virtual machines, for example), but Docker Swarm works with containers.

The Docker Swarm orchestrator uses a declarative model. This means that we define the desired state for our services and Docker Swarm will take care of the rest. If the defined number of replicas or tasks for a service is wrong – for example, if one of them died – Docker Swarm will take action to recover the correct state of the service. In this example, it will deploy a new replica to keep all the required nodes healthy.

The following diagram represents services and tasks in relation to containers. The colors service has five replicas (colors.1 to colors.5). Each replica runs on one container from the same image, codegazers/colors:1.13, and these containers run distributed cluster-wide across node1, node2, and node3:

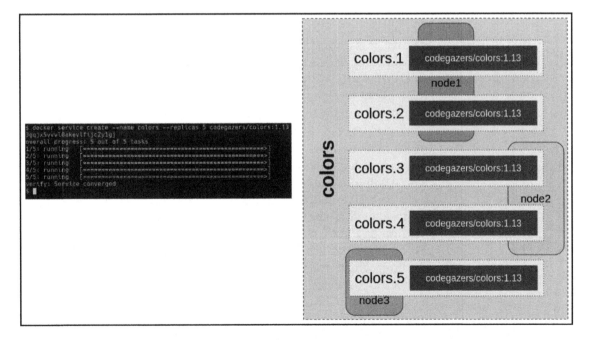

Service creation requires the following information:

- Which image will run the associated containers?
- How many containers does this service require to be healthy?
- Should the service be available to users on any port and protocol?
- How should service updates be managed?
- Is there any preferred location for this service to run?

Service creation will require all this information to be entered on the command line. Since services are Docker objects, we can use common actions such as listing, creating, removing, updating, and inspecting their properties. Docker Swarm will manage all our tasks' integration with services. We will never deploy tasks or containers. We will just create and manage services. Let's take a look at Docker command-line actions and options related to services:

- `create`: This is common to other objects, but services have many non-standard properties. We will not list and review all service arguments because most of them are inherited from containers. Here, we'll review the most important ones related to service behavior:
    - `--config`: We can create a service configuration only, not a real service. This will create all service environments and requirements but without running any task.
    - `--container-label/--label`: We added this option here because it is important to understand that services and containers are different objects and that we can add labels to both. By default, Docker Swarm will create many labels on each service container to relate them to each other. We can easily use those labels to filter information regarding our services' containers on any host.
    - `--constraint/--placement-pref`: As we mentioned previously, we can specify which nodes should run a given service's tasks. We use a list of key-value pairs as constraints to do this. All defined keys must be fulfilled to schedule the service's tasks on a given node. If no node satisfies the defined constraints, the tasks will not be run because Docker Swarm's scheduler will not find any node with those requirements. On the other hand, `placement-pref` will provide a placement preference. This will not limit which nodes will run the tasks, but we can use this to spread our services' tasks across different nodes using a defined key. For example, we might distribute a given service's tasks across different physical locations (such as data centers).

- `--mode`: There are two different service modes (in fact, there are three, as we will find out later in the *Networking in Docker Swarm* section, but at this point, just keep the following two in mind). By default, all services will use replication mode. This means that we will set a number of replicas to be healthy (by default, this is one replica). We also have global services. In this case, we will create as many replicas as nodes in the cluster, but we will just run one replica per node. This mode is very interesting for monitoring applications, for example, because all the nodes will receive their monitoring process. One important thing about these services is that every node that gets into the cluster will receive its own replica. Docker Swarm will deploy it on the new node for us automatically.

- `--with-registry-auth`: This is a very important option because it allows us to distribute credentials among cluster nodes so that we can use private images. It is also important to understand that Docker Swarm requires external or internal registries to work. We will not work with local images on cluster nodes anymore. Local images will lead to inconsistent deployments because image names can match, while content could be completely different across nodes.

- `--endpoint-mode`: This option sets how services announce or manage their tasks. We can use `vip` and `dnsrr` for this. Services will default to `vip`, so each service will receive a virtual IP associated with its name, and an internal load balancer will route traffic to each replicated process (container/task) associated with it. On the other hand, `dnsrr` will use internal name resolution to associate each replica IP address whenever we ask for a service name. This way, internal name resolution will give us a different IP address when a given service has been deployed with more than one task.

- `--network`: We can attach new services to an existing network. As we did with containers, we can also use a host network namespace. The difference here is that we can't execute privileged services, so our services will have to expose ports numbered higher than `1024`.

- `--publish`: We will use this option to publish ports externally. Docker Swarm will expose ports using Docker Swarm's router mesh on every node. If external requests arrive on a host that does not execute any service tasks, Docker Swarm will internally reroute requests to an appropriate node.

- `--replicas`/`--replicas-max-per-node`: Services are defined by how many replicas or tasks are deployed to maintain their healthy state. By default, all services deploy one single replica. As we will see later, we can change the number of replicas at any time we need. Not all application components (processes) will work well if we scale up or down their replicas. Imagine, for example, a SQL database. It is a completely stateful component because the database process will write data. If we add a new database replica accessing the same storage, the database will become corrupted. If each database replica has its own storage, they will manage different data. As a result, not all services can be scaled up or down.

- `--reserve-cpu`/`--reserve-memory`: We can reserve the amount of resources required for a service to work. If no node presents enough resources, it will not be scheduled.

- `--update-delay`/`--update-failure-action`/`--update-max-failure-ratio`/`--update-monitor`/`--update-order`/`--update-parallelism`: `update` options manage how changes are executed for a service. We will set how many services' tasks will be updated at once, how many seconds we will wait between instances' updates, and how the update process will be done. The `--update-order` option sets how this update process will be executed. By default, the running container will be stopped and a new one will be created after the old one is completely finished. With this setting, the service will be impacted. We can set a different order by starting a new container first. Then, once everything is fine, the old one will be stopped. This way, the service will not be impacted, but your application process must be able to allow for this situation. For example, it will not work on a standard SQL database, as we mentioned previously. We will also set what to do when some of the updates fail, either by executing an automatic rollback or by pausing the rest of the service updates until manual action is taken.

- `--rollback-delay`/`--rollback-failure-action`/`--rollback-max-failure-ratio`/`--rollback-monitor`/`--rollback-order`/`--rollback-parallelism`: If the update process goes wrong, we can set an automatic rollback. These settings modify how rollbacks will be done. We have the same options we reviewed for the `update` process, but this time, the arguments will refer to the `rollback` process.

- `ps`: With this, we can review all our service's tasks and their distributions in the cluster. We can also use filters and output format. We will see a couple of examples of this in the *Chapter labs* section.

- `logs`: This is a very useful action because Docker Swarm will retrieve the logs of all our tasks for us. We can then review them from the manager command line instead of going to wherever the tasks were running to read the container's logs.

- `update`: Service properties can be updated. For example, we can change image release versions, publish new ports, and change the number of replicas, among other things.

- `rollback`: With this, we can return to the service's previous properties. It is important to understand that images from previous executions should be kept in our hosts to allow for the application's rollbacks.

- `inspect/ls/rm`: These are the common actions we encounter with all other kinds of objects. We've already learned how to use them.

 It is important to note that privileged containers are not allowed on services. Therefore, if we want to use the host network namespace, container processes should expose and use non-privileged ports (higher than `1024`).

Docker service constraints can be set with custom labels, but there are some internal ones that are created by default that are very useful:

Label	Attribute
`node.id`	Node ID
`node.hostname`	Node hostname; for example, `node.hostname==antares`
`node.role`	Node Swarm role; for example, `node.role!=manager`
`node.labels`	Swarm node-assigned labels; for example, `node.labels.environment==production`
`engine.labels`	Docker Engine-defined labels; for example, `engine.labels.operatingsystem==ubuntu 18.04`

We can use variables to define service properties. In the following example, we're using internal Docker Swarm variables in the container's hostname:

```
$ docker service create --name "top" --hostname="{{.Service.Name}}-{{.Task.ID}}" busybox top
```

To summarize, before continuing with other Swarm resources: services are a group of tasks, each executing one container. All these containers run together to maintain the service's state. Docker Swarm will monitor the service's state and if one container dies, it will run a new container to maintain the number of instances. It is important to note that a container's IDs and names will change. However, while new tasks can be created, the task's name will not be changed.

Let's have a look at a quick example before moving on to the next topic. We will create a simple NGINX web server service using docker service create:

```
$ docker service create --name webserver --publish 80 nginx:alpine
lkcig20f3wpfcbfpe68s72fas
overall progress: 1 out of 1 tasks
1/1: running [==================================================>]
verify: Service converged
```

We can review where the created task is running by using docker service ps:

```
$ docker service ps webserver
ID NAME IMAGE NODE DESIRED STATE CURRENT STATE ERROR PORTS
lb1akyp4dbvc webserver.1 nginx:alpine sirius Running Running about a minute
ago
```

Then, we move to the node where the task is running. Once there, we kill the associated container using docker container kill:

```
$ docker container ls
CONTAINER ID IMAGE COMMAND CREATED STATUS PORTS NAMES
6aeaee25ff9b nginx:alpine "nginx -g 'daemon of..." 6 minutes ago Up 6 minutes
80/tcp webserver.1.lb1akyp4dbvcqcfznezlhr4zk

$ docker container kill 6aeaee25ff9b
6aeaee25ff9b
```

After a few seconds, a new task will be created automatically with a new container. The task name hasn't changed, but it is a new task, as we can tell from its ID:

```
$ docker service ps webserver
ID NAME IMAGE NODE DESIRED STATE CURRENT STATE ERROR PORTS
lnabvvg6k2ne webserver.1 nginx:alpine sirius Running Running less than a
second ago
lb1akyp4dbvc \_ webserver.1 nginx:alpine sirius Shutdown Failed 7 seconds
ago "task: non-zero exit (137)"
```

Finally, we can review some of the labels that were created by Swarm to fully identify containers using their services. We use `docker container inspect` for this:

```
$ docker container ls
CONTAINER ID IMAGE COMMAND CREATED STATUS PORTS NAMES
1d9dc2407f74 nginx:alpine "nginx -g 'daemon of..." 13 minutes ago Up 13
minutes 80/tcp webserver.1.1nabvvg6k2ne6boqv3hvqvth8

$ docker container inspect 1d9dc2407f74 --format "{{.Config.Labels}}"
map[com.docker.swarm.node.id:ev4ocuzk611j0375z80mkba5f
com.docker.swarm.service.id:1kcig20f3wpfcbfpe68s72fas
com.docker.swarm.service.name:webserver com.docker.swarm.task:
com.docker.swarm.task.id:1nabvvg6k2ne6boqv3hvqvth8
com.docker.swarm.task.name:webserver.1.1nabvvg6k2ne6boqv3hvqvth8
maintainer:NGINX Docker Maintainers <docker-maint@nginx.com>]
```

There are some service options that can be set using strings to help us identify their configuration and other associated resources. This is very important when we need to isolate resources attached to a specific service's tasks or use some special information to access other services, such as the container's hostname. We can use labels to add meta-information to containers, but there are also Docker Swarm-defined variables that we can use within strings. These variables use Go's template syntax (as we also learned when formatting the listing command's output) and can be used with `docker service create` and the `--hostname`, `--mount`, and `--env` arguments.

Therefore, we can set an associated service container's hostname to be unique between tasks using these variables; for example, `--hostname="{{.Service.Name}}-{{.Task.ID}}"`. We can even use the node's name to identify this task with the node in which it is running using `--hostname="{{.Node.Hostname}}"`. This can be very useful with global services.

The following is a quick list of valid service template substitutions:

- **Service**: `.Service.ID`, `.Service.Name`, and `.Service.Labels`
- **Node**: `.Node.ID` and `.Node.Hostname`
- **Task**: `.Task.ID`, `.Task.Name`, and `.Task.Slot`

In the next section, we will introduce some new Docker Swarm objects that will help us deploy our applications on clusters.

Deploying applications using Stacks and other Docker Swarm resources

In this section, we will learn about other Docker Swarm objects that will help us to fully deploy applications within the cluster.

We've already learned how to configure applications using environment variables. This is not recommended for production because anyone with system Docker access can read their values. To avoid this situation, we will use external data sources. We also learned how to integrate host resources inside containers. We can set configurations and passwords in files shared between hosts and containers. This will work on standalone environments but not for distributed workloads, where containers can run on different hosts. We will need to sync those files on all cluster nodes.

To avoid syncing files on multiple nodes, Docker Swarm provides two different objects for managing them. We can have private files or secrets and configurations. Both objects store their values in the Swarm key-value store. Stored values will be available for every cluster node that requires them. These objects are similar, but secrets are used for passwords, certificates, and so on, while config objects are used for application configuration files. Now, let's examine them in depth.

Secrets

A secret is a blob of data that contains passwords, certificates, and any other information that should not be shared over the network. They will be stored in an encrypted fashion so that they're safe from snoopers. Docker Swarm will manage and store secrets for us. Because this kind of data is stored in the key-value store, only managers will have access to any secrets we create. When a container needs to use that stored secret, the host responsible for running that container (a service task container) will have access too. The container will receive a temporal filesystem (in-memory `tmpfs` on Linux hosts) containing that secret. When the container dies, the secret will not be accessible on the host. Secrets will only be available to running containers when they are required.

Since secrets are Docker Swarm objects, we can use all of the usual actions (`list`, `create`, `remove`, `inspect`, and so on). Do not expect to read secret data with the `inspect` action. Once created, it is not possible to read or change a secret's content. We create secrets with files or by using standard input for data. We can add labels for easy listing in big cluster environments.

Once a secret has been created, we can use it within our services. We have both short and long notations. By default, using the short format, a file with secret data will be created under /run/secrets/<SECRET_NAME>. This file will be mounted in a tmpfs filesystem on Linux. Windows is different because it does not support on-memory filesystems. We can use the long format to specify the filename to be used for the secret file under /run/secrets, along with its ownership and file permissions. This will help us avoid root usage inside the container in order to access the file. Let's create a secret with docker secret create and then use it on a service:

```
$ echo this_is_a_super_secret_password|docker secret create app-key -
o9sh44stjm3kxau4c5651ujvr

$ docker service create --name database \
  --secret source=ssh-key,target=ssh \
  --secret source=app-key,target=app,uid=1000,gid=1001,mode=0400 \
  redis:3.0
```

As we mentioned previously, it is not possible to retrieve secret data. We can inspect previously created secrets using the common docker secret inspect action:

```
$ docker secret inspect app-key
[
    {
        "ID": "o9sh44stjm3kxau4c5651ujvr",
        "Version": {
            "Index": 12
        },
        "CreatedAt": "2019-12-30T20:42:59.050992148Z",
        "UpdatedAt": "2019-12-30T20:42:59.050992148Z",
        "Spec": {
            "Name": "app-key",
            "Labels": {}
        }
    }
]
```

In the next section, we will learn about configuration objects.

Config

Config objects are similar to secrets, but they aren't encrypted on the Docker Swarm Raft log and will not be mounted on a `tmpfs` filesystem in containers. Configs can be added or removed while service tasks are running. In fact, we can even update service configurations. We will use these objects to store configurations for applications. They can contain strings or binaries (up to 500 KB, which is more than enough for configurations).

When we create a config object, Docker Swarm will store it in the Raft log, which is encrypted, and it will be replicated to other managers by mutual TLS. Therefore, all the managers will have the new config object value.

Using config files on services requires there to be a mount path inside the containers. By default, the mounted configuration file will be world-readable and owned by the user running the container, but we can adjust both properties should we need to.

Let's look at a quick example. We will create a configuration file using `docker config create` and then use it inside a service:

```
$ echo "This is a sample configuration" | docker config create sample-config -
d0nqny24g5y1tiogwggxmesox

$ docker service create \
  --name sample-service \
  --config source=sample-config,target=/etc/sample.cfg,mode=0440 \
  nginx:alpine
```

In this case, we can review the config content and see that it is readable. Using `docker config inspect`, we get the following output:

```
$ docker config inspect sample-config --pretty
ID: d0nqny24g5y1tiogwggxmesox
Name: sample-config
Created at: 2019-12-10 21:07:51.350109588 +0000 utc
Updated at: 2019-12-10 21:07:51.350109588 +0000 utc
Data:
This is a sample configuration
```

Let's move on to stacks.

Stacks

Stacks help us deploy complete applications. They are **Infrastructure-as-Code (IaC)** files with all their component definitions, their interactions, and the external resources required to deploy an application. We will use `docker-compose` file definitions (`docker-compose.yaml`). Not all `docker-compose` file primitive keys will be available. For example, `depends_on` will not be available for stacks because they don't have dependency declarations. This is something you have to manage in your own application logic.

As we learned with the `docker-compose` command in `Chapter 5`, *Deploying Multi-Container Applications*, every application that's deployed will run by default in its own network. When using stacks on Docker Swarm, application components are deployed cluster-wide. Overlay networks will be used because each component should reach others, regardless of where they are running. Stacks will also be deployed on their own networks by default.

Stacks deploy applications based on services. Therefore, we will keep our service definitions in the `docker-compose` file. To be able to identify these services from other stacks, we will set the stacks' names.

 It is important to understand that `docker-compose` will deploy multi-container applications on one Docker Engine, while `docker stack` will deploy multi-service applications on a Swarm cluster. Note that, nonetheless, both use the same kind of IaC file.

Let's have a quick look at the `docker stack` command line:

- `deploy`: Deploying Stacks requires a `docker-compose` file version of 3.0 and above. We will use the `deploy` action to create and run all application components at once. It is also possible to use a Docker Application Bundle file, which is something that will not be covered in this book, but it is good to know that we have multiple options with Docker Stacks for deploying applications on Docker Swarm. As we mentioned previously, we will need to name our stack's deployment to fully identify all its components within the cluster. All of the stack's resources will receive the stack's name as a prefix unless they were externally created from the stack's file definition. In this latter case, they will retain their original names.

- These are the main options for `docker stack deploy`:

  - `--compose-file/-c`: We use `docker-compose.yaml` as the stack definition file unless we specify a custom filename with this option.
  - `--orchestrator`: This option was recently added and allows us to choose which orchestrator will deploy and manage the stack. We will be able to choose between Docker Swarm and Kubernetes when both are available in our environment.
  - `--with-registry-auth`: As we learned with services, sharing authentication is vital when using private registries. Without this option, we can't ensure all the nodes are using the same image or that they have access to the registry because this will depend on locally stored authentication.

- `services`: The `services` option shows us a list of the deployed stack's services. As with all other listing actions, we can format and filter its output.
- `ps`: This action lists all the services and where tasks were deployed. It is easy to filter and format its output, as we will see in the *Chapter labs* section of this chapter.
- `ls/rm`: These are common object actions for listing and removing them.

There is not much more to say about stacks. IaC requires that every deployment is reproducible. Even for a simple standalone service, make sure to use a stack file to deploy it. The *Chapter labs* section will cover these actions and options with some more examples. In the next section, we will learn how Swarm can change application networking cluster-wide.

Networking in Docker Swarm

When we talk about Docker Swarm, we need to introduce a new concept regarding networks: *overlay* networks. As we mentioned at the beginning of this chapter, a new network driver will be available because Docker Swarm will distribute all application components across multiple nodes. They have to be reachable no matter where they run. The overlay network will work over VXLAN tunnels using the **User Datagram Protocol (UDP)**. We will be able to encrypt this communication, but some overhead should normally be expected.

The overlay network driver will create a distributed network across cluster nodes and automatically provides routing of packets to interconnect distributed containers.

When Swarm is first initialized, two networks are created:

- `docker_gwbridge`: This bridge network will connect all Docker daemons that are part of the cluster.
- `ingress`: This is an overlay network that will manage Docker Swarm services' control and data traffic. All the services will be connected to this network so that they can reach each other if we do not specify any custom overlay network.

Docker Swarm will only manage overlay networks. We can create new overlay networks for our applications that will be isolated from each other. The same happens when working locally with custom bridged networks. We will be able to connect services to different networks at once, as we did with bridged environments. We will also be able to connect containers to overlay networks, although this is not something that's commonly done. Remember that we will not run standalone containers in Docker Swarm.

If firewalls are enabled in your environment, you'll need to allow the following traffic:

Port or Range of Ports	Protocol	Purpose
2377	TCP	Cluster management traffic
7946	TCP/UDP	Swarm node intercommunication
4789	UDP	Overlay networking

Docker Swarm management traffic is always encrypted by default, as we learned in previous sections. We can also encrypt overlay networking. When we use encryption arguments on overlay network creation, Docker Swarm creates **Internet Protocol Security (IPSEC)** encryption on overlay VXLANs. It adds security, though a performance overhead is to be expected. It is up to you to manage the balance between security and performance in your applications. As encryption is done upon network creation, it can't be changed once the network has been created.

Creating overlay networks is easy – we just specify the overlay driver with `docker network create`:

```
$ docker network create -d overlay testnet
1ff11sixrjj7cqppgoxhrdu3z
```

By default, it is created unencrypted and non-attachable. This means that containers will not be able to connect to this network. Only services will be allowed. Let's verify this by trying to attach a simple container to the created network using `docker container run`:

```
$ docker container run -ti --network testnet alpine
Unable to find image 'alpine:latest' locally
latest: Pulling from library/alpine
Digest:
sha256:2171658620155679240babee0a7714f6509fae66898db422ad803b951257db78
Status: Downloaded newer image for alpine:latest
docker: Error response from daemon: Could not attach to network testnet:
rpc error: code = PermissionDenied desc = network testnet not manually
attachable.
```

To avoid this, we need to declare the network as attachable from the very beginning. This second example also adds an encryption option using `docker network create --attachable --opt encrypted`:

```
$ docker network create -d overlay testnet2 --attachable --opt encrypted
9blpskhcvahonytkifn31w91d

$ docker container run -ti --network testnet2 alpine
/ #
```

We connected to the newer sample encrypted network without any problem because it was created with the `attachable` property.

All services that are connected to the same overlay network will see each other by their names, and all their exposed ports will be available internally, regardless of whether they are published.

> By default, all Swarm overlay networks will have 24-bit masks, which means we will be able to allocate 255 IP addresses. Each service that's deployed may consume multiple IP addresses, as well as one for each node peering on a given overlay network. You may run into IP exhaustion in some situations. To avoid this, consider creating bigger networks if many services need to use them.

In the next section, we will take a closer look at service discovery and how Docker routes traffic to all service replicas.

Service discovery and load balancing

Docker Swarm has internal **Internet Protocol Address Management (IPAM)** and **Domain Name System (DNS)** components to automatically assign a virtual IP address and a DNS entry for each service that's created. Internal load balancing will distribute requests among a service's tasks based on the service's DNS name. As we mentioned earlier, all the services on the same network will know each other and will be reachable on their exposed ports.

Docker Swarm managers (in fact, the leader) will use the created ingress overlay network to publish the services we declared as accessible from outside the cluster. If no port was declared during service creation, Docker Swarm will automatically assign one for each exposed port that's declared in the `30000-32767` range. We have to manually declare any port above `1024` because we can't create privileged services.

All the nodes will participate in this ingress router mesh. Therefore, the nodes will accept connections on the published port, regardless of whether they run one of the requested tasks. The router mesh will route all incoming requests to published ports on all the nodes to running tasks (containers). Therefore, published ports will be allocated on all Swarm nodes and hence only one service will be able to use declared ports. In other words, if we publish a service on port `8080`, we will not be able to reuse that port for another service. This will limit the maximum number of services that can run on the cluster to the number of free ports available on the Linux or Windows systems used. We learned that Docker Engine will not be able to publish more than one container on the same port using NAT. In this case, all the nodes will fix ports to published services.

The router mesh listens on the published ports on all the node's available IP addresses. We will use cluster-external load balancers to route traffic to the cluster's hosts. We usually use a couple of them for publishing, with the load balancer forwarding all requests to them.

 We can use `docker service update` to modify or remove already declared ports or add new ones.

The following schema shows how a router mesh works on a three-node cluster publishing a service with two replicas. The **colors** service runs two tasks. Therefore, one container runs on **NODE1** and **NODE2**, respectively (these are Docker Swarm-scheduled tasks on the nodes in the following diagram). Internally, these containers expose their application on port 3000. The service that defined that container's port as 3000 will be published on the host's port; that is, 8080. This port will be published on all the nodes, even if they do not run any service tasks. Internal load balancing will route requests to the appropriate containers using the ingress overlay network. Finally, users will access the published service through an external load balancer. This is not part of the Docker Swarm environment, but it helps us to provide high-availability forwarding requests to a set of available nodes:

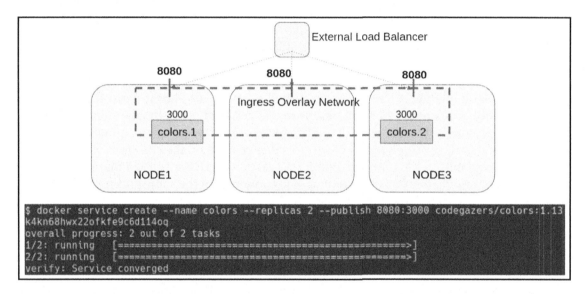

We will have short and long formats for publishing services. Long formats always provide more options. In the following example, we're publishing an NGINX process on cluster port 8080 and forwarding its traffic to the container's port, 80, using docker service create --publish:

```
$ docker service create --name webserver \
  --publish published=8080,target=80,protocol=tcp \
nginx:alpine
```

On any node, we will be able to access the NGINX service on port `8080`. We can test this using the `curl` command:

```
$ curl -I 0.0.0.0:8080
HTTP/1.1 200 OK
Server: nginx/1.17.6
Date: Tue, 31 Dec 2019 17:51:26 GMT
Content-Type: text/html
Content-Length: 612
Last-Modified: Tue, 19 Nov 2019 15:14:41 GMT
Connection: keep-alive
ETag: "5dd406e1-264"
Accept-Ranges: bytes
```

We can retrieve the current service tasks' IP addresses by querying the DNS for `tasks.<SERVICE_NAME>`.

By default, all the services use the router mesh. However, we can avoid this default behavior, as we will see in the following section.

Bypassing the router mesh

Using host mode or a **Round-Robin DNS (RRDNS)** endpoint, we can bypass the router mesh. This will allow us to access instances on given nodes on defined ports or apply our own load balancer. In some situations, we need to include special load balancing features such as weights or persistence of users' sessions. The default Docker Swarm's router mesh behavior will route requests to all available services' backend instances. It is important to identify your application's requirements to determine whether you should deploy its components using Docker Swarm's default load balancing.

Docker's internal load balancer will just do L3 routing. It will not provide any weight-based routing or special features.

Using host mode

Using host mode, only nodes with running instances will receive traffic. We can label nodes so that they only schedule some tasks on them and route traffic to them from load balancers. In this case, we can't run more replicas for this service than the defined and labeled number of nodes.

In the following example, we will run one NGINX process on each node in the cluster since we defined a global service. We will use `docker service create --mode global --publish mode=host`:

```
$ docker service create --name webserver \
  --publish published=8080,target=80,protocol=tcp,mode=host \
  --mode global \
nginx:alpine
```

The service's defined port will be available on all the nodes in the cluster.

Using Round-Robin DNS mode

We can also use RRDNS mode to avoid the service's virtual IP address. In this situation, Docker Swarm will not assign a virtual IP for the service, so it will create a service DNS entry with all its replicas' IP addresses. This is useful when we want to use our own load balancer inside the Docker Swarm cluster to deploy this load balancer as another service. It is not easy to maintain the IP addresses of replicas inside the load balancer service. We will probably use DNS resolution inside the load balancer's configuration, querying the DNS to retrieve all instances' IP addresses.

The next section will help us understand the concepts we've learned in this chapter with some labs.

Chapter labs

Now, we will complete this chapter's lab to help us improve our understanding of the concepts we've learned. Deploy environments/swarm-environment from this book's GitHub repository (https://github.com/PacktPublishing/Docker-Certified-Associate-DCA-Exam-Guide.git) if you have not done so yet. You can use your own Linux server. Use vagrant up from the environments/swarm folder to start your virtual environment.

Wait until all your nodes are running. We can check the nodes' status using `vagrant status`. Connect to your lab node using `vagrant ssh swarm-node1`. Vagrant has deployed four nodes for you. You will be using the `vagrant` user with root privileges using `sudo`. You should get the following output:

```
Docker-Certified-Associate-DCA-Exam-Guide/environments/swarm$ vagrant up
----------------------------------------------------------------------
------------------
Docker SWARM MODE Vagrant Environment
Engine Version: current
Experimental Features Enabled
----------------------------------------------------------------------
------------------
Bringing machine 'swarm-node1' up with 'virtualbox' provider...
Bringing machine 'swarm-node2' up with 'virtualbox' provider...
Bringing machine 'swarm-node3' up with 'virtualbox' provider...
Bringing machine 'swarm-node4' up with 'virtualbox' provider...

...
Docker-Certified-Associate-DCA-Exam-Guide/environments/swarm$
```

Nodes will have three interfaces (IP addresses and virtual hardware resources can be modified by changing the `config.yml` file):

- `eth0` [10.0.2.15]: Internal, required for Vagrant.
- `eth1` [10.10.10.X/24]: Prepared for Docker Swarm internal communication. The first node will get the IP address `10.10.10.11`, and so on.
- `eth2` [192.168.56.X/24]: A host-only interface for communication between your host and the virtual nodes. The first node will get the IP address `192.168.56.11`, and so on.

We will use the `eth1` interface for Docker Swarm and we will be able to connect to published applications using the `192.168.56.X/24` IP address range. All nodes have Docker Engine Community Edition installed and the `vagrant` user is allowed to execute `docker`.

Now, we can connect to the first deployed virtual node using `vagrant ssh swarm-node1`. This process may vary if you've already deployed a Docker Swarm virtual environment before and just started it using `vagrant up`:

```
Docker-Certified-Associate-DCA-Exam-Guide/environments/swarm$ vagrant ssh
swarm-node1
vagrant@swarm-node1:~$
```

Now, you are ready to start the labs. Let's start by creating a Docker Swarm cluster.

Creating a Docker Swarm cluster

Once Vagrant (or your own environment) has been deployed, we will have four nodes (named node<index>, from 1 to 4) with Ubuntu Xenial and Docker Engine installed.

First, review your lab node's IP addresses (10.10.10.11 to 10.10.10.14 if you used Vagrant since the first interface will be Vagrant's internal host-to-node interface). Once you are familiar with the environment's IP addresses, we can initiate a cluster on node1, for example.

 If you are using Linux as a VirtualBox host, you can execute alias vssh='vagrant ssh' on your Terminal to use vssh instead of vagrant ssh to connect to nodes as it will be more familiar with non-Vagrant-based real environments.

Now that we have our environment ready for the labs, along with four nodes and Docker Engine already installed, let's get started:

1. Connect to node1 and initialize a new cluster using docker swarm init:

```
Docker-Certified-Associate-DCA-Exam-Guide/environments/swarm$
vagrant ssh swarm-node1
-------------------------------------------------------------
--------------------------
 Docker SWARM MODE Vagrant Environment
 Engine Version: current
 Experimental Features Enabled
-------------------------------------------------------------
--------------------------
 . . .
 . . .

vagrant@swarm-node1:~$ docker swarm init
Error response from daemon: could not choose an IP address to
advertise since this system has multiple addresses on different
interfaces (10.0.2.15 on eth0 and 10.10.10.11 on eth1) - specify
one with --advertise-addr
```

This is normal if you are using Vagrant as nodes will have at least two interfaces. The first interface is internal to Vagrant, while the other is the one fixed for the labs. In this case, we will need to specify which interface to use for the cluster with `--advertise-addr`. We will execute `docker swarm init --advertise-addr`:

```
vagrant@swarm-node1:~$ docker swarm init --advertise-addr
10.10.10.11
Swarm initialized: current node (b1t5o5x8mqbz77e9v4ihd7cec) is now
a manager.

To add a worker to this swarm, run the following command:

    docker swarm join --token
SWMTKN-1-3xfi4qggreh811br98d63x7299gtz1fanwfjkselg9ok5wroje-
didcmb39w7apwokrah6xx4cus 10.10.10.11:2377

To add a manager to this swarm, run 'docker swarm join-token
manager' and follow the instructions.
```

Now, Swarm is initialized correctly.

2. Add a second node that's connecting to `node2` and executing the command described in the initialization output. We will join the cluster using the `docker swarm join` command with the obtained token:

```
Docker-Certified-Associate-DCA-Exam-Guide/environments/swarm$
vagrant ssh swarm-node2

vagrant@swarm-node2:~$ docker swarm join --token
SWMTKN-1-3xfi4qggreh811br98d63x7299gtz1fanwfjkselg9ok5wroje-
didcmb39w7apwokrah6xx4cus 10.10.10.11:2377
This node joined a swarm as a worker.
```

With this, a node is added as a worker.

3. On `node1`, verify that the new node was added by using `docker node ls`:

```
Docker-Certified-Associate-DCA-Exam-Guide/environments/swarm$
vagrant ssh swarm-node1

vagrant@swarm-node1:~$ docker node ls
ID HOSTNAME STATUS AVAILABILITY MANAGER STATUS ENGINE VERSION
b1t5o5x8mqbz77e9v4ihd7cec * swarm-node1 Ready Active Leader 19.03.5
rj3rgb9egnb256cms0zt8pqew swarm-node2 Ready Active 19.03.5
```

Notice that `swarm-node1` is the leader because this is the node that initialized the cluster. We couldn't have executed `docker node ls` on `swarm-node2` because it was not a manager node.

4. We will execute the same joining process on `swarm-node3`, using `docker swarm join` again:

```
vagrant@swarm-node1:~$ docker node ls
ID HOSTNAME STATUS AVAILABILITY MANAGER STATUS ENGINE VERSION
b1t5o5x8mqbz77e9v4ihd7cec * swarm-node1 Ready Active Leader 19.03.5
rj3rgb9egnb256cms0zt8pqew swarm-node2 Ready Active 19.03.5
ui67xyztnw8kn6fjjezjdtwxd swarm-node3 Ready Active 19.03.5
```

5. Now, we will review the token for managers, so the next node will be added as a manager. We will use `docker swarm join-token manager`:

```
vagrant@swarm-node1:~$ docker swarm join-token manager
To add a manager to this swarm, run the following command:

    docker swarm join --token
SWMTKN-1-3xfi4qggreh81lbr98d63x7299gtz1fanwfjkselg9ok5wroje-
aidvtmglkdyvvqurnivcsmyzm 10.10.10.11:2377
```

Now, we connect to `swarm-node4` and execute the shown joining command (`docker swarm join`) with the new token:

```
vagrant@swarm-node4:~$ docker swarm join --token
SWMTKN-1-3xfi4qggreh81lbr98d63x7299gtz1fanwfjkselg9ok5wroje-
aidvtmglkdyvvqurnivcsmyzm 10.10.10.11:2377
This node joined a swarm as a manager
```

6. The cluster now has four nodes: two managers and two workers. This will not provide high availability should the leader fail. Let's promote `swarm-node2` to the manager role too, for example, by executing `docker node update --role manager`:

```
vagrant@swarm-node4:~$ docker node update --role manager swarm-
node2
swarm-node2
```

We can change node roles using the `promote` and `demote` commands as well, but it is more convenient to know what they really mean for node property updates. Also, notice that we can change node roles whenever we want, but we should maintain the number of healthy managers.

We can review the node's status again. Managers are shown as `Reachable` or `Leader`, indicating that this node is the cluster leader. Using `docker node ls`, we get the following output:

```
vagrant@swarm-node4:~$ docker node ls
ID HOSTNAME STATUS AVAILABILITY MANAGER STATUS ENGINE VERSION
b1t5o5x8mqbz77e9v4ihd7cec swarm-node1 Ready Active Leader 19.03.5
rj3rgb9egnb256cms0zt8pqew swarm-node2 Ready Active Reachable
19.03.5
ui67xyztnw8kn6fjjezjdtwxd swarm-node3 Ready Active 19.03.5
jw9uvjcsyg05u1slm4wu0hz61 * swarm-node4 Ready Active Reachable
19.03.5
```

Notice that we executed these commands on `node4`. We can do this because it is a manager (not a leader, but a manager). We can use any manager to manage the cluster, but only the leader will perform updates on the internal database.

7. We will just leave one manager for the rest of the labs, but first, we will kill the `node1` Docker Engine daemon to see what happens in the cluster. We will stop the Docker daemon using `systemctl stop docker`:

```
Docker-Certified-Associate-DCA-Exam-Guide/environments/swarm$
vagrant ssh swarm-node1

vagrant@swarm-node1:~$ sudo systemctl stop docker
```

Connect to the other manager (`node2`, for example; that is, the recently promoted node). Now, let's review the node's status with `docker node ls`:

```
Docker-Certified-Associate-DCA-Exam-Guide/environments/swarm$
vagrant ssh swarm-node2

vagrant@swarm-node2$ docker node ls
ID HOSTNAME STATUS AVAILABILITY MANAGER STATUS ENGINE VERSION
b1t5o5x8mqbz77e9v4ihd7cec swarm-node1 Down Active Unreachable
19.03.5
rj3rgb9egnb256cms0zt8pqew * swarm-node2 Ready Active Reachable
19.03.5
ui67xyztnw8kn6fjjezjdtwxd swarm-node3 Ready Active 19.03.5
jw9uvjcsyg05u1slm4wu0hz61 swarm-node4 Ready Active Leader 19.03.5
```

A new leader was elected from among the other running managers. Now, we can start the `node1` Docker Engine daemon again using `systemctl start docker`:

```
Docker-Certified-Associate-DCA-Exam-Guide/environments/swarm$
vagrant ssh swarm-node1

vagrant@swarm-node1$ sudo systemctl start docker

vagrant@swarm-node1$ docker node ls
ID HOSTNAME STATUS AVAILABILITY MANAGER STATUS ENGINE VERSION
b1t5o5x8mqbz77e9v4ihd7cec * swarm-node1 Ready Active Reachable
19.03.5
rj3rgb9egnb256cms0zt8pqew swarm-node2 Ready Active Reachable
19.03.5
ui67xyztnw8kn6fjjezjdtwxd swarm-node3 Ready Active 19.03.5
jw9uvjcsyg05u1slm4wu0hz61 swarm-node4 Ready Active Leader 19.03.5
```

The node remains as a manager but is no longer the leader of the cluster because a new one was elected when it failed.

8. Let's demote all non-leader nodes to workers for the rest of the labs using `docker node update --role worker`:

```
vagrant@swarm-node1$ docker node update --role worker swarm-node2
swarm-node2

vagrant@swarm-node1:~$ docker node update --role worker swarm-node1
swarm-node1

vagrant@swarm-node1:~$ docker node ls
Error response from daemon: This node is not a swarm manager.
Worker nodes can't be used to view or modify cluster state. Please
run this command on a manager node or promote the current node to a
manager.
```

Notice the error when listing again. `node1` is not a manager now, so we can't manage the cluster from this node anymore. All management commands will now run from `node4` for the rest of the labs. `node4` is the only manager, which makes it the cluster leader, as we can observe using `docker node ls` once more:

```
Docker-Certified-Associate-DCA-Exam-Guide/environments/swarm$
vagrant ssh swarm-node4

vagrant@swarm-node4:~$ docker node ls
ID                               HOSTNAME     STATUS   AVAILABILITY
MANAGER STATUS    ENGINE VERSION
b1t5o5x8mqbz77e9v4ihd7cec        swarm-node1  Ready    Active
```

```
19.03.5
rj3rgb9egnb256cms0zt8pqew        swarm-node2      Ready      Active
19.03.5
ui67xyztnw8kn6fjjezjdtwxd        swarm-node3      Ready      Active
19.03.5
jw9uvjcsyg05u1slm4wu0hz6l *      swarm-node4      Ready      Active
Leader                  19.03.5
```

In the next lab, we will deploy a simple web server service.

Deploying a simple replicated service

From `swarm-node4`, we will create a replicated service (by default) and test how we can distribute more replicas on different nodes. Let's get started:

1. Deploy the `webserver` service using a simple `nginx:alpine` image by executing `docker service create`:

   ```
   vagrant@swarm-node4:~$ docker service create --name webserver
   nginx:alpine
   kh906v3xg1ni98xk466kk48p4
   overall progress: 1 out of 1 tasks
   1/1: running [==================================================>]
   verify: Service converged
   ```

   Notice that we had to wait a few seconds until all the instances were correctly running. The amount of time this takes may vary if the image has some configured health check.

    We can overwrite the image-defined health checks on service creation or by updating the configuration using `--health-cmd` and other related arguments. In fact, we can change almost everything on a used image, just as we did with containers.

2. Once it is deployed, we can review where the replica was started by using `docker service ps`:

   ```
   vagrant@swarm-node4:~$ docker service ps webserver
   ID                    NAME                 IMAGE                 NODE
   DESIRED STATE         CURRENT STATE              ERROR
   PORTS
   wb4knzpud1z5          webserver.1          nginx:alpine          swarm-
   node3                 Running              Running 14 seconds ago
   ```

In this case, `nginx` was deployed on `swarm-node3`. This may vary in your environment.

3. We can scale the number of replicas to 3 and review how they were distributed. We will use `docker service update --replicas` for this:

```
$ docker service update --replicas 3 webserver
webserver
overall progress: 3 out of 3 tasks
1/3: running [==================================================>]
2/3: running [==================================================>]
3/3: running [==================================================>]
verify: Service converged
```

If we review the replicas' distribution, we can discover where the containers are running using `docker service ps webserver`:

```
vagrant@swarm-node4:~$ docker service ps webserver
ID NAME IMAGE NODE DESIRED STATE CURRENT STATE ERROR PORTS
wb4knzpud1z5 webserver.1 nginx:alpine swarm-node3 Running Running 2
minutes ago
ie9br2pblxu6 webserver.2 nginx:alpine swarm-node4 Running Running
50 seconds ago
9d021pmvnnrq webserver.3 nginx:alpine swarm-node1 Running Running
50 seconds ago
```

Notice that, in this case, `swarm-node2` did not receive a replica, but we can force replicas to run there.

4. To force specific locations, we can add labels to specific nodes and add constraints to nodes. We'll add a label using `docker node update --label-add`:

```
vagrant@swarm-node4:~$ docker node update --label-add tier=front
swarm-node2
swarm-node2
```

Now, we can modify the current service so that it runs on specific nodes labeled as `tier==front`. We will use `docker service update --constraint-add node.labels.tier` and then review its distributed tasks again with `docker service ps`:

```
vagrant@swarm-node4:~$ docker service update --constraint-add
node.labels.tier==front webserver
webserver
overall progress: 3 out of 3 tasks
```

```
1/3: running
[==================================================>]
2/3: running
[==================================================>]
3/3: running
[==================================================>]
verify: Service converged

vagrant@swarm-node4:~$ docker service ps webserver
ID                      NAME                    IMAGE               NODE
DESIRED STATE           CURRENT STATE               ERROR
PORTS
wjgkgkn0ullj            webserver.1             nginx:alpine        swarm-
node2                   Running                 Running 24 seconds ago
wb4knzpud1z5              \_ webserver.1        nginx:alpine        swarm-
node3                   Shutdown                Shutdown 25 seconds ago
bz2b4dw1emvw            webserver.2             nginx:alpine        swarm-
node2                   Running                 Running 26 seconds ago
ie9br2pb1xu6             \_ webserver.2         nginx:alpine        swarm-
node4                   Shutdown                Shutdown 27 seconds ago
gwzvykixd5oy            webserver.3             nginx:alpine        swarm-
node2                   Running                 Running 28 seconds ago
9d021pmvnnrq             \_ webserver.3         nginx:alpine        swarm-
node1                   Shutdown                Shutdown 29 seconds ago
```

Now, all the replicas are running on `swarm-node2`.

5. Now, we will perform some maintenance tasks on `node2`. In this situation, we will remove the `service` constraint before draining `swarm-node2`. If we do not do that, no other node will receive workloads because they are restricted to `tier=front` node labels. We removed the service's constraints using `docker service update --constraint-rm node.labels.tier`:

```
vagrant@swarm-node4:~$ docker service update --constraint-rm
node.labels.tier==front webserver
webserver
overall progress: 3 out of 3 tasks
1/3: running
[==================================================>]
2/3: running
[==================================================>]
3/3: running
[==================================================>]
verify: Service converged

vagrant@swarm-node4:~$ docker service ps webserver
ID                      NAME                    IMAGE               NODE
```

DESIRED STATE	CURRENT STATE	ERROR	
PORTS			
wjgkgkn0ullj	webserver.1	nginx:alpine	swarm-
node2	Running	Running 4 minutes ago	
wb4knzpud1z5	_ webserver.1	nginx:alpine	swarm-
node3	Shutdown	Shutdown 4 minutes ago	
bz2b4dw1emvw	webserver.2	nginx:alpine	swarm-
node2	Running	Running 4 minutes ago	
ie9br2pblxu6	_ webserver.2	nginx:alpine	swarm-
node4	Shutdown	Shutdown 4 minutes ago	
gwzvykixd5oy	webserver.3	nginx:alpine	swarm-
node2	Running	Running 4 minutes ago	
9d021pmvnnrq	_ webserver.3	nginx:alpine	swarm-
node1	Shutdown	Shutdown 4 minutes ago	

The tasks did not move to other nodes because the tasks were already satisfying the service constraints (no constraint in the new situation).

 Docker Swarm will never move tasks if it is not really necessary because it will always try to avoid any service disruption. We can force an update regarding service task redistribution by using `docker service update --force <SERVICE_NAME>`.

6. In this step, we will pause `swarm-node3` and drain `swarm-node2`. We will use `docker node update --availability pause` and `docker node update --availability drain` to do so, respectively:

```
vagrant@swarm-node4:~$ docker node update --availability pause
swarm-node3
swarm-node3

vagrant@swarm-node4:~$ docker node update --availability drain
swarm-node2
swarm-node2
```

Now, let's review our service replica distribution again using `docker service ps`:

```
vagrant@swarm-node4:~$ docker service ps webserver --filter
desired-state=running
```

ID	NAME	IMAGE	NODE
DESIRED STATE	CURRENT STATE	ERROR	
PORTS			
6z55nch0q8ai	webserver.1	nginx:alpine	swarm-
node4	Running	Running 3 minutes ago	
8i159udc4iey	webserver.2	nginx:alpine	swarm-
node4	Running	Running 3 minutes ago	

```
1y4q96hb3hik          webserver.3          nginx:alpine          swarm-
node1                 Running              Running 3 minutes ago
```

Notice that only `swarm-node1` and `swarm-node4` get some tasks because `swarm-node3` is paused and we removed all tasks on `swarm-node2`.

We can use `docker node ps <NODE>` to get all the tasks from all the services running on the specified node.

7. We will remove the `webserver` service and enable nodes `node2` and `node3` again. We will execute `docker service rm` to remove the service:

    ```
    vagrant@swarm-node4:~$ docker service rm webserver
    webserver

    vagrant@swarm-node4:~$ docker node update --availability active
    swarm-node2
    swarm-node2

    vagrant@swarm-node4:~$ docker node update --availability active
    swarm-node3
    swarm-node3
    ```

In the next lab, we will create a global service.

Deploying a global service

In this lab, we will deploy a global service. It will run one task on each cluster node. Let's learn how to use `global` mode:

1. In this chapter, we learned that global services will deploy one replica on each node. Let's create one and review its distribution. We will use `docker service create  --mode global`:

    ```
    vagrant@swarm-node4:~$ docker service create --name webserver --
    mode global nginx:alpine
    4xww1in0ozy3g8q6yb6rlbidr
    overall progress: 4 out of 4 tasks
    ui67xyztnw8k: running
    [==================================================>]
    b1t5o5x8mqbz: running
    [==================================================>]
    rj3rgb9egnb2: running
    ```

```
[===========================================>]
jw9uvjcsyg05: running
[===========================================>]
verify: Service converged
```

All the nodes receive their own replicas, as we can see with `docker service ps`:

```
vagrant@swarm-node4:~$ docker service ps webserver --filter
desired-state=running
ID                      NAME                                        IMAGE
NODE                    DESIRED STATE          CURRENT STATE
ERROR                   PORTS
0jb3tolmta6u            webserver.ui67xyztnw8kn6fjjezjdtwxd
nginx:alpine            swarm-node3            Running
Running about a minute ago
im69ybzgd879            webserver.rj3rgb9egnb256cms0zt8pqew
nginx:alpine            swarm-node2            Running
Running about a minute ago
knh5ntkx7b3r            webserver.jw9uvjcsyg05u1slm4wu0hz61
nginx:alpine            swarm-node4            Running
Running about a minute ago
26kzify7m7xd            webserver.b1t5o5x8mqbz77e9v4ihd7cec
nginx:alpine            swarm-node1            Running
Running about a minute ago
```

2. We will now drain `swarm-node1`, for example, and review the new task distribution. We will drain the node using `docker node update --availability drain`:

```
vagrant@swarm-node4:~$ docker node update --availability drain
swarm-node1
swarm-node1

vagrant@swarm-node4:~$ docker service ps webserver --filter
desired-state=running
ID                      NAME                                        IMAGE
NODE                    DESIRED STATE          CURRENT STATE
ERROR                   PORTS
0jb3tolmta6u            webserver.ui67xyztnw8kn6fjjezjdtwxd
nginx:alpine            swarm-node3            Running
Running 3 minutes ago
im69ybzgd879            webserver.rj3rgb9egnb256cms0zt8pqew
nginx:alpine            swarm-node2            Running
Running 3 minutes ago
knh5ntkx7b3r            webserver.jw9uvjcsyg05u1slm4wu0hz61
nginx:alpine            swarm-node4            Running
Running 3 minutes ago
```

None of the nodes received the `swarm-node1` task because global services will only run one replica of a defined service.

3. If we enable `swarm-node1` once more using `docker node update --availability active`, its replica will start to run again:

```
vagrant@swarm-node4:~$ docker node update --availability active
swarm-node1
node1
vagrant@swarm-node4:~$ docker service ps webserver --filter
desired-state=running
ID                      NAME                                            IMAGE
NODE                    DESIRED STATE           CURRENT STATE
ERROR                   PORTS
sun8lxwu6p3k            webserver.b1t5o5x8mqbz77e9v4ihd7cec
nginx:alpine            swarm-node1             Running
Running 1 second ago
0jb3tolmta6u            webserver.ui67xyztnw8kn6fjjezjdtwxd
nginx:alpine            swarm-node3             Running
Running 5 minutes ago
im69ybzgd879            webserver.rj3rgb9egnb256cms0zt8pqew
nginx:alpine            swarm-node2             Running
Running 5 minutes ago
knh5ntkx7b3r            webserver.jw9uvjcsyg05u1slm4wu0hz6l
nginx:alpine            swarm-node4             Running
Running 5 minutes ago
```

Swarm will run one task of any global service on each node. When a new node joins the cluster, it will also receive one replica of each global service defined in the cluster.

4. We will remove the `webserver` service again to clear the cluster for the following labs by using `docker service rm webserver`:

```
vagrant@swarm-node4:~$ docker service rm webserver
webserver
```

We will now take a quick look at service updates to learn how to update a service's base image.

Updating a service's base image

Let's learn how to refresh a new image version of a deployed and running service while *avoiding* user access interruption:

1. First, we create a 6-replica `webserver` service using `docker service create --replicas 6`:

```
vagrant@swarm-node4:~$ docker service create --name webserver \
--replicas 6 --update-delay 10s --update-order start-first \
nginx:alpine
vpllw7cxlma7mwojdyswbkmbk
overall progress: 6 out of 6 tasks
1/6: running
[==================================================>]
2/6: running
[==================================================>]
3/6: running
[==================================================>]
4/6: running
[==================================================>]
5/6: running
[==================================================>]
6/6: running
[==================================================>]
verify: Service converged
```

2. Next, we update to a specific `nginx:alpine` version with `perl` support, for example. We use `docker service update --image` to change only its base image:

```
vagrant@swarm-node4:~$ docker service update --image nginx:alpine-perl webserver
webserver
overall progress: 6 out of 6 tasks
1/6: running [==================================================>]
2/6: running [==================================================>]
3/6: running [==================================================>]
4/6: running [==================================================>]
5/6: running [==================================================>]
6/6: running [==================================================>]
verify: Service converged
```

The update took more than 60 seconds because Swarm updated tasks one by one at 10-second intervals. It will first start the new container with the newly defined image. Once it is healthy, it will stop the old version of the container. This must be done on each task and therefore takes more time, but this way, we can ensure that there is always a `webserver` task running. In this example, we have not published any `webserver` ports, so no user interaction is expected. It is just a simple lab – but real-life environments will be the same, and internal Docker Swarm load balancing will always guide the user's requests to alive instances while an update is running.

The new version is running now, as we can observe by using `docker service ps` again:

```
vagrant@swarm-node4:~$ docker service ps webserver --filter
desired-state=running
ID                      NAME                    IMAGE                   NODE
DESIRED STATE           CURRENT STATE             ERROR
PORTS
n9s6lrk8zp32            webserver.1             nginx:alpine-perl     swarm-
node4                   Running                 Running 4 minutes ago
68istkhse4ei            webserver.2             nginx:alpine-perl     swarm-
node1                   Running                 Running 5 minutes ago
j6pqig7njhdw            webserver.3             nginx:alpine-perl     swarm-
node1                   Running                 Running 6 minutes ago
k4vlmeb56kys            webserver.4             nginx:alpine-perl     swarm-
node2                   Running                 Running 5 minutes ago
k50fxl1gms44            webserver.5             nginx:alpine-perl     swarm-
node3                   Running                 Running 5 minutes ago
apur3w3nq95m            webserver.6             nginx:alpine-perl     swarm-
node3                   Running                 Running 5 minutes ago
```

3. We will remove the `webserver` service again to clear the cluster for the following labs using `docker service rm`:

```
vagrant@swarm-node4:~$ docker service rm webserver
webserver
```

In the next lab, we will deploy applications using stacks instead of creating services manually, which might lead to us making configuration errors, for example. Using stacks will provide environment reproducibility because we will always run the same IaC definitions.

Deploying using Docker Stacks

In this lab, we will deploy a PostgreSQL database using secrets, configurations, and volumes on an IaC file. This file will contain all the application's requirements and will be used to deploy the application as a Docker Stack. Let's get started:

1. First, we will create a secret for the required PostgreSQL admin user password. We will execute `docker service create` with the standard input as the secret content:

   ```
   vagrant@swarm-node4:~$ echo SuperSecretPassword|docker secret
   create postgres_password -
   u21mmo1zoqqguh01u8guys9gt
   ```

   We will use it as an external secret inside the `docker-compose` file.

2. We are going to create a simple initialization script to create a new database when PostgreSQL starts. We will create a simple file in the current directory named `create-docker-database.sh` with the following content and appropriate `755` permissions:

   ```
   #!/bin/bash
   set -e

   psql -v ON_ERROR_STOP=0 --username "$POSTGRES_USER" --dbname
   "$POSTGRES_DB" <<-EOSQL
       CREATE USER docker;
       CREATE DATABASE docker;
       GRANT ALL PRIVILEGES ON DATABASE docker TO docker;
   EOSQL
   ```

   Then, we create a config file with the file's content. We will use this file to create a database named `docker` on starting up PostgreSQL. This is something we can use because it is provided by the official Docker Hub PostgreSQL image. We will use `docker config create` with the `create-docker-database.sh` file:

   ```
   vagrant@swarm-node4:~$ docker config create create-docker-database
   ./create-docker-database.sh
   uj6zvrdq0682anzr0kobbyhk2
   ```

3. We will add labels to some of the nodes to ensure the database is always running there since we will create an external volume only on that node. For this example, we will use `node2`. We will create a volume using `docker volume create`:

```
Docker-Certified-Associate-DCA-Exam-Guide/environments/swarm$
vagrant ssh swarm-node2

vagrant@swarm-node2:~$ docker volume create PGDATA
PGDATA
```

This volume will only exist on `swarm-node2`, so we will create a constraint based on a node label to run the service task only on `swarm-node2`. We will use `docker node update --label-add tier=database` for this:

```
vagrant@swarm-node4:~$ docker node update --label-add tier=database
swarm-node2
swarm-node2
```

This is a simple sample. In your production environment, you will never use local volumes. We will need to define and use some plugin that allows us to share the same volume on different hosts, such as NFS and RexRay.

4. Now, we will create the following Docker Compose file, named `postgres-stack.yaml`:

```
version: '3.7'
services:
  database:
    image: postgres:alpine
    deploy:
      placement:
        constraints:
          - node.role == worker
          - node.labels.tier == database
    environment:
      - POSTGRES_PASSWORD_FILE=/run/secrets/postgres_password
    secrets:
      - source: postgres_password
        target: "/run/secrets/postgres_password"
    configs:
      - source: create-docker-database
        target: "/docker-entrypoint-initdb.d/create-db.sh"
        mode: 0755
        uid: "0"
```

```
        volumes:
          - type: volume
            source: PGDATA
            target: /var/lib/postgresql/data
        ports:
          - target: 5432
            published: 15432
            protocol: tcp
        networks:
          net:
            aliases:
              - postgres
              - mydatabase
configs:
  create-docker-database:
    external: true
secrets:
  postgres_password:
    external: true
volumes:
  PGDATA:
    external: true
networks:
  net:
    driver: overlay
    attachable: true
```

Take note of the following things in this file; we added a lot of learned information here:

- We defined the `postgres:alpine` image for the `database` service.
- The `database` service will only be scheduled on worker nodes with a `tier` label key and a value of `database`. In this case, it will run tasks only on `node2`.
- The `postgres` image can use Docker Swarm secret files as environment variables, and in this case, it will use `postgres_password` mounted on `/run/secrets/postgres_password`. The secret is declared externally because it was previously created outside of this file.
- We also added a config file to create an initial database called `docker`. The config file is external as well because we added it outside the `postgres-stack.yaml` file.
- We also added an external volume named `PGDATA`. We will use this volume for the database but it will only exist on `node2`. It is defined as external because we manually create the `PGDATA` volume locally on `node2`.

- We published the PostgreSQL application's port 5432 on the host's port; that is, 15432. We changed the published port to recognize that they are not the same because 5432 will be an internal port on the defined network named net.
- Finally, we defined the net network as attachable to be able to test our database with a simple container running a postgres client. We added two aliases to the database service inside this network: postgres and mydatabase.

 Notice that all the objects that were created for the stack will use the stack's name as a prefix. This will not happen on externally defined objects. They will be used, but we create them manually, outside of the stack's life cycle.

5. We deploy the postgres stack using docker stack deploy:

```
vagrant@swarm-node4:~$ docker stack deploy -c postgres-stack.yaml
postgres
Creating network postgres_net
Creating service postgres_database
```

We can easily review the stack's status using docker stack ps.

```
vagrant@swarm-node4:~$ docker stack ps postgres
ID NAME IMAGE NODE DESIRED STATE CURRENT STATE ERROR PORTS
53in2mik27r0 postgres_database.1 postgres:alpine swarm-node2
Running Running 19 seconds ago
```

It is running on swarm-node2, as we expected.

6. We published port 5432 on port 15432. We can connect to this port from any node IP address in the cluster because Swarm uses a routing mesh. We use the curl command to review the port's availability:

```
vagrant@swarm-node4:~$ curl 0.0.0.0:15432
curl: (52) Empty reply from server

vagrant@swarm-node2:~$ curl 0.0.0.0:15432
curl: (52) Empty reply from server

vagrant@swarm-node3:~$ curl 0.0.0.0:15432
curl: (52) Empty reply from server
```

We get this response to curl because we are not using the right software client (but the ports are listening). Let's run a simple alpine container with the postgres client.

7. Now, we can run a simple `alpine` container attached to the stack's deployed network. In this example, it is `postgres_net`:

```
vagrant@swarm-node4:~$ docker network ls --filter name=postgres_net
NETWORK ID NAME DRIVER SCOPE
mh53ek97pi3a postgres_net overlay swarm
```

Here, we ran a simple `alpine` container and installed the `postgresql-client` package using `docker container run` with an appropriate network:

```
vagrant@swarm-node4:~$ docker container run -ti --network
postgres_net alpine
Unable to find image 'alpine:latest' locally
latest: Pulling from library/alpine
e6b0cf9c0882: Pull complete
Digest:
sha256:2171658620155679240babee0a7714f6509fae66898db422ad803b951257
db78
Status: Downloaded newer image for alpine:latest
/ # apk add --update --no-cache postgresql-client --quiet
```

Remember that we added the `mydatabase` and `postgres` aliases to the `database` service. Therefore, any of them will be valid for testing database connectivity since Swarm added these entries to the internal DNS. We can test this by running a simple `ping` command inside the container:

```
/ # ping -c 1 mydatabase
PING mydatabase (10.0.3.2): 56 data bytes
64 bytes from 10.0.3.2: seq=0 ttl=64 time=0.237 ms
--- mydatabase ping statistics ---
1 packets transmitted, 1 packets received, 0% packet loss
round-trip min/avg/max = 0.237/0.237/0.237 ms

/ # ping -c 1 postgres
PING postgres (10.0.3.2): 56 data bytes
64 bytes from 10.0.3.2: seq=0 ttl=64 time=0.177 ms
--- postgres ping statistics ---
1 packets transmitted, 1 packets received, 0% packet loss
round-trip min/avg/max = 0.177/0.177/0.177 ms

/ # ping -c 1 database
PING database (10.0.3.2): 56 data bytes
64 bytes from 10.0.3.2: seq=0 ttl=64 time=0.159 ms
--- database ping statistics ---
1 packets transmitted, 1 packets received, 0% packet loss
round-trip min/avg/max = 0.159/0.159/0.159 ms
```

We will use the installed client to test our deployed PostgreSQL. Remember to use the previously defined password that we created as a secret, `SuperSecretPassword`. We will test our database's connectivity using the `psql` command:

```
/ # psql -h mydatabase -U postgres
Password for user postgres:
psql (12.1)
Type "help" for help.

postgres=# \l
                            List of databases
   Name    |  Owner   | Encoding |  Collate   |   Ctype    | Access privileges
-----------+----------+----------+------------+------------+-------
------------------
 docker    | postgres | UTF8     | en_US.utf8 | en_US.utf8 | =Tc/postgres
+
           |          |          |            |            | postgres=CTc/postgres+
           |          |          |            |            | docker=CTc/postgres
 postgres  | postgres | UTF8     | en_US.utf8 | en_US.utf8 |
 template0 | postgres | UTF8     | en_US.utf8 | en_US.utf8 |
=c/postgres +
           |          |          |            |            | postgres=CTc/postgres
 template1 | postgres | UTF8     | en_US.utf8 | en_US.utf8 |
=c/postgres +
           |          |          |            |            | postgres=CTc/postgres
(4 rows)

postgres=#
```

We listed the deployed databases using `\l` and the `docker` database, which was created with our `create-db.sh` script. Notice that we used the default PostgreSQL database port `5432` (we omitted any port customization on client request) instead of `15432`. This is because the `docker` container was connecting to the database internally. Both the `postgres_database.1` task and the externally run container are using the same network, `postgres_net`.

Notice that we can use all learned options with the created stack service, `postgres_database`. Anyway, we can modify the Docker Compose file and redeploy the same stack again with some changes. Swarm will review the required updates and take the necessary actions on all components.

Let's exit the running container by executing the `exit` command, and then remove the `postgres` stack and `node2` volume to clean up for the following labs using `docker stack rm`:

```
postgres=# exit
/ # exit

vagrant@swarm-node4:~$ docker stack rm postgres
Removing service postgres_database
Removing network postgres_net
```

In the next lab, we will launch a simple replicated service and review internal ingress load balancing.

Swarm ingress internal load balancing

In this lab, we will use the `codegazers/colors:1.13` image. This is a simple application that will show different random front page colors or texts. Let's get started:

1. Let's create a service named `colors` based on the `codegazers/colors:1.13` image. Since we won't be setting any specific color using environment variables, random ones will be chosen for us. Use `docker service create --constraint node.role==worker`, as follows:

    ```
    vagrant@swarm-node4:~$ docker service create --name colors \
      --publish 8000:3000 \
    --constraint node.role==worker \
    codegazers/colors:1.13

    mkyz0d94ovb144xmvo0q4py41
    overall progress: 1 out of 1 tasks
    1/1: running [==================================================>]
    verify: Service converged
    ```

    We chose not to run a replica on the manager node because we will use `curl` from `node4` in this lab.

2. Let's test local connectivity from the `swarm-node4` manager with `curl`:

    ```
    vagrant@swarm-node4:~$ curl 0.0.0.0:8000/text
    APP_VERSION: 1.0
    COLOR: orange
    CONTAINER_NAME: d3a886d5fe34
    CONTAINER_IP: 10.0.0.11 172.18.0.3
    ```

```
CLIENT_IP: ::ffff:10.0.0.5
CONTAINER_ARCH: linux
```

We deployed one replica and it is running the `orange` color. Take note of the container's IP address and its name.

3. Let's run five more replicas by executing `docker service update --replicas 6`:

```
vagrant@swarm-node4:~$ docker service update --replicas 6 colors --quiet
colors
```

4. If we test service port `8080` with `curl` once more, we will get different colors. This is because the containers were launched without color settings:

```
vagrant@swarm-node4:~$ curl 0.0.0.0:8000/text
APP_VERSION: 1.0
COLOR: red
CONTAINER_NAME: 64fb2a3009b2
CONTAINER_IP: 10.0.0.12 172.18.0.4
CLIENT_IP: ::ffff:10.0.0.5
CONTAINER_ARCH: linux

vagrant@swarm-node4:~$ curl 0.0.0.0:8000/text
APP_VERSION: 1.0
COLOR: cyan
CONTAINER_NAME: 73b07ee0c287
CONTAINER_IP: 10.0.0.14 172.18.0.3
CLIENT_IP: ::ffff:10.0.0.5
CONTAINER_ARCH: linux
```

We get different colors on different containers. The router mesh is guiding our requests to the `colors` tasks' containers using the ingress overlay network.

> We can access all the `colors` service task logs using `docker service logs colors`.

5. Let's remove the `colors` service for the next and final lab using `docker service rm`:

```
vagranr@swarm-node4:~$ docker service rm colors
colors
```

In the next lab, we will review service endpoint modes and consider how DNS resolves `vip` and `dnsrr` situations.

Service discovery

In this lab, we will create a test overlay attachable network and review DNS entries for the `vip` and `dnsrr` endpoint modes. Let's get started:

1. First, we need to create an attachable overlay `test` network using `docker network create --attachable -d overlay`, as follows:

   ```
   vagrant@swarm-node4:~$ docker network create --attachable -d
   overlay test
   32v9pibk7cqfseknrctmyxfsw
   ```

2. Now, let's create two different `colors` services. Each one will use different endpoint modes. For the `vip` mode, we will use `docker service create`:

   ```
   vagrant@swarm-node4:~$ docker service create --replicas 2 \
   --name colors-vip --network test --quiet codegazers/colors:1.13
   4m2vvbnqo9wgf8awnf53zr5b2
   ```

   Let's create the second one for `dnsrr` using `docker service create --endpoint-mode dnsrr`, as follows:

   ```
   vagrant@swarm-node4:~$ docker service create --replicas 2 \
   --name colors-dnsrr --network test --quiet --endpoint-mode dnsrr
   codegazers/colors:1.13
   wqpv929pe5ehniviclzkdvcl0
   ```

3. Now, let's run a simple `alpine` container on the `test` network using `docker container run` and test the internal name resolution functionality. We will need to install the `bind-tools` package to be able to use the `host` and `nslookup` tools:

   ```
   vagrant@swarm-node4:~$ docker run -ti --rm --network test alpine
   / # apk add --update --no-cache bind-tools --quiet
   / # host colors-vip
   colors-vip has address 10.0.4.2
   / # host colors-dnsrr
   colors-dnsrr has address 10.0.4.7
   colors-dnsrr has address 10.0.4.8
   / #exit
   ```

As expected, when using the `vip` endpoint mode, the service receives a virtual IP address. All requests will be redirected to that address and ingress will route to the appropriate container using internal load balancing.

On the other hand, using the `dnsrr` endpoint will not provide a virtual IP address. The internal DNS will add an entry for each container IP.

4. We can also take a look at the containers attached to the `test` network. These containers will get one internal IP address and one that will be routed on the overlay network. We can launch the `ip add show` command attached to one of the running `colors-dnsrr` tasks' containers using `docker container exec`:

```
vagrant@swarm-node4:~$ docker exec -ti colors-
dnsrr.1.vtmpdf0w82daq6fdyk0wwzqc7 ip add show
1: lo: <LOOPBACK,UP,LOWER_UP> mtu 65536 qdisc noqueue state UNKNOWN
qlen 1
 link/loopback 00:00:00:00:00:00 brd 00:00:00:00:00:00
 inet 127.0.0.1/8 scope host lo
 valid_lft forever preferred_lft forever
111: eth0@if112: <BROADCAST,MULTICAST,UP,LOWER_UP,M-DOWN> mtu 1450
qdisc noqueue state UP
 link/ether 02:42:0a:00:04:07 brd ff:ff:ff:ff:ff:ff
 inet 10.0.4.7/24 brd 10.0.4.255 scope global eth0
 valid_lft forever preferred_lft forever
113: eth1@if114: <BROADCAST,MULTICAST,UP,LOWER_UP,M-DOWN> mtu 1500
qdisc noqueue state UP
 link/ether 02:42:ac:12:00:04 brd ff:ff:ff:ff:ff:ff
 inet 172.18.0.4/16 brd 172.18.255.255 scope global eth1
 valid_lft forever preferred_lft forever
```

All Vagrant environments can easily be removed by executing `vagrant destroy -f` to remove all previously created nodes for this lab. This command should be executed on your `environments/swarm` local directory.

Remove all the services that you created for this last lab with `docker service rm colors-dnsrr colors-vip`.

Summary

In this chapter, we reviewed how to deploy and work with the Docker Swarm orchestrator. This is the default orchestrator in Docker as it comes out of the box with Docker Engine.

We learned about Docker Swarm's features and how to deploy applications using stacks (IaC files) and services instead of containers. Orchestration will manage the application's components to keep them running, helping us to even upgrade them without impacting users. Docker Swarm also introduced new objects such as secrets and config, which help us distribute workloads within cluster nodes. Volumes and networks should be managed cluster-wide. We also learned about overlay networking and how Docker Swarm's router mesh has simplified application publishing.

In the next chapter, we will learn about the Kubernetes orchestrator. Currently, Kubernetes is a small part of the Docker Certified Associate exam, but this will probably be increased in the following releases. It is also useful for you to know and understand the concepts of Kubernetes alongside Docker Swarm. Docker Enterprise provides both and we can make them work together.

Questions

1. Choose all of the false statements from the following options:

   a) Docker Swarm is the only orchestrator that can work with Docker.
   b) Docker Swarm comes included out of the box with Docker Engine.
   c) Docker Swarm will allow us to deploy applications on a pool of nodes working together, known as a cluster.
   d) All of the preceding statements are false.

2. Which of the following statements are false regarding what Swarm provides by default?

   a) Service discovery
   b) Internal load balancing
   c) Overlay networking among distributed containers on cluster nodes
   d) All of the preceding statements are false

3. Which of the following statements are true in relation to managers?

   a) We can't create replicated services with tasks running on managers.
   b) There is just one leader node on each cluster that manages all Swarm cluster changes and object statuses.
   c) If the leader node dies, all the changes will be frozen until the leader node is healthy again.
   d) All of the preceding statements are true.

4. Which of the following statements are false in relation to workers?

   a) Worker nodes just run workloads.
   b) If we drain a worker node, all the workloads running on that node will be moved to other available nodes.
   c) Swarm roles can be changed for any node in the cluster whenever this is required.
   d) All of the preceding statements are true.

5. Which of the following statements are false about Swarm Stacks?

   a) By default, all Stacks will be deployed on their own networks.
   b) Stacks will use Docker Compose files to define all application components.
   c) Everything that's used for a Stack should be defined inside the `docker-compose` file. We can't add external objects.
   d) All of the preceding statements are true.

Further reading

Refer to the following links for more information regarding the topics that were covered in this chapter:

- Docker Swarm overview: `https://docs.docker.com/engine/swarm/`
- Deploying applications on Docker Swarm: `https://docs.docker.com/get-started/swarm-deploy/`
- Orchestration with Docker Swarm: `https://hub.packtpub.com/orchestration-docker-swarm/`
- Native Docker clustering with Swarm: `https://www.packtpub.com/virtualization-and-cloud/native-docker-clustering-swarm`

Orchestration Using Kubernetes

9

This chapter is dedicated to the most widely used container orchestrator today—Kubernetes. In 2018, Kubernetes was adopted by 51% of container users as their main orchestrator. Kubernetes adoption has increased in recent years, and it is now at the core of most **Container-as-a-Service (CaaS)** platforms.

Cloud providers have followed the expansion of Kubernetes, and most of them (including Amazon, Google, and Azure) now provide their own **Kubernetes-as-a-Service (KaaS)** platforms where users do not have to take care of Kubernetes' administrative tasks. These services are designed for simplicity and availability on cloud platforms. Users just run their workloads on them and the cloud providers manage complicated maintenance tasks.

In this chapter, we will learn how Kubernetes works and what features it provides. We'll review what is required to deploy a Kubernetes cluster with high availability. We will then learn about Kubernetes objects, such as pods and services, among others. Networking is key to distributing workloads within a cluster; we will learn how Kubernetes networking works and how it provides service discovery and load balancing. Finally, we will review some of the special security features provided by Kubernetes to manage cluster authentication and authorization.

In this chapter, we will cover the following topics:

- Deploying Kubernetes
- High availability with Kubernetes
- Pods, services, and other Kubernetes resources
- Deploying orchestrated resources
- Kubernetes networking
- Publishing applications

Kubernetes is not part of the Docker Certified Associate exam yet, but it probably will be in the next release as Docker Enterprise comes with a fully compatible Kubernetes platform deployed on top of the Docker Swarm orchestrator. Docker Enterprise is the only container platform that provides both orchestrators at the same time. We will learn about Docker Enterprise's components and features in the third section of this book, with a chapter dedicated to each component.

Technical requirements

In this chapter, we will learn about the features of the Docker Swarm orchestrator. We also provide some labs at the end of the chapter to help you to understand and learn about the concepts that we will cover. These labs can be run on your laptop or PC using the provided Vagrant *Kubernetes environment* or any already-deployed Docker Swarm cluster by yourself. You can view additional information in this book's GitHub code repository, which is available at `https://github.com/PacktPublishing/Docker-Certified-Associate-DCA-Exam-Guide.git`.

Check out the following video to see the Code in Action:

`"https://bit.ly/3gzAnS3"`

Deploying Kubernetes using Docker Engine

Kubernetes has many features and is more complex than Docker Swarm. It provides additional features not available on Docker Swarm without having to modify our application code. Docker Swarm is more aligned with microservices logic, while Kubernetes is closer to the virtual machine application's **lift and shift** approach (move application as is to a new infrastructure). This is because the Kubernetes pod object can be compared to virtual machines (with application processes running as containers inside a pod).

Before we begin discussing Kubernetes architecture, let's review some of the concepts that we've learned about orchestration.

Orchestration should provide all that's required for deploying a solution to execute, manage, and publish applications based on the containers distributed on a pool of nodes. Therefore, it should provide a control plane to ensure cluster availability, a scheduler for deploying applications, and a network plane to interconnect distributed applications. It should also provide features for publishing cluster-distributed applications. Application health will also be managed by the orchestrator. As a result, if one application component dies, a new one will be deployed to ensure the application's health.

Kubernetes provides all of these features, and so does Docker Swarm too. However, Kubernetes has many more features, is extensible, and has a bigger community behind the project. Docker also adopted Kubernetes in its Docker Enterprise 2.0 release. It is the only platform that supports Docker Swarm and Kubernetes on the same infrastructure.

Kubernetes provides more container density because it is able to run more than one container at once for each application component. It also provides autoscale features and other advanced scheduling features.

Because Kubernetes is a big community project, some of its components have also been decoupled on different projects to provide faster deployment. The main open source project is hosted by the **Cloud Native Computing Foundation** (**CNCF**). Kubernetes releases a new version every 6 months—imagine updating old legacy applications in production every 6 months. As previously mentioned, it is not easy to follow this application life cycle for many other products, but Kubernetes provides a methodology to upgrade to new software releases easily.

Kubernetes' architectural model is based on the usual orchestration components. We deploy master nodes to execute management tasks and worker nodes (also known as minions) to run application workloads. We also deploy an `etcd` key-value database to store all of the cluster object data.

Let's introduce the Kubernetes components. Masters and workers run different processes, and their number may vary depending on the functionalities provided by each role. Most of these components could be installed as either system services or containers. Here is a list of Kubernetes cluster components:

- `kube-apiserver`
- `kube-scheduler`
- `kube-controller-manager`
- `etcd`
- `kubelet`

- `kube-proxy`
- Container runtime

Note that this list is very different from what we learned about Docker Swarm, where everything was built-in. Let's review each component's features and properties. Remember, this is not a Kubernetes book—we will only learn the basics.

We will run dedicated master nodes to provide an isolated cluster control plane. The following components will run on these nodes:

- `kube-apiserver`: This is the Kubernetes core, and it exposes the Kubernetes API via HTTP (HTTPS if we use TLS certificates). We will connect to this component in order to deploy and manage applications.
- `kube-scheduler`: When we deploy an application's components, the scheduler will decide where to run each one if no node-specific location has been defined. To decide where to run deployed workloads, it will review workload properties, such as specific resources, limits, architecture requirements, affinities, or constraints.
- `kube-controller-manager`: This component will manage controllers, which are processes that are always watching for a cluster object's state changes. This, for example, will manage the node's and workload's states to ensure the desired number of instances are running.
- `etcd`: This is the key-value store for all Kubernetes objects' information and states. Some production environments will run `etcd` out of the master nodes' infrastructure to avoid performance issues and to improve components' high availability.

Worker processes, on the other hand, can run on any node. As we learned with Docker Swarm, we can decide to run application workloads on worker and master nodes. These are the required components for compute nodes:

- `kubelet`: This is the core Kubernetes agent component. It will run on any cluster node that is able to execute application workloads. This process will also ensure that node-assigned Kubernetes workloads are running and are healthy (it will only manage pods created within Kubernetes).

 We are talking about scheduling containers or workloads on a Kubernetes cluster. The fact is that we will schedule pods, which are Kubernetes-specific objects. Kubernetes will run pods; it will never run standalone containers.

- `kube-proxy`: This component will manage the workload's network interactions using operating system packet filtering and routing features. `kube-proxy` should run on any worker node (that is, nodes that run workloads).

Earlier, we mentioned the container runtime as one of the Kubernetes cluster's components. In fact, it is a requirement because Kubernetes itself does not provide one. We will use Docker Engine as it is the most widely used engine, and we have already discussed it in previous chapters.

The following workflow represents all Kubernetes components distributed on five nodes (notice that the master has worker components too and that `etcd` is also deployed out of it):

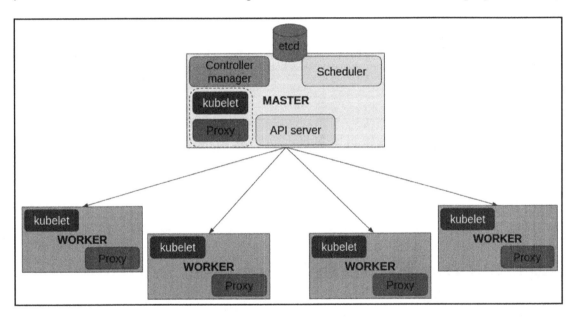

As discussed in `Chapter 8`, *Orchestration Using Docker Swarm*, external load balancers will provide L4 and L7 routing on replicated services. In this case, cluster management components do not use router mesh-like services. We will provide high availability for core components using replicated processes on different nodes. A virtual IP address will be required and we will also use **Fully Qualified Domain Name (FQDN)** names for **Transport Layer Security (TLS)** certificates. This will ensure secure communications and access to and from Kubernetes components.

The following diagram shows the TLS certificates that will be created to ensure secure communication between components:

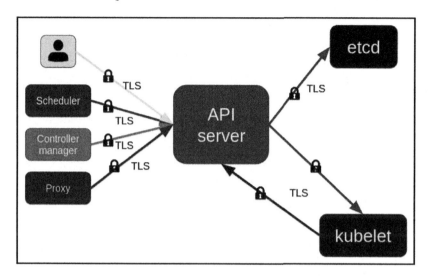

We will use the `kubectl` command line to interact with the Kubernetes cluster, and we will always connect to the `kube-apiserver` processes.

In the next section, we will learn how to implement high-availability Kubernetes cluster environments.

Deploying a Kubernetes cluster with high availability

Docker Swarm was easy to implement. To provide high availability, we simply changed the node roles to accomplish the required odd number of managers. In Kubernetes, this is not so easy; roles cannot be changed, and, usually, administrators do not change the initial number of master nodes.

Therefore, installing a Kubernetes cluster with high-availability components requires some planning. The good thing here is that Docker Enterprise will deploy the cluster for you (since the 2.0 release). We will review this method in Chapter 11, *Universal Control Plane*, as **Universal Control Plane (UCP)** will deploy Kubernetes on top of Docker Swarm.

To provide high availability, we will deploy an odd number of control plane components. It is usual to deploy `etcd` on three additional nodes. In this scenario, nodes would be neither masters nor workers because `etcd` will be deployed out of the Kubernetes nodes. We will require access to this external `etcd` from the master nodes only. Therefore, in this situation, we will run a cluster of eight nodes: three nodes will run `etcd`, three masters nodes will run all of the other control plane components (cluster management), and there will be at least two workers to provide redundancy if one of them dies. This is appropriate for many Kubernetes environments. We isolate `etcd` from the control plane components to provide better management performance.

We can deploy `etcd` on master nodes. This is similar to what we learned about Docker Swarm. We can have *pure masters*—running only management components—and worker nodes for workloads.

Installing Kubernetes is not easy, and there are many software vendors that have developed their own KaaS platforms to provide different methods of installation.

For high availability we will run distributed copies of `etcd`. In this scenario, `kube-apiserver` will connect to a list of nodes instead of just one `etcd` node. The `kube-apiserver`, `kube-scheduler`, and `kube-controller-manager` processes will run duplicated on different master nodes (one instance on each master node).

We will use `kube-apiserver` to manage the cluster. The Kubernetes client will connect to this server process using the HTTP/HTTPS protocol. We will use an external load balancer to distribute traffic between different replicas running on the master nodes. Kubernetes works with the Raft algorithm because `etcd` uses it.

Applications deployed in the cluster will have high availability based on resilience by default (just like in Docker Swarm clusters). Once an application is deployed with all of its components, if one of them fails, `kube-controller-manager` will run a new one. There are different controllers processes, for different deployments that are responsible for executing applications based on replicas, on all nodes at the same time, and other specific execution situations.

In the next section, we will introduce the pod concept, which is key to understanding the differences between Kubernetes and Docker Swarm.

Pods, services, and other Kubernetes resources

The pod concept is key to understanding Kubernetes. A pod is a group of containers that run together. It is very simple. All of these containers share a network namespace and storage. It is like a small logical host because we run many processes together, sharing the same IP addresses and volumes. The isolation methods that we learned about in `Chapter 1`, *Modern Infrastructures and Applications with Docker*, are applicable here.

Pods

Pods are the smallest scheduling unit in Kubernetes environments. Containers within a pod will share the same IP address and can find each other using `localhost`. Therefore, assigned ports must be unique within pods. We cannot reuse ports for other containers and inter-process communication because processes will run as if they were executed on the same logical host. A pod's life relies on the healthiness of a container.

Pods can be used to integrate full application stacks, but it is true that they are usually used with a few containers. In fact, microservices rely on small functionalities; therefore, we will run just one container per node. As pods are the smallest Kubernetes scheduling unit, we scale pods up and down, not containers. Therefore, complete stacks will be replicated if many grouped application components are executed together within a pod.

On the other hand, pods allow us, for example, to execute a container in order to initialize some special features or properties for another container. Remember the *Deploying using Docker Stacks* section from `Chapter 8`, *Orchestration Using Docker Swarm*? In that lab, we launched a PostgreSQL database and we added an initialization script to create a specific database. We can do this on Kubernetes using the initial containers within a pod.

Terminating and removing pods will depend on how much time it will take to stop or delete all of the containers running within a pod.

The following diagram represents a pod with some containers inside, sharing the same IP address and volume, among other features (we will be able to apply a special security context to all containers within a pod):

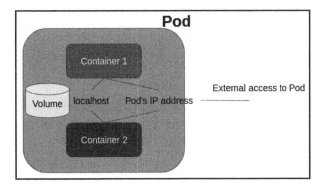

Let's now review the service resources on Kubernetes.

Services

Services have a different meaning in Kubernetes. Services are abstract objects for the cluster; we do not schedule services in Kubernetes. They define a logical set of pods that work together to serve an application component. We can also associate a service with an external resource (endpoint). This service will be used inside a cluster like any other, but with external IP addresses and ports, for example.

We also use services to publish applications inside and outside a Kubernetes cluster. For these purposes, there are different types of services. All of them, except headless services, provide internal load balancing between all pod replicas for a common service:

- **Headless**: We use headless services to interface with non-Kubernetes service discovery solutions. No virtual IP will be allocated. There will be no load balancing or proxy to reach the service's pods. This behavior is similar to Docker Swarm's DNSRR mode.
- **ClusterIP**: This is the default service type. Kubernetes will provide an internal virtual IP address chosen from a configurable pool. This will allow only internal cluster objects to reach the defined service.
- **NodePort**: NodePort services also receive a virtual IP (ClusterIP), but exposed services' ports will be available on all cluster nodes. Kubernetes will route requests to the service's ClusterIP address, no matter which node received them. Therefore, the service's defined port will be available on `<ANY_CLUSTER_NODE>:<NODEPORT_PORT>`. This effectively reminds us of the routing mesh's behavior on Docker Swarm. In this case, we need to add some cluster nodes to external load balancers to reach the defined and exposed service's ports.

- **LoadBalancer**: This service type is available only in a cloud provider's Kubernetes deployment. We expose a service externally using automatically created (using the cloud provider's API integration) load balancers. It uses both a ClusterIP virtual IP for internal routing and a NodePort concept for reaching service-defined ports from load balancers.
- **ExternalName**: This is not very common nowadays because it relies on DNS CNAME records and is a new implementation. It is used to add external services, out of the Kubernetes cluster. External services will be reachable by their names as if they were running inside Kubernetes cluster.

The following schema represents the NodePort service type's usual configuration. In this example, the service is reachable on port 7000 from an external load balancer, while pods are reachable internally on port 5000. All traffic will be internally load balanced between all of the service's pod endpoints:

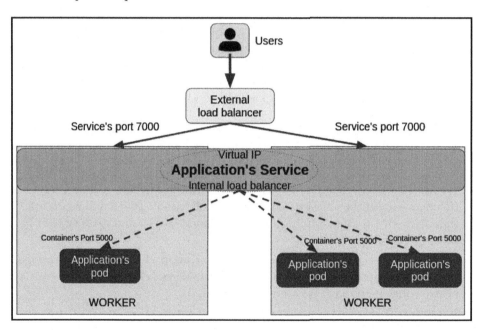

There are many other resources in Kubernetes. We will take a quick look at some of them before going into how we deploy applications on Kubernetes clusters in depth.

ConfigMaps and secrets

We learned how to distribute the required application information cluster-wide with Docker Swarm. Kubernetes also provides solutions for this. We will use ConfigMaps, instead of Docker Swarm config objects, and secrets.

In both cases, we can use either files or standard input (using the `--from-literal` option) to create these resources. The literal option will allow us to create these objects using the command line instead of a YAML file.

 The Kubernetes `kubectl` command line provides two different approaches to create cluster resources/objects (imperative and declarative). We will use either command-line generators or resource files, usually in YAML format. The first method is usually known as imperative, but is not available for all kinds of resources, and using files is known as declarative. This will apply to all Kubernetes resources; therefore, we will be able to use either `kubectl create pod` with arguments or `kubectl create -f <POD_DEFINITION_FILE_IN_YAML_FORMAT>`. We can export a previously generated command-line object into YAML format easily to allow resource reproducibility, to save its definition somewhere safe.

ConfigMaps and secrets allow us to decouple configurations from image content without using unsecured runtime-visible variables or local files shared on some nodes. We will use secrets for sensitive data, while ConfigMaps will be used for common configurations.

Namespaces

Namespaces can be understood as scopes based on names. They allow us to isolate resources between them. The names of resources are unique within each namespace. Resources can only be within one namespace; therefore, we can divide access to them using namespaces.

One of the simplest uses for namespaces is to limit user access and the usage of Kubernetes' objects and resources' quotas. Based on namespaces, we will allow a specific set of host resources for users. For example, different groups of users or teams will have their own resources and a quota that will limit their environment's behavior.

Persistent volumes

We learned about volumes in `Chapter 4`, *Container Persistency and Networking*. In Kubernetes, volumes are attached to pods, not containers; therefore, volumes will follow a pod's life cycle.

There are many volume types in Kubernetes and we can mix them inside pods. Volumes are available to any container running within a pod. There are volumes specially designed for cloud providers and storage solutions that are available in most data centers. Let's review a couple of interesting, commonly used volumes:

- `emptyDir`: This volume is created when a pod is assigned to a node and is removed with the pod. It starts off empty and is usually used to share information between containers running within a pod.
- `hostPath`: We have already used this type of volume on Docker. These volumes allow us to mount a file or directory from the host into pods.

Each volume type has its own special options to enable its unique features.

These volumes are designed to be used within pods, but they are not prepared for Kubernetes clustering and storing permanent data. For these situations, we use **Persistent Volumes (PVs)**.

PVs allow us to abstract how storage is provided. It doesn't matter how storage hosts arrive in the cluster; we only care about how to use them. A PV is provisioned by an administrator, for example, and users are allowed to use it. PVs are Kubernetes resources; hence, we can associate them with namespaces and they have their own life cycle. They are pod-independent.

PVs are requested by **Persistent Volume Claims (PVCs)**. Therefore, PVCs consume defined PVs. This is the way to associate a pod with a PV.

Therefore, PVCs allow users to consume storage. We can designate storage according to internal properties, such as speed, how it is provided on the hosts, and more, and allow dynamic provisioning using **storage classes**. With these objects, we describe all of the storage solutions available in the cluster with their properties as profiles and Kubernetes prepares the persistent storage to be used.

It is important to know that we can decide the behavior of the PV data once pods die. The **retail reclaim** policy describes what to do with volumes and their content once pods no longer use them. Therefore, we will choose between deleting the volume, retaining the volume and its content, and recycling it.

We can say that PVs are Kubernetes cluster resources designated for application persistent storage and PVCs are the requests to use them.

Storage classes are a new feature that allow administrators to integrate dynamic provisions into our cluster. This helps us to provide storage without having to manually configure each volume. We will just define profiles and features for storage and the provisioners will give the best solution for the required volume.

In the next section, we will learn how to deploy workloads on Kubernetes clusters.

Deploying orchestrated resources

Deploying workloads in Kubernetes is easy. We will use `kubectl` to specify the resources to be created and interact with `kube-apiserver`.

As mentioned earlier, we can use the command line to either use built-in generators or YAML files. Depending on the Kubernetes API version, some options may not be available, but we will assume Kubernetes 1.11 or higher.

In this chapter, all examples use Kubernetes 1.14 because it is the version available on the current Docker Enterprise release, 3.0, at the time of writing this book.

Let's start by creating a simple pod. We will review both options—imperative, using the command-line, and declarative, using YAML manifests.

Using the pod generator, we will run the `kubectl run --generator=run-pod/v1` command:

```
$ kubectl run --generator=run-pod/v1 --image=nginx:alpine myfirstpod --
labels=example=myfirstpod
pod/myfirstpod created
```

Using a YAML definition file, we will describe all of the required properties of the pod:

```
apiVersion: v1
kind: Pod
metadata:
 name: myfirstpod
  labels:
     example: myfirstpod
spec:
  containers:
  - name: myfirstpodcontainer
    image: nginx:alpine
```

To deploy this `.yaml` definition file, we will just run `kubectl create -f <YAML_DEFINITION_FILE>`. This will create all of the defined resources in the file on the specified namespace. Because we are not using an argument to specify a namespace, they will be created on the user-defined one. In our case, we are using the `default` namespace by default.

We can define the namespace either on each YAML file or by using a command-line argument. The latter will overwrite the YAML definition.

Both examples will create the same pod, with one container inside, running an `nginx:alpine` image.

Take care when using the `args` and `command` definitions on Kubernetes. These keys differ from the definitions we used for Docker containers or images. Kubernetes' `command` will represent `ENTRYPOINT`, while `args` will represent the container/image `CMD` definition.

We can kill this pod by simply removing it using `kubectl delete`. To get a list of pods running within a namespace, we will use `kubectl get pods`. If the namespace is omitted on the `kubectl` execution, the user-assigned namespace will be used:

```
$ kubectl get pods
NAME           READY    STATUS     RESTARTS    AGE
myfirstpod     1/1      Running    0           11s
```

But this just created a simple pod; we cannot create more NGINX replicas with this kind of resource. To use replicas, we will use ReplicaSets instead of single pods.

We will set up a pod template section and pod selectors to identify which deployed pods belong to this `ReplicaSet` resource within a new YAML file. This will help the controller to watch the pods' health.

Here, to the previous pod definition, we add a `template` section and a `selector` key with labels:

```
apiVersion: apps/v1
kind: ReplicaSet
metadata:
  name: myfirstrs
  labels:
    example: myfirstrs
spec:
  replicas: 3
  selector:
    matchLabels:
      example: myfirstrs
  template:
    metadata:
      name: myfirstpod
      labels:
        example: myfirstrs
    spec:
      containers:
      - name: myfirstpodcontainer
        image: nginx:alpine
```

Therefore, we created three replicas using the same pod definition as we did earlier. This pod's definition was used as a template for all of the replicas. We can review all of the resources deployed using `kubectl get all`. In the following command, we filter the results to retrieve only resources with the `example` label and the `myfirstrs` value:

```
$ kubectl get all -l example=myfirstrs
NAME                     READY   STATUS    RESTARTS   AGE
pod/myfirstrs-2xrpk      1/1     Running   0          47s
pod/myfirstrs-94rb5      1/1     Running   0          47s
pod/myfirstrs-jm6lc      1/1     Running   0          47s

NAME                           DESIRED   CURRENT   READY   AGE
replicaset.apps/myfirstrs      3         3         3       47s
```

Each replica will have the same prefix name, but its own ID will be part of the name. This uniquely identifies the resource in the Kubernetes cluster.

We are using `kubectl get all -l <KEY=VALUE>` to filter all of the resources we labeled with the `example` key and the `myfirstrs` value.

We can use `DaemonSet` to deploy a replica on each node in the cluster, just as we did with Docker Swarm's global services:

```
apiVersion: apps/v1
kind: DaemonSet
metadata:
  name: myfirstds
  labels:
    example: myfirstds
spec:
  selector:
    matchLabels:
      example: myfirstds
  template:
    metadata:
      name: myfirstpod
      labels:
        example: myfirstds
    spec:
      containers:
      - name: myfirstpodcontainer
        image: nginx:alpine
        resources:
          limits:
            memory: 100Mi
          requests:
            cpu: 100m
            memory: 10Mi
```

We can now review the pod distribution again using `kubectl get all`.

Notice that we added the container's resource limits and resource requests. The `limits` key allows us to specify resource limits for each container. On the other hand, `requests` informs the scheduler about the minimal resources required to run this component. A pod will not be able to run on a node if there are not enough resources to achieve the requested CPU, memory, and more. If any containers exceed their limits, they will be terminated:

```
$ kubectl get all -l example=myfirstds -o wide
NAME READY STATUS RESTARTS AGE IP NODE NOMINATED NODE READINESS GATES
pod/myfirstds-cr7xc 1/1 Running 0 84s 192.168.135.5 node3 <none> <none>
```

```
pod/myfirstds-f6x8n 1/1 Running 0 84s 192.168.104.6 node2 <none> <none>

NAME DESIRED CURRENT READY UP-TO-DATE AVAILABLE NODE SELECTOR AGE
CONTAINERS IMAGES SELECTOR
daemonset.apps/myfirstds 2 2 2 2 2 <none> 84s myfirstpodcontainer
nginx:alpine example=myfirstds
```

The `Deployment` resource is a higher-level concept, as it manages `ReplicaSet` and allows us to issue application component updates. It is recommended that you use `Deployment` instead of `ReplicaSet`. We will again use the `template` and `select` sections:

```
apiVersion: apps/v1
kind: Deployment
metadata:
  name: myfirstdeployment
  labels:
    example: myfirstds
spec:
  replicas: 3
  selector:
    matchLabels:
      example: myfirstdeployment
  template:
    metadata:
      name: myfirstpod
      labels:
        example: myfirstdeployment
    spec:
      containers:
      - name: myfirstpodcontainer
        image: nginx:alpine
        ports:
        - containerPort: 80
```

Therefore, the deployment will run three replicas of `nginx:alpine`, distributed again on cluster nodes:

```
$  kubectl get all -l example=myfirstdeployment -o wide
NAME                                         READY   STATUS    RESTARTS   AGE
IP               NODE    NOMINATED NODE   READINESS GATES
pod/myfirstdeployment-794f9bfcd7-9m8vg       1/1     Running   0          12s
192.168.135.9    node3   <none>           <none>
pod/myfirstdeployment-794f9bfcd7-f7499       1/1     Running   0          12s
192.168.104.10   node2   <none>           <none>
pod/myfirstdeployment-794f9bfcd7-kfzfk       1/1     Running   0          12s
192.168.104.11   node2   <none>           <none>

NAME                                                     DESIRED   CURRENT   READY
```

```
AGE     CONTAINERS          IMAGES          SELECTOR
replicaset.apps/myfirstdeployment-794f9bfcd7   3            3          3
12s    myfirstpodcontainer    nginx:alpine    pod-template-
hash=794f9bfcd7,example=myfirstdeployment
```

Notice that replicas are only running on some nodes. This is because we have some taints on the other nodes (some Kubernetes deployments avoid workloads on master nodes by default). Taints and tolerations help us to allow the scheduling of pods on only specific nodes. In this example, the master node will not run a workload, although it also has a worker role (it runs the Kubernetes worker processes that we learned about, `kubelet` and `kube-proxy`). These features remind us of Docker Swarm's node availability concepts. In fact, we can also execute `kubectl cordon <NODE>` to set a node as non-schedulable.

 This chapter is a brief introduction to the main concepts of Kubernetes. We highly recommend that you view the Kubernetes documentation for further information: `https://kubernetes.io`.

We can set replication based on a pod's performance and limits. This is known as **autoscaling**, and it is an interesting feature that is not available in Docker Swarm.

When an application's replicated components require persistence, we use another kind of resource. StatefulSets guarantee the order and uniqueness of pods.

Now that we know how to deploy applications, let's review how Kubernetes manages and deploys a network locally with components distributed on different nodes.

Kubernetes networking

Kubernetes, like any other orchestrator, provides local and distributed networking. There are a few important communication assumptions that Kubernetes has to accomplish:

- Container-to-container communication
- Pod-to-pod communication
- Pod-to-service communication
- User access and communication between external or internal applications

Container-to-container communication is easy because we learned that containers within a pod share the same IP and network namespace.

We know that each pod gets its own IP address. Therefore, Kubernetes needs to provide routing and accessibility to and from pods running on different hosts. Following the Docker concepts that we learned about in `Chapter 4`, *Container Persistency and Networking*, Kubernetes also uses bridge networking for pods running on the same host. Therefore, all pods running on a host will be able to talk with each other using bridge networking.

Remember how Docker allowed us to deploy different bridge networks on a single host? This way, we were able to isolate applications on a host using different networks. Using this local concept, overlaying networks on a Docker Swarm cluster also deployed bridged interfaces. And these interfaces will be connected using tunnels created between hosts using VXLAN. Isolation was something simple on Docker standalone hosts and Docker Swarm. Docker Engine had to manage all of the backstage magic to make this work with firewall rules and routing, but overlay networking is available out of the box.

Kubernetes provides a simpler approach. All pods run on the same network; hence, every pod will see other pods within the same host. In fact, we can go further—pods are locally accessible from hosts.

Let's consider this concept with a couple of pods. We will run `example-webserver` and `example-nettools` at the same time, executing simple `nginx:alpine` and `frjaraur/nettools:minimal` (this is a small alpine image with some helpful network tools) pods. First, we will create a deployment for `example-webserver` using `kubectl create deployment`:

```
$ kubectl create deployment example-webserver --image=nginx:alpine
deployment.apps/example-webserver created
```

We review the pod's IP address using `kubectl get pods`:

```
$ kubectl get pods -o wide
NAME                                   READY    STATUS    RESTARTS    AGE    IP
NODE        NOMINATED NODE    READINESS GATES
example-webserver-7789c6d697-kts71    1/1      Running   0           69s
192.168.104.16    node2    <none>              <none>
```

As we said, `localhost` communications to the pod will work. Let's try a simple `ping` command from the host to the pod's IP address:

```
node3:~$ ping -c 2 192.168.104.16
PING 192.168.104.16 (192.168.104.16) 56(84) bytes of data.
64 bytes from 192.168.104.16: icmp_seq=1 ttl=63 time=0.483 ms
64 bytes from 192.168.104.16: icmp_seq=2 ttl=63 time=0.887 ms
```

```
--- 192.168.104.16 ping statistics ---
2 packets transmitted, 2 received, 0% packet loss, time 1001ms
rtt min/avg/max/mdev = 0.483/0.685/0.887/0.202 ms
```

Additionally, we can also have access to its running `nginx` process. Let's try `curl` using the pod's IP again, but this time, we will use port `80`:

```
node3:~$ curl -I 192.168.104.16:80
HTTP/1.1 200 OK
Server: nginx/1.17.6
Date: Sun, 05 Jan 2020 22:20:42 GMT
Content-Type: text/html
Content-Length: 612
Last-Modified: Tue, 19 Nov 2019 15:14:41 GMT
Connection: keep-alive
ETag: "5dd406e1-264"
Accept-Ranges: bytes
```

Therefore, the host can communicate with all of the pods running on top of Docker Engine.

We can get a pod's IP address using `jsonpath`, to format the pod's information output, which is very interesting when we have hundreds of pods: `kubectl get pod example-webserver -o jsonpath='{.status.podIP}'`.

Let's execute an interactive pod with the aforementioned `frjaraur/nettools:minimal` image. We will use `kubectl run --generator=run-pod/v1` to execute this new pod. Notice that we added `-ti -- sh` to run an interactive shell within this pod. From this pod, we will run `curl` again, connecting to the `example-webserver` pod's IP address:

```
$ kubectl run --generator=run-pod/v1 example-nettools --
image=frjaraur/nettools:minimal -ti -- sh
If you don't see a command prompt, try pressing enter.
/ # ping -c 2 192.168.104.16
PING 192.168.104.16 (192.168.104.16): 56 data bytes
64 bytes from 192.168.104.16: seq=0 ttl=62 time=0.620 ms
64 bytes from 192.168.104.16: seq=1 ttl=62 time=0.474 ms

--- 192.168.104.16 ping statistics ---
2 packets transmitted, 2 packets received, 0% packet loss
round-trip min/avg/max = 0.474/0.547/0.620 ms

/ # curl -I 192.168.104.16:80
HTTP/1.1 200 OK
Server: nginx/1.17.6
Date: Sun, 05 Jan 2020 22:22:16 GMT
```

```
Content-Type: text/html
Content-Length: 612
Last-Modified: Tue, 19 Nov 2019 15:14:41 GMT
Connection: keep-alive
ETag: "5dd406e1-264"
Accept-Ranges: bytes
```

We have successfully accessed the deployed `example-webserver` pod using `ping` and `curl`, sending some requests to its `nginx` running process. It is clear that both containers can see each other.

There is something even more interesting in this example: we have not reviewed where these pods are running. In fact, they are running on different hosts, as we can read from the `kubectl get pods -o wide` command's output:

```
$ kubectl get pods -o wide
NAME                                READY     STATUS      RESTARTS    AGE     IP
NODE        NOMINATED NODE      READINESS GATES
example-nettools                     1/1      Running     1           85s
192.168.135.13    node3    <none>                  <none>
example-webserver-7789c6d697-kts7l   1/1      Running     0           5m8s
192.168.104.16    node2    <none>                  <none>
```

Networking between hosts is controlled by another component that will allow these distributed communications. In this case, this component is Calico, which is a **container network interface** (**CNI**) applied to this Kubernetes cluster. The Kubernetes network model provides a flat network (all pods are distributed on the same network), and data plane networking is based on interchangeable plugins. We will use the plugin that best affords all of the required features in our environment.

There are other CNI implementations apart from Calico, such as Flannel, Weave, Romana, Cillium, and more. Each one provides its own features and host-to-host implementations. For example, Calico uses **Border Gateway Protocol** (**BGP**) to route real container IP addresses inside the cluster. Once a CNI is deployed, all of the container IP addresses will be managed by its implementation. They are usually deployed at the beginning of a Kubernetes cluster implementation. Calico allows us to implement network policies, which are very important to ensure security in this flat network where every pod sees other pods.

We have not looked at any service networking yet, which is also important here. If a pod dies, a new IP will be allocated, hence access will be lost on the previous IP address; that is why we use services. Remember, services are logical groupings of pods, usually with a virtual IP address. This IP address will be assigned from another pool of IP addresses (the service IP addresses pool). Pods and services do not share the same IP address pool. A service's IP will not change when new pods are recreated.

Service discovery

Let's create a service associated with the currently deployed example-webserver deployment. We'll use kubectl expose:

```
$ kubectl expose deployment example-webserver \
--name example-webserver-svc --type=NodePort --port=80

service/example-webserver-svc exposed
```

We could have done this using either kubectl create service (imperative format) or a YAML definition file (declarative format). We used kubectl expose because it's simpler to quickly publish any kind or resource. We can review a service's IP addresses using kubectl get services:

```
$ kubectl get services -o wide
NAME                     TYPE        CLUSTER-IP      EXTERNAL-IP   PORT(S)
AGE      SELECTOR
kubernetes               ClusterIP   10.96.0.1       <none>        443/TCP
11h      <none>
example-webserver-svc    NodePort    10.98.107.31    <none>
80:30951/TCP    39s     app=example-webserver
```

Remember that we define the services associated with pods using selectors. In this case, the service will group all pods with the app label and the example-webserver value. This label was automatically created because we created Deployment. As a result, all pods grouped for this service will be accessible on the 10.98.107.31 IP address and the internal TCP port 80. We defined which pod's port will be associated with this service—in both cases, we set port 80:

```
$ curl -I 10.98.107.31:80
HTTP/1.1 200 OK
Server: nginx/1.17.6
Date: Sun, 05 Jan 2020 22:26:09 GMT
Content-Type: text/html
Content-Length: 612
Last-Modified: Tue, 19 Nov 2019 15:14:41 GMT
Connection: keep-alive
ETag: "5dd406e1-264"
Accept-Ranges: bytes
```

It is accessible, as expected. Kubernetes' internal network has published this service on the defined ClusterIP address.

Because we created this service as `NodePort`, a random port has been associated with the service. In this case, it is port `30951`. As a result, requests will be routed to the application's pods within the cluster when we reach the cluster nodes' IP addresses in the randomly chosen port.

> `NodePort` ports are assigned randomly by default, but we can set them manually in the range between `30000` and `32767`.

Let's verify this feature. We will send some requests to the port that is listening on cluster nodes. In this example, we'll use the `curl` command on the local `0.0.0.0` IP address and port `30951` on various nodes:

```
node1:~$ curl -I 0.0.0.0:30951
HTTP/1.1 200 OK
Server: nginx/1.17.6
Date: Sun, 05 Jan 2020 22:26:57 GMT
Content-Type: text/html
Content-Length: 612
Last-Modified: Tue, 19 Nov 2019 15:14:41 GMT
Connection: keep-alive
ETag: "5dd406e1-264"
Accept-Ranges: bytes


node3:~$ curl -I 0.0.0.0:30951
HTTP/1.1 200 OK
Server: nginx/1.17.6
Date: Sun, 05 Jan 2020 22:27:41 GMT
Content-Type: text/html
Content-Length: 612
Last-Modified: Tue, 19 Nov 2019 15:14:41 GMT
Connection: keep-alive
ETag: "5dd406e1-264"
Accept-Ranges: bytes
```

Communication between pods happens even if they are not running on the same node. The following output shows that pods are not running in either `node1` or `node3`. The application's pod is running on `node2`. The internal routing works:

```
$ kubectl get pods -o wide -l app=example-webserver
NAME                                 READY   STATUS    RESTARTS   AGE   IP
NODE        NOMINATED NODE    READINESS GATES
example-webserver-7789c6d697-kts7l   1/1     Running   0          10m
192.168.104.16   node2   <none>            <none>
```

There is something more interesting, though—services create a DNS entry with their names following this pattern:

```
<SERVICE_NAME>.<NAMESPACE>.svc.<CLUSTER>.<DOMAIN>
```

In our example, we have not used a namespace or a domain. The service resolution will be simple: `example-webserver.default.svc.cluster.local`. This resolution is only available in the Kubernetes cluster by default. Therefore, we can test this resolution by executing a pod with the `host` or `nslookup` tools. We will attach our terminal interactively to the running `example-nettools` pod using `kubectl attach` and run `host` and `curl` to test the DNS resolution:

```
$ kubectl attach example-nettools -c example-nettools -i -t
If you don't see a command prompt, try pressing enter.
/ # host example-webserver.default.svc.cluster.local
example-webserver.default.svc.cluster.local has address 10.101.195.251
/ # curl -I example-webserver.default.svc.cluster.local:80
HTTP/1.1 200 OK
Server: nginx/1.17.6
Date: Sun, 05 Jan 2020 21:58:37 GMT
Content-Type: text/html
Content-Length: 612
Last-Modified: Tue, 19 Nov 2019 15:14:41 GMT
Connection: keep-alive
ETag: "5dd406e1-264"
Accept-Ranges: bytes
```

We have confirmed that the service has a DNS entry that is reachable by any other Kubernetes cluster resource. We have also published the service using `NodePort`, so it is accessible on any node IP address. We could have an external load balancer routing requests to this deployed service on any cluster node's IP address and a chosen (or manually set) port. This port will be fixed for this service until it is removed.

 Notice that we used `kubectl attach example-nettools -c example-nettools -i -t` to reconnect to a running pod left in the background.

In the next section, we will learn how scaling will change the described behavior.

Load balancing

If we now scale up to three replicas, without changing anything on the deployed service, we will add load balancing features. Let's scale up using `kubectl scale`:

```
$ kubectl scale --replicas=3 deployment/example-webserver
deployment.extensions/example-webserver scaled
```

Now we will have three running instances or pods for the `example-webserver` deployment.

 Notice that we have scaled from the command line using the resource's type and its name: `kubectl scale --replicas=<NUMBER_OF_REPLICAS> <RESOURCE_TYPE>/<NAME>`.

We can review deployment pods using `kubectl get pods` with the associated label:

```
$ kubectl get pods -o wide -l app=example-webserver
NAME                                     READY   STATUS    RESTARTS   AGE    IP
NODE        NOMINATED NODE    READINESS GATES
example-webserver-7789c6d697-dnx61   1/1     Running   0          4m8s
192.168.135.14    node3    <none>            <none>
example-webserver-7789c6d697-kts71   1/1     Running   0          23m
192.168.104.16    node2    <none>            <none>
example-webserver-7789c6d697-zdrtr   1/1     Running   0          4m8s
192.168.104.17    node2    <none>            <none>
```

If we now test the service's access again, we will reach each one of the three replicas. We execute the next simple loop to reach the service's backend pods five times:

```
$ for I in $(seq 5);do curl -I 10.98.107.31:80;done
```

If we review one of the deployed pod's logs using `kubectl logs`, we will notice that not all requests were logged. Although we made more than two requests using the service's IP address, we just logged a few:

```
$ kubectl logs example-webserver-7789c6d697-zdrtr
192.168.166.128 - - [05/Jan/2020:22:44:32 +0000] "HEAD / HTTP/1.1" 200 0 "-
" "curl/7.47.0" "-"
192.168.166.128 - - [05/Jan/2020:22:45:38 +0000] "HEAD / HTTP/1.1" 200 0 "-
" "curl/7.47.0" "-"
```

Only one-third of the requests are logged on each pod; therefore, the internal load balancer is distributing the traffic between all available applications' pods. Internal load balancing is deployed by default between all pods associated with a service.

As we have seen, Kubernetes provides flat networks for pods and services, simplifying networking and internal application accessibility. On the other hand, it is insecure because any pod can reach any other pods or services. In the next section, we will learn how to avoid this situation.

Network policies

Network policies define rules to allow communication between groups of pods and other components. Using labels, we apply specific rules to matching pods for ingress and egress traffic on defined ports. These rules can be set using IP ranges, namespaces, or even other labels to include or exclude resources.

Network policies are applied using network plugins; therefore, the CNI deployed on our cluster must support them. For example, Calico supports NetworkPolicy resources.

 We will be able to define default rules to all pods in the cluster, isolating all internet traffic, for example, or a defined group of hosts.

This YAML file represents an example of a NetworkPolicy resource applying ingress and egress traffic rules:

```
apiVersion: networking.k8s.io/v1
kind: NetworkPolicy
metadata:
  name: database-traffic
spec:
  podSelector:
    matchLabels:
      tier: database
  policyTypes:
  - Ingress
  - Egress
  ingress:
  - from:
    - ipBlock:
        cidr: 172.17.10.0/24
    - podSelector:
        matchLabels:
          tier: frontend
    ports:
    - protocol: TCP
      port: 5432
```

```
egress:
- to:
  - ipBlock:
      cidr: 10.0.0.0/24
  ports:
  - protocol: TCP
    port: 5978
```

In this example, we will apply defined ingress and egress rules to all pods including the `tier` label with the `database` value.

The ingress rule allows traffic from any pod on the same namespace with the `tier` label and the `frontend` value. All IP addresses in subnet `172.17.10.0/24` will also be allowed to access defined `database` pods.

The egress rule allows traffic from defined `database` pods to port `5978` on all IP addresses on subnet `10.0.0.0/24`.

If we do not apply a `NetworkPolicy` resource to a namespace, all traffic is allowed. We can change this behavior using `podSelector: {}`. This will match all pods in the namespace. For example, to disallow all egress traffic, we can use the following `NetworkPolicy` YAML definition:

```
apiVersion: networking.k8s.io/v1
kind: NetworkPolicy
metadata:
  name: default-deny
spec:
  podSelector: {}
  policyTypes:
  - Egress
```

So, we have learned that we can ensure security even on a Kubernetes flat network with `NetworkPolicy` resources. Let's review the ingress resources.

Publishing applications

Ingress resources help us to publish applications deployed on Kubernetes clusters. They work very well with HTTP and HTTPS services, providing many features for distributing and managing traffic between services. This traffic will be located on the OSI model's transport and application layers; they are also known as layers 4 and 7, respectively. It also works with raw TCP and UDP services; however, in these cases, traffic will be load balanced at layer 4 only.

These resources route traffic from outside the cluster to services running within the cluster. Ingress resources require the existence of a special service called an **ingress controller**. These services will load balance or route traffic using rules created by ingress resources. Therefore, publishing an application using this feature requires two components:

- **Ingress resource**: The rules to apply to incoming traffic
- **Ingress controller**: The load balancer that will automatically convert or translate ingress rules to load balance configurations

A combination of both objects provides the dynamic publishing of applications. If one application's pod dies, a new one will be created and the service and ingress controller will automatically route all traffic to the new one. This will also isolate services from external networks. We will publish one single endpoint instead of the `NodePort` or `LoadBalancer` service types for all services, which will consume many nodes' ports or cloud IP addresses. This endpoint is the load balancer that will use the ingress controller and ingress resource rules to route traffic internally to deployed services:

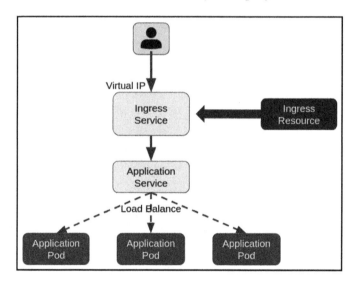

This chapter's labs show us an interesting load balancing example using **NGINX Ingress Controller**. Let's review a quick example YAML configuration file:

```
apiVersion: networking.k8s.io/v1beta1
kind: Ingress
metadata:
  name: simple-fanout-example
  annotations:
    nginx.ingress.kubernetes.io/rewrite-target: /
```

```
spec:
  rules:
  - host: example.local
    http:
      paths:
      - path: /example1
        backend:
          serviceName: example-webserver
          servicePort: 80
      - path: /example2
        backend:
          serviceName: another-service
          servicePort: 8080
```

This example outlines the rules that should be applied to route requests to a specific
example.local-specific host header. Any request containing /example1 in its URL will
be guided to example-webserver, while another-service will receive requests
containing the /example2 path in its URL. Notice that we have used the internal service's
ports; therefore, no additional service exposure is required. One ingress controller endpoint
will redirect traffic to the example-webserver and another-service services. This saves
up the host's ports (and/or IP addresses on the cloud providers because
the LoadBalancer service type uses one published public IP address per service).

 We can provide as many ingress controllers as needed. In fact, in multi-
tenant environments, we usually deploy more than just one to isolate
publishing planes between different tenants.

This brief look at publishing applications on Kubernetes has finished this review of the
main Kubernetes networking features. Let's now move on to Kubernetes security
properties.

Kubernetes security components and features

Kubernetes provides mechanisms to authenticate and authorize access to its API. This
allows us to apply different levels of privileges for users or roles within a cluster. This
prevents unauthorized access to some core resources, such as scheduling or nodes in the
cluster.

Once users are allowed to use cluster resources, we use namespaces to isolate their own resources from other users. This works even in multi-tenant environments where a higher level of security is required.

Kubernetes works with the very elaborate **Role-Based Access Control (RBAC)** environment, which provides a great level of granularity to allow specific actions on some resources while other actions are denied.

We manage the `Role` and `ClusterRole` resources to describe permissions for different resources. We use `Role` to define permissions within namespaces and `ClusterRole` for permissions on cluster-wide resources. Rules are supplied using some defined verbs, such as `list`, `get`, `update`, and more, and these verbs are applied to resources (or even specific resource names). The `RoleBinding` and `ClusterRoleBinding` resources grant permissions defined in roles to users or sets of users.

Kubernetes also provides the following:

- Service accounts to identify processes within pods to other resources
- Pod security policies to control the special behaviors of pods, such as privileged containers, host namespaces, restrictions on running containers with root users, or enabling read-only root filesystems on containers, among other features
- Admission controllers to intercept API requests, allowing us to validate or modify them to ensure image freshness and security, forcing the creation of pods to always pull from registries, to set the default storage, to deny the execution of processes within privileged containers, or to specify the default host resource limit ranges if none are declared, among other security features

 It is very important in production environments to limit a host's resource usage because non-limited pods can consume all of their resources by default.

Kubernetes provides many features to ensure cluster security at all levels. It is up to you to use them because most of them are not applied by default. We will learn more about the roles and grants applied to resources in `Chapter 11`, *Universal Control Plane*, because many of these configurations are integrated into Docker Enterprise.

We are not going to go deeper into this topic because Kubernetes is not part of the current Docker Certified Associate curriculum, and this is just a quick introduction.

It is recommended that you take a closer look at Kubernetes' security features because it has many more compared to Docker Swarm. On the other hand, it is true that Docker Enterprise provides many of these features to Docker Swarm.

Comparing Docker Swarm and Kubernetes side by side

In this section, we will compare the Docker Swarm and Kubernetes features side by side to get a good idea of how they solve common problems. We have discussed these concepts in both this chapter and in `Chapter 8`, *Orchestration Using Docker Swarm*. They have common approaches to many problems:

Parameters	Docker Swarm	Kubernetes
High-availability solution	Provides high availability for core components.	Provides high availability for core components.
Resilience	All services run with resilience based on the state definition.	All resources based on replication controllers will provide resilience (`ReplicaSet`, `DaemonSet`, `Deployment`, and `StatefulSet`) based on the state definition.
Infrastructure as code	The Docker Compose file format will allow us to deploy stacks.	We will use YAML to format resource files. These will allow us to deploy workloads using a declarative format.
Dynamic distribution	Application components and their replicas will be automatically distributed cluster-wide, although we can provide some constraints.	Kubernetes also distributes components, but we can provide advanced constraints using labels and other features.
Automatic updates	Application components can be upgraded using rolling updates and rollbacks in the case of a failure.	Kubernetes also provides rolling updates and rollbacks.
Publishing applications	Docker Swarm provides internal load balancing between service replicas and **router mesh** to publish an application's service's ports on all of the cluster nodes at the same time.	Kubernetes also provides internal load balancing, and `NodePort` type services will also publish the application's components on all of the nodes at the same time. But Kubernetes also provides load balancing services (among other types) to auto-configure external load balancers to route requests to deployed services.

Cluster-internal networking	Containers that are deployed as tasks for each service can communicate with other containers deployed in the same network. Internal IP management will provide their IP addresses, and services can be consumed by their names so that there is internal DNS resolution.	Pod-to-pod communication works and IP addresses are provided by internal **Internet Protocol Address Management** (IPAM). We will also have service-to-service communication and resolution.
Key-value store	Docker Swarm provides an internal store to manage all objects and their statuses. This store will have high availability with an odd number of master nodes.	Kubernetes also requires a key-value store to manage its resources. This component is provided using `etcd` and we can deploy it externally out of Kubernetes cluster nodes. We should provide an odd number of `etcd` nodes to provide high availability.

The preceding table showed us the main similarities regarding solving common problems. The next table will show the main differences:

Parameters	Docker Swarm	Kubernetes
Pods versus tasks	Docker Swarm deploys tasks for services. Each task will run one container at a time. If the container dies, a new one will be created to ensure the required number of replicas (tasks).Services are the smallest unit of deployment. We will deploy applications running their components as services.	Kubernetes has the concept of a pod. Each pod can run more than one container inside. All of them share the same IP address (networking namespace). Containers inside a pod share volumes and will always run on the same host. A pod's life relies on containers. If one of them dies, a pod is unhealthy. Pods are the smallest unit of deployment in Kubernetes; therefore, we scale pods up and down, with all of their containers.
Services	Services in Docker Swarm are objects with an IP address for internal load balancing between replicas (by default, we can avoid this using the `dnsrr` endpoint mode). We create services to execute our application components, and we scale up or down the number of replicas required to be healthy.	In Kubernetes, services are different. They are logical resources. This means that they are deployed only to publish a group of pod resources. Kubernetes services are logical groupings of pods that work together. Kubernetes services also get an IP address for internal load balancing (`clusterIP`), and we can also avoid this situation by using the "headless" feature.

Networking	Docker Swarm deploys overlay networking by default. This ensures communications between an application's components are deployed on different hosts.Stacks in Docker Swarm will be deployed on different networks. This means that we can provide a subnet for each application. Multiple networks for deployments will provide a good level of security because they are isolated from each other. This can be improved using available network encryption (disabled by default). However, on the other hand, they are difficult to manage and things can get complicated when we need to provide isolation on services integrated into multiple stacks.	Kubernetes provides a flat network using a common interface called a CNI. Networking has been decoupled from Kubernetes' core to allow us to use multiple and different networking solutions. Each solution has its own features and implementation for routing on a cluster environment. A flat network makes things easier. All pods and services will see each other by default. On the other hand, security is not provided. We will deploy `NetworkPolicy` resources to ensure secure communications between resources in the cluster. These policies will manage who can talk to who in the Kubernetes world.
Authentication and authorization	Docker Swarm, by default, does not provide any mechanism to authenticate or authorize specific requests. Once a Docker Swarm node has published its daemon access (in a `daemon.json` configuration file), anyone can connect to it and manage the cluster if we use a manager node. This is a security risk that should always be avoided. We can create a secure client configuration with SSL/TLS certificates. But certificates in Docker Swarm will ensure secure communication only. There is no authorization validation. Docker Enterprise will provide the required features to provide RBAC to Docker Swarm's clusters.	Kubernetes does provide authentication and authorization. In fact, it includes a full-featured RBAC system to manage users' and applications' accesses to the resources deployed within the Kubernetes cluster. This RBAC system allows us to set specific permissions for a user's or team's access. Using Kubernetes namespaces will also improve security in multi-tenant or team scenarios.
Secrets	Docker encrypts secrets by default. They will only be readable inside containers while they are running.	Kubernetes will encode secrets using the Base64 algorithm by default. We will need to use external secret providers or additional encryption configuration (`EncryptionConfig`) to ensure a secret's integrity.

Publishing applications	Docker Swarm just provides a router mesh for publishing applications. This will publish application ports on all cluster nodes. This can be insecure because all nodes will have all the applications published and we will use a lot of ports (at least one for each published application). Docker Enterprise will provide Interlock, which has many features in common with ingress controllers.	Kubernetes provides ingress controller resources. Ingress controllers publish a few endpoints (using NodePort or any other cloud service definition), and this internal ingress will talk to services' backends (pods). This will require fewer ports for applications (only those required to publish ingress controllers). Requests will be routed by these resources to real backend services. Security is improved because we add a smart piece of software in the middle of the requests to help us to decide which backends will process requests. The ingress controller acts as a reverse-proxy and it will verify whether a valid host header is used on every request. If none is used, requests will be forwarded to a default backend. If requests contain a valid header, they will be forwarded to the defined service's virtual IP and the internal load balancer will choose which pod will finally receive them. The orchestrator will manage defined rules and clusters, and the internal or external load balancer will interpret them to ensure the right backend receives the user's request.

So far, we have learned that there are several similarities and differences between Docker Swarm and Kubernetes. We can note the following:

- Kubernetes provides more container density.
- Docker Swarm provides cluster-wide networking with subnets for isolation by default.
- Kubernetes provides role-based access to cluster resources.
- Publishing applications in Kubernetes is better using ingress controllers.

Let's now review some of the topics we have learned by applying them to some easy labs.

Chapter labs

We will now work through a long lab that will help us to review the concepts we've learned so far.

Deploy `environments/kubernetes` from this book's GitHub repository (`https://github.com/PacktPublishing/Docker-Certified-Associate-DCA-Exam-Guide.git`) if you have not done so yet. You can use your own Linux server. Use `vagrant up` from the `environments/kubernetes` folder to start your virtual environment. All files used during these labs can be found inside the `chapter9` folder.

Wait until all of the nodes are running. We can check the status of the nodes using `vagrant status`. Connect to your lab node using `vagrant ssh kubernetes-node1`. Vagrant deploys three nodes for you, and you will be using the `vagrant` user with root privileges using `sudo`. You should have the following output:

```
Docker-Certified-Associate-DCA-Exam-Guide/environments/kubernetes$ vagrant
up
-------------------------------------------------------------------------
------------------
 KUBERNETES Vagrant Environment
 Engine Version: current
 Kubernetes Version: 1.14.0-00
 Kubernetes CNI: https://docs.projectcalico.org/v3.8/manifests/calico.yaml
-------------------------------------------------------------------------
------------------
Bringing machine 'kubernetes-node1' up with 'virtualbox' provider...
Bringing machine 'kubernetes-node2' up with 'virtualbox' provider...
Bringing machine 'kubernetes-node3' up with 'virtualbox' provider...


...
Docker-Certified-Associate-DCA-Exam-Guide/environments/kubernetes$
```

Nodes will have three interfaces (IP addresses and virtual hardware resources can be modified by changing the `config.yml` file):

- `eth0 [10.0.2.15]`: This is an internal interface, required for Vagrant.
- `eth1 [10.10.10.X/24]`: This is prepared for Docker Kubernetes' internal communication. The first node will get the `10.10.10.11` IP address and so on.
- `eth2 [192.168.56.X/24]`: This is a host-only interface for communication between your host and the virtual nodes. The first node will get the `192.168.56.11` IP address and so on.

We will use the `eth1` interface for Kubernetes, and we will be able to connect to published applications using the `192.168.56.X/24` IP address' range. All nodes have Docker Engine Community Edition installed and a Vagrant user is allowed to execute `docker`. A small Kubernetes cluster with one master (`kubernetes-node1`) and two worker nodes (`kubernetes-node2` and `kubernetes-node3`) will be deployed for you.

We can now connect to the first deployed virtual node using `vagrant ssh kubernetes-node1`. The process may vary if you have already deployed a Kubernetes virtual environment and have just started it using `vagrant up`:

```
Docker-Certified-Associate-DCA-Exam-Guide/environments/kubernetes$ vagrant
ssh kubernetes-node1
vagrant@kubernetes-node1:~$
```

Now you are ready to start the labs. We will start these labs by deploying a simple application.

Deploying applications in Kubernetes

Once Vagrant (or your own environment) is deployed, we will have three nodes (named `kubernetes-node<index>` from 1 to 3) with Ubuntu Xenial and Docker Engine installed. Kubernetes will also be up and running for you, with one master node and two workers. The Calico CNI will also be deployed for you automatically.

First, review your node IP addresses (`10.10.10.11` to `10.10.10.13` if you used Vagrant, because the first interface will be Vagrant-internal).

The steps for deploying our application are as follows:

1. Connect to `kubernetes-node1` and review the deployed Kubernetes cluster using `kubectl get nodes`. A file, named `config`, including the required credentials and the Kubernetes API endpoint will be copied under the `~/.kube` directory automatically. We'll also refer to this file as **Kubeconfig**. This file configures the `kubectl` command line for you:

   ```
   Docker-Certified-Associate-DCA-Exam-Guide/environments/kubernetes$
   vagrant ssh kubernetes-node1

   vagrant@kubernetes-node1:~$ kubectl get nodes
   NAME STATUS ROLES AGE VERSION
   kubernetes-node1 Ready master 6m52s v1.14.0
   kubernetes-node2 Ready <none> 3m57s v1.14.0
   kubernetes-node3 Ready <none> 103s v1.14.0
   ```

   Kubernetes cluster version 1.14.00 has been deployed and is running. Notice that `kubernetes-node1` is the only master node in this cluster; therefore, we are not providing high availability.

Currently, we are using the `admin` user, and, by default, all deployments will run on the `default` namespace, unless another is specified. This configuration is also done in the `~/.kube/config` file.

The Calico CNI was also deployed; hence, host-to-container networking should work cluster-wide.

2. Create a deployment file, named `blue-deployment-simple.yaml`, using your favorite editor with the following content:

```yaml
apiVersion: extensions/v1beta1
kind: Deployment
metadata:
  name: blue-app
  labels:
    color: blue
    example: blue-app
spec:
  replicas: 2
  selector:
    matchLabels:
      app: blue
  template:
    metadata:
      labels:
        app: blue
    spec:
      containers:
      - name: blue
        image: codegazers/colors:1.12
        env:
        - name: COLOR
          value: blue
        ports:
        - containerPort: 3000
```

This will deploy two replicas of the `codegazers/colors:1.12` image. We will expect two running pods after it is deployed. We set the `COLOR` environment variable to `blue` and, as a result, all of the application components will be `blue`. Containers will expose port `3000` internally within the cluster.

3. Let's deploy this `blue-app` application using `kubectl create -f <KUBERNETES_RESOURCES_FILE>.yaml`:

```
vagrant@kubernetes-node1:~$ kubectl create -f blue-deployment-
simple.yaml
deployment.extensions/blue-app created
```

This command line has created a deployment, named `blue-app`, with two replicas. Let's review the deployment created using `kubectl get deployments`:

```
vagrant@kubernetes-node1:~$ kubectl get deployments -o wide
NAME READY UP-TO-DATE AVAILABLE AGE CONTAINERS IMAGES SELECTOR
blue-app 2/2 2 2 103s blue codegazers/colors:1.12 app=blue
```

Therefore, two pods will be running, associated with the `blue-app` deployment. Let's now review the deployed pods using `kubectl get pods`:

```
vagrant@kubernetes-node1:~$ kubectl get pods -o wide
NAME READY STATUS RESTARTS AGE IP NODE NOMINATED NODE READINESS
GATES
blue-app-54485c74fc-wgw7r 1/1 Running 0 2m8s 192.168.135.2
kubernetes-node3 <none> <none>
blue-app-54485c74fc-x8p92 1/1 Running 0 2m8s 192.168.104.2
kubernetes-node2 <none> <none>
```

In this case, one pod runs on `kubernetes-node2` and another one runs on `kubernetes-node3`. Let's try to connect to their virtual assigned IP addresses on the exposed port. Remember that IP addresses will be assigned randomly, hence they may vary on your environment. We will just use `curl` against the IP address of `kubernetes-node1` and the pod's internal port:

```
vagrant@kubernetes-node1:~$ curl 192.168.104.2:3000/text
APP_VERSION: 1.0
COLOR: blue
CONTAINER_NAME: blue-app-54485c74fc-x8p92
CONTAINER_IP: 192.168.104.2
CLIENT_IP: ::ffff:192.168.166.128
CONTAINER_ARCH: linux
```

We can connect from `kubernetes-node1` to pods running on other hosts correctly. So, Calico is working correctly.

We should be able to connect to any pods' deployed IP addresses. These IP addresses will change whenever a container dies and a new pod is deployed. We will never connect to pods to consume their application processes. We will use services instead of pods to publish applications, as we have already discussed in this chapter. They will not change their IP addresses when application components, running as pods, have to be recreated.

4. Let's create a service to load balance requests between deployed pods with a fixed virtual IP address. Create the `blue-service-simple.yaml` file with the following content:

```
apiVersion: v1
kind: Service
metadata:
  name: blue-svc
spec:
  ports:
  - port: 80
    targetPort: 3000
    protocol: TCP
    name: http
  selector:
    app: blue
```

A random IP address will be associated with this service. This IP address will be fixed, and it will be valid even if pods die. Notice that we have exposed a new port for the service. This will be the service's port, and requests reaching the defined port 80 will be routed to port 3000 on each pod. We will use `kubectl get svc` to retrieve the service's port and IP address:

```
vagrant@kubernetes-node1:~$ kubectl create -f blue-service-
simple.yaml
service/blue-svc created

vagrant@kubernetes-node1:~$ kubectl get svc
NAME TYPE CLUSTER-IP EXTERNAL-IP PORT(S) AGE
blue-svc ClusterIP 10.100.207.49 <none> 80/TCP 7s
kubernetes ClusterIP 10.96.0.1 <none> 443/TCP 53m
```

5. Let's verify the internal load balance by sending some requests to the `blue-svc` service using `curl` against its IP address, accessing port 80:

```
vagrant@kubernetes-node1:~$ curl 10.100.207.49:80/text
APP_VERSION: 1.0
COLOR: blue
CONTAINER_NAME: blue-app-54485c74fc-x8p92
```

```
CONTAINER_IP: 192.168.104.2
CLIENT_IP: ::ffff:192.168.166.128
CONTAINER_ARCH: linux
```

6. Let's try again using `curl`. We will test the internal load balancing by executing some requests to the service's IP address and port:

```
vagrant@kubernetes-node1:~$ curl 10.100.207.49:80/text
APP_VERSION: 1.0
COLOR: blue
CONTAINER_NAME: blue-app-54485c74fc-wgw7r
CONTAINER_IP: 192.168.135.2
CLIENT_IP: ::ffff:192.168.166.128
CONTAINER_ARCH: linux
```

The service has load-balanced our requests between both pods. Let's now try to expose this service to be accessible to the application's users.

7. Now we will remove the previous service's definition and deploy a new one with the service's `NodePort` type. We will use `kubectl delete -f <KUBERNETES_RESOURCES_FILE>.yaml`:

```
vagrant@kubernetes-node1:~$ kubectl delete -f blue-service-simple.yaml
service "blue-svc" deleted
```

Create a new definition, `blue-service-nodeport.yaml`, with the following content:

```yaml
apiVersion: v1
kind: Service
metadata:
  name: blue-svc
spec:
  type: NodePort
  ports:
  - port: 80
    targetPort: 3000
    protocol: TCP
    name: http
  selector:
    app: blue
```

8. We now just create a service definition and notice a random port associated with it. We will also use `kubectl create` and `kubectl get svc` after it is deployed:

```
vagrant@kubernetes-node1:~$ kubectl create -f blue-service-
nodeport.yaml
service/blue-svc created

vagrant@kubernetes-node1:~$ kubectl get svc
NAME TYPE CLUSTER-IP EXTERNAL-IP PORT(S) AGE
blue-svc NodePort 10.100.179.60 <none> 80:32648/TCP 5s
kubernetes ClusterIP 10.96.0.1 <none> 443/TCP 58m
```

9. We learned that the `NodePort` service will act as Docker Swarm's router mesh. Therefore, the service's port will be fixed on every node. Let's verify this feature using `curl` against any node's IP address and assigned port. In this example, it is `32648`. This port may vary on your environment because it will be assigned dynamically:

```
vagrant@kubernetes-node1:~$ curl 0.0.0.0:32648/text
APP_VERSION: 1.0
COLOR: blue
CONTAINER_NAME: blue-app-54485c74fc-x8p92
CONTAINER_IP: 192.168.104.2
CLIENT_IP: ::ffff:192.168.166.128
CONTAINER_ARCH: linux
```

10. Locally, on `node1` port `32648`, the service is accessible. It should be accessible on any of the nodes on the same port. Let's try on `node3`, for example, using `curl`:

```
vagrant@kubernetes-node3:~$ curl 10.10.10.13:32648/text
APP_VERSION: 1.0
COLOR: blue
CONTAINER_NAME: blue-app-54485c74fc-wgw7r
CONTAINER_IP: 192.168.135.2
CLIENT_IP: ::ffff:10.0.2.15
CONTAINER_ARCH: linux
```

We learned that even if a node does not run a related workload, the service will be accessible on the defined (or, in this case, random) port using `NodePort`.

11. We will finish this lab by upgrading the deployment images to a newer version. We will use `kubectl set image deployment`:

```
vagrant@kubernetes-node1:~$ kubectl set image deployment blue-app
blue=codegazers/colors:1.15
deployment.extensions/blue-app image updated
```

12. Let's review the deployment again to verify that the update was done. We will use `kubectl get all -o wide` to retrieve all of the created resources and their locations:

```
vagrant@kubernetes-node1:~$ kubectl get all -o wide
NAME READY STATUS RESTARTS AGE IP NODE NOMINATED NODE READINESS
GATES
pod/blue-app-787648f786-4tz5b 1/1 Running 0 76s 192.168.104.3 node2
<none> <none>
pod/blue-app-787648f786-98bmf 1/1 Running 0 76s 192.168.135.3 node3
<none> <none>

NAME TYPE CLUSTER-IP EXTERNAL-IP PORT(S) AGE SELECTOR
service/blue-svc NodePort 10.100.179.60 <none> 80:32648/TCP 22m
app=blue
service/kubernetes ClusterIP 10.96.0.1 <none> 443/TCP 81m <none>

NAME READY UP-TO-DATE AVAILABLE AGE CONTAINERS IMAGES SELECTOR
deployment.apps/blue-app 2/2 2 2 52m blue codegazers/colors:1.15
app=blue

NAME DESIRED CURRENT READY AGE CONTAINERS IMAGES SELECTOR
replicaset.apps/blue-app-54485c74fc 0 0 0 52m blue
codegazers/colors:1.12 app=blue,pod-template-hash=54485c74fc
replicaset.apps/blue-app-787648f786 2 2 2 76s blue
codegazers/colors:1.15 app=blue,pod-template-hash=787648f786
```

13. Notice that new pods were created with a newer image. We can verify the update using `kubectl rollout status`:

```
vagrant@kubernetes-node1:~$ kubectl rollout status
deployment.apps/blue-app
deployment "blue-app" successfully rolled out
```

14. We can go back to the previous image version just by executing `kubectl`
    `rollout undo`. Let's go back to the previous image version:

    ```
    vagrant@kubernetes-node1:~$ kubectl rollout undo
    deployment.apps/blue-app
    deployment.apps/blue-app rolled back
    ```

15. And now, we can verify that the current `blue-app` deployment runs
    the `codegazers/colors:1.12` images again. We will again review deployment
    locations using `kubectl get all`:

    ```
    vagrant@kubernetes-node1:~$ kubectl get all -o wide
    NAME READY STATUS RESTARTS AGE IP NODE NOMINATED NODE READINESS
    GATES
    pod/blue-app-54485c74fc-kslgw 1/1 Running 0 62s 192.168.104.4 node2
    <none> <none>
    pod/blue-app-54485c74fc-lrkxv 1/1 Running 0 62s 192.168.135.4 node3
    <none> <none>

    NAME TYPE CLUSTER-IP EXTERNAL-IP PORT(S) AGE SELECTOR
    service/blue-svc NodePort 10.100.179.60 <none> 80:32648/TCP 29m
    app=blue
    service/kubernetes ClusterIP 10.96.0.1 <none> 443/TCP 87m <none>

    NAME READY UP-TO-DATE AVAILABLE AGE CONTAINERS IMAGES SELECTOR
    deployment.apps/blue-app 2/2 2 2 58m blue codegazers/colors:1.12
    app=blue

    NAME DESIRED CURRENT READY AGE CONTAINERS IMAGES SELECTOR
    replicaset.apps/blue-app-54485c74fc 2 2 2 58m blue
    codegazers/colors:1.12 app=blue,pod-template-hash=54485c74fc
    replicaset.apps/blue-app-787648f786 0 0 0 7m46s blue
    codegazers/colors:1.15 app=blue,pod-template-hash=787648f786
    ```

    Going back to the previous state was very easy.

> We can set comments for each change using the `--record` option on the
> `update` commands.

Using volumes

In this lab, we will deploy a simple web server using different volumes. We will use `webserver.deployment.yaml`.

We have prepared the following volumes:

- `congigMap`: **Config volume with** `/etc/nginx/conf.d/default.conf`—**the configuration file)**
- `emptyDir`: **Empty volume for NGINX logs,** `/var/log/nginx`
- `secret`: **Secret volume to specify some variables to compose the** `index.html` **page**
- `persistentVolumeClaim`: **Data volume bound to the** `hostPath` **defined as** `persistentVolume` **using the host's** `/mnt` **content**

We have declared one specific node for our web server to ensure the `index.html` file location under the `/mnt` directory. We have used `nodeName: kubernetes-node2` in our deployment file, `webserver.deployment.yaml`:

1. First, we verify that there is no file under the `/mnt` directory in the `kubernetes-node2` node. We connect to `kubernetes-node2` and then we review the `/mnt` content:

   ```
   $ vagrant ssh kubernetes-node2

   vagrant@kubernetes-node2:~$ ls  /mnt/
   ```

2. Then, we change to `kubernetes-node1` to clone our repository and launch the web server deployment:

   ```
   $ vagrant ssh kubernetes-node1

   vagrant@kubernetes-node1:~$ git clone
   https://github.com/PacktPublishing/Docker-Certified-Associate-DCA-E
   xam-Guide.git
   ```

   We move to `chapter9/nginx-lab/yaml`:

   ```
   vagrant@kubernetes-node1:~$ cd Docker-Certified-Associate-DCA-Exam-
   Guide/chapter9/nginx-lab/yaml/
   vagrant@kubernetes-node1:~/Docker-Certified-Associate-DCA-Exam-
   Guide/chapter9/nginx-lab/yaml$
   ```

3. We will use the `ConfigMap`, `Secret`, `Service`, `PersistentVolume`, and `PersistentVolumeClaim` resources in this lab using YAML files. We will deploy all of the resource files in the `yaml` directory:

```
vagrant@kubernetes-node1:~/Docker-Certified-Associate-DCA-Exam-
Guide/chapter9/nginx-lab/yaml$ kubectl create -f .
configmap/webserver-test-config created
deployment.apps/webserver created
persistentvolume/webserver-pv created
persistentvolumeclaim/werbserver-pvc created
secret/webserver-secret created
service/webserver-svc created
```

4. Now we will review all of the resources created. We have not defined a namespace; therefore, the `default` namespace will be used (we omitted it in our commands because it is our default namespace). We will use `kubectl get all` to list all of the resources available in the default namespace:

```
vagrant@kubernetes-node1:~/Docker-Certified-Associate-DCA-Exam-
Guide/chapter9/nginx-lab/yaml$ kubectl get all
NAME                             READY    STATUS     RESTARTS    AGE
pod/webserver-d7fbbf4b7-rhvvn    1/1      Running    0           31s
NAME                     TYPE        CLUSTER-IP       EXTERNAL-IP
PORT(S)          AGE
service/kubernetes       ClusterIP   10.96.0.1        <none>
443/TCP          107m
service/webserver-svc    NodePort    10.97.146.192    <none>
80:30080/TCP     31s
NAME                         READY    UP-TO-DATE   AVAILABLE   AGE
deployment.apps/webserver    1/1      1            1           31s
NAME                                 DESIRED   CURRENT   READY
AGE
replicaset.apps/webserver-d7fbbf4b7  1         1         1
31s
```

However, not all of the resources are listed. The `PersistentVolume` and `PersistentVolumeClaim` resources are not shown. Therefore, we will ask the Kubernetes API about these resources using `kubectl get pv` (`PersisteVolumes`) and `kubectl get pvs` (`PersistenVolumeClaims`):

```
vagrant@kubernetes-node1:~/Docker-Certified-Associate-DCA-Exam-
Guide/chapter9/nginx-lab/yaml$ kubectl get pv
NAME            CAPACITY   ACCESS MODES   RECLAIM POLICY   STATUS
CLAIM                      STORAGECLASS   REASON   AGE
webserver-pv    500Mi      RWO                             Retain            Bound
default/werbserver-pvc     manual                  6m13s
```

```
vagrant@kubernetes-node1:~/Docker-Certified-Associate-DCA-Exam-
Guide/chapter9/nginx-lab/yaml$ kubectl get pvc
NAME                STATUS   VOLUME          CAPACITY    ACCESS MODES
STORAGECLASS    AGE
werbserver-pvc      Bound    webserver-pv    500Mi       RWO
manual          6m15s
```

5. Let's send some requests to our web server. You can see, in `kubectl get all` output, that `webserver-svc` is published using `NodePort` on port `30080`, associating the host's port `30080` with the service's port `80`. As mentioned earlier, all hosts will publish port `30080`; therefore, we can use `curl` on the current host (`kubernetes-node1`) and port `30080` to try to reach our web server's pods:

```
vagrant@kubernetes-node1:~/Docker-Certified-Associate-DCA-Exam-
Guide/chapter9/nginx-lab/yaml$ curl 0.0.0.0:30080
<!DOCTYPE html>
<html>
<head>
<title>DEFAULT_TITLE</title>
<style>
    body {
        width: 35em;
        margin: 0 auto;
        font-family: Tahoma, Verdana, Arial, sans-serif;
    }
</style>
</head>
<body>
<h1>DEFAULT_BODY</h1>
</body>
</html>
```

6. We have used ;a `ConfigMap` resource to specify an NGINX configuration file, `webserver.configmap.yaml`:

```
apiVersion: v1
kind: ConfigMap
metadata:
  creationTimestamp: null
  name: webserver-test-config
data:
  default.conf: |+
      server {
          listen        80;
          server_name   test;
          location / {
              root    /wwwroot;
```

```
        index   index.html index.htm;
    }
    error_page   500 502 503 504   /50x.html;
    location = /50x.html {
        root   /usr/share/nginx/html;
    }
}
```

This configuration is included inside our deployment file,
`webserver.deployment.yaml`. Here is the piece of code where it is defined:

```
...
        volumeMounts:
        - name: config-volume
          mountPath: /etc/nginx/conf.d/
...
      volumes:
      - name: config-volume
        configMap:
          name: webserver-test-config
...
```

The first piece declares where this configuration file will be mounted, while the
second part links the defined resource: `webserver-test-config`. Therefore, the
data defined inside the `ConfigMap` resource will be integrated inside the web
server's pod as `/etc/nginx/conf.d/default.conf` (take a look at the data
block).

7. As mentioned earlier, we also have a `Secret` resource
   (`webserver.secret.yaml`):

```
apiVersion: v1
data:
  PAGEBODY: SGVsbG9fV29ybGRfZnJvbV9TZWNyZXQ=
  PAGETITLE: RG9ja2VyX0NlcnRpZmllZF9EQ0FfRXhhbV9HdWlkZQ==
kind: Secret
metadata:
  creationTimestamp: null
  name: webserver-secret
```

We can verify, here, that keys are visible while values are not (encoded using the
Base64 algorithm).

We can also create this secret using the imperative format with the `kubectl` command line:

```
kubectl create secret generic webserver-secret \
--from-
literal=PAGETITLE="Docker_Certified_DCA_Exam_Guide" \
--from-literal=PAGEBODY="Hello_World_from_Secret"
```

We also used this secret resource in our deployment:

```
...
        env:
...

      - name: PAGETITLE
        valueFrom:
          secretKeyRef:
            name: webserver-secret
            key: PAGETITLE
      - name: PAGEBODY
        valueFrom:
          secretKeyRef:
            name: webserver-secret
            key: PAGEBODY
...
```

In this case, the `PAGETITLE` and `PAGEBODY` keys will be integrated as environment variables inside the web server's pod. These values will be used in our lab as values for the `index.html` page. `DEFAULT_BODY` and `DEFAULT_TITLE` will be changed from the pod's container process.

8. This lab has another volume definition. In fact, we have `PersistentVolumeclaim` included as a volume in our deployment's definition:

```
...
        volumeMounts:
...

      - mountPath: /wwwroot
        name: data-volume
...

    - name: data-volume
      persistentVolumeClaim:
        claimName: werbserver-pvc
...
```

The volume claim is used here and is mounted in `/wwwroot` inside the web server's pod. `PersistentVolume` and `PersistentVolumeClaim` are defined in `webserver.persistevolume.yaml` and `webserver.persistevolumeclaim.yaml`, respectively.

9. Finally, we have an `emptyDir` volume definition. This will be used to bypass the container's filesystem and save the NGINX logs:

```
...
        volumeMounts:
...

        - mountPath: /var/log/nginx
          name: empty-volume
          readOnly: false
...
      volumes:
...
      - name: empty-volume
        emptyDir: {}
...
```

10. The first pod execution will create a default `/wwwroot/index.html` file inside it. This is mounted inside the `kubernetes-node2` node's filesystem, inside the `/mount` directory. Therefore, after this first execution, we find that `/mnt/index.html` was created (you can verify this by following *step 1* again). The file was published, and we get it when we execute `curl 0.0.0.0:30080` in *step 5*.

11. Our application is quite simple, but it is prepared to modify the content of the `index.html` file. As mentioned earlier, the default title and body will be changed with the values defined in the secret resource. This will happen after the creation of the container if the `index.html` file already exists. Now that it has been created, as verified in *step 10*, we can delete the web server's pod. Kubernetes will create a new one, and, therefore, the application will change its content. We use `kubectl delete pod`:

```
vagrant@kubernetes-node1:~/Docker-Certified-Associate-DCA-Exam-
Guide/chapter9/nginx-lab/yaml$ kubectl delete pod/webserver-
d7fbbf4b7-rhvvn
pod "webserver-d7fbbf4b7-rhvvn" deleted
```

After a few seconds, a new pod is created (we are using a deployment and Kubernetes takes care of the application's component resilience):

```
vagrant@kubernetes-node1:~/Docker-Certified-Associate-DCA-Exam-
Guide/chapter9/nginx-lab/yaml$ kubectl get pods
NAME READY STATUS RESTARTS AGE
webserver-d7fbbf4b7-sz6dx 1/1 Running 0 17s
```

12. Let's again verify the content of our web server using `curl`:

```
vagrant@kubernetes-node1:~/Docker-Certified-Associate-DCA-Exam-
Guide/chapter9/nginx-lab/yaml$ curl 0.0.0.0:30080
<!DOCTYPE html>
<html>
<head>
<title>Docker_Certified_DCA_Exam_Guide</title>
<style>
 body {
 width: 35em;
 margin: 0 auto;
 font-family: Tahoma, Verdana, Arial, sans-serif;
 }
</style>
</head>
<body>
<h1>Hello_World_from_Secret</h1>
</body>
</html>
```

Now the content has changed inside the defined `PersistentVolume` resource.

13. We can also verify the `/mnt/index.html` content in `kubernetes-node2`:

```
$ vagrant ssh kubernetes-node2

vagrant@kubernetes-node2:~$ cat /mnt/index.html
<!DOCTYPE html>
<html>
<head>
<title>Docker_Certified_DCA_Exam_Guide</title>
<style>
 body {
 width: 35em;
 margin: 0 auto;
 font-family: Tahoma, Verdana, Arial, sans-serif;
 }
</style>
</head>
```

```
<body>
<h1>Hello_World_from_Secret</h1>
</body>
</html>
```

In this lab, we have used four different volume resources, with different definitions and features. These labs were very simple, showing you how to deploy a small application on Kubernetes. All of the labs can be easily removed by destroying all the Vagrant nodes using `vagrant destroy` from the `environments/kubernetes` directory.

We highly recommend going further with Kubernetes because it will become a part of the exam in the near future. However, right now, Kubernetes is outside the scope of the Docker Certified Associate exam.

Summary

In this chapter, we quickly reviewed some of Kubernetes' main features. We compared most of the must-have orchestration features with those discussed in `Chapter 8`, *Orchestration Using Docker Swarm*. Both provide workload deployment and the management of a distributed pool of nodes. They monitor an application's health and allow us to upgrade components without service interruption. They also provide networking and publishing solutions.

Pods provide higher container density, allowing us to run more than one container at once. This concept is closer to applications running on virtual machines and makes container adoption easier. Services are logical groups of pods and we can use them to expose applications. Service discovery and load balancing work out of the box dynamically.

Cluster-wide networking requires additional plugins in Kubernetes, and we also learned that a flat network can facilitate routing on different hosts and make some things easier; however, it does not provide security by default. Kubernetes provides enough mechanisms to ensure network security using network policies and single endpoints for multiple services with ingress. Publishing applications is even easier with ingress. It adds internal load balancing features dynamically with rules managed using ingress resources. This allows us to save up node ports and public IP addresses within the environment.

At the end of the chapter, we reviewed a number of points about Kubernetes security. We discussed how RBAC provides different environments to users running their workloads on the same cluster. We also talked about some features provided by Kubernetes to ensure default security on resources.

There is much more to learn about Kubernetes, but we will have to end this chapter here. We highly recommend that you follow the Kubernetes documentation and the release notes on the project's website (`https://kubernetes.io/`).

In the next chapter, we'll look at the differences and similarities between Swarm and Kubernetes, side by side.

Questions

1. Which of these features is not included in Kubernetes by default?

    a) An internal key-value store.
    b) Network communication between containers distributed on different Docker hosts.
    c) Controllers for deploying workload updates without service interruptions.
    d) None of these features are included.

2. Which of these statements is true about pods?

    a) Pods always run in pairs to provide an application with high availability.
    b) Pods are the minimum unit of deployment on Kubernetes.
    c) We can deploy more than one container per pod.
    d) We need to choose which containers in a pod should be replicated when pods are scaled.

3. Which of these statements is true about pods?

    a) All pod containers run using a unique network namespace.
    b) All containers within a pod can share volumes.
    c) All pods running on Docker Engine are accessible from the host using their IP addresses.
    d) All of these statements are true.

4. Kubernetes provides different controllers to deploy application workloads. Which of these statements is true?

    a) `DaemonSet` will run one replica on each cluster node.
    b) `ReplicaSet` will allow us to scale application pods up or down.
    c) Deployments are higher-level resources. They manage `ReplicaSet`.
    d) All of these statements are true.

5. How can we expose services to users in Kubernetes? (Which of these statements is false?)

    a) ClusterIP services provide a virtual IP accessible to users.
    b) NodePort services listen on all nodes and route traffic using the provided ClusterIP to reach all service backends.
    c) LoadBalancer creates simple load balancers on cloud providers to load balance requests to service backends.
    d) Ingress controllers help us to use single endpoints (one per ingress controller) to load balance requests to non-published services.

Further reading

You can refer to the following links for more information on topics covered in this chapter:

- Kubernetes documentation: `https://kubernetes.io/docs/home/`
- Kubernetes concepts: `https://kubernetes.io/docs/concepts/`
- Kubernetes learning tasks: `https://kubernetes.io/docs/tasks/`
- Kubernetes on Docker Enterprise: `https://docs.docker.com/ee/ucp/kubernetes/kube-resources`
- *Getting Started with Kubernetes*: `https://www.packtpub.com/virtualization-and-cloud/getting-started-kubernetes-third-edition`

Section 3 - Docker Enterprise

This section introduces Docker Enterprise **Containers as a Service (CaaS)** platform, including a deep dive review of all its components. We will cover Docker Enterprise runtime, Universal Control Plane, and Docker Trusted Registry. In each section, we will take a closer look at all of the components, the management of each feature provided, and the installation of each product in a production environment.

This section comprises the following chapters:

- Chapter 10, *Introduction to the Docker Enterprise Platform*
- Chapter 11, *Universal Control Plane*
- Chapter 12, *Publishing Applications in Docker Enterprise*
- Chapter 13, *Implementing an Enterprise-Grade Registry with DTR*

10
Introduction to the Docker Enterprise Platform

In the previous chapters, we talked about Docker's features and Docker environments. We introduced the concepts of containers and looked at how we can deploy applications to orchestrated environments. All the features we saw were based on Docker Community Edition. In this chapter, we will learn about all the various Docker editions and their differences before introducing the Docker Enterprise platform.

In this chapter, we will introduce the different Docker editions and tools. We will also review the concept of **Container as a Service (CaaS)** and learn about what we need in these kinds of environments. Docker provides an enterprise-ready CaaS platform and we will review all of its components.

We will cover the following topics in this chapter:

- Reviewing the Docker editions
- Understanding CaaS
- The Docker Enterprise platform
- Planning your Docker Enterprise deployment

Let's start this chapter by learning about all the different Docker editions and their specific features.

Reviewing the Docker editions

In this section, we will have a quick review of the different Docker editions. We have been using Docker Community in previous chapters, but now, it is time to learn about Docker Enterprise. This is because it is very important for the Docker Certified Associate exam. In fact, it could relate to more than 50% of the knowledge required for the exam because all of the concepts you'll be learning about will relate to this platform.

Docker Community is the Docker platform we use while developing container-based applications. It is free to use and is supported on GitHub (`https://github.com/docker/docker-ce`) and Docker Forums (`https://forums.docker.com/`).

Docker Enterprise is an enterprise-ready solution. Docker/Mirantis provides 24/7 support and is licensed by subscription.

Docker Community

When we talk about Docker Community Edition, also known as **docker-ce**, we are just referring to Docker Engine (daemon), although there are other community software products made by Docker's team:

- **Docker Toolbox**: This was the first approach available for Microsoft Windows and Apple Mac users. Before Windows containers, this was the only way of using Docker on Windows nodes. It provides a desktop environment with many tools and shortcuts for most components and actions.
- **Docker Machine**: Docker Machine allows us to provision Docker hosts. It comes with some predefined provisioners and we can extend this list with external binaries to deploy nodes with the most popular cloud providers and on-premises infrastructures.
- **Docker Desktop**: This was an evolution of the Docker Toolbox environment on Windows Professional environments. Developers were very happy with the experience they had with Docker Toolbox. In response, Docker created a desktop environment capable of launching a small Kubernetes environment, while also including application templates to help developers create simple applications with just a few mouse clicks.

Docker Community Edition provides a complete Docker Engine platform. Hence, we can create a cluster with either Docker Swarm or Kubernetes. All Community Edition features have been covered in previous chapters – we have never talked about any Enterprise-specific integrations. Docker Swarm does not provide **role-based access control** (**RBAC**) for user management. We also have to provide a solution for publishing applications securely. Remember that Docker just provides a router mesh and host publishing features and that they are not secure. For many users, Docker Swarm, with a couple of tweaks, is more than enough. It is easy to learn and manage and also provides resilience and high availability for core components.

Kubernetes can be deployed on top of Docker Community Edition. We will just use Docker Engine as the runtime for the Kubernetes cluster. This is quite common as it's the most-used solution nowadays. Kubernetes provides a rich ecosystem and comes with some out-of-the-box features required for production. But, on the other hand, some details, such as networking, require third-party solutions. Kubernetes has a different approach to the world of containers. Docker follows the *"batteries included but interchangeable"* approach, providing everything required to work out of the box, although we can change most of its components. On the other hand, Kubernetes was made with the *"everything should be pluggable"* mindset. Kubernetes has a richer ecosystem because there are many solutions around its core pieces. These help it grow faster and bigger than Docker.

Docker Enterprise

Docker Enterprise has everything that's missing from Docker Swarm. It provides a full CaaS platform that's based on two components: Docker **Universal Control Plane** (**UCP**) and **Docker Trusted Registry** (**DTR**). During the last European DockerCon, in December 2018, Docker Desktop Enterprise was announced and it was stated that it would include desktop functionality for developers. Docker Desktop Enterprise allows developers to create applications easily using Docker. They can also test their developed containers on Kubernetes locally or even choose which production environment they want to test in to ensure that their applications will run smoothly in production. Docker Desktop was created with developers in mind and Enterprise helps them avoid friction between development and production.

At the time of writing this book, Docker can be found under two different product brands. Mirantis bought the Docker Enterprise product, while Docker maintains Docker Community software and their desktop product. The complete Enterprise platform will be part of the Mirantis catalog.

Therefore, Docker Enterprise Edition covers the following products:

- **Docker Enterprise Engine**: Docker Engine is required for the Docker Enterprise platform; it provides all the required runtime features. There are slight differences between the Community and Enterprise editions. In fact, the most important one is to do with support. Docker Enterprise provides an enterprise 24/7 support subscription option and a working hours support subscription option. The Docker Community edition does not provide such support. This slight difference will probably persuade enterprise users to use Docker Enterprise Edition.

- **Docker UCP**: The control plane for the cluster is also included in Docker Enterprise Edition. This product is called Docker UCP. It also provides a Kubernetes production-ready platform out of the box, on top of a production-ready Docker Swarm cluster. It is probably the best option for getting a Kubernetes cluster with minimal effort. This cluster distribution is also supported by Docker, which means that all Kubernetes integrations have been fully tested on the Docker Enterprise platform. The bad thing about this is that Kubernetes releases have to be frozen during a product's lifetime. At the time of writing this book, the currently supported and distributed Kubernetes release is 1.14, while it is generally available as 1.17 in the Community edition. This is normal for enterprise products. Everything must be tested and verified before moving to a newer release, and this takes time.

- **Docker Trusted Registry**: A registry is always required to work with containers. Although Docker developed **Docker Registry** and it is open source, it is not enough for production. It provides neither authentication nor authorization, which are fundamental to ensure secure access to images. We can integrate **Docker Trusted Content**, but this is not easy. We will need to include Notary services and integrate them into the rest of the deployed platform. Believe me, this is not easy. I have done it in the past and it was hard to implement and even harder to maintain. DTR includes authentication and authorization based on the RBAC model. We can have organizations, teams, and different access for different users, and we can make some of our images publicly available. We get fully featured access and image publishing control. It also includes a Docker Trusted Content implementation, with all the required components and integrations. It includes CI/CD workflow integrations for different stages and security image scanning. These features will allow us to ensure that only approved images that are free from vulnerabilities run in our production CaaS platform.

- **Docker Desktop Enterprise**: This is the most recently added feature at the time of writing this book. The Docker Certified Associate exam does not include any questions about it right now. Due to this, we will just provide a basic Docker Desktop introduction. This is a desktop application that provides developers with full Docker Swarm and Kubernetes environments so that they can develop and test their applications on their laptops before moving their artifacts to other stages.

As we can see, there's a number of different components that are packaged in a Docker Enterprise release. If we go to `https://success.docker.com/article/compatibility-matrix`, we can review which component releases are verified and are supported to work together. At the time of writing this book, these are the latest supported releases of each component for Docker Enterprise Edition 3.0:

- Docker Engine 19.03.x
- Universal Control Plane 3.2.x
- Docker Trusted Registry 2.7.x

Docker Engine is supported on many Linux distributions (such as Red Hat/CentOS, SUSE SLES, Oracle Linux, and Ubuntu) and Windows (2016 and 2019 releases).

Windows nodes are only supported as worker nodes and they will only be part of a Docker Swarm orchestration. Kubernetes is not available on the Windows platform on Docker Enterprise 3.0.

In the next section, we will discuss what a CaaS platform is and how Docker provides all the expected features.

Understanding CaaS

A CaaS platform is a platform that can be used to provide container services to users. The term *as a Service* is usually associated with cloud providers and their solutions. We will extend this terminology to on-premises environments here. We will talk about CaaS as a framework or compound of applications designed to provide a complete container-based solution to users. A CaaS solution must provide the full container workflow (build, ship, and run). There is also another new term these days: **KaaS** solutions. This terminology refers to **Kubernetes as a Service** platforms, where Kubernetes is the core of the environment. These solutions add some facilities that are not included with Kubernetes out of the box, such as monitoring, logging, and CI/CD.

CaaS and KaaS environments are aimed at users that require a complete solution. There will be administrators of the solution and clients that will consume the services provided in the environment.

These platforms must provide the following:

- **Authentication**: Users accessing the platform should be authenticated so as to only allow approved users.
- **Authorization**: Roles will provide different access to different users. There should be administrators and users. Each should have different levels of access and views within the platform. Actions that can be performed on containers should be inaccessible to non-authorized users.
- **Runtime**: All containers will run on container engines. This is a requirement. There are different engines, but Docker Engine is still the most common nowadays.
- **Publishing**: We use these platforms to create and run applications based on containers, but people have to be able to consume our deployed services. CaaS/KaaS platforms must provide a component that allows us to publish applications that are deployed inside our environment.
- **Registry**: All images must be stored somewhere. Remember, images are always required. There are no containers without images, and versioning them alongside code changes will help you track issues and new functionalities. Having a registry included in your CaaS/KaaS platform is vital.
- **Status**: We need to have a complete view of the statuses of all our platform components. If there's a failure, we need to know which components will be affected, whether we'll be able to push new images, and whether our services work, for instance.
- **Integrations**: Although, in my opinion, logging and monitoring are not strictly required, it is good to at least provide integrations to external platforms for these features. Some CaaS platforms include these services in their deployment (such as Red Hat's OpenShift, among others), but it should be easy to integrate our logging and monitoring environments. Sometimes, operations teams will have their own monitoring platforms; a CaaS platform should just forward all required events to them. CI/CD workflows are another interesting integration. If a CaaS platform can integrate development and test stages within the platform, users will be able to just code. Everything else can be automated with CI/CD tools.

As we mentioned previously, these platforms will require some administrators to do all the maintenance tasks and configurations, while users will just consume the provided services to create and run their applications. There are some cloud providers that have taken a different approach. **Azure Kubernetes Service (AKS)**, Amazon's **Elastic Kubernetes Service (EKS)**, and **Google Kubernetes Service (GKS)** are the most well-known examples of these environments.

On these platforms, we just select the number of workers to deploy in our cluster. All maintenance tasks are managed by the cloud provider; we just configure user access and prepare some of the cloud provider's load balancers to route the traffic. Everything else is configured and deployed in Kubernetes. This is great because we get to just focus on deploying applications. We don't have to care about high availability in the environment, backups, or platform upgrades. The cloud provider will manage all these tasks for us. Such platforms also include monitoring and logging facilities that are integrated into their **Platform as a Service (PaaS)** environments.

In this section, we reviewed what we need to provide in a CaaS or KaaS platform. In the next section, we will learn about how Docker Enterprise implements these concepts.

The Docker Enterprise platform

Docker Enterprise provides a CaaS platform. In this section, we will try to apply everything we know about CaaS platforms to what we understand about Docker Enterprise. We will cover many concepts in order to help you to understand how we implement end-to-end container-based solutions with Docker Enterprise. We will not cover Docker Desktop Enterprise because it is not part of the Docker Certified Associate exam.

Docker Engine

Docker Engine is a core piece of the platform. It provides the runtime for executing the platform. Unlike Kubernetes, Docker Swarm requires Docker Engine to work. Kubernetes provides the option to use `containerd` directly or a **Container Runtime Interface Optimized** (**CRI-O** for OCI-compatible containers). Docker Engine includes Swarm mode, and we do not need any other software to implement a fully functional distributed orchestration environment. Docker Engine provides the underlying layer of execution of all platform components.

On top of Docker Engine, we will create a Docker Swarm cluster, and other Docker Enterprise components will run either as Docker Swarm services or multi-container applications. This is key because there are a few components that will run as agents in the platform, and we will automatically deploy them as **global services** (remember these concepts). But there are also some components that must be unique within the cluster. They will run as **multi-container** applications on top of some defined hosts. These components will use different schemas for their execution.

For Docker Enterprise, we will deploy Docker Enterprise Engine, along with support for specific releases. Enterprise releases have to be supported for a long time, so this affects release times. As we saw in the *Docker Enterprise Engine* section, the currently supported release is 19.03.x (at the time of writing this book), while for the Community Edition, the supported release can be different (it's currently also 19.03.6, but it was only until recently that there could be big differences between releases). This is normal because Docker engineers and support teams must verify all components' integrations and solve any issues for current Docker Enterprise releases, while at the same time evolving the product by adding new features. These features always appear on Docker Community Edition before they are fully tested and implemented for Docker Enterprise Edition.

Because we will be working in a cluster environment, we will be able to execute maintenance tasks and move workloads between nodes without service interruption. Docker Engine updates will be smooth and easy.

Universal Control Plane

UCP provides the control plane for the Docker Enterprise platform. It provides all the processes and tools you need in order to manage all your cluster components and their statuses. UCP will deploy components on master and worker nodes, as we will learn in Chapter 11, *Universal Control Plane*. It is based on Docker Swarm orchestration, but, as we mentioned previously, the core components will run as multi-container applications. The master nodes will run the control plane processes. These processes will not run on any other node if they fail. It is important to understand that these core processes can only run on defined nodes. No other nodes can take these workloads. If we have a problem occurring on a master node and we cannot recover the master node, we need to create a new master. We will promote a worker node or install a new master after removing the old one.

UCP will deploy some distributed databases, and it is important to maintain their quorum. We will review a couple of common issues in Chapter 11, *Universal Control Plane*. Remember, UCP manager nodes are very important and processes need to run on defined nodes.

All internal cluster communications will be encrypted using TLS. UCP manages all nodes, all components, and all their certificates. It will also provide certificates for authenticated and authorized users. We can ensure secure client-to-server communications by default.

The Kubernetes cluster will also be deployed with the required **Container Network Interface (CNI)**, Calico, by default, and secured configurations. UCP provides a production-ready Docker Swarm and Kubernetes platform.

Cluster authentication and authorization will be managed by UCP. We will be able to integrate third-party authentication systems, such as **Lightweight Directory Access Protocol (LDAP)**, and Active Directory. All authorization mechanisms and implementations are also included in UCP. We can provide a unified login, delegating all DTR authentication requests to UCP. This is the usual and preferred configuration. UCP provides a complete RBAC system based on resources, roles, and grants. We will have high levels of granularity to specify customized access to any resource within the cluster.

UCP provides a management web UI and also an API interface to access a cluster's resources. We will be able to configure all Docker Swarm and Kubernetes resources. For Kubernetes, a simple interface is provided to deploy resources' YAML files. We will use the cluster remotely. We will never allow a user access to either manager or worker nodes.

 It is very important to disallow any non-authorized access to cluster nodes. Access via SSH to Docker hosts or directly to Docker Engine's daemon will bypass all security implementations applied by UCP.

The web UI will also provide some simple monitoring capabilities to verify the entire cluster's state. We can review the status of all containers, pods, services, and, in general, all resources managed by the cluster. We can also export the cluster's metrics using Prometheus' standard integrations. The web UI also provides access to container logs, and we can even use them to review the application's behavior. All this access will be managed by UCP's RBAC system.

Docker Swarm and Kubernetes will be available through their APIs. Kubernetes provides its own RBAC, as we learned in `Chapter 9`, *Orchestration Using Kubernetes*. Docker Swarm requires external tools. UCP provides these external tools, proxying all API requests to UCP's internal RBAC integration and providing appropriate authentication and authorization mechanisms.

UCP also provides an integrated component for publishing applications deployed within the cluster. This component is Interlock and, at the time of writing this book, is based on NGINX. Interlock only works with Docker Swarm deployments, monitoring the cluster's API for changes on defined services. We will define which services will be published and which headers, names, and routes should be available. All changes that are applied to the services will be automatically populated to Interlock's reverse proxy component, which will forward requests to the associated backends. We will learn about this in more depth in `Chapter 12`, *Publishing Applications in Docker Enterprise*.

Docker Trusted Registry

As we mentioned when we were talking about CaaS requirements, we need a registry to store images. This registry must provide secure access and roles because we need some granularity when publishing images. Some users will be owners of their images, while others will only use them. We need to ensure image immutability. DTR provides this. It is built on top of the open source Docker Registry, but many improvements were added to provide an enterprise-ready solution.

DTR provides a secured store for all CaaS/KaaS images. We will be able to ensure provenance and immutability. We will also provide different access levels to images. Some users will be maintainers of base images, while others will be able to use them for their own projects. We also have teams and organizations. We can publish images within organizations in a multi-tenant environment, ensuring that all users within an organization are able to use their public images. Teams will share image maintenance responsibilities, but only some members will be able to modify image content.

Because security is key in CaaS environments, DTR will provide image scanning and signing. Image scanning will review all images, searching for binary vulnerabilities. It will use a **Common Vulnerabilities and Exposures (CVE)** database to find any vulnerable files. All vulnerable content will be reported and administrators will manage these issues within the platform. We can decide to only execute clean images; that is, images that are without any reported vulnerabilities. Image signing will allow us to forbid any unsigned images into our infrastructure. This ensures that we will only execute images that have been created and signed within our organization. If an image has been externally modified, it will not be allowed to run a container.

DTR can also be integrated into a CI/CD pipeline, along with its image promotion features. Image tags can be modified with triggers. This process can also tell external applications to track and help us implement special stages in our deployment workflow. Images are the new code artifacts for applications and we can integrate DTR in our CI/CD pipelines.

In the next section, we will describe a minimal environment for production using Docker Enterprise Edition.

Planning your Docker Enterprise deployment

Docker Enterprise provides a production-ready CaaS platform, as we have been discussing throughout this chapter. In this section, we will review the minimum logical requirements for deploying Docker Enterprise in production.

We learned that Docker Swarm and Kubernetes require an odd number of master nodes to work properly. Docker Swarm does not require an external key-value store, while Kubernetes does. Docker Enterprise will deploy this key-value store with UCP, so a minimum of three manager nodes will be required to provide high availability. All managers will run the same services. In Docker Swarm and Kubernetes, we have a leader node that writes cluster changes in the database. Other managers will sync their data, but we can also run administration commands on any of them. We need to integrate an external load balancer to distribute API requests on all manager nodes.

> Remember, three nodes only protect the cluster if one of them fails. The cluster will work fine with two manager nodes, but if another one fails, the cluster will become inconsistent.

UCP requires at least three manager nodes. But what about DTR? This component has its own distributed database: it uses **RethinkDB**. This database also requires an odd number of replicas; therefore, three nodes will be required. DTR will be deployed on worker nodes using a multi-container architecture. We can then say that we will need at least three worker nodes for DTR. Image scanning can consume a lot of CPU resources, and it is recommended to isolate DTR nodes from other worker nodes to avoid application impact. A DTR cluster requires shared storage between nodes because only the node receiving the application's requests will write changes to the database. But all nodes must write to the same storage location, so shared storage is required. We will use an external load balancer in front of DTR's API to distribute requests between service nodes.

We will add workers to this platform as needed. In fact, we will start with a minimum of two worker nodes for high availability. All application workloads must have resilience; hence, a minimum of two nodes for Windows and Linux workloads will be required if we deploy on both architectures. The following diagram represents the described scenario:

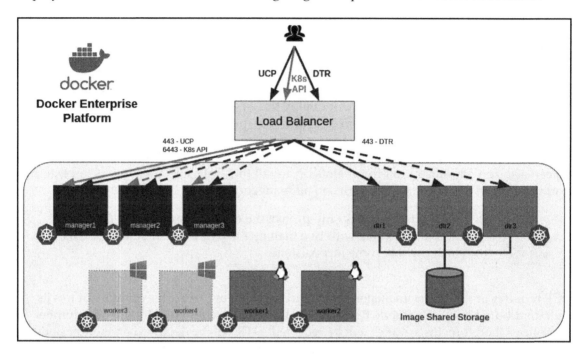

We will use fixed IP addresses for the manager and worker nodes. This is preferred, although worker nodes can be deployed using DHCP. We will isolate the control plane from the data plane, as we discussed in `Chapter 8`, *Orchestration Using Docker Swarm*. The data plane will be used for applications, while the control plane will be used for internal cluster communications.

Calico will be used by default as the Kubernetes CNI, and it is important to check for any possible IP range conflicts. The following table shows the default IP addresses used for Docker Engine, Docker Swarm, and Kubernetes:

Component	Subnet	Range	Default IP address
Engine	`fixed-cidr`	CIDR range for the `docker0` interface and local containers	`172.17.0.0/16`

Engine	`default-address-pools`	CIDR range for the `docker_gwbridge` interface and bridge networks	`172.18.0.0/16`
Swarm	`default-addr-pool`	CIDR range for Docker Swarm overlay networks	`10.0.0.0/8`
Kubernetes	`pod-cidr`	CIDR range for Kubernetes pods	`192.168.0.0/16`
Kubernetes	`service-cluster-ip-range`	CIDR range for Kubernetes services	`10.96.0.0/16`

To avoid any firewall issues, take a look at the following link, which describes some of the configurations required on some Linux platforms: `https://docs.docker.com/ee/ucp/admin/install/plan-installation`.

We will use **Fully Qualified Domain Names** (**FQDNs**) for the virtual IP addresses associated with UCP/Kubernetes and DTR APIs.

We will review all required ports in `Chapter 11`, *Universal Control Plane,* and `Chapter 13`, *Implementing an Enterprise-Grade Registry with DTR*. But clients consume cluster services using specific exposed ports. By default, UCP and DTR will expose their APIs and web UI on port `443`, while Kubernetes will be exposed on port `6443`.

We will usually require internet access during product installation, although we can execute an offline installation. Internet access is needed for DTR if we need to provide automatic image-scanning database synchronization. We can download a compressed database file from Docker's site once a week, for example, to avoid this required connectivity.

Licensing processes can also be automated, and subscription renewal can synchronize product licenses before they expire.

This was a brief description of the deployment of Docker Enterprise components to production. We will cover these components in more depth in the following chapters.

Summary

In this chapter, we provided an introduction to the Docker Enterprise platform. We reviewed the main differences between Docker Community tools and Docker Enterprise products.

We also covered the concepts of the CaaS and KaaS platforms. We looked at what we should expect from these platforms and how different manufacturers and cloud providers deploy their implementations.

We also described the most important features of Docker Enterprise, namely Docker Enterprise Engine, UCP, and DTR. These components provide Docker's CaaS solution. With that, we've covered the most important things to consider when planning a Docker Enterprise production environment.

In the next chapter, we will explore UCP in more depth.

Questions

1. Which of these components is not part of the Docker Enterprise platform?

    a) DTR.
    b) Docker Enterprise Engine.
    c) Docker Machine.
    d) All of these are part of the Docker Enterprise platform.

2. Which of these statements are true about Docker Community and Docker Enterprise?

    a) Docker Enterprise provides an enterprise-ready platform.
    b) We cannot deploy Docker Swarm to production.
    c) Kubernetes is not supported in Docker Enterprise; only Docker Swarm is supported.
    d) Docker Registry is an enterprise-ready registry.

3. Which Docker components are required to deploy a KaaS solution?

    a) Docker Enterprise Engine.
    b) UCP.
    c) Kubernetes.
    d) DTR.

4. Which of the following statements are true for deploying a Docker Enterprise environment?

    a) We use fixed IP addresses for manager nodes only.
    b) We just route traffic to one of the manager nodes.
    c) We need to deploy a CNI after UCP completes the Kubernetes installation.
    d) None of the above.

5. What is the minimum number of nodes required to execute Linux workloads on a Docker Enterprise platform with high availability?

    a) We need to deploy three managers, three workers with DTR, and one Linux worker with enough resources to run all workloads.
    b) We need to deploy three managers with DTR running on them and two Linux workers.
    c) We need to deploy three managers, three workers with DTR, and two Linux workers.
    d) All these options are valid.

Further reading

You can refer to the following references for more information about the topics that were covered in this chapter:

- Introduction to Docker Enterprise: `https://docs.docker.com/ee/`
- Docker Enterprise components: `https://docs.docker.com/ee/docker-ee-architecture/`
- Mirantis Docker Enterprise website: `https://www.mirantis.com/software/docker/docker-enterprise/`
- Mirantis Docker acquisition: `https://www.mirantis.com/company/press-center/company-news/mirantis-acquires-docker-enterprise/`

Universal Control Plane

11

In this chapter, we will learn everything about Docker's **Universal Control Plane** (UCP) that's required for the Docker Certified Associate exam. Universal Control Plane is the Docker Enterprise component in charge of managing clusters. First, we will introduce UCP's components and their features. It is important to know that UCP has changed a lot in recent years. The Docker Enterprise platform was previously known as Docker Datacenter. Docker changed its name when version 2.0 was released. That version was also important because it was the first one to include Kubernetes as a second orchestrator. In this chapter, we will learn how Kubernetes is integrated and how to deploy a production-ready platform.

In November 2019, Mirantis Inc. acquired the Docker Enterprise platform business, including its products, customers, and employees. Therefore, Docker Enterprise is currently a Mirantis Inc. product.

We will discover UCP's main components and learn how to deploy a production-ready environment with high availability. Enterprise environments have many security requirements and UCP includes its own authentication and authorization systems based on RBAC, all of which can be easily integrated with an enterprise's user management platform. Docker Enterprise is based on Docker Swarm but also includes an enterprise-ready Kubernetes environment within the cluster. We will learn about UCP's administration tasks, security configurations, special features, and how to provide a disaster recovery strategy based on backup and restore features. We will finish this chapter by reviewing what should be monitored on this platform to ensure its health.

We will cover the following topics in this chapter:

- Understanding UCP components and features
- Deploying UCP with high availability
- Reviewing Docker UCP's environment

- Role-based access control and isolation
- UCP's Kubernetes integration
- UCP administration and security
- Backup strategies
- Upgrades, health checks, and troubleshooting

Let's get started!

Technical requirements

You can find the code for this chapter in the GitHub repository: `https://github.com/PacktPublishing/Docker-Certified-Associate-DCA-Exam-Guide.git`

Check out the following video to see the Code in Action:

`"https://bit.ly/34BHHdj"`

Understanding UCP components and features

Docker's UCP provides the control plane for the Docker Enterprise platform. It is based on Docker Swarm but also integrates the Kubernetes orchestrator. The following is a quick list of its current features:

- A centralized cluster management interface
- A cluster resource environment
- Role-based access control
- A client environment via WebGUI or the CLI

As we mentioned previously, UCP is based on Docker Swarm orchestration. We will deploy a Docker Swarm cluster with managers and worker roles.

First, we will install a manager node. This will be the leader during the installation process. All the components will be deployed as containers, so we only require a Docker Enterprise Engine to run them.

Once the first manager has been installed, and with all the UCP components up and running, we will continue adding nodes to the cluster. This is a really simple process.

All the components will be managed by a master agent process called `ucp-agent`. This process will deploy all the other components according to the role of the installed node.

Let's review the different components that are deployed on manager and worker role nodes.

UCP components on manager nodes

In `Chapter 8`, *Orchestration Using Docker Swarm*, we learned how these clusters work. Manager nodes run all management processes. We will deploy an odd number of manager nodes to provide high availability because Docker Swarm is based on the Raft protocol and requires consensus or quorum in the management plane.

Manager nodes run all UCP core services, including the web UI and data stores that persist the state of UCP. These are the UCP services running on manager nodes:

Component	Description
ucp-agent	This component is the agent running on each node to monitor and ensure the required services are running.
ucp-swarm-manager	To provide compatibility with a Docker Swarm environment, this component runs on manager nodes.
ucp-proxy	This component provides secure access to each Docker Engine on the platform using TLS and forwarding requests to a local socket.
ucp-auth-api	Authentication is managed with this component running on manager nodes, exposing its API to authorize access.
ucp-auth-store	This component stores data and the configurations of users, organizations, and teams on the UCP platform.
ucp-auth-worker	An authentication worker periodically runs synchronization tasks with external authentication backends.

`ucp-client-root-ca`	This component provides a certificate authority to sign users' bundles on the platform. Bundles are packages issued by the management platform to provide users with access.
`ucp-cluster-root-ca`	To ensure secure communication between platform components, this component provides a CA for signing TLS certificates.
`ucp-kv`	This component provides a key-value database to store cluster configurations. It was only used for Legacy Swarm (we have not seen how Docker Swarm was deployed in the past, but it is similar to Kubernetes these days) but currently, it is also used as a Kubernetes key value.
`ucp-controller`	The UCP web UI is key for management. `ucp-controller` provides this feature. It is the first point of failure when users cannot access the cluster.
`ucp-reconcile`	To monitor components' health, UCP runs `ucp-agent`, and if some of them fail, it will try to restart them. This component will just run when something goes wrong.
`ucp-dsinfo`	UCP can run troubleshooting reports. It executes this component to retrieve all available information. We use support dumps to send information to support services.
`ucp-metrics`	This component recovers node metrics. This data can be used in other monitoring environments.
`ucp-interlock/ucp-interlock-proxy`	Interlock components allow advanced users to publish applications deployed in the cluster. `ucp-interlock` queries the UCP API for changes to be configured to publish services in the `ucp-interlock-proxy` component, as well as a reverse proxy to be deployed and configured automatically for you by UCP.

The following processes also run on master nodes but are separated into a different table because they are related to Kubernetes:

Process	Description
ucp-kube-apiserver	This is the Kubernetes master API component. All Kubernetes processes will be deployed as containers in our host. Using containers to deploy applications helps us to maintain applications' components and their upgrades.
ucp-kube-controller-manager	This Kubernetes process will manage all controllers required to control, replicate, and monitor Pods.
ucp-kube-scheduler	kube-scheduler schedules workloads within cluster nodes.
ucp-kubelet	kubelet is the Kubernetes agent. It is the endpoint used by Kubernetes to manage nodes and their interactions.
ucp-kube-proxy	kube-proxy manages a Pod's publishing and communications.
k8s_ucp-kube-dns/ k8s_ucp-kubedns-sidecar/ k8s_ucp-dnsmasq-nanny	These containers manage and monitor DNS procedures and the resolution required for UCP and Kubernetes.
k8s_calico-node/ k8s_install-cni_calico-node/ k8s_calico-kube-controllers	Calico is the default **container network interface (CNI)** for Kubernetes and it is automatically deployed during UCP installation.

There is also an important component on newer releases to help with the interaction between Docker Swarm and Kubernetes interactions:

Process	Description
k8s_ucp-kube-compose	kube-compose allows us to deploy Docker Compose's workloads either on Docker Swarm as stacks or Kubernetes.

These are the components that can be deployed on manager nodes. We will usually deploy at least three manager nodes because either Docker Swarm or Kubernetes requires an odd number of nodes for a distributed consensus.

Now, let's review worker components.

UCP components on worker nodes

The following are the components that are deployed on worker nodes once they are joined to the cluster:

Components	Description
`ucp-agent`, `ucp-proxy`, `ucp-dsinfo`, and `ucp-reconcile`	These processes have the same functionality that was described for manager nodes.
`ucp-interlock-extension`	`interlock-extension` prepares configurations for `interlock-proxy` based on changes retrieved from Docker Swarm service configurations. This process is based on templates reconfigured dynamically to accomplish all updates that happen within cluster-wide published workloads.
`ucp-interlock-proxy`	`interlock-proxy` runs a proxy process configured dynamically thanks to all other Interlock processes. These prepare a configuration file for the proxy component with all the running backends required for each published service.

For Kubernetes to work, worker nodes also execute the following processes:

Processes	Description
`ucp-kubelet` and `ucp-kube-proxy`	Only these two processes are required for Kubernetes on worker nodes.
`k8s_calico-node` and `k8s_install-cni_calico-node`	Networking within cluster nodes requires Calico, so its processes are also deployed on worker nodes.

From these lists, it is easy to understand how Kubernetes is deployed on Docker Enterprise. Manager nodes run Kubernetes' control plane while workers receive workloads. Notice that managers run `kube-proxy` and `kubelet`, so they are also able to receive workloads. This is also true for Docker Swarm, as we learned in Chapter 8, *Orchestration Using Docker Swarm*. Docker Enterprise allows managers to execute application workloads by default.

We will also review the volumes that are deployed on UCP. We will divide them into two categories:

- **Volumes for certificates**: All these volumes are associated with certificate management within the cluster. Take care of them because if we lose them, we will have serious authentication problems between UCP/Kubernetes processes:
  - `ucp-auth-api-certs`
  - `ucp-auth-store-certs`
  - `ucp-auth-worker-certs`
  - `ucp-client-root-ca`
  - `ucp-cluster-root-ca`
  - `ucp-controller-client-certs`
  - `ucp-controller-server-certs`
  - `ucp-kv-certs`
  - `ucp-node-certs`

- **Volumes for data**: These are data volumes and are used to store different databases deployed within the cluster, as well as the metrics that have been retrieved from different components:
  - `ucp-auth-store-data`
  - `ucp-auth-worker-data`
  - `ucp-kv`
  - `ucp-metrics-data`
  - `ucp-metrics-inventory`

All these volumes are important for the cluster. Key-value pairs, common certificates, and authentication data volumes are replicated on control plane nodes. They are created using the default local volume driver unless we have already created them using a different driver. Keep in mind that they should be created before deploying the cluster if we want to store data in a non-standard location (`/var/lib/docker/volumes` or the defined `data-root` path in your environment).

This section is very important for the Docker Certified Associate exam because we need to know where components are distributed and their functionality on the platform.

Now that we know what components will be deployed on each cluster role, we will learn how to install production-ready environments.

Deploying UCP with high availability

First, we will take a look at the hardware and software requirements for the platform. We will use version 3.0 – the current version at the time of writing this book. It is known that the DCA exam was prepared even before Docker Enterprise version 2.0 was released. Neither Docker Desktop nor Kubernetes were part of the Docker Enterprise platform on that release. We will deploy the current version because the exam has evolved to cover important topics in newer versions. Let's quickly review the current maintenance life cycle:

Docker Enterprise 2.1	Docker Enterprise 3.0
End of life on 2020-11-06	End of life on 2021-07-21
Components: - Enterprise Engine 18.09.z - Universal Control Plane 3.1.z - Docker Trusted Registry 2.6.z	Components: - Enterprise Engine 19.03.z - Universal Control Plane 3.2.z - Docker Trusted Registry 2.7.z

Docker provides 2 years of support from the release date. We recommend taking a look at Docker's website for updated information on the maintenance life cycle and compatibility matrix:

- `https://success.docker.com/article/maintenance-lifecycle`
- `https://success.docker.com/article/compatibility-matrix`

All of the listed versions include Kubernetes, but the deployed version will be different. At the time of writing this book, Docker Enterprise deploys Kubernetes v1.14.8.

We can deploy the Docker Enterprise platform on-premises or on cloud providers. Before deploying the first node, let's review the minimum node requirements:

- 8 GB and 4 GB of RAM for the manager and worker nodes, respectively.
- 2 vCPUs for manager nodes. Worker nodes' vCPUs will depend on the applications to be deployed.
- 10 GB of free disk space for the `/var` partition for manager nodes (a minimum of 6 GB is recommended because Kubernetes will verify disk space before installation) and at least 500 MB of free disk space for the `/var` partition for worker nodes. Worker node space will depend on the applications to be deployed, how big their images are, and how many image releases should be present on our nodes.

A more realistic approach to resources for control plane and image management would probably be the following:

- 16 GB of RAM for manager nodes and workers with DTR (we will learn about DTR in `Chapter 13`, *Implementing an Enterprise-Grade Registry with DTR*).
- Four vCPUs for manager nodes and workers with DTR. Control plane CPU and image scanning can take forever if there is not enough CPU available.

Keep in mind that a cluster's size will really depend on the applications being deployed. It is usually recommended to distribute application components in several nodes because clusters with fewer nodes are harder to maintain. A few nodes with many resources is worse than having the same resources distributed on many nodes. It gives you better cluster life cycle management and a better workload distribution when some nodes fail.

On control plane nodes, we will deploy Docker Enterprise Engine version 19.03 (the latest release at the time of writing). These nodes should be deployed with static IP addresses and Linux kernel version 3.10 or higher. Because we will deploy more than one replica, we will require an external load balancer to route control plane requests to any of the available manager nodes. We will use a virtual IP address and a **Fully Qualified Domain Name (FQDN)** associated with this load balancer. We will add them as **Subject Alternative Names (SANs)** to ensure valid certificates. Certificates should be associated (as a SAN) with any node that can be reached as part of UCP's service. In this case, manager nodes will run control plane components, so certificates should be valid for any of them, including all possible FQDN names associated with UCP's management endpoints (ports `443` and `6443` by default for Docker Swarm and Kubernetes, respectively).

We will expose TCP ports `443` and `6443` to users by default. Both can be changed to other ones more appropriate for our environment. The first port allows user interaction with UCP's control plane either using the web browser, the API, or the Docker command line. The second port described publishes the Kubernetes API server. It allows us to interact directly with the Kubernetes orchestrator.

Worker nodes do not require static IP addresses but they should be accessible by their names using DNS.

We cannot deploy user namespaces within UCP. (We learned about the user namespaces that are used to improve host security in `Chapter 3`, *Running Docker Containers*.) It is not easy to use this feature under UCP conditions, which is why it is not supported.

A minimum environment with high availability will include three managers and at least two workers. The following diagram shows the smallest environment (DTR nodes are not included). We can say that UCP has three major logical components:

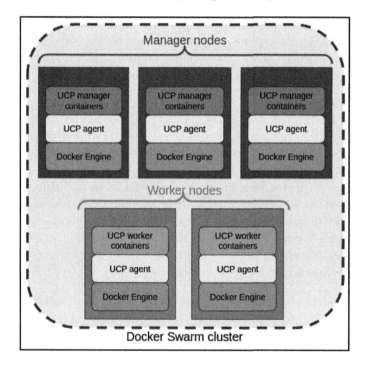

Therefore, as a summary, we will need the following logical requirements for the deployment:

- Static IP addresses for manager nodes
- A VIP address and FQDN for the control plane
- An external load balancer owning a VIP and TCP pass through to managers on ports 443 and 6443 (by default)

The following ports and protocols should be permitted (TCP ports unless explicitly described):

- On managers:
    - Port 443 for the UCP web UI and API
    - Port 6443 for the Kubernetes API server
    - Ports 2376 and 2377 for Docker Swarm communication
    - Ports ranging from 12379 to 12388 for internal UCP component communication
- On workers and managers:
    - Port 7946 (TCP and UDP) for Docker Swarm gossip
    - Port 4789 (UDP) for overlay networking
    - Port 12376 for TLS authentication proxy to access Docker Engine
    - Port 6444 for the Kubernetes API reverse proxy
    - Port 179 for BGP peers for Kubernetes networking
    - Port 9099 for Calico health checks
    - Port 10250 for Kubernetes Kubelet

Users will use ports 443 and 6443 to access UCP services via the HTTPS protocol.

All cluster nodes will run containers. Some of these nodes will act as managers and they will run management components while others just run a few worker components and workloads. But there are two common elements on managers and workers: UCP agent and Docker Engine.

Docker Engine is always required because we need to run containers. Docker Enterprise requires Docker Enterprise Engine. The installation process is easy and it will be based on the license key file and the specific packages available for each customer at https://hub.docker.com/u/<YOUR_USER_OR_ORGANIZATION>/content. First, we will go to https://hub.docker.com/ and register for a Docker Hub account. Docker provides a 1-month trial of the Docker Enterprise platform, available at https://hub.docker.com/editions/enterprise/docker-ee-trial. In Chapter 11, *Universal Control Plane*, Chapter 12, *Publishing Applications in Docker Enterprise*, and Chapter 13, *Implementing an Enterprise-Grade Registry with DTR*, we will show my own account (frjaraur) for example purposes, as well as the different steps and pictures to help you understand this.

The following screenshot shows the `frjaraur` content URL. You will have your own content once you log into the Docker Hub website. We will find the required license and our package repository URL on this page after signing up for a Docker Enterprise 30-day trial:

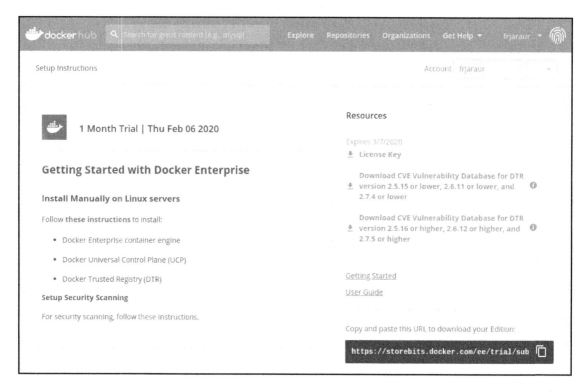

At the bottom right, we will read our package's URL. Click on the copy button and follow the next procedure to install Docker Enterprise Engine. This procedure will be different for each Linux distribution. In this book, we will follow Ubuntu's procedure. The process is described at the previously provided customer content URL. Microsoft Windows nodes are also supported within the Docker Enterprise platform, although they can just be used as workers at the time of writing this book.

These are the steps to follow to install UCP with high availability on Ubuntu nodes:

1. Export the Docker Engine version and the previously shown URL on the `DOCKER_EE_VERSION` and `DOCKER_EE_URL` variables, respectively. At the time of writing this book, the latest Docker Enterprise Engine version is 19.03:

```
# export
DOCKER_EE_URL="https://storebits.docker.com/ee/trial/sub-76c16081-2
```

```
98d-4950-8d02-7f5179771813"
# export DOCKER_EE_VERSION=19.03
```

Notice that your `DOCKER_EE_URL` will be completely different. You can ask for a trial license to follow these steps.

2. Then, we need to add the Docker customer's package repository to our environment:

```
# curl -fsSL "${DOCKER_EE_URL}/ubuntu/gpg" | sudo apt-key add -
# apt-key fingerprint 6D085F96
# add-apt-repository \
"deb [arch=$(dpkg --print-architecture)] $DOCKER_EE_URL/ubuntu \
$(lsb_release -cs) \    stable-$DOCKER_EE_VERSION"
# apt-get update -qq
```

3. Finally, we will install the required packages:

```
# apt-get install -qq docker-ee docker-ee-cli containerd.io
```

These procedures must be applied to all cluster nodes before installing UCP. As we mentioned previously, we will have different procedures for different Linux flavors, but we will also be able to include Microsoft Windows nodes in the cluster. Microsoft Windows Docker Engine's installation is completely different and is shown at `https://hub.docker.com/u/<YOUR_USER_OR_ORGANIZATION>/content`.

> Always review your Docker customer's content page before installing Docker Enterprise Engine because the installation procedure may change.

When all the cluster nodes have Docker Engine installed, we can continue with Docker UCP's installation. This workflow is not required but it is recommended because we can avoid any problems before installing UCP. This is because its components will run as containers in your hosts.

Docker provides support for different infrastructures and also certifies running the Docker Enterprise platform on them. Amazon Web Services and Microsoft Azure are the certified environments at the time of writing this book. In both cases, Docker also provides infrastructure scripts and/or step-by-step documentation for successfully deploying the Docker Enterprise platform on them.

The Docker Enterprise platform is based on Docker Swarm, although Kubernetes is also deployed. Therefore, we will create a Docker Swarm cluster using the UCP installer, and then we will add other nodes as managers or workers.

The installation will require launching a container named `ucp`. This is very important because it ensures just one installation at once. We will also use Docker Engine's local socket as the volume inside the installation container. The UCP installation process has many options – we will cover the most important ones here.

To install UCP, we will launch `docker container run --name ucp docker/ucp:<RELEASE_TO_INSTALL>`. It is important to install a specific release because the `docker/ucp` container will also be used for backup/recovery and other tasks.

Let's write down and execute a usual installation command line for the first manager in the cluster:

```
(first manager node) # docker container run --rm -it --name ucp \
  -v /var/run/docker.sock:/var/run/docker.sock \
  docker/ucp:3.2.5 install \
  --host-address <MANAGEMENT_HOST_IP_ADDRESS> \
  --san <LOAD_BALANCED_FQDN> \
  --san <OTHER_FQDN_ALIAS_OR_IP> \
  --admin-username <ADMIN_USER> \
  --admin-password <ADMIN_USER_PASSWORD>

 INFO[0000] Your Docker daemon version 19.03.5, build 2ee0c57608
 (4.4.0-116-generic) is compatible with UCP 3.2.5 (57c1024)
   WARN[0000] None of the Subject Alternative Names we'll be using in the
 UCP certificates ["<NODE_IP_ADDRESS>" "<NODE_NAME>"] contain a domain
 component. Your generated certs may fail TLS validation unless you only use
 one of these short names or IP addresses to connect. You can use the --san
 flag to add more aliases
 INFO[0000] Checking required ports for connectivity
 INFO[0004] Checking required container images
 INFO[0007] Running install agent container ...
 INFO[0000] Loading install configuration
 INFO[0000] Running Installation Steps
 INFO[0000] Step 1 of 35: [Setup Internal Cluster CA]
 . . .
 INFO[0014] Step 16 of 35: [Deploy UCP Controller Server]
 INFO[0016] Step 17 of 35: [Deploy Kubernetes API Server]
 . . .
 INFO[0033] Step 24 of 35: [Install Kubernetes CNI Plugin]
 INFO[0063] Step 25 of 35: [Install KubeDNS]
 INFO[0064] Step 26 of 35: [Create UCP Controller Kubernetes Service
 Endpoints]
```

```
INFO[0066] Step 27 of 35: [Install Metrics Plugin]
INFO[0067] Step 28 of 35: [Install Kubernetes Compose Plugin]
INFO[0073] Step 29 of 35: [Deploy Manager Node Agent Service]
INFO[0073] Step 30 of 35: [Deploy Worker Node Agent Service]
INFO[0073] Step 31 of 35: [Deploy Windows Worker Node Agent Service]
INFO[0073] Step 32 of 35: [Deploy Cluster Agent Service]
INFO[0073] Step 33 of 35: [Set License]
INFO[0073] Step 34 of 35: [Set Registry CA Certificates]
INFO[0073] Step 35 of 35: [Wait for All Nodes to be Ready]
INFO[0078] All Installation Steps Completed
```

After 35 steps, your UCP's environment will be installed on the first Linux node. Take care and use DNS resolution and an external load balancer. As we mentioned in the previous sections, all the managers will run the same control plane components. Therefore, an external load balancer is required to guide requests to any of them. This can be done by following the round-robin algorithm, for example (it does not matter which UCP manager node receives the requests, but at least one should be reachable).

The external load balancer will provide a virtual IP address to the UCP control plane and we will also provide pass-through port-routing for ports 443 and 6443 (or customized ones if you changed them). We will add this external load balancer's virtual IP address and the associated fully qualified domain name as a SAN. In fact, we will add as many SANs as required for our environment using the --san argument.

These steps are key for your organization access and **Docker Trusted Registry** (DTR) because it is usual to integrate both within UCP. In this case, DTR will ask UCP for user authentication, so it has to have access and resolution to UCP's FQDN and ports.

 We will use a pass-through or transparent proxy on external load balancers to allow UCP's backends to manage TLS certificates and connections.

The UCP image will allow us to do the following:

- Install and uninstall UCP using the `install` and `uninstall-ucp` actions. The uninstall option will remove all UCP components from all cluster nodes. We do not have to execute any other procedure to completely remove UCP from our nodes. Docker Engine will not be removed.
- Download the required Docker images from Docker Hub using the `images` option.
- Backup and restore UCP manager nodes using the `backup` and `restore` actions.

- Provide a UCP cluster ID and its certificates using the `id` and `dump-certs` options. Dumping certificates allows us to store them securely to avoid certificate problems if we accidentally remove any required volume.
- Create a support-dump using the `support` action. These dumps will contain all the useful information about our environment, including application/container logs.
- Upgrade the UCP platform by executing the `upgrade` option. This option will upgrade all UCP components and may impact our services. It is preferred to add the `--manual-worker-upgrade` argument to avoid worker nodes from being auto-upgraded. We will need to take care of our workloads and move them within worker nodes and manually upgrade UCP on them.
- Create an example UCP configuration file and verify the required port status. UCP can be configured using either the provided web UI or using configuration files. Using configuration files will allow us to maintain reproducibility, and changes can be managed with any configuration management application. This method can be achieved once UCP is installed or during installation by customizing the example config file generated with the `example-config` option and using `docker/ucp install --existing-config` with this modified file. The available options are described at the following link: `https://docs.docker.com/ee/ucp/admin/configure/ucp-configuration-file`.

The following are the most commonly used UCP installation options:

Options	Description
`--swarm-grpc-port`, `--controller-port`, `--kube-apiserver-port`, and `--swarm-port`	These options allow us to modify the default ports used in several services. The most important ones, probably customized in your environment, will be `kube-apiserver-port` (defaults to `6443`) and `controller-port` (defaults to `443`). They publish Kubernetes and UCP user endpoints to allow us to interact with the cluster.
`--host-address` and `--data-path-addr`	The first option sets which node's IP address will be allocated for publishing the control plane. The second option allows us to isolate the control plane from the data plane. We set a different interface or IP address for the data plane.
`--pod-cidr`, `--service-cluster-ip-range` and `--nodeport-range`	These options allow us to customize Kubernetes Pods' and Services' IP address ranges and publishing ports for `NodePort` services.
`--external-server-cert`	With this option, we configure our own certificate within the UCP cluster.

`--san`	We include as many SANs as required to add these aliases to UCP certificates. Ask yourself how users and admins will consume the UCP cluster and add the FQDN names related to these services.
`--admin-username` and `--admin-password`	It is recommended to set up an admin username and password during installation to provide a reproducible workflow. We will avoid the `--interactive` option to have an **Infrastructure-as-Code** (**IaC**) UCP installation process.

Once UCP is installed on the first manager node, we will just join other manager nodes and workers to the cluster, as we learned in `Chapter 8`, *Orchestration Using Docker Swarm*. To get the required `docker join` command line, we just execute `docker swarm join-token manager` for manager nodes and `docker swarm join-token worker` for worker nodes. We just copy their output and execute the `docker join` command on each manager and worker node. It is quite easy.

It is also possible to obtain the required joining instructions from the web UI by going to the **Shared Resources** | **Nodes** menu.

Nodes in a UCP cluster can work with either Docker Swarm or Kubernetes, or even in mixed mode. This allows nodes to run Docker Swarm and Kubernetes workloads at the same time.

Mixed mode is not recommended in production because orchestrators do not share their load information. Therefore, a node can be almost full for one orchestrator and empty for another. In this situation, it can continue receiving new workloads for a non-full orchestrator, hence impacting other orchestrator's application performance.

As a summary, we installed Docker Engine and then we installed UCP. We reviewed this process and the main arguments required to install the Docker Enterprise platform in our environment.

If you plan to install Docker Enterprise on Amazon AWS or the Microsoft Azure cloud, you should read the specific instructions and options in the Docker documentation (for AWS, `https://docs.docker.com/ee/ucp/admin/install/cloudproviders/install-on-aws`; for Azure, `https://docs.docker.com/ee/ucp/admin/install/cloudproviders/install-on-azure`).

Now, we will review the UCP environment.

Reviewing the Docker UCP environment

In this section, we will review the Docker UCP environment. We will be able to use either the web UI, the command line, or its published REST API. In this book, we will cover the web application interface and how to integrate our `docker` client command line with UCP.

First, we will introduce the web UI.

The web UI

The web UI will run on all manager nodes. We will use UCP's fully qualified domain name, which is associated with its virtual IP address. Port `443` will be used unless you manually configured a different one. If we open `https://<UCP_FQDN>:<UCP_PORT>` on our browser, we will access the UCP login page. If we have used autogenerated certificates, the browser will warn us about an untrusted CA. This is normal because UCP generates an internal CA automatically for us to sign all internal and external certificates. We can upload our corporate or private certificates into UCP.

> Remember to apply a passthrough (or transparent proxy) configuration on your external load balancer to access UCP backends. We will use `https://<MANAGER_IP>:<UCP_PORT>/_ping` for the backend's health check.

Let's have a quick review of UCP's web UI. The following screenshot shows the main login interface. We set the admin's password during installation, either executing this process interactively with the `--interactive` argument or automating these settings by adding the `--admin-username` and `--admin-password` arguments. The username and password that are used during installation should be used to log into UCP.

The main page will also ask us to add a license file if we have not applied it during installation. This can be done using the `--license` argument for `docker run docker/ucp:<RELEASE> install`:

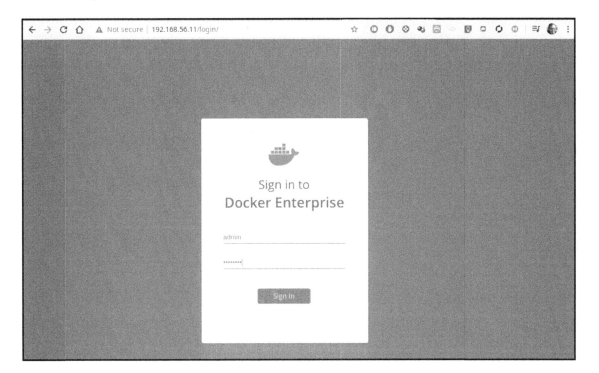

The following screenshot shows the UCP **Dashboard**. Each user will have access to their own. The left panel will provide access to the user's profile, **Dashboard**, **Access Control**, **Shared Resources**, and resources specific to **Kubernetes** and **Swarm**:

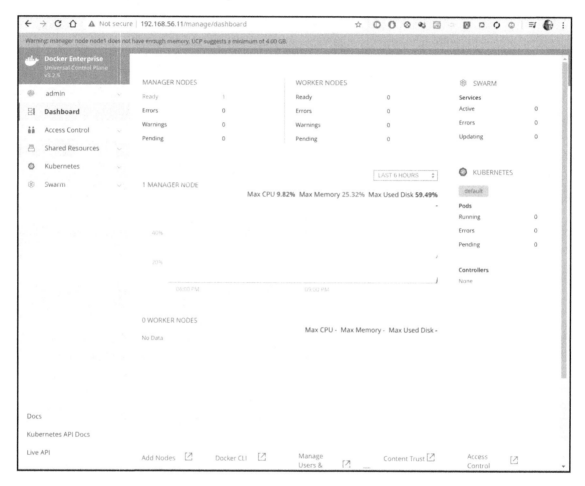

The **Dashboard** screen shows us a quick review of the cluster's components' status. It also provides a summary of the Swarm and Kubernetes workloads and an overview of the cluster's load. Do not think this is enough for monitoring as this is too simple. We should add monitoring tools to improve alerting, performance reporting, and capacity planning features.

Access Control will only appear when UCP administrators access the cluster's Web UI. Administrators will be able to manage all of RBAC's behavior:

- **Orgs & Teams** provides an interface to create organizations and teams and we will integrate users into them from these entries.
- The **Users** endpoint will allow us to manage users as expected. We will learn how to create and manage users in the next topic.
- **Roles** provides an interface for Kubernetes and UCP roles. Kubernetes resources should be managed using declarative methods using YAML resource files, while Docker Swarm's resources (managed by UCP) will be created using the web UI.
- **Grants** helps us manage Kubernetes role bindings and Swarm roles and collection integrations.

Shared Resources provides access to resources for either Kubernetes or Docker Swarm. We will manage collections, stacks, containers, images, and nodes:

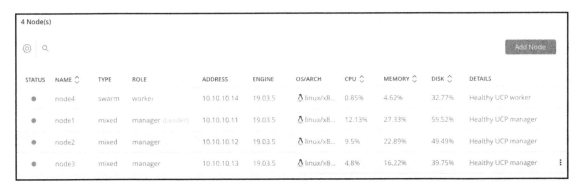

Nodes can be managed from the **Nodes** entry point. We will set node properties and the orchestrator mode. Adding new nodes is easy, as we have seen. The **Add Node** option shows us the cluster's `docker join` command line. We will just copy this instruction to the new node's Terminal. This will also apply to Microsoft Windows nodes.

Stacks will show either multi-container or multi-service applications deployed on a Docker Swarm cluster. This view also shows Kubernetes workloads.

Kubernetes and **Swarm** endpoints show us each orchestrator's specific resources:

- Kubernetes shows namespaces, service accounts, controllers, services, ingress resources, Pod configurations, and storage. We will be able to change which namespace will be used for all users' web UI endpoints. We will also review and create Kubernetes resources using the declarative method.

- Swarm allows us to create and review services, volumes, networks, secrets, and configurations.

We can review the UCP documentation as well as Kubernetes' and the UCP API. This will help us implement automation procedures based on REST API integrations.

The command line using the UCP bundle

The UCP bundle is probably the most important part to access for your users and administrators. Although every user can have access to UCP's web UI, CI/CD, monitoring tools, and DevOps, users will review and launch their workloads using the Docker command line. Therefore, this access should be secure. Remember that Docker Swarm deploys an encrypted control plane. All its internal communications will be secured by TLS. Users' access is not secured. UCP, on the other hand, provides a completely secure solution. Security is ensured using TLS for users and admin access. This is managed using personalized certificates. Each user will get their own group of certificates. Kubernetes access is also secured using the UCP user bundle.

To obtain this UCP bundle, users will use either the web UI or a simple `curl` command – or any command-line web client – to download this package file, compressed as a ZIP folder:

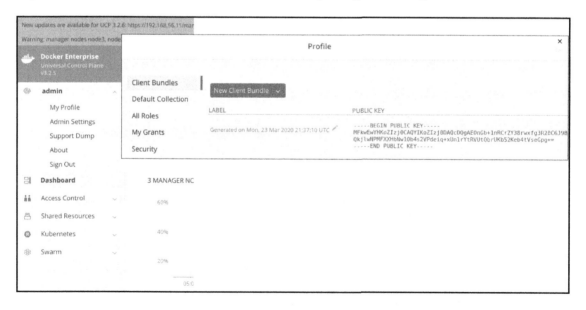

The preceding screenshot shows web GUI access to the user bundle file. We will just download it using a web browser. Once it is on our computer, we will decompress it. This file contains certificates, configuration, and scripts to load the client environment on our computer, regardless of whether it is running Linux, Mac, or Windows operating systems. There is an environment file for each one. We will look at its content and the procedure in Linux, but it is similar in Windows (the commands will vary).

We can use `curl` and `jq` to download the user bundle from the command line:

```
$ AUTHTOKEN=$(curl -sk -d
'{"username":"<username>","password":"<password>"}'
https://<UCP_FQDN>:<UCP_PORT>/auth/login | jq -r .auth_token)

$ curl -k -H "Authorization: Bearer $AUTHTOKEN"
https://<UCP_FQDN>:<UCP_PORT>/api/clientbundle -o ucp-bundle-admin.zip
```

If we decompress the admin bundle file, `ucp-bundle-admin.zip`, using `unzip`, we will obtain all the files required to connect to our cluster:

```
$ unzip ucp-bundle-admin.zip
```

We will then load this environment. We will use `env.ps1` in Microsoft Windows PowerShell or the `env.cmd` Command Prompt. On Linux hosts, we will use `env.sh`. When we load the environment on our shell, we will be able to connect remotely to the UCP cluster using the `docker` or `kubectl` client software:

```
$ source env.sh
 Cluster "ucp_<UCP_FQDN>:6443_admin" set.
 User "ucp_<UCP_FQDN>:6443_admin" set.
 Context "ucp_<UCP_FQDN>:6443_admin" created.
```

Notice that the Kubernetes context has also been set. Therefore, we will be able to manage the cluster and deploy workloads on either Kubernetes or Docker Swarm. Each user's UCP bundle must be stored securely. We can generate a new one if we remove it, but keep it safe; someone could potentially use it and obtain access to your environment files.

UCP provides client software for Microsoft Windows and Linux on our manager nodes at `https://<UCP_FQDN>:<UCP_PORT>/manage/dashboard/dockercl i`. We can download them to connect to the cluster.

It is key to use the UCP bundle instead of connecting to the cluster using SSH or any other local access. We will never allow local access to cluster nodes. Everyone must access the cluster either using the command line or the web UI.

 UCP's REST API is also secured using certificates. We will require the UCP bundle's certificate files to access the cluster using its API.

We will review UCP's access control in the next section and provide a simple example that will help us understand RBAC concepts.

Role-based access control and isolation

Role-based access control (RBAC) manages authorization for Docker Swarm and Kubernetes. Docker Enterprise lets us manage users' access to resources. We use roles to allow users to view, edit, and use cluster resources.

Authorization is based on the following concepts:

- **Subjects**: We manage users, teams, and service accounts within organizations. Users are part of teams, included in organizations.
- **Resources**: These are the groups of Docker objects we were talking about in Chapter 1, *Modern Infrastructures and Applications with Docker*. As Kubernetes is also integrated into the UCP cluster, Kubernetes resources are also part of these groupings. UCP manages resources grouped in collections.
- **Collections**: These are sets of resources, including different kinds of objects, such as volumes, secrets, configs, networks, services, and so on.
- **Roles**: These group sets of permissions and we assign them to different subjects. Roles define what can be done by whom.
- **Grants**: Combining subjects with roles and resource sets, we obtain grants. They are effective user permissions applied to groups of resources.

 Service accounts are only valid for Kubernetes. These are not user accounts; they are associated with applications or APIs assigned to manage their access.

There are some predefined roles but we can create our own. This is a list of the default ones included with Docker Enterprise's UCP:

- **None**: This role does not provide access to any Docker Swarm resources. This should be the default role for new users.
- **View Only**: Users with this role can view resources such as services, volumes, and networks but they cannot create new resources.
- **Restricted Control**: Users with this role can view and edit resources but they cannot use bind mounts (hosts' directories) or execute new processes within containers using `docker exec`. They cannot run privileged containers or with enhanced capabilities.
- **Scheduler**: This role allows users to view nodes so that they can schedule workloads on them. By default, all users get a grant with the `Scheduler` role against the `/Shared` collection.
- **Full Control**: This role should be restricted to advanced users only. These can view and edit volumes, networks, and images. They also can create privileged containers.

 Users will only be able to manage their own containers or Pods. This behavior allows integrating namespaces (Kubernetes) and collections (Docker Swarm) in this equation. Therefore, users with full control access to a set of resources included in a collection will have all privileges on them in Docker Swarm. The same will happen if we add resources within a namespace and the user is included in a fully privileged role in Kubernetes.

There is also a more advanced role that's assigned to Docker Enterprise administrators. They will have full control and management privileges for the UCP environment. This can be managed using the **Is Admin** checkbox on the user's properties page.

Grants interconnect users and permissions with the set of resources where they should be applied. The grants management workflow includes their creation, user assignment, the role that should be applied, and resource association. This way, we ensure that the appropriate privileges are applied to a collection of resources assigned to a group of users (or just one user).

Collections are hierarchical and contain resources. They are represented by using a directory-like structure and every user has their own private collection, along with the user's default permissions. Using this, we can nest collections. Once a user has been granted access to a collection, they will have access to all its hierarchical children. There are three main collections: /, /System, and /Shared.

Under the /System collection, we will find UCP's manager nodes and UCP's and DTR's system services. By default, only administrators will have access to this collection. On the other hand, the /Shared collection will contain all the worker nodes ready for running workloads. We can add additional collections and move some workers to isolate them and provide multi-tenant features. Distributing workers on different collections will also distribute workload execution for different groups or tenants.

Each user has a private collection by default under /Collections/Swarm/Shared/Private/<USER_NAME>. This ensures that users' workloads are secure by default and only administrators will have access. Therefore, users have to deploy workloads on their team-shared collections.

Labels associated with collections manage users' access to resources, which makes it easy to allow or disallow a user's visibility dynamically.

Let's review these concepts with a short example.

We have two projects in our organization (myorganization): projectA and projectB. We will also assume that we have three teams in our organization: developers, quality and assurance, and DevOps. Let's describe some users and their roles within our organization:

- **Developers**: dev1 and dev2
- **Quality and assurance:** qa1 and qa2
- **DevOps:** devops1 and devops2
- **UCP Admin**

The following image shows some screenshots of the user creation process. First, we create an organization and then teams and users inside the previously created organization:

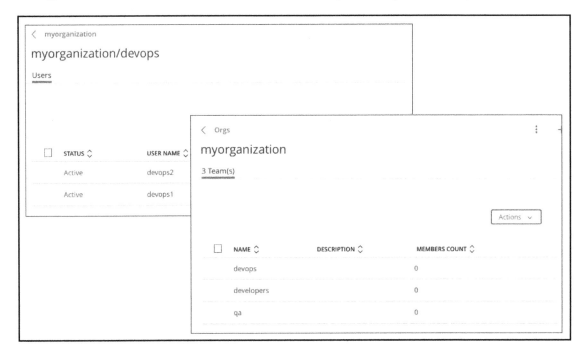

Each user will have their own user account in UCP. We will create developers, quality and assurance, and DevOps teams and we will add their users. We will also create three main collections as stages and child collections for each project. Therefore, we will have the following:

- `development/projectA` and `development/projectB`
- `certification/projectA` and `certification/projectB`
- `production/projectA` and `production/projectB`

Let's suppose that each developer works on one project at a time. They should have full access to their projects during the development stage but they should have view-only access in the certification stage. Quality and assurance users will only have access to create and modify their deployments in the certification stage. DevOps will have access to create and modify resources in production and they will allow view-only access to developers, but only on `projectA`. In fact, `projectB` should be secure and only a `devops2` user should be able to modify resources for this project.

The following screenshots show the process of adding grants to allow a user access to collections. First, we create a collection, and then we add that collection to a new role:

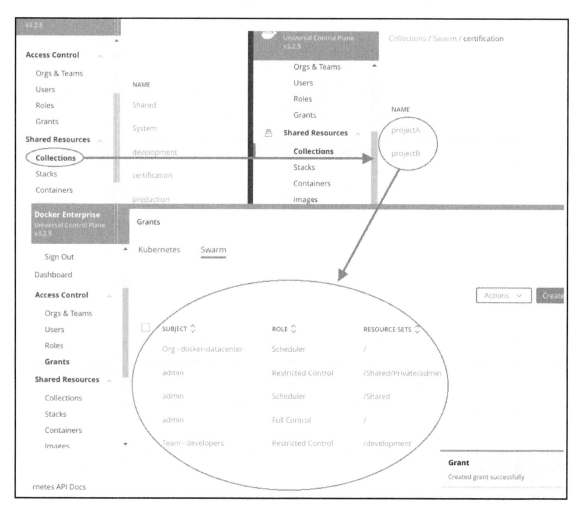

We will launch two deployments with different users and will review how they view these deployments.

We will assume that all the required users have been created and that each user's ucp-bundle has been downloaded. As user dev1, we will create a simple nginx deployment for projectB, using com.docker.ucp.access.label=/development/projectB as the label:

```
(as user dev1)$ source env.sh
Cluster "ucp_192.168.56.11:6443_dev1" set.
User "ucp_192.168.56.11:6443_dev1" set.
Context "ucp_192.168.56.11:6443_dev1" modified.

(as user dev1)$ docker service create --name nginx-dev --label
com.docker.ucp.access.label=/development/projectB nginx
k7hsizrvlc0cmy9va78bri06k
overall progress: 1 out of 1 tasks
1/1: running [==================================================>]
verify: Service converged

(as user dev1)$ $ docker service ls
ID NAME MODE REPLICAS IMAGE PORTS
k7hsizrvlc0c nginx-dev replicated 1/1 nginx:latest
```

If we now impersonate user qa1, we will get different results:

```
(as user qa1)$ source env.sh
Cluster "ucp_192.168.56.11:6443_qa1" set.
User "ucp_192.168.56.11:6443_qa1" set.
Context "ucp_192.168.56.11:6443_qa1" modified.

(as user qa1)$ docker service ls
ID NAME MODE REPLICAS IMAGE PORTS
```

User qa1 will not list any services because it does not have access to the dev1 collection. But if we review this list with the devops2 user, we will obtain a list that includes the dev1 user's services:

```
(as user devops2)$ docker service ls
ID NAME MODE REPLICAS IMAGE PORTS
k7hsizrvlc0c nginx-dev replicated 1/1 nginx:latest
```

If we try to modify this resource (the nginx-dev service), we will obtain an access error because we only have view authorization. On the other hand, the dev2 user can scale up the number of replicas because they are in the developer group:

```
(as user devops2)$ docker service update --replicas 2 nginx-dev
Error response from daemon: access denied:
no access to Service Create, Service Update, on collection
8185981a-5e15-4906-9fbf-465e9f712918
```

```
no access to Service Create, Service Update, on collection
8185981a-5e15-4906-9fbf-465e9f712918
no access to Service Update, on collection
8185981a-5e15-4906-9fbf-465e9f712918

(as user dev2)$ docker service update --replicas 2 nginx-dev
nginx-dev
overall progress: 2 out of 2 tasks
1/2: running [==================================================>]
2/2: running [==================================================>]
verify: Service converged
```

To finish off this example, we will create two different services as user `devops2`. We will deploy secure and unsecured services from `projectB` and `projectA`, respectively:

```
(as user devops2)$ docker service create --quiet --name nginx-prod-secure \
--label com.docker.ucp.access.label=/production/projectB nginx

4oeuld63v96ck26efype57320

(as user devops2)$ docker service create --quiet --name nginx-prod-unsecure
\
--label com.docker.ucp.access.label=/production/projectA nginx

txmuqfcr751n8cb445hqu73td

(as user devops2)$ docker service ls
ID NAME MODE REPLICAS IMAGE PORTS
k7hsizrvlc0c nginx-dev replicated 2/2 nginx:latest
4oeuld63v96c nginx-prod-secure replicated 1/1 nginx:latest
txmuqfcr751n nginx-prod-unsecure replicated 1/1 nginx:latest
```

In this case, the `devops1` user should only be able to manage `nginx-prod-unsecure`, which is associated with `projectA`:

```
(as user devops1)$ docker service ls
ID NAME MODE REPLICAS IMAGE PORTS
k7hsizrvlc0c nginx-dev replicated 2/2 nginx:latest
txmuqfcr751n nginx-prod-unsecure replicated 1/1 nginx:latest
```

This was a simple example of authorization management using labels. In this case, we manually added these labels, but we can set a default collection for each user if we wish. This will provide a default label associated with their workflows, instead of us using the out-of-the-box `/Collections/Swarm/Shared/Private/<USER>` collection. We can also associate constraints with collections to ensure specific locations. This is very important in multi-tenant environments.

UCP's Kubernetes integration

As we have learned, Kubernetes is deployed alongside Docker Swarm when installing UCP. If we take a look at all the required Kubernetes components, we will notice that all of them run as containers within our cluster. The required key-value store will also be provided. Port 6443 (by default) will provide Kubernetes access, and users and administrators will use this port to manage the cluster or execute their workloads.

We will use the Docker bundle's certificates and configuration file, kube.yml. As we learned in this chapter, we will load our user's bundle environment and then get access to the Kubernetes cluster using the kubectl command line.

Once env.sh has been loaded using source env.sh, we will have the required environment variables and access to our certificates. If we get Kubernetes cluster nodes using kubectl get nodes, we will obtain their status:

```
$ kubectl get nodes
NAME STATUS ROLES AGE VERSION
node1 Ready master 4d13h v1.14.8-docker-1
node2 Ready master 4d13h v1.14.8-docker-1
node3 Ready master 4d13h v1.14.8-docker-1
node4 Ready <none> 4d12h v1.14.8-docker-1
```

If we review the running Pods in the kube-system namespace using kubectl get pods -n kube-system, we will notice that calico and compose for Kubernetes are also deployed:

```
$ kubectl get pods -n kube-system
NAME READY STATUS RESTARTS AGE
calico-kube-controllers-5c48d7d966-cncw2 1/1 Running 3 4d13h
calico-node-8sxh2 2/2 Running 6 4d13h
calico-node-k2fgh 2/2 Running 6 4d13h
calico-node-nrk62 2/2 Running 6 4d13h
calico-node-wgl9c 2/2 Running 6 4d13h
compose-779494d49d-wk8m4 1/1 Running 3 4d13h
compose-api-85c67b79bd-7sbhj 1/1 Running 4 4d13h
kube-dns-6b8f7bdd9-g6tfq 3/3 Running 9 4d13h
kube-dns-6b8f7bdd9-ls2z2 3/3 Running 9 4d13h
ucp-metrics-6nfz4 3/3 Running 9 4d13h
ucp-metrics-hnsfb 3/3 Running 9 4d13h
ucp-metrics-xdl24 3/3 Running 9 4d13h
```

These components are very important because Calico is the default CNI deployed with UCP. This allows us to deploy applications distributed cluster-wide. Pods and services are able to communicate within the cluster even if they do not run on the same host. This is not required in Docker Swarm because overlay networking is included by default. Calico allows us also to improve Kubernetes security because it can deploy network policies to isolate and manage Pods' and services' communications.

On the other hand, Compose for Kubernetes provides a standard interface for Docker Swarm and Kubernetes. Docker stacks could be deployed either on Docker Swarm or Kubernetes.

We can also notice that `ucp-metrics` also runs Kubernetes workloads as other system-related deployments, obtained using `kubectl get deployments -A`:

```
$ kubectl get deployments -A
NAMESPACE NAME READY UP-TO-DATE AVAILABLE AGE
kube-system calico-kube-controllers 1/1 1 1 4d14h
kube-system compose 1/1 1 1 4d14h
kube-system compose-api 1/1 1 1 4d14h
kube-system kube-dns 2/2 2 2 4d14h
```

Kubernetes roles and role bindings are managed from the command line and the web UI. All Kubernetes features from the 1.14.8 release are available. This is also very important. Docker Enterprise provides a vanilla Kubernetes release and product releases also upgrade Kubernetes, but you cannot upgrade Kubernetes manually.

In the next section, we will review the main administration tasks and security improvements.

UCP administration and security

UCP administrators manage Docker Swarm and Kubernetes clusters. They integrate external LDAP/AD authentication. Authentication can be delegated but UCP manages authorizations, as we learned in the *Role-based access control and isolation* section.

The following screenshot shows the **Admin Settings** endpoint:

Docker Enterprise license can be introduced during installation, but it also can be manage from the web UI in **Admin Settings**. This endpoint also allow us to do the following administration tasks:

- Rotate Docker Swarm's tokens to improve a cluster's security. Tokens are only used to join nodes to the cluster; we can change them whenever we need to.
- Manage Interlock's ports and enable publishing applications using this feature. We will talk about Interlock in Chapter 12, *Publishing Applications in Docker Enterprise.*
- Configure some cluster configurations such as UCP's port and key-value database snapshots.
- Integrate external LDAP and configure the default role to apply for new users and some session settings. This option delegates authentication to external LDAP/AD systems and UCP will just be used as an authentication cache if it is not available. We set user filters using attributes to only integrate subsets of users in the UCP environment. UCP synchronizes LDAP changes periodically.
- Change UCP's application and audit logging levels.
- Execute and configure backups from the web UI.
- Integrate Docker Trusted Registry and Docker Content Trust to allow only signed images. This will be applied to all the nodes within the cluster.
- Set the default orchestrator for new nodes. We can choose between Docker Swarm, Kubernetes, and mixed mode.
- Authorize administrators or users to execute workloads on UCP managers or worker nodes running DTR. We will decide who can run workloads on management nodes. It is recommended to avoid any non-control-plane workload on managers.
- Customize and launch platform upgrades. This will allow us to decide between a completely automated process and deploying manual upgrades to worker nodes to avoid impacting an application's service.

It is recommended to disallow application workloads on UCP managers. These nodes should only run on the UCP system and DTR containers. This will avoid any application performance issues due to UCP's control plane. On the other hand, if any application component consumes too many resources, this will not affect the control plane.

Allowing only signed images in production is key. This will ensure image provenance and a CI/CD workflow. It is also possible to require some specific signs for images. For example, we can ensure that only images signed by `Operations Team`, `Developer's Chief`, and `IT manager` will run in production. This will apply to all the nodes in the cluster.

Many of UCP's and Kubernetes' features can be queried or modified via UCP's REST API. We should review the documentation at `https://<UCP_FQDN>[:443]/apidocs/` and `https://<UCP_FQDN>[:443]/kubernetesdocs/`.

UCP also provides some Pod security policies that are applied by default on a Kubernetes cluster. These Pod security policies will do the following:

- Manage privileged containers
- Configure the host's namespaces (IPC, PID, network, and ports)
- Manage the host's paths and their permissions and volume types
- Manage users and groups for the container process execution and `setuid` capabilities inside the container
- Change the default container's capabilities
- Integrate Linux security modules
- Allow host kernel configurations using `sysctl`

By default, only administrators will be able to deploy privileged containers in UCP's Kubernetes. This is configured on a privileged Pod security policy. By default, UCP just provides two special policies, as we can see in the `kubectl get PodSecurityPolicies` output:

```
$ kubectl get PodSecurityPolicies
NAME PRIV CAPS SELINUX RUNASUSER FSGROUP SUPGROUP READONLYROOTFS VOLUMES
privileged true * RunAsAny RunAsAny RunAsAny RunAsAny false *
unprivileged false RunAsAny RunAsAny RunAsAny RunAsAny false *
```

You can read more about the Pod security policies included with Docker Enterprise and how to create new ones in the Kubernetes documentation or by going to this blog post: `https://www.mirantis.com/blog/understanding-kubernetes-security-on-docker-enterprise-3-0/`.

Admission controllers are other valuable pieces in Kubernetes' security. They intercept Kubernetes API requests to allow or modify them before scheduling or executing any action. This allows us to enforce default security on resources, even if users try to execute an action that isn't allowed. Admission controllers are applied to the Kubernetes API process. Therefore, we should inspect the `ucp-kube-apiserver` container's command-line options to verify which admission controllers have been applied to our environment. As Kubernetes is not part of the DCA exam yet, we will stop here regarding this topic. But it is important to understand that Docker Enterprise applies security in Kubernetes using well-known Kubernetes mechanisms. UCP applies three special admission controllers to prevent anyone from removing core Kubernetes roles required by UCP, to ensure image signing if required, and to manage the execution of non-system Kubernetes Pods only on non-mixed nodes.

In the next section, we will review how to create and restore UCP's backups.

Backup strategies

In this section, we will learn how to backup and restore the Docker Enterprise UCP platform.

As UCP runs on top of Docker Swarm, this is the first component to review when preparing a good backup strategy.

We should run periodic backups of Docker Swarm. These backups will allow us to recover cluster configuration and workloads.

Docker Swarm's backup

We introduced how to execute a Docker Swarm backup in Chapter 8, *Orchestration Using Docker Swarm*. In that chapter, we described the content we should take care of. Let's learn about the steps to follow to implement a production-ready backup of Docker Swarm for the Docker Enterprise platform.

Make sure you have applied the auto-lock feature to improve secure access to Docker Swarm data as we will need it. The lock key will not be stored with a backup. You should store it in a safe place.

We will execute the backup steps on all non-leader manager nodes. This will ensure that any of the managers except the leader (at that moment) can be restored. In fact, it should not be easy to completely destroy a cluster, so backing up just a node should be fine. If all the clusters are completely lost, we will recover that node and then add others, as we did during the installation process. Your cluster health should not rely on backup-restore features. That is why we run the Raft protocol for cluster components syncing and running more than one manager node.

Application deployments and their configuration should be stored in code repositories, as we have recommended a couple of times in this book. Sometimes, it is even easier to deploy a new cluster and launch all the applications again using automation tools.

The following steps are recommended to create a good backup of Docker Swarm orchestrator data:

1. Verify that the platform is healthy before executing this backup procedure.
2. We will stop Docker Engine on the non-leader manager by executing `systemctl stop docker`.
3. Create a `.tar` file with `/var/lib/docker/swarm` directory content: `tar -cvzf "<DIRECTORY_FOR_YOUR_BACKUPS>/swarm-backup-$(hostname -s)-$(date +%y%m%d).tgz" /var/lib/docker/swarm/`.
4. Start Docker Engine again executing `systemctl start docker`.
5. We can execute this procedure on other non-leader manager nodes, although we will be able to restore Docker Swarm with one node only if the backup was successful.

UCP runs on top of Docker Swarm. Let's review the required steps for backing up UCP.

Backing up UCP

Unlike in Docker Swarm, in UCP, there is no need to pause or stop any platform components to execute a backup. This feature is quite new. In older releases, components had to be paused on nodes while performing a backup. We will just execute this backup on a single node because UCP data will allow us to recover the entire cluster. But there are a few important notes about this backup:

- This backup does not include Docker Swarm deployed workloads, networks, configurations, or secrets.
- We cannot recover an updated UCP using a backup from an older release.
- Neither `ucp-metrics-data` nor `ucp-node-certs` volumes are included.

- Kubernetes data will be covered in a UCP backup.
- Neither Router Mesh's nor Interlock settings will be stored. Once the restored components have been redeployed, configurations will also be recovered.
- Backup content will be stored in a `.tar` file in a user-defined location. It can be secured using a passphrase.

We can create UCP backups using the web UI, command line, or its API (on the latest releases).

Using the command line, we will need to use the `ucp` release container. For the current version at the time of writing this book, we will use the `docker/ucp:3.2.4` image. To create a backup from the command line, we will execute `docker container run docker/ucp:<RELEASE> backup`:

```
$ docker container run \
--rm \
--interactive \
--log-driver none \
--name ucp \
--volume /var/run/docker.sock:/var/run/docker.sock \
--volume <FULL_PATH_FOR_UCP_BACKUP_DIRECTORY>:/backup \
docker/ucp:3.2.4 backup \
--file <BACKUP_FILENAME>.tar \
--passphrase "<PASSPHRASE>" \
--include-logs=false
```

In this example, we are not including UCP platform logs (they will be included by default). If SELinux is enabled, which is recommended, we will also add `--security-opt label=disable`.

Using the web UI, we will first navigate to **Admin Settings**. Then, we'll select **Backup Admin**, and finally, we'll click on **Backup Now** to immediately launch the backup execution.

We will not cover the API method in this book and how to verify backup content when the process has finished, but it is described on the Docker documentation website. It is also recommended to review the latest backup information provided at `https://docs.docker.com/ee/admin/backup/back-up-ucp/`.

To restore a UCP backup, we can start from one of these situations:

- We can start from scratch, restoring a UCP backup on a new, recently installed Docker Enterprise Engine.
- We can also recover a UCP backup on an initiated Docker Swarm, restoring UCP so that it has a new, fully functional cluster.
- We can restore UCP on the Docker Swarm cluster where it was created. We will just choose one of its manager nodes and run the recovery process after the previous UCP deployment is completely uninstalled. This is the only case where the previously created user's bundle will continue to work.

> If recovery is started from scratch or using a new Docker Swarm cluster, the IP addresses and SAN that were used will not be valid. Therefore, we will need to regenerate server certificates after the UCP restore.
>
> After you have successfully restored UCP, you can add new managers and workers the same way you would after a fresh installation.

To restore a previously created backup, we will execute `docker container run docker/ucp:<RELEASE> restore`. We need to use the same image release that was used to create the backup. This is very important because we cannot restore from a different release:

```
$ docker container run \
  --rm \
  --interactive \
  --name ucp \
  --volume /var/run/docker.sock:/var/run/docker.sock \
  docker/ucp:3.2.4 restore \
  --passphrase "<PASSPHRASE>" <
<FULL_PATH_FOR_UCP_BACKUP_DIRECTORY>/<BACKUP_FILENAME>.tar
```

It is important to know that backup and restore are processes that you should execute when everything else is not working. We deploy UCP environments with high availability to avoid unexpected situations. You have to actively monitor your cluster environments and not leave unattended errors or alarms on monitoring systems. In the event of a manager node failure, a cluster will continue working, but we must reestablish a healthy status as soon as possible. From my experience, most of the issues found in production Docker Enterprise environments are related to filesystems growing without control, processes eating all the resources, or communication problems. Take care of these possible issues, monitor cluster health, and do periodic backups (and update their processes) to ensure you are able to recover your environment if everything fails.

In the next section, we will learn what to monitor and how to check different components' statuses to avoid unnoticed failures.

Upgrades, monitoring, and troubleshooting

In this section, we will review how cluster upgrades must be deployed. We will work in a cluster environment. There are some steps to follow in order to execute platform updates without service interruption. Monitoring and troubleshooting are critical in production. We will learn about what important keys and values we should review to ensure a cluster's health and what steps we should follow to troubleshoot a degraded or faulty environment.

Upgrading your environment

We must review the Docker UCP release notes and upgrade procedure for each version. At the time of writing this book, the current release documentation is available on Docker's website: `https://docs.docker.com/reference/ucp/3.2/cli/upgrade`.

We should always perform a backup before any procedure, and we usually start by upgrading Docker Engine. You should review the Docker documentation to ensure that these steps are not changed between releases. Node upgrades should be done one at time. We will begin with non-leader manager nodes. Once all the managers have been upgraded, we will move the running services between different worker nodes to ensure minimal service interruption between upgrades.

Once all the Docker Engine instances have been updated, we will start with the UCP upgrade. We can execute this process from the web UI and from the command line. We recommend following the command-line steps because the process will give you more information. We can execute this process offline if all the required images have been previously downloaded on all the nodes. We can check the required images at this link: `https://docs.docker.com/ee/ucp/admin/install/upgrade-offline/`. We will preload all the images using `docker image load -i <PACKAGE_WITH_ALL_IMAGES>.tar.gz`.

We will run `docker container run docker/ucp upgrade` with the appropriate arguments to upgrade our UCP environment. Docker Engine should be upgraded before executing this command:

```
docker container run --rm -it \
  --name ucp \
  -v /var/run/docker.sock:/var/run/docker.sock \
```

```
docker/ucp:3.2.X \
upgrade --interactive
```

If your nodes work with more than one interface, we will also add `--host-address` with an appropriate IP address.

> We can run and upgrade the process with the debug option, `--debug`, which is very useful for identifying errors if something goes wrong.

There is an interesting option on the current release because we can upgrade workers manually using `--manual-worker-upgrade`. This helps us control the impact we have on services that are deployed in the environment.

All UCP processes will be upgraded in all nodes unless the `--manual-worker-upgrade` option is used. Once the upgrade process ends, the environment will be completely upgraded to the new release. At that moment, it is important to verify the health of the cluster.

Monitoring a cluster's health

We can use either the command line or the web UI to review the environment's health. We will use common Docker Swarm commands because we are running the environment on top of this orchestrator. We can review the node status with `docker node ls`. If we use the Docker UCP bundle to connect to the environment, we might miss some components. Make sure you are using an administrator user in the environment to be able to retrieve its health. Using the bundle, we can list all the control plane processes and use `docker container ls` to verify their statuses.

We can retrieve a manager's status from the `https://<ucp-manager-url>/_ping` endpoint, on each manager node's IP address or FQDN name. Requests to this URL can give us a `200` code if a node is healthy and a `500` code if there are some faulty components.

> It is important to understand that this endpoint must be verified on each node because we are accessing the cluster through a load balancer to each manager. This configuration helps us provide high availability to the environment.

The web UI also provides cluster status information. The **Dashboard** page shows us a clear status overview of the environment. This page includes counters for errors, warnings, or pending states for managers and workers. We will quickly notice errors on platform nodes. A performance summary for managers and worker nodes allows us to verify cluster sizing and its usage. We will also see information about deployed services on Docker Swarm and Kubernetes. This way, we can drill down to different UCP sections to deep dive into encountered errors. The following screenshot shows how the UCP **Dashboard** looks when showing the described platform overview:

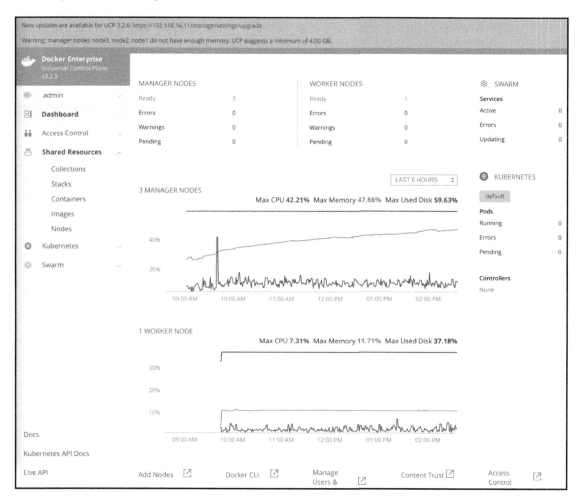

In each UCP resource section, we will see the resources' statuses, along with their properties. To monitor the cluster node's health, we will review the **Nodes** section, which can be found under **Shared Resources**. In this section, we will review the CPU and memory usage per node. This view will also help us find possible service degradation when node resource usage is too high.

Troubleshooting UCP

Throughout this chapter, we have been reviewing the main monitoring endpoints for UCP components. There are some critical endpoints in the cluster. We also described some database processes that manage important clusters' persistent data. These components run on managers and they replicate their data between them. It should be enough for the UCP environment, but sometimes, things can go wrong and they lose node synchronization. Network latency and performance problems can lead to these situations.

Troubleshooting UCP-KV

If we lose some manager nodes, `ucp-kv` can show the incorrect number of nodes. We can check the number of configured nodes with `etcdctl`. We can execute `etcdctl` on the `ucp-kv` container directly:

```
$ docker exec -it ucp-kv etcdctl \
  --endpoint https://127.0.0.1:2379 \
  --ca-file /etc/docker/ssl/ca.pem \
  --cert-file /etc/docker/ssl/cert.pem \
  --key-file /etc/docker/ssl/key.pem \
  cluster-health
```

This will show us `cluster is healthy` messages if the configured number of managers are healthy. If `ucp-kv` is unhealthy, we should review whether all the manager nodes are fine. If we deleted one manager but this change was not correctly updated on the other nodes, we could end up with an unhealthy cluster. To recover from this situation, we would need to remove the deleted node from the `etcd` database using `etcdctl member remove` (check the `etcd` documentation at `https://etcd.io/docs/v3.4.0/op-guide/runtime-configuration/`).

Update the component configurations and their states (deleting nodes, for example) one by one. Wait until the changes are synced in the cluster before executing a new update command.

We can also have problems with the authentication database. In the next section, we will learn how to correct the number of nodes if we lose one manager node.

Troubleshooting UCP-Auth

First, we will review the current number of healthy manager nodes. If some of them are still unhealthy, we should correct that situation first. Once the managers are healthy, if the authentication database continues to be in an inconsistent state, we will follow this procedure:

```
$ docker container run --rm -v ucp-auth-store-certs:/tls \
docker/ucp-auth:<RUNNING_VERSION> \
--db-addr=<HEALTHY_MANAGER_IP_ADDRESS>:12383 \
--debug reconfigure-db --num-replicas <NUMBER_OF_MANAGERS>
```

This command will run a `docker/ucp-auth` container using the RethinkDB `reconfigure-db` command to fix the right number of managers.

Troubleshooting nodes

As we mentioned previously, network latency and performance can lead you to problematic situations. Take care of node resources and filesystems. If manager nodes become exhausted, the cluster will end up in an unhealthy state.

We can observe heartbeat failures if nodes cannot be contacted in 10 seconds. Worker nodes will reach a pending state if they cannot contact a manager node. We check these nodes locally. We also take a look at possible network or performance issues.

Managers can also become unhealthy. If other managers cannot reach them, `ucp-controller` processes will be impacted. We can check container logs for network issues.

These are some of the most common issues found on the Docker UCP platform. We usually start by reviewing the web UI dashboard and the `ucp-controller` container logs. If any other component seems unhealthy, we review its logs.

In the next chapter, we will learn how to publish applications deployed within the Docker Enterprise platform using the Interlock feature.

Summary

This chapter covered the main Docker UCP features. We learned how to deploy a cluster with high availability and how to manage and deploy workloads using either UCP's web UI or the user bundle with the Docker and Kubernetes command line. We also introduced UCP's role-based access control, which helps us provide fine-grained access to cluster resources. We also took a look at the web UI and the main configurations available for managing Docker Enterprise's control plane.

We also learned about UCP's components and how to deploy and manage Docker Enterprise's control plane and user resources in production. Finally, we learned how to ensure platform availability by verifying a cluster's components' status and executing backups.

In the next chapter, we will learn how to publish a deployed application using Docker's integrated tools and features.

Questions

1. Which of these sentences are true?

    a) The Docker UCP installation process will also install the Docker Enterprise Engine on our hosts.
    b) UCP provides an integrated RBAC system that will help us to authenticate and authorize our users against its database.
    c) Docker UCP provides two kinds of access: the web UI and the UCP bundle.
    d) All of the above sentences are true.

2. Which of these sentences is not true about a docker/ucp image?

    a) This image will provide UCP's backup and restore.
    b) We should always use the latest docker/ucp release version in our environment.
    c) Docker UCP can be completely removed using a docker/ucp image.
    d) The upgrade process must be executed manually on each cluster's node.

3. What have we learned about the UCP installation process (which of the following is true)?

> a) We can change the UCP controller and Kubernetes ports using special arguments.
> b) We can isolate the control plane using `--data-path-addr` to specify an interface or an IP address for the data plane.
> c) We can only have one subject alias name for the UCP environment and, by default, this will be the manager's IP address.
> d) We will install UCP on the manager using the `docker/ucp install` procedure and then we will join worker nodes.

4. Which of the following is true about high availability in UCP?

> a) UCP is deployed on top of a Docker Swarm cluster, so we will need an odd number of nodes to provide high availability.
> b) We will need to deploy Kubernetes with high availability once UCP is installed.
> c) An external load balancer is required to distribute client requests between different nodes using a transparent-proxy (passthrough) to allow managers to provide end-to-end TLS tunnels.
> d) We can check a manager's availability using the `https://<ucp-manager-url>/_ping` endpoint.

5. Which one of these roles is not included in UCP by default?

> a) `Privileged`
> b) `Full Control`
> c) `Administrator`
> d) `Scheduler`

Further reading

Refer to the following links for more information regarding the topics that were covered in this chapter:

- Universal Control Plane overview: `https://docs.docker.com/ee/ucp/`
- Docker Enterprise architecture: `https://docs.docker.com/ee/docker-ee-architecture/`
- Docker Enterprise products: `https://docs.docker.com/ee/supported-platforms/`

- UCP's access control mode: `https://docs.docker.com/ee/ucp/authorization/`
- Deploying applications on UCP's Kubernetes: `https://docs.docker.com/ee/ucp/kubernetes/`
- UCP access using the command line: `https://docs.docker.com/ee/ucp/user-access/cli/`
- Troubleshooting UCP node states: `https://docs.docker.com/ee/ucp/admin/monitor-and-troubleshoot/troubleshoot-node-messages/`
- Docker UCP's API: `https://docs.docker.com/reference/ucp/3.2/api/`
- Docker Enterprise best practices and design considerations: `https://success.docker.com/article/docker-enterprise-best-practices`
- Designing a disaster recovery strategy: `https://success.docker.com/article/dr-failover-strategy`

12
Publishing Applications in Docker Enterprise

The previous chapter helped us to understand Docker Enterprise's control plane components. Docker UCP deploys Docker Swarm and Kubernetes clusters over the same nodes. Both orchestrators share host components and devices. Each orchestrator will manage its own hardware resources. Information such as available memory and CPU is not shared between orchestrators. Therefore, we have to take care if we use both on a host simultaneously.

But what about publishing applications deployed on them? We learned how to publish applications on Docker Swarm and Kubernetes, but working on enterprise environments must be secure. In this chapter, we will learn how to publish applications on Docker Enterprise environments using either UCP-provided or community tools.

This chapter will show us the main publishing resources and features provided by UCP for Docker Swarm and Kubernetes. These components will help us to publish only front services, thereby ensuring an application's security. We will learn about ingress controllers, which is the preferred solution for publishing applications in Kubernetes, and Interlock, an enterprise-ready solution provided by UCP to publish applications in Docker Swarm.

We will cover the following topics in this chapter:

- Understanding publishing concepts and components
- Deep diving into your application's logic
- Ingress controllers
- Interlock
- Chapter labs

We will begin this chapter by reviewing some of the concepts learned in connection with Docker Swarm and Kubernetes deployments.

Technical requirements

You can find the code for this chapter in the GitHub repository: `https://github.com/ PacktPublishing/Docker-Certified-Associate-DCA-Exam-Guide.git`

Check out the following video to see the Code in Action:

`"https://bit.ly/2EHobBy"`

Understanding publishing concepts and components

`Chapter 8`, *Orchestration Using Docker Swarm*, showed us how applications work when deployed on top of a Docker Swarm cluster.

We will use service objects to deploy applications in Docker Swarm. Internal communication between services is always allowed if they run in the same network. Therefore, we will deploy an application's components in the same network and they will interact with other published applications. If two applications have to interact, they should share the network or be published.

Publishing applications is easy; we will just specify the ports that should be listening on the host where the process is running. However, we learned that Docker Swarm will publish an application's ports on all cluster hosts, and Router Mesh will route internal traffic to reach an appropriate service's tasks. Let's go back to these topics relating to containers and services before reviewing multi-service applications.

We have different options to publish container applications, as we learned in `Chapter 4`, *Container Persistency and Networking*. To make processes visible out of a container's isolated network namespace, we will use different network strategies:

- **Bridge networking**: This is the default option. A container's processes will be exposed using the host's **Network Address Translation (NAT)** features. Therefore, a container's process listening on a port will be attached to a host's port. NAT rules will be applied either to Linux or Microsoft Windows containers. This allows us to execute more than one container's instances using different hosts' ports.

We will publish container processes using the `--publish` or `-p` (or even `--publish-all` or `-P` to publish all image-declared exposed ports) option with the optional Docker host's IP address and port alongside the published port and protocol (TCP/UDP): `docker container run -p` `[HOST_IP:HOST_PORT:]<CONTAINER_PORT>[/PROTOCOL]`. By default, all the host's IP addresses and random ports within the `32768-65000` range will be used.

- **The host's network namespace**: In this situation, we will use the host's network namespace. Processes will be directly available, listening on the host's ports. No port translation will be used between the container and the host. Since the process port is attached directly, only one container's instance is allowed per host. We will use `docker container run --net=host` to associate a new container with the host's network namespace.
- **MacVLAN**: This is a special case where a container will use its own namespace, but it will be available at the host's network level. This allows us to attach VLANs (Virtual LANs) directly to containers and make them visible within an actual network. Containers will receive their own MACs; hence, services will be available in the network as if they were nodes.

These were the basic options. We will use external DNS to announce how they will be reached. We can also deploy containers on customized bridge networks. Custom networks have their own DNS namespace and containers will reach one another within the same network through their names or aliases. Services won't be published for other services running in the same network. We will just publish them for other networks or user access. In these cases, we will use NAT (common bridge networking), a host's namespace, or MacVLAN.

These will work on standalone hosts, but things will change if we distribute our workloads cluster-wide. We will now introduce the Kubernetes network model. This model must cover these situations:

- Pods running on a node should be able to communicate with others running on other hosts without NAT.
- System components (kubelet and control plane daemons) should be able to communicate with pods running on a host.
- Pods running in the host network of a node can communicate with all pods running on other hosts without NAT.

As we have learned, all containers within a pod share its IP address and all pods run on a flat network. We do not have network segmentation in Kubernetes, so we need other tools to isolate them. We will use network policies to implement firewall-like or network ACL-like rules. These rules are also applied to publishing services (ingress traffic).

Docker's network model is based on the **Container Network Model (CNM)** standard, while Kubernetes' network model is implemented using the **Container Network Interface (CNI)** model.

Docker's CNM manages **Internet Protocol Address Management (IPAM)** and network plugins. IPAM will be used to manage address pools and containers' IP addresses, while network plugins will be responsible for managing networks on each Docker Engine. CNM is implemented on Docker Engine via its `libnetwork` library, although we can add third-party plugins to replace this built-in Docker driver.

On the other hand, CNI modes expose an interface for managing a container's network. CNI will assign IP addresses to pods, although we can also add external IPAM interfaces, describing its behavior using JSON format. These describe how any CNI plugin must provide cluster and standalone networking when we add third-party plugins. As mentioned previously, Docker Enterprise's default CNI plugin is Calico. It provides cluster networking and security features using IP in IP encapsulation (although it also provides VXLAN mode).

Let's move on. Docker Engine provides all the networking features for hosts, and Kubernetes will also provide cluster-wide networking using CNI. Docker Swarm includes cluster-wide networking out of the box using VXLAN. An overlay network driver creates a distributed network between all hosts using their bridge network interfaces. We will just initialize a Docker Swarm cluster and no additional operations will be required. An ingress overlay network and a `docker_gwbridge` bridge network will be created. The former will manage control and data traffic related to Swarm services, while `docker_gwbridge` will be used to interconnect Docker hosts within Docker Swarm overlay networks.

We improved cluster's security by encrypting overlay networks, but we will expect some overhead and a minor negative impact on performance. As demonstrated in standalone networking and containers sharing networks, all services connected to the same overlay network will be able to talk to one another, even if we have not published any ports. Ports that should be accessible outside of a service's network must be explicitly published using `-p [ HOSTS_PORT:]<CONTAINER_PORT>[/PROTOCOL]`.

> There is a long format for publishing a service's ports. Although you have to write more, it is clearer. We will write `-p published=<HOSTS_PORT>,target=<CONTAINER_PORT>,protocol=<PROTOCOL>`.

Publishing services within Docker Swarm will expose a defined service's port on all hosts in the cluster. This feature is **Router Mesh**. All hosts will publish this service even if they do not really run any service's processes. Docker will guide traffic to a service's tasks within the cluster using an internal ingress overlay network.

Remember that all services received a virtual IP address. This IP address will be fixed during a service's lifetime. Each service is composed of tasks associated with the containers. Docker will run as many tasks, and thus containers, as are required for this service to work. Each task will run just one container, with its IP address. As containers can run everywhere in the cluster and they are ephemeral (between different hosts), they will receive different IP addresses. A service's IP addresses are fixed and will create a DNS entry in Docker Swarm's embedded DNS. Therefore, all services within an overlay network will be reachable and known by their names (and aliases).

A similar approach is present in Kubernetes. In this case, services are just a grouping of pods. Pods will get different dynamic IP addresses because resilience will manage their life cycle, creating new ones if they die. But services will always have a fixed IP address during their life. This is also true for Docker Swarm. Therefore, we will publish services and internal routing and load balancing will guide traffic to pods or tasks' containers.

Both orchestrators will allow us to bypass these default behaviors, but we are not going to dive deep into these ideas because we have covered them in `Chapter 8`, *Orchestration Using Docker Swarm*, and `Chapter 9`, *Orchestration Using Kubernetes*.

Now that we have a basic understanding, we can introduce ingress controllers. These are pieces of software that will allow us to publish fewer ports within our cluster. They will help us to ensure security by default access, publishing fewer ports and only specific application routes. Ingress controllers will provide reverse proxy with load balancing capacities to help us publish an application's backends running as services inside a container's infrastructure. We will use internal networking instead of publishing an application's services. We will just publish the ingress controller and all the application's traffic will become internal from this endpoint.

The ingress controller concept can be applied to both Kubernetes and Docker Swarm. Kubernetes has special resources for this to work, but Docker Swarm has nothing already prepared. In this case, we will have to use external applications. Docker Enterprise does provide an out-of-the-box solution for Docker Swarm services. Interlock integrates the ingress controller features described but applied to Docker Swarm's behavior.

In the next section, we will talk a little about application logic and expected behavior on container platforms.

Understanding an application's logic

We have reviewed how publishing will work for our application's components, but should they all be published? The short answer is probably no. Imagine a three-layer application. We will have a middle layer for some kind of backend that will consume a database and should be accessed through a frontend. In a legacy data center, this layered application will probably run each service on a separate node. These nodes will run on different subnets to isolate accesses between them with firewalls. This architecture is quite common. Backend components will be in the middle, between the database and the frontend. The frontend should not access the database. In fact, the database should only be accessible from the backend component. Therefore, should we publish the database component service? The frontend component will access the backend, but do we have to publish the backend component? No, but the frontend should be able to access the backend service. Users and other applications will use frontend components to consume our application. Therefore, only frontend components should be published. This guarantees security by using a container's features instead of firewalls and subnets, but the final outcome is the same.

Docker Swarm allows us to implement multi-networking applications using overlay custom networks. These will allow us to interconnect components of applications from different applications sharing some networks. This can become complex if many services from different applications have to consume one service. This many-to-one networking behavior may not work correctly in your environment. To avoid this complexity, you have two options:

- Use flat networks, either moving to Kubernetes or defining large overlay subnets. The first option is better in this case as Kubernetes provides network policies to improve flat network security. Large networks in Docker Swarm do not provide any security for their components. It is up to you to improve it with external tools.
- Publish this common service and allow other applications to consume it as if they were cluster-external. We will use DNS entries for our service and other applications will know how to access it. We will use load balancers and/or API managers to improve availability and security. These external components are beyond the scope of this book, but they will provide non-container-based application behavior.

Now that we understand how applications can be deployed and published, we will introduce the concept of ingress controllers and their components before getting into Docker Enterprise's Interlock.

Publishing applications in Kubernetes using ingress controllers

As mentioned previously, ingress controllers are special Kubernetes components that are deployed to publish applications and services.

Ingress resources will define rules and routes required to expose HTTP and HTTPS deployed services.

An ingress controller will complete this equation as a reverse proxy, adding load-balancing capabilities. These features can be arranged by an external edge router or a cluster-deployed software proxy. Any of these will manage traffic using dynamic configurations built using ingress resource rules.

We can also use ingress for TCP and UDP raw services. This will depend on which ingress reverse proxy has been deployed. It is customary to publish an application's services using protocols other than HTTP and HTTPS. In this case, we can use either Router Mesh on Docker Swarm or NodePort/LoadBalancer on Kubernetes.

An ingress resource may look like the following YAML file:

```
apiVersion: networking.k8s.io/v1beta1
kind: Ingress
metadata:
  name: test-ingress
  annotations:
    nginx.ingress.kubernetes.io/rewrite-target: /
spec:
  rules:
  - http:
      paths:
      - path: /testpath
        pathType: Prefix
        backend:
          serviceName: test
          servicePort: 80
```

Ingress rules contain an optional host key used to associate this resource with a proxied host header for inbound traffic. All subsequent rules will be applied to this host.

It will also contain a list of paths, associated with different services, defined as proxied backends. All requests matching the host and path keys will be redirected to listed backends. Deployed services and ports will define each backend for an application.

> We will define a default backend to route any request not matching any ingress resource's rules.

As mentioned, ingress controllers will deploy ingress rules on different proxy services. We will either use existing external hardware or software load balancers or we will deploy these components within the cluster. As these pieces are interchangeable, different deployments will provide different behaviors, although ingress resource configurations will be similar. These deployments should be published, but backend services do not require direct external access. Ingress controller pieces will manage routes and rules required to access services.

Ingress controllers will be published using any of this chapter's described methods, although we will usually use NodePort- and LoadBalancer-type services.

> We can deploy multiple ingress controllers on any Kubernetes cluster. This is important because we can improve isolation on multi-tenant environments using specific ingress controllers for each customer.

We have described a layer 7 routing architecture for Kubernetes. The following diagram shows an example of ingress controller deployment. An external load balancer will route a user's requests to the ingress controller. This component will review ingress resource tables and route traffic to the appropriate internal service's ClusterIP. Then, Kubernetes will manage internal service-to-pod communications to ensure that a user's requests reach the service's associated pods:

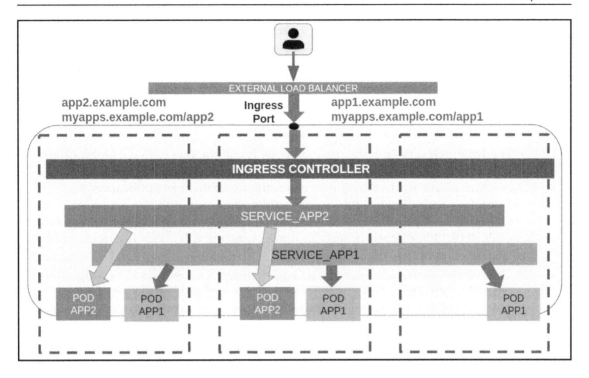

In the next section, we will learn how Docker Enterprise deploys this publishing logic for Docker Swarm services.

Using Interlock to publish applications deployed in Docker Swarm

Interlock is based on the ingress controller's logic described previously. Docker Swarm architecture is different. Its differences are even more pronounced when we talk about Kubernetes and Docker Swarm networking implementations. Kubernetes provides a flat network architecture, as we have seen. Multiple networks within the cluster will add additional security features, but also more complexity.

 Interlock substitutes the previous Docker Enterprise's router mesh L7 routing implementation. Router mesh was available in previous UCP releases. Interlock appeared in the 2.0 release of Docker Enterprise.

Interlock will integrate Docker Swarm and Docker Remote API features to isolate and configure dynamically an application proxy such as NGINX or HA-Proxy using extensions. Interlock will use Docker Swarm's well-known objects, such as configs and secrets, to manage proxy required configurations. We will be able to manage TLS tunnels and integrate rolling updates (and rollbacks) and zero-downtime reconfigurations.

Interlock's logic is distributed in three main services:

- The **Interlock service** is the main process. It will interact with the Docker Remote API to monitor Docker Swarm events. This service will create all the configurations required by a proxy to route requests to an application's endpoints, including headers, routes, and backends. It will also manage extensions and proxy services. The Interlock service will be consumed via its gRPC API. Other Interlock services and extensions will access Interlock's API to get their prepared configurations.
- The **Interlock-extension** service will query Interlock's API for the configurations created upstream. Extensions will use this pre-configuration to prepare real configurations for the extension-associated proxy. For proxy services such as NGINX or HA-Proxy, deployed within the cluster, the Interlock-extension service will create its configurations and then these will be sent to the Interlock service via its API. The Interlock service will then create a config object within the Docker Swarm cluster for the deployed proxy services.
- The **Interlock-proxy** is the proxy service. It will use configurations stored in config objects to route and manage HTTP and HTTPS requests.

Docker Enterprise deploys NGINX as the Interlock-proxy. Docker Swarm cluster changes affecting published services will be updated dynamically.

> Interlock allows DevOps groups to implement **Blue-Green** and **Canary** service deployment. These will help DevOps to deploy application upgrades without impacting access on the part of users.

The following diagram shows a basic Interlock schema. As mentioned, Interlock looks like an ingress controller. The following schema represents common applications' traffic. User requests will be forwarded by the external load balancer to the Interlock proxy instances. This component will review its rules and forward requests to the configured service's IP address. Then, Docker Swarm will use internal routing and load balancing to forward requests to the service's tasks:

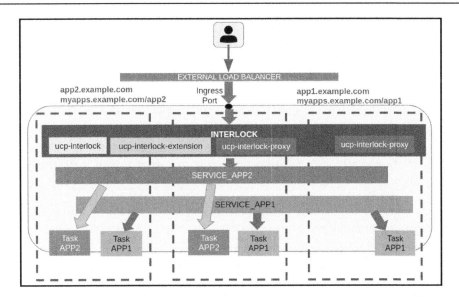

Interlock's layer 7 routing supports the following features:

- Since Interlock services run as Docker Swarm services, high availability based on resilience is granted.
- Interlock interacts with the Docker API, hence, dynamic and automatic configuration is provided.
- Automatic configuration: Interlock uses the Docker API for configuration. You do not have to manually update or restart anything to make services available. UCP monitors your services and automatically reconfigures proxy services.
- We can scale a proxy service up and down because it is deployed as a separate component.
- Interlock provides TLS tunneling, either for TLS termination or TCP passthrough. Certificates will be stored using Docker Swarm's secret objects.
- Interlock supports request routing by context or paths.
- We can deploy multiple extensions and proxy configurations simultaneously to isolate accesses on multi-tenant or multi-region environments.

Interlock-proxy and Interlock-extension services' instances run on worker nodes. This will improve security, isolating the control plane from publishing services.

 We can use host mode networking to bypass default routing mesh services' behavior for the Interlock-proxy service. This will improve network performance.

Publishing services using Interlock are based on label customization. We will require at least the following:

- `com.docker.lb.hosts`: This label will manage the host header, hence the service's published name.
- `com.docker.lb.port`: The internal service's port is also required and associated using this label. Remember that this port should not be published.
- `com.docker.lb.network`: This defines which network the Interlock-proxy service should attach to in order to be able to communicate with the defined service.

Other labels will allow us to modify configured-proxy behavior and features. This is a list of some other important labels:

Labels	Description
`com.docker.lb.ssl_cert` and `com.docker.lb.ssl_key`	These keys allow us to integrate the backend's certificate and key.
`com.docker.lb.sticky_session_cookie`	We will set a cookie to allow sticky sessions to define a service instance's backends.
`com.docker.lb.backend_mode`	This stipulates how requests reach different backends (it defaults to `vip`, which is also the default mode for Docker Swarm services).
`com.docker.lb.ssl_passthrough`	We can close tunnels on application backends, thereby enabling SSL passthrough.
`com.docker.lb.redirects`	This key allows us to redirect requests to different FQDNs using host header definitions.

You can review all the available labels in Docker Enterprise's documentation (`https://docs.docker.com/ee/ucp/interlock/usage/labels-reference`).

If a service is isolated on just one network, we don't need to add `com.docker.lb.network`, but it will be required if it is combined with `com.docker.lb.ssl_passthrough`. If we publish services using stacks, we will use the stack's name.

There are many options and configurations available for Interlock's described components. We will be allowed to change the proxy's default port, the Docker API socket, and the polling interval, among other things. Extensions will have many features and configurations depending on external load balancing integrations. We recommend that you review all the available keys and configurations in Docker Enterprise's documentation (`https://docs.docker.com/ee/ucp/interlock/config`).

We recommend reviewing this link, `https://success.docker.com/article/how-to-troubleshoot-layer-7-loadbalancing`, to get some interesting tips regarding the troubleshooting of Interlock-related issues.

In the next chapter, we will introduce Docker Trusted Registry. This tool provides a secure image store, integrating image signing features and vulnerability scanning. These features, among others, provide a production-ready image store solution.

Reviewing Interlock usage

We will now review some examples of Interlock usage.

We will need to enable Interlock in Docker Enterprise. It is disabled by default and is part of the **Admin Settings** section. We can change the default ports (`8080` for HTTP and `8443` for secure access using HTTPS), as shown in the following screenshot:

Once enabled, Interlock's services are created, which we can verify by using the admin's UCP bundle and executing `docker service ls`:

```
$ docker service ls --filter name=ucp-interlock
ID NAME MODE REPLICAS IMAGE PORTS
onf2z2i5ttng ucp-interlock replicated 1/1 docker/ucp-interlock:3.2.5
nuq8eagch4in ucp-interlock-extension replicated 1/1 docker/ucp-interlock-
extension:3.2.5
x2554tcxb7kw ucp-interlock-proxy replicated 2/2 docker/ucp-interlock-
proxy:3.2.5 *:8080->80/tcp, *:8443->443/tcp
```

It is important to observe that, by default, Interlock-proxy will not be isolated on worker nodes if there are not enough nodes to run the required number of instances. We can change this behavior by using simple location constraints (`https://docs.docker.com/ee/ucp/interlock/deploy/production`).

For this example, we will use the `colors` application again. We used this simple application in Chapter 5, *Deploying Multi-Container Applications*. This is a simple `docker-compose` file prepared to deploy a `colors` service. We will use a random color, leaving the `COLORS` variable empty. We will create a `colors-stack.yml` file with the following content:

```
version: "3.2"

services:
 colors:
 image: codegazers/colors:1.16
 deploy:
 replicas: 3
       labels:
         com.docker.lb.hosts: colors.lab.local
         com.docker.lb.network: colors-network
         com.docker.lb.port: 3000
     networks:
       - colors-network

networks:
  colors-network:
    driver: overlay
```

We will connect to Docker Enterprise with a valid user using their bundle. For this lab, we will use the `admin` user that we created during installation. We will download the user's `ucp` bundle using any of the procedures described in `Chapter 11`, *Universal Control Plane*. Once downloaded and unzipped, we will just load UCP's environment using `source env.sh`:

```
$ source env.sh
Cluster "ucp_<UCP_FQDN>:6443_admin" set.
User "ucp_<UCP_FQDN>:6443_admin" set.
Context "ucp_<UCP_FQDN>:6443_admin" modified.
```

Once the UCP environment is loaded, we will use the book's Git repository (`https://github.com/frjaraur/dca-book-code.git`). Interlock's labs can be found under the `interlock-lab` directory. We will deploy the `colors` stack using `docker stack deploy -c colors-stack.yml lab`:

```
interlock-lab$ docker stack deploy -c colors-stack.yml lab
Creating network lab_colors-network
Creating service lab_colors
```

We will review how `colors` instances are distributed within the cluster by using `docker stack ps`:

```
$ docker stack ps lab
ID NAME IMAGE NODE DESIRED STATE CURRENT STATE ERROR PORTS
ksoie4oin10e lab_colors.1 codegazers/colors:1.16 node4 Running Running 8
seconds ago
b0dykjgp8ack lab_colors.2 codegazers/colors:1.16 node2 Running Preparing 9
seconds ago
m13tvfbw5cgb lab_colors.3 codegazers/colors:1.16 node3 Running Preparing 9
seconds ago
```

We enabled Interlock on UCP's **Admin Settings** section. We used the default port, so we should access our deployed service on the `8080` port (because we are using HTTP in this lab). Notice that we have not used any `port` key in the `docker-compose` file. We have not published any service's port. Let's check whether Interlock is working by specifying the required host header, `colors.lab.local`:

```
$ curl -H "host: colors.lab.local" http://<UCP_NODE>:8080/text
APP_VERSION: 1.15
COLOR: black
CONTAINER_NAME: e69a7ca3b74f
CONTAINER_IP: 10.0.5.15 172.18.0.4
CLIENT_IP: 10.0.0.2
CONTAINER_ARCH: linux
$ curl -H "host: colors.lab.local" http://<UCP_NODE>:8080/text
```

```
APP_VERSION: 1.15
COLOR: yellow
CONTAINER_NAME: 69ebb6f349f6
CONTAINER_IP: 10.0.5.14 172.18.0.3
CLIENT_IP: 10.0.0.2
CONTAINER_ARCH: linux
```

The output may change and we will launch some requests to ensure that we get different backends (we deployed three instances). If we do not specify any host header, a default one will be used. If none was configured (default behavior), we will get a proxy error. As we are using NGINX (default), we will get a `503` error:

```
$ curl -I http://<UCP_NODE>:8080/text
HTTP/1.1 503 Service Temporarily Unavailable
Server: nginx/1.14.2
Date: Tue, 31 Mar 2020 19:51:05 GMT
Content-Type: text/html
Content-Length: 537
Connection: keep-alive
ETag: "5cad421a-219"
```

We can change the default Interlock's backend using the special label `com.docker.lb.default_backend: "true"`, associated with one of our services. This will act as a default site when headers don't match any configured service.

Let's remove this lab before continuing. We will use `docker stack rm`. We will probably get an error because stacks will now have to be removed carefully:

```
$ docker stack rm lab
Removing service lab_colors
Removing network lab_colors-network
Failed to remove network 97bgcu0eo445sz8ke10bacbge: Error response from
daemon: Error response from daemon: rpc error: code = FailedPrecondition
desc = network 97bgcu0eo445sz8ke10bacbge is in use by service
x2554tcxb7kwv0wzsasvfjh6dFailed to remove some resources from stack: lab
```

This error is normal. The Interlock-proxy component is attached to our application's network, hence it cannot be removed. Interlock will refresh configurations every few seconds (Docker API polls will be launched every 3 seconds and, after these intervals, Interlock will manage the required changes). If we just wait a few seconds and launch the removal command again, it will delete the stack's remaining components (network):

```
$ docker stack rm lab
Removing network lab_colors-network
```

We will now test a simple redirection using the `com.docker.lb.redirects` key.

Simple application redirection

In this example, we will review how we can redirect requests from one service to another. This can be interesting when we want to migrate users from an old application to a newer release, at application level. We are not talking about an image upgrade in this case. We will simply create a new overlay network using `docker network create`:

```
$ docker network create -d overlay redirect
```

We will now create a simple web server application service (the smallest NGINX image, `nginx:alpine`). Notice that we will add to host headers inside the `com.docker.lb.hosts` label. We have also added `com.docker.lb.redirects` to ensure that all requests sent to `http://old.lab.local` will be redirected to `http://new.lab.local`. This is how this service definition will appear:

```
$ docker service create --name redirect --network redirect \
--label com.docker.lb.hosts=old.lab.local,new.lab.local \
--label com.docker.lb.port=80 \
--label com.docker.lb.redirects=http://old.lab.local,http://new.lab.local
nginx:alpine
```

If we test access to one of our UCP nodes on port `8080`, using `old.lab.local` as the host header, we will be redirected to `http://new.lab.local`. We added `-L` to the `curl` command to allow the required redirection:

```
$ curl -vL http://<UCP_NODE>:8080/ -H Host:old.lab.local
* Trying <UCP_NODE>...
* TCP_NODELAY set
* Connected to <UCP_NODE> (<UCP_NODE>) port 8080 (#0)
> GET / HTTP/1.1
> Host:old.lab.local
> User-Agent: curl/7.58.0
> Accept: */*
>
< HTTP/1.1 302 Moved Temporarily
< Server: nginx/1.14.2
< Date: Tue, 31 Mar 2020 22:21:26 GMT
< Content-Type: text/html
< Content-Length: 161
< Connection: keep-alive
< Location: http://new.lab.local/
< x-request-id: d4a9735f8880cfdc99e0478b7ea7d583
< x-proxy-id: 1bfde5e3a23e
< x-server-info: interlock/v3.0.0 (27b903b2) linux/amd64
<
* Ignoring the response-body
```

```
* Connection #0 to host <UCP_NODE> left intact
* Issue another request to this URL: 'http://new.lab.local/'
* Could not resolve host: new.lab.local
* Closing connection 1
curl: (6) Could not resolve host: new.lab.local
```

Notice that new.lab.local was a dummy FQDN, hence we cannot resolve it, but the test request was forwarded to this new application site.

We will now deploy an example service that is protected using TLS certificates. Interlock will manage its certificates and access will be secure.

Publishing a service securely using Interlock with TLS

In this example, we will deploy a service that should be published securely using TLS. We can create tunnels from users directly to our service, configuring Interlock as a transparent proxy, or we can allow Interlock to manage tunnels. In this case, a service can be deployed using HTTP, but HTTPS will be required from the user's perspective. Users will interact with the Interlock-proxy component before reaching the defined service's backends.

For this example, we will use the colors application again with random configuration. We will use the colors-stack-https.yml file with the following content:

```
version: "3.2"

services:
  colors:
    image: codegazers/colors:1.16
    deploy:
      replicas: 1
      labels:
        com.docker.lb.hosts: colors.lab.local
        com.docker.lb.network: colors-network
        com.docker.lb.port: 3000
        com.docker.lb.ssl_cert: colors_colors.lab.local.cert
        com.docker.lb.ssl_key: colors_colors.lab.local.key
    networks:
    - colors-network

networks:
  colors-network:
    driver: overlay
secrets:
```

```
colors.lab.local.cert:
    file: ./colors-lab-local.cert
colors.lab.local.key:
    file: ./colors-lab-local.key
```

We will create a sample key and an associated certificate and these will be integrated inside Interlock's configuration automatically.

 It is always relevant to review Interlock's component logs using Docker service logs; for example, we will detect configuration errors using `docker service logs ucp-interlock`.

We will use `openssl` to create a certificate that is valid for 365 days:

```
$ openssl req \
 -new \
 -newkey rsa:4096 \
 -days 365 \
 -nodes \
 -x509 \
 -subj "/C=US/ST=CA/L=SF/O=colors/CN=colors.lab.local" \
 -keyout colors.lab.local.key \
 -out colors.lab.local.cert
```

Once these keys and certificates are created, we will connect to Docker Enterprise using the `admin` user again. Although the admin's environment will probably already be loaded (if you are following these labs one by one), we will load the `ucp` environment using `source env.sh`:

```
$ source env.sh
Cluster "ucp_<UCP_FQDN>:6443_admin" set.
User "ucp_<UCP_FQDN>:6443_admin" set.
Context "ucp_<UCP_FQDN>:6443_admin" modified.
```

Once the UCP environment is loaded, we will use this book's example `colors-stack-ssl.yaml` file. We will deploy the `colors` stack with HTTPS using `docker stack deploy -c colors-stack-https.yml lab`. This directory also contains a prepared certificate and key:

```
interlock-lab$ $ docker stack deploy -c colors-stack-https.yml colors
Creating network colors_colors-network
Creating secret colors_colors.lab.local.cert
Creating secret colors_colors.lab.local.key
Creating service colors_colors
```

We will review how `colors` instances are distributed within the cluster using `docker stack ps`:

```
$ docker stack ps colors
ID NAME IMAGE NODE DESIRED STATE CURRENT STATE ERROR PORTS
xexbvl18d454 colors_colors.1 codegazers/colors:1.16 node4 Running Running 4
minutes ago
```

We enabled Interlock on UCP's **Admin Settings** section. We used the default port, hence we should access our deployed service on the 8443 port (because we are using HTTPS). Notice that we have not used any `port` key on the `docker-compose` file. We have not published any service's port.

We can review Interlock's proxy configuration by reading the associated `com.docker.interlock.proxy.<ID>` configuration object. We can use `docker config inspect` and filter its output. First, we will obtain the current `ucp-interlock-proxy` configuration object:

```
$ export CFG=$(docker service inspect --format '{{(index
.Spec.TaskTemplate.ContainerSpec.Configs 0).ConfigName}}' ucp-interlock-
proxy)
```

Then, we will just inspect this object:

```
$ docker config inspect --pretty ${CFG}
```

Inspecting the Interlock-proxy configuration can be very useful when it comes to troubleshooting Interlock issues. Try to include one service or stack at a time. This will avoid the mixing of configurations and help us to follow incorrect configuration issues.

Summary

This chapter covered Docker Enterprise's publishing features. We learned different publishing strategies for Docker Swarm and Kubernetes and how these tools can be integrated inside Docker Enterprise.

We have seen how these methods also improve an application's security by isolating different layers and allowing us to publish only frontend and requisite services.

The next chapter will teach us how Docker Enterprise implements a fully secure and production-ready image store solution.

Questions

1. Which labels are required to publish a service using Interlock?

   a) `com.docker.lb.backend_mode`
   b) `com.docker.lb.port`
   c) `com.docker.lb.hosts`
   d) `com.docker.lb.network`

2. Which one of these processes is not part of Interlock?

   a) `ucp-interlock`
   b) `ucp-interlock-controller`
   c) `ucp-interlock-extension`
   d) `ucp-interlock-proxy`

3. Where do Interlock processes run within Docker Enterprise nodes?

   a) `ucp-interlock` runs on Docker Swarm's leader.
   b) `ucp-interlock-extension` runs on any manager.
   c) `ucp-interlock-proxy` runs only on workers.
   d) None of the above answers are correct.

4. Which features does Interlock support?

   a) SSL/TLS endpoint management
   b) Transparent proxy or SSL/TLS passthrough
   c) Dynamic configuration using the Docker API
   d) TCP/UDP publishing

5. Which of the following statements regarding the publishing of applications on container-orchestrated environments are true?

   a) Ingress controllers and Interlock have a common logic using reverse proxy services for publishing applications.
   b) Ingress controllers help us to publish applications securely by exposing only required services.
   c) Interlock requires access to an application's front service networks.
   d) None of these premises are true.

Further reading

Refer to the following links for more information regarding the topics covered in this chapter:

- Docker Interlock documentation: `https://docs.docker.com/ee/ucp/interlock/`
- Universal Control Plane Service Discovery and Load Balancing for Swarm: `https://success.docker.com/article/ucp-service-discovery-swarm`
- Universal Control Plane Service Discovery and Load Balancing for Kubernetes: `https://success.docker.com/article/ucp-service-discovery-k8s`

13
Implementing an Enterprise-Grade Registry with DTR

Docker Enterprise is a complete **Container as a Service (CaaS)** platform. In previous chapters, we have learned how **Universal Control Plane (UCP)** provides a complete control plane solution for the Docker Swarm and Kubernetes orchestrators. We also learned about how UCP includes publishing features using Interlock. An enterprise-ready platform should also cover the storage of images. In this chapter, we will learn about **Docker Trusted Registry (DTR)**, a component of the Docker Enterprise platform designed to manage and ensure security in Docker images.

In this chapter, we will learn about DTR components and how to deploy and manage a secure registry with high availability in terms of its components. We will also learn about how DTR provides an enterprise solution using **Role-Based Access Control (RBAC)**, image scanning, and other security features. The final topics covered will demonstrate how we can integrate DTR automation and promotion features in our CI/CD workflow and strategies to ensure DTR's health. By the end of this series of chapters about Docker Enterprise, you will have good knowledge of this platform.

We will cover the following topics in this chapter:

- Understanding DTR components and features
- Deploying DTR with high availability
- Learning about RBAC
- Image scanning and security features
- Integrating and automating image workflow
- Backup strategies
- Updates, health checks, and troubleshooting

Technical requirements

You can find the code for this chapter in the GitHub repository: `https://github.com/PacktPublishing/Docker-Certified-Associate-DCA-Exam-Guide.git`

Check out the following video to see the Code in Action:

`"https://bit.ly/32tg6sn"`

Understanding DTR components and features

DTR is the Docker Enterprise's platform registry, used to store and manage images. It is deployed on top of defined UCP worker nodes. DTR will run as a multi-container application. This means that all containers will run together, associated with just one defined node. In the case of node failure, no other nodes will take its DTR containers. This is very important because we need to deploy multiple DTR deployments, on different nodes.

DTR uses RethinkDB as a database to store and sync data between registry nodes. To provide high availability to DTR, we need to deploy an odd number of replicas. We will use three replicas, so we need to deploy DTR workloads on three worker nodes. Synchronization will be done using overlay networking. DTR installation will create a `dtr-ol` overlay network and this will be used internally for replica synchronization.

Each replica will deploy the following processes:

Replica (DTR instance)	Process
`dtr-api-<replica_id>`	This process exposes DTR's API internally.
`dtr-garant-<replica_id>`	DTR's authentication is managed by means of this component.
`dtr-jobrunner-<replica_id>`	`jobrunner` is used to schedule different internal DTR maintenance tasks.
`dtr-nginx-<replica_id>`	The `nginx` process acts as a reverse proxy, publishing DTR's API and web UI on ports 80 and 443 (secure).

`dtr-notary-server-<replica_id>` and `dtr-notary-signer-<replica_id>`	These processes help us to sign and maintain users' signatures.
`dtr-registry-<replica_id>`	A community-based registry will be installed as a core component in DTR.
`dtr-rethinkdb-<replica_id>`	RethinkDB is the database used to store DTR's repository information.
`dtr-scanningstore-<replica_id>`	This component manages and stores scanning data.

Notice that all processes will have a common suffix to identify each replica within the cluster. We will deploy different replicas, but their data will be synchronized.

Notary server processes will also receive requests whenever any user pushes or pulls images using a client with content trust enabled. A notary signer will execute server-side timestamps and snapshots for image signatures.

Volumes will be used to persist DTR data. Each node running a DTR replica will manage its own volumes. If DTR detects their existence, they will be used. This prevents the destruction of previous installations (we have to use the previous `replica_id` identification):

Replica (DTR instance)	Process
`dtr-ca-<replica_id>`	This volume manages the required key and root information to issue DTR's CA.
`dtr-notary-<replica_id>`	This volume stores notary keys and certificates.
`dtr-postgres-<replica_id>`	This volume is used by images' vulnerability scanning.
`dtr-registry-<replica_id>` and `dtr-nfs-registry-<replica_id>`	A registry's data is stored on this volume. This is the default option, but we are able to integrate third-party storage. In fact, shared storage will be required to provide DTR processes with high availability. `dtr-nfs-registry-<replica_id>` will be used if the storage's backend is NFS.
`dtr-rethink-<replica_id>`	This volume stores repository information.

DTR's data storage is key because this is where images will live. Take care of your images' layers because DTR's backup does not back up their data and meta-information. You have to deploy your own backup to be able to restore your images' data.

DTR can be deployed either on-premises or in the cloud. We can use Amazon, Google, or Microsoft Azure. It supports the following storage backends:

- NFS
- Amazon S3
- Cleversafe
- Google Cloud Storage
- OpenStack Swift
- Microsoft Azure

We can use any S3 object's storage-compatible solution (Minio, for example). Object storage works great with an image's data if we have big layers with a lot of content.

DTR provides image caching for multi-site environments where communication latency between users and the registry can become a problem. Image caching will be used to ensure that users get the required images from the nearest registry node.

RBAC is provided with DTR as it is in UCP. Both applications can be integrated to have a single sign-on solution, but RBAC is independent. DTR will forward authentication to UCP and this will verify a user's authentication, but each application will manage different roles and profiles. This way, a UCP's power user can have limited access to images in DTR.

Security in DTR is based on image security scanning and Docker Content Trust. Image security scanning will search for an image's content vulnerabilities using binaries' and libraries' **bills of materials (BOMs)**. A **Common Vulnerabilities and Exposures (CVE)** database is used to search for well-known issues in our images.

 A BOM is a detailed list of all the files present inside an image. A CVE database is a public database of well-known vulnerabilities found in files around the world. It is community-driven and there are many contributors reporting and looking for vulnerabilities in applications' code.

DTR also includes image promotion and task scheduling. These features allow us to monitor image tagging and security to trigger different modifications or interactions with either external or DTR-integrated tools.

Repository mirroring and caching will help us to integrate DTR in enterprise environments.

We will learn how to deploy DTR with high availability in the next section.

Deploying DTR with high availability

Deploying DTR with high availability requires more than one replica executing all DTR components. We will deploy an odd number of replicas to ensure high availability.

DTR should be deployed on dedicated worker nodes. This will ensure that none of the non-system processes will impact DTR's behavior and vice versa. DTR's processes can take a lot of CPU during scanning and other procedures. Therefore, we will use three dedicated worker nodes. We usually admit DHCP on worker nodes, but we will ask for fixed IP addresses on DTR's worker nodes. We will also require fixed hostnames.

We can deploy the Docker Enterprise platform on-premises or in the cloud. DTR requirements were described in brief in `Chapter 11`, *Universal Control Plane*.

To deploy DTR on dedicated workers, these nodes require at least the following:

- 16 GB of RAM
- 2 vCPUs (virtual CPUs)

For production, we will ask for bigger nodes with more resources:

- 32 GB of RAM
- 4 vCPUs

This increment of hardware resources is due to image-scanning features. This will take a bunch of CPU and memory resources because it will load the content of all images and create all binary and library `md5-checksum-hashes` to compare these values against the CVE database.

An image's data will be downloaded by default in the `dtr-registry-<REPLICA_ID>` volume. If you deploy a standalone replica for testing, for example, ensure that you have sufficient space for your images. A minimum of 25 GB is required, but we recommend having at least 500 GB if you plan to manage Microsoft Windows images.

At the time of writing this book, the latest DTR release is 2.7.6. We will first install a DTR replica. Once the first replica is installed, we will join two other replicas. We recommend that you configure the first replica before continuing with others. This will ensure the synchronization of configuration changes between replicas. This is important for configuring DTR's data storage.

If we configured a license on UCP, this will be copied to the DTR. If not, we will need to configure it in both environments.

As we have seen in Docker's UCP installation, `installation-container` will have many actions associated with it, such as `backups/restore`, `install`, and `join`:

Command	Action
`install`	DTR will be installed using the `docker/dtr` image. We will launch this process from any UCP node because the UCP URL will be used and the process will be executed from manager nodes once the connection is established.
`join`	We will execute more than one DTR replica to provide high availability. In this case, we will install the first replica and then we will join others to this one.
`reconfigure`	We can modify DTR configurations using the DTR image. Some configurations require restarting. We will configure DTR replicas to avoid downtime.
`remove`	Sometimes, we need to remove a number of DTR replicas. We will use the `remove` action, available in the `docker/dtr` image, to delete replicas from the DTR environment. This action will neatly remove replicas, updating other replicas about this change.
`destroy`	This command will be used to forcefully remove all DTR replicas' containers and volumes. This procedure should be used with care because replica removal is forced and does not inform others about this condition, meaning that a cluster can be left in an unhealthy state. Use this option to completely remove DTR from your cluster.
`backup/restore`	This command creates a TAR file with all the information and files required to restore a DTR replica, including non-image volumes and configurations. This will not back up an image's data layers. An image's data must be stored using third-party tools. Take care with this because you should be able to restore your DTR cluster to a running state, but you could lose all your images.
`upgrade`	The `upgrade` option will help us to automatically deploy platform upgrades. All DTR components will be updated to a defined upgrade release. If we have deployed DTR with high availability, this process should not impact our users.

`images`	We can download DTR's required images prior to installation. This is very useful, for example, when we have to execute an offline installation. We will download DTR images using a Docker Engine instance with internet access.
`emergency-repair`	When all the replicas of DTR are unhealthy, but one replica is running with healthy core processes, we will use the `emergency-repair` action with this replica to recover the cluster.

We will usually have the following common arguments for the majority of the actions:

Arguments	Actions
`--ucp-url`	This should be our valid UCP's URL. We will use the cluster's **Fully Qualified Domain Name** (**FQDN**) and port (443 by default).
`--ucp-ca` and `--ucp-insecure-tls`	We will choose either of these options, using UCP's valid CA or insecure TLS, avoiding any CA authentication.
`--ucp-username` and `--ucp-password`	These options will provide UCP's user authentication. If none are used, we will be asked for them during execution. These should be valid and must have administrator privileges.

> Always use the appropriate `docker/dtr:<RELEASE>` version for all actions. Do not mix releases unless you are doing a DTR upgrade. The current release, at the time of writing this book, is 2.7.6.

DTR installation requires UCP's URL and one administrator's username and password. We can use these interactively, but as we learned in previous sections, it is preferable to include installation as part of script-like structures. This will help us to provide a reproducible configuration and installation methodology.

We will now describe DTR's installation process. The first replica will be installed using `docker container run docker/dtr:<RELEASE> install`. We will launch the installation process from any cluster node. In fact, we can deploy DTR from our laptop because we will include UCP's URL and the administrator's username and password. Installation can be done using an interactive or automated process. We will also choose which UCP node will run the first replica's processes using `--ucp-node`:

```
$ docker run -it --rm \
  docker/dtr:<RELEASE> install \
  --dtr-external-url <DTR_COMPLETE_URL>\
  --ucp-node <UCP_NODE_TO_INSTALL> \
  --ucp-username <UCP_USERNAME> \
  --ucp-password <UCP_PASSWORD> \
  --ucp-url <UCP_COMPLETE_URL> \
```

```
   --ucp-ca "$(curl -s -k <UCP_COMPLETE_URL>/ca)"

INFO[0000] Beginning Docker Trusted Registry installation
INFO[0000] Validating UCP cert
INFO[0000] Connecting to UCP
INFO[0000] health checking ucp
INFO[0000] The UCP cluster contains the following nodes without port
conflicts: <LIST_OF_UCP_CLUSTER_NODES>
INFO[0000] Searching containers in UCP for DTR replicas
...
...
INFO[0000] Creating network: dtr-ol
INFO[0000] Connecting to network: dtr-ol
INFO[0000] Waiting for phase2 container to be known to the Docker daemon
INFO[0001] Setting up replica volumes...
...
...
INFO[0011] License config copied from UCP.
INFO[0011] Migrating db...
...
...
INFO[0004] Migrated database from version 0 to 10
INFO[0016] Starting all containers...
...
...
INFO[0114] Successfully registered dtr with UCP
INFO[0114] Installation is complete
INFO[0114] Replica ID is set to: c8a9ec361fde
INFO[0114] You can use flag '--existing-replica-id c8a9ec361fde' when
joining other replicas to your Docker Trusted Registry Cluster
```

Since DTR's installation process will connect to UCP's API, TLS will be used, and certificates will be sent. We added UCP's CA to validate its certificates.

Once the first replica is installed, we will configure and then join other replicas. It is important to configure shared storage and other settings if you have not changed them during the installation process.

 Notice the last line of the installation's output. It shows the You can use flag '--existing-replica-id c8a9ec361fde' when joining other replicas to your Docker Trusted Registry Cluster text message. Keep this replica's ID; we will use it for reconfiguring it and joining other replicas.

We can configure the shared storage we need to execute the `reconfigure` action. We can use either filesystem or object storage types:

- **Filesystem storage types**: **Network File System** (**NFS**), bind mount, and volume
- **Object storage (cloud) types**: Amazon S3, Openstack's Swift, Microsoft Azure, and Google Cloud Storage

Object storage and NFS are valid options for shared storage. Each cloud provider will require its own specifications. Common parameters will be the user or account name, password, and bucket. Object storage is the preferred option for DTR shared image storage. There are some on-premises solutions, such as Minio, that are easy to implement in our data center. NFS is also valid and it is quite common in current data centers. In this case, we will use the `--nfs-storage-url` parameter with the `reconfigure` action. `nfs-storage-url` will require the following format: `nfs://<ip|hostname>/<mountpoint>`.

DTR's storage backend configuration can also be managed using YAML format.

 Many DTR options can be set using environment variables. To review available variables, execute `docker container run docker/dtr:<RELEASE> <ACTION> --help` to retrieve an action's help. Variables will be shown on each argument or option.

Joining replicas will provide high availability to DTR's processes. Replication requires external storage for sharing images' blobs (data layers) and meta-information. Therefore, we will reconfigure the first replica's storage if we did not choose shared storage during installation. We have the first replica's ID and we will use `docker/dtr:<RELEASE> reconfigure --existing-replica-id <FIRST_REPLICA'S_ID>` to reconfigure the storage's backend. In this example, we will just use NFS, which is common in our data centers.

Before executing the storage's configuration, we will copy the registry volume's data into our NFS filesystem.

The following lines provide us with a quick example of this migration mounting NFS endpoint as a local directory on DTR's host (we have used a sample IP address and the ID of the replica created previously):

```
$ sudo mount -t nfs 10.10.10.11:/data /mnt
$ sudo cp -pR /var/lib/docker/volumes/dtr-registry-c8a9ec361fde/_data/* /mnt/
```

This step will guarantee previous data if we use `--storage-migrated` with the `reconfigure` action. If you are using NFS as a local volume, you should guarantee that it is mounted on reboot using the appropriate line in your `fstab` file. This was just an example. We will never use NFS locally mounted for DTR; we can use NFS directly, using appropriate command-line options, to mount an NFS endpoint as a DTR volume.

The following screenshot shows Amazon's S3 options integrated in DTR's web UI. Each backend type will integrate different options:

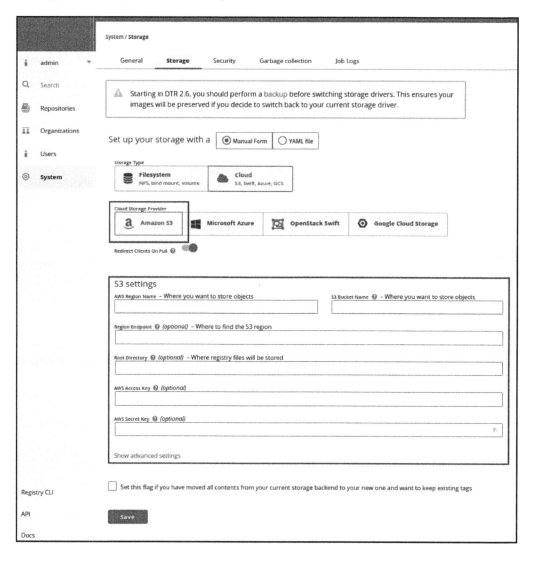

We have used variables for command parameters, but we have left the command's output intact because it is interesting how NFS and the current replica's ID are present:

```
$ docker container run --rm -it docker/dtr:<RELEASE> reconfigure \
--existing-replica-id <FIRST_REPLICA'S_ID> \
--nfs-storage-url nfs://<NFS_SERVER>/<NFS_SHARED_DIR> \
--storage-migrated \
--ucp-username <UCP_USERNAME> \
--ucp-password <UCP_PASSWORD> \
--ucp-url <UCP_COMPLETE_URL> \
--ucp-insecure-tls
INFO[0000] Starting phase1 reconfigure
INFO[0000] Validating UCP cert
INFO[0000] Connecting to UCP
INFO[0000] health checking ucp
INFO[0000] Searching containers in UCP for DTR replicas
INFO[0000] Cluster reconfiguration will occur on all DTR replicas
...
...
INFO[0000] Connecting to network: dtr-ol
INFO[0000] Waiting for phase2 container to be known to the Docker daemon
INFO[0000] Establishing connection with Rethinkdb
...
...
INFO[0003] Getting container configuration and starting containers...
INFO[0003] Waiting for database to stabilize for up to 600 seconds before
attempting to reconfigure replica c8a9ec361fde
INFO[0003] Establishing connection with Rethinkdb
INFO[0003] Configuring NFS
...
...
INFO[0004] Recreating volume node4/dtr-registry-nfs-c8a9ec361fde
...
...
INFO[0009] Recreating dtr-registry-c8a9ec361fde...
INFO[0013] Recreating dtr-garant-c8a9ec361fde...
INFO[0017] Changing dtr-api-c8a9ec361fde mounts from [dtr-ca-
c8a9ec361fde:/ca dtr-registry-c8a9ec361fde:/storage] to [dtr-ca-
c8a9ec361fde:/ca dtr-registry-nfs-c8a9ec361fde:/storage]
...
...
INFO[0038] Recreating dtr-scanningstore-c8a9ec361fde...
INFO[0042] Trying to get the kv store connection back after reconfigure
INFO[0042] Establishing connection with Rethinkdb
INFO[0042] Verifying auth settings...
INFO[0042] Successfully registered dtr with UCP
INFO[0042] The `--storage-migrated` flag is set. Not erasing tags.
```

Notice the `--storage-migrated` argument. If we migrate storage after the creation of a number of repositories, all this work will be lost if we do not migrate the registry volume's data. In this case, we have just copied the volume's content.

Now that we have a shared registry's storage backend, we can join new replicas. We will use the current replica's ID because new replicas require a base replica to sync with. We will use the `join` action on any cluster node because we will select another worker node for this replica (we have mocked our example using <NEW_UCP_NODE>):

```
$ docker container run --rm -it docker/dtr:<RELEASE> \
join \
--ucp-node <NEW_UCP_NODE> \
--ucp-username <UCP_USERNAME> \
--ucp-password <UCP_PASSWORD> \
--ucp-url <UCP_COMPLETE_URL> \
--ucp-insecure-tls \
--existing-replica-id c8a9ec361fde
INFO[0000] Beginning Docker Trusted Registry replica join
INFO[0000] Validating UCP cert
INFO[0000] Connecting to UCP
INFO[0000] health checking ucp
INFO[0000] The UCP cluster contains the following nodes without port
conflicts: <UCP_NODES_AVAILABLE>
INFO[0000] Searching containers in UCP for DTR replicas
INFO[0001] Searching containers in UCP for DTR replicas
INFO[0001] verifying [80 443] ports on node3
INFO[0012] Waiting for running dtr-phase2 container to finish
INFO[0012] starting phase 2
INFO[0000] Validating UCP cert
...
...
INFO[0057] Recreating dtr-scanningstore-c8a9ec361fde...
INFO[0061] Configuring NFS
INFO[0062] Using NFS storage: nfs://10.10.10.11/data
INFO[0062] Using NFS options:
...
...
INFO[0176] Transferring data to new replica: cc0509711d05
INFO[0000] Establishing connection with Rethinkdb
...
...
INFO[0183] Database successfully copied
INFO[0183] Join is complete
INFO[0183] Replica ID is set to: cc0509711d05
INFO[0183] There are currently 2 replicas in your Docker Trusted Registry
cluster
INFO[0183] You currently have an even number of replicas which can impact
```

```
cluster availability
  INFO[0183] It is recommended that you have 3, 5 or 7 replicas in your
cluster
```

All values apart from the first replica's ID were mocked and the outputs of the `join` command have been reduced for this book. Notice that we have used `--ucp-insecure-tls` instead of adding UCP's CA. After `183` steps, the new replica was joined. At least three replicas are required for high availability. All replicas are deployed as multi-container applications on defined worker nodes.

 Starting in DTR 2.6, you should perform a backup before switching storage drivers. This ensures that your images will be preserved if you decide to switch back to your current storage driver.

DTR will expose its API securely, using TLS. Therefore, certificates will be used to create secure tunnels. By default, DTR will create a CA to sign server certificates. We can use our corporation's private or public certificates. They can be applied during installation using `--dtr-ca` and `--dtr-cert`, but we can change them later in DTR's web UI or by using the `reconfigure` action. If you used your custom certificate, your certificate will probably be included in your system. If Docker created auto-signed certificates for us, these will not be trusted in your system. Docker created a CA for use to sign DTR certificates and you will probably get the following error message when you try to execute any registry action from your command line:

```
Error response from daemon: Get https://<DTR_FQDN>[:DTR_PORT]/v2/: x509:
certificate signed by unknown authority.
```

To avoid this issue, we can either avoid SSL verification, define an insecure registry, or add DTR's CA as trusted on our system:

- **Insecure registry**: To set up an insecure registry for our client, we will add `"insecure-registries" : ["<DTR_FQDN>[:DTR_PORT]"]` to our Docker Engine `daemon.json` file. This is not recommended and should be avoided in production because someone could hijack our server's identity.
- **Adding DTR's CA to our system**: This procedure may change depending on the Docker Engine host's operating system. We will describe procedures for Ubuntu/Debian and Red Hat/CentOS nodes. They are very common in our data centers:

  ```
  CA updating procedure on Ubuntu/Debian nodes:
  $ openssl s_client -connect <DTR_FQDN>:<DTR_PORT> -showcerts
  </dev/null 2>/dev/null | openssl x509 -outform PEM | sudo tee
  /usr/local/share/ca-certificates/<DTR_FQDN>.crt
  ```

```
$ sudo update-ca-certificates
$ sudo systemctl restart docker

CA updating procedure on Red Hat/CenOS nodes:
$ openssl s_client -connect <DTR_FQDN>:<DTR_PORT> -showcerts
</dev/null 2>/dev/null | openssl x509 -outform PEM | sudo tee
/etc/pki/ca-trust/source/anchors/<DTR_FQDN>.crt
$ sudo update-ca-trust
$ sudo systemctl restart docker
```

Including DTR's CA in our client systems is the preferred method because we will still validate its certificates.

We can log in to DTR's web UI using the defined DTR's URL. Since login is integrated with UCP by default, redirections will be integrated into this process and UCP will authorize users.

The following screenshot shows DTR's main interface once we are logged in. Repositories will be shown in a tree-like structure. Users will only have access to their resources:

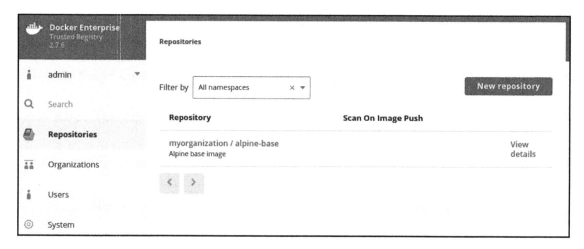

DTR's web UI is quite simple. It allows administrators to manage users, teams, organizations, and RBAC integrations. The following is a screenshot of the system's endpoint:

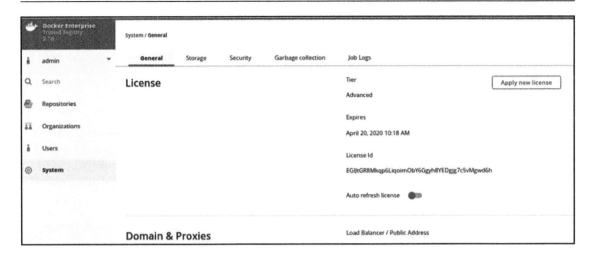

The system's endpoint provides access to the following resources and configurations:

- **The General tab**:
  - Allows us to manage DTR's license.
  - DTR's load-balanced URL.
  - Integration of corporate proxies to download the required image-scanning CVE database.
  - Single sign-on integration within UCP and DTR.
  - Configures browser cookies for clients. This will help us to forward requests to specific DTR backends.
  - Allows us to set whether repositories can be created on push. This allows users to push images, and repositories will automatically be created if they do not exist.
- **The Storage tab**: This tab allows us to configure all of DTR's storage backends. We can choose between filesystem or object storage (cloud), and each backend will have different options.
- **The Security tab**: Security is key for images. This tab allows us to configure DTR's image-scanning features.
- **The Garbage collection tab**: Untagged images consume space and will increase the risk if some use non-referenced layers. This tab allows us to schedule the automatic removal of untagged images.
- **The Job logs tab**: The logs of internal tasks can be reviewed on this tab. This log will show us information regarding mirroring and image pruning, among other internal features.

The following section will show us how to manage different access to consume images stored in your DTR repositories.

Learning about RBAC

DTR provides a complete RBAC environment. DTR will authenticate and authorize valid users. We can integrate third-party authentication solutions as we learned in Chapter 11, *Universal Control Plane*. Integrating external **Lightweight Directory Access Protocol (LDAP)/Active Directory (AD)** authentication mechanisms will allow us to delegate users' passwords to them, while UCP and DTR will manage user authorization.

By default, DTR redirects user authentications to UCP because single sign-on is included. We can change this behavior in the **System | General** menu. It is recommended to keep this setting so as to manage users in just one application. All authentication will be delegated to UCP and this will route users to its integrated third-party authentication mechanism (if configured).

Once we are authenticated to the DTR environment, we will get different permissions to allow us to manage images from repositories or just pull different releases from them.

 By default, anonymous users will be able to pull images from public repositories. You must ensure that only allowed images are stored in public repositories.

We can create users on either UCP or DTR because, by default, we will have a single sign-on environment and users will be shared between both applications.

Users are managed in teams and organizations, as we also learned in Chapter 11, *Universal Control Plane*. These allow us to integrate teams into organizations, while users will be integrated in those teams:

- **Organizations** will provide a logical level of abstraction and isolation. They allow us to namespace other resources.
- **Teams** will allow us to assign user access to repositories.

Users will be integrated into organizations and teams. These allow us to restrict access to images within organizations and with the permissions and allowed actions given using teams.

Repositories' accesses are managed by two concepts:

- **Ownership**: Repository creators
- **Public accessibility**: Public or private repositories

Owners of repositories can decide about access for others. As has been mentioned, we can have public and private images.

Private repositories can only be consumed by owners and DTR administrators. Other users cannot pull images from these repositories. Only repositories' owners can push images to them.

Within organizations, we will provide read and write access for specific teams in an organization's private repositories. These teams will be able to push images to these repositories. These teams are owners of these repositories and we can provide read-only access to some teams. They will only be able to pull images. All other teams will not have any access because we are talking about an organization's private repositories.

Public repositories are different. Users' public repositories allow other users to pull images from them, while only owners are able to push. They have read-write access. An organization's public repositories will allow users to also pull images. In these cases, only teams with read-write access will be allowed to push images.

The following table represents permissions that can be applied to repositories:

Permissions	Description
Read-only	A user can browse/search and pull images from a repository. Users will not be able to push to this repository.
Read and write	A user can browse/search, pull, and push images to a repository.
Owner	The owner has read-write access to their repositories, but they are also allowed to manage their permissions and descriptions. They can also set a repository's privacy level (public/private).

Organizations' members have read-only access to public images within this organization. Therefore, an organization's users can always pull their public images. Organizations' members can see other members and view all teams included within their organization. But we need to integrate users within an organization's teams to provide management and read-write access.

An organization's members who are not included in any team cannot manage an organization's repositories. They can only pull its public images.

An organization's owners, on the other hand, will be able to manage the organization and all its repositories. We can include any user within an organization as an owner. These users can also manage teams within an organization and their level of access.

We will use a simple example to help you understand how permissions and access will be given to users in different repositories.

Let's imagine an organization named **myorganization**. Let's include a team for **devops** and others for **developers** and **operations**. In this example, the **devops** team will define core images, while **developers** will use them for their applications.

devops group members will have read-write access, while **developers** will have read-only access. These will just pull images to create their own ones. They will use enterprise-defined core images, created by the **devops** team. In this case, the **operations** team does not have access to these application core images.

On the other hand, the **devops** team created a series of images for testing the platform, under the **testing image** repository. This repository is public and all users within the organization will be able to use it on the Docker Enterprise platform. The following diagram shows the RBAC situation described:

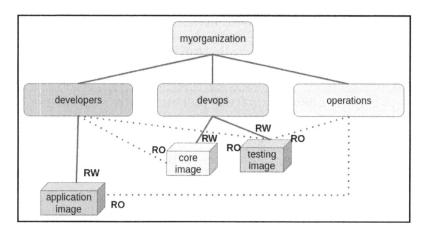

In the next section, we will review image scanning and other security features included in the DTR platform.

Image scanning and security features

In this section, we will review DTR's security features, such as security scanning and image signing.

Security scanning

DTR includes image security scanning as a built-in feature. It will scan each image's layer for binaries and libraries. A scan report will include the aggregated BOM for each layer. We now have a complete picture of an image's files and its MD5 hashes. This ensures the immutability of each layer's content between image releases. If we change a file within a layer, its hash changes and scanning will be executed against the new layer's content. Image scanning will also download and manage a CVE database provided by Docker. This will be used to correlate an image's layer reports with the vulnerability information given.

Scanning will show us a report regarding the health of our image, reporting all detected well-known vulnerabilities found on the image's layers.

This CVE database should be updated frequently because new threats appear almost daily. We can use either online synchronization or offline manual updates. In both cases, we require a valid Docker Enterprise license. Online synchronization requires a valid internet connection (we can use our corporate's proxies within DTR, configuring the `--http-proxy` and/or `--https-proxy` options either on DTR's installation or by reconfiguring the environment following the installation process).

 Do not forget to use the `--no-proxy` option to configure all your enterprise's internal FQDNs.

Image scanning consumes a lot of DTR's hosts' resources. In fact, the first security scan for each layer requires a lot of resources. Subsequent scans will use previous layers' reports. If an image's layer size is large, scanning will take a lot of resources to create the layer's report. All files' hashes should be included in the report to correlate them with the database's data. If we use common layers in our images, this process will only be executed once. A layer's report will be updated if we change that layer's content. That layer will become old and a new scan will be executed. Take care of these processes between image changes.

Scanning can be executed whenever an image is updated or created within DTR's registry automatically. This will be set on each repository using the **Scan on push** feature. We can periodically execute images' scans manually, but this could prove hard to maintain without using DTR's API.

The image's scanning report will be shown on each repository's tag. We will have a report of the health of the image's vulnerabilities, as can be seen in the following screenshot:

The vulnerability status of the image can be as follows:

- **Green**: No vulnerability was found. The image is secure.
- **Orange**: Some minor or major vulnerabilities were found.
- **Red**: Critical vulnerabilities were found and security could be compromised.

We can dive into each tag's report by clicking on its details. We will be able to review the full scan results, including the image's metadata, size, owner, and the most recent scan.

We have two different views for a tag's scan details:

- The **Layers** view will show us a list of the image's layers in the order of the image's construction. We will see each layer with the vulnerabilities identified on it. We can click on each layer to drill down into its components.
- The **Components** view will list all the image's components. Components will be sorted according to the number of vulnerabilities identified because a file can have multiple issues.

We can integrate triggers to inform other processes or applications regarding the scanning results once they are finished.

Image immutability

Another interesting feature can be enabled for each image's repository. An image's immutability will mean that the overwriting of tags will be avoided. This will ensure the uniqueness of tags. This is interesting in terms of production releases. No one will reuse a tag that has already been used, so the development life cycle is not compromised because each release will have a unique ID.

Content trust in DTR

DTR has integration with **Docker Content Trust** (**DCT**). We have covered this topic in `Chapter 6`, *Introduction to Docker Content Trust*. We learned that image signing improves cluster and application security, ensuring image ownership, immutability, and provenance. If we have a CI/CD pipeline that creates images as application artifacts, we can ensure that the correct image will run in production. UCP allowed us to run only signed images within our organization.

DTR provides a notary server and a notary signer. These components are required for DCT. Both application components will be accessed through an internal proxy and integrated with UCP's roles and access environment. This integration enables the signing of images that UCP can trust and execute securely.

The Docker client will allow us to configure content trust for repositories and sign images. We will use a simple Docker client command line to sign images. The main difference in a corporate environment is that we need to ensure that images are signed by enterprise users. We will use our own certificates, included in our user's bundle. We will use `key.pem` and `cert.pem` as private and public keys, respectively.

We will now describe the steps necessary for signing images in the Docker Enterprise environment:

1. First, we will download the user's bundle. We have already described this process in `Chapter 11`, *Universal Control Plane*. Once we have our bundle in our system (already decompressed and ready to use), we will add a private key to our laptop's or Docker client node's trust store. We will use `docker trust load`:

```
$ docker trust key load --name <MY_USERNAME> key.pem
Loading key from "key.pem"...
Enter passphrase for new <MY_USERNAME> key with ID ....:
Repeat passphrase for new <MY_USERNAME> key with ID ....:
Successfully imported key from key.pem
```

2. We will then initialize trust metadata for a specific repository. We should add ourselves as signers on each repository where we will push images. Remember that repositories should contain the registry's FQDN and port. We will use the `docker trust signer add` command:

```
$ docker trust signer add \
--key cert.pem \
<MY_USERNAME>
<DTR_FQDN>[:DTR_PORT][/ORGANIZATION][/USERNAME][/REPOSITORY]
Adding signer "<MY_USERNAME>" to
<DTR_FQDN>[:DTR_PORT][/ORGANIZATION][/USERNAME][/REPOSITORY]...
Initializing signed repository for
<DTR_FQDN>[:DTR_PORT][/ORGANIZATION][/USERNAME][/REPOSITORY]...
Enter passphrase for root key with ID ....:
Enter passphrase for new repository key with ID ....:
Repeat passphrase for new repository key with ID .....:
Successfully initialized
"<DTR_FQDN>[:DTR_PORT][/ORGANIZATION][/USERNAME][/REPOSITORY]"
Successfully added signer: <MY_USERNAME> to
<DTR_FQDN>[:DTR_PORT][/ORGANIZATION][/USERNAME][/REPOSITORY]
```

3. With these few steps, we are ready to sign an image. Let's review a simple example with an `alpine` image. We will tag our image ready for our registry and we will sign it using `docker trust sign`:

```
$ docker tag alpine
<DTR_FQDN>[:DTR_PORT]/myorganization/alpine:signed-test
$ docker trust sign
<DTR_FQDN>[:DTR_PORT]/myorganization/alpine:signed-test
Signing and pushing trust data for local image
<DTR_FQDN>[:DTR_PORT]/myorganization/alpine:signed-test, may
overwrite remote trust data
The push refers to repository
[<DTR_FQDN>[:DTR_PORT]/myorganization/alpine]
beee9f30bc1f: Layer already exists
signed-test: digest:
sha256:cb8a924afdf0229ef7515d9e5b3024e23b3eb03ddbba287f4a19c6ac90b8
d221 size: 528
Signing and pushing trust metadata
Enter passphrase for <MY_USERNAME> key with ID c7690cd:
Successfully signed
<DTR_FQDN>[:DTR_PORT]/myorganization/alpine:signed-test
```

4. Once signed, we can push our image to the registry. Notice that we are using `<DTR_FQDN>[:DTR_PORT]` as DTR's registry:

```
$ docker push <DTR_FQDN>[:DTR_PORT]/myorganization/alpine:signed-test
The push refers to repository [192.168.56.14/myorganization/alpine-base]
beee9f30bc1f: Layer already exists
signed-test: digest:
sha256:cb8a924afdf0229ef7515d9e5b3024e23b3eb03ddbba287f4a19c6ac90b8d221 size: 528
```

We now have our signed image in the registry, as we can observe in the following screenshot:

Repositories / myorganization / alpine-base / Tags

myorganization / alpine-base

Alpine base image

Info	Permissions	**Tags**	Webhooks	Promotions	Pruning	Mirrors	Settings	Activity

	Image	**Type**	**ID**	**Size**	**Signed**	**Last Pushed**	**Vulnerabilities**	
☐	1.0-signed	linux amd64	cb8a924afdf0	2.8 MB	**Signed**	54 seconds ago by admin	Pending	View details
☐	1.0	linux amd64	cb8a924afdf0	2.8 MB	Not signed	16 hours ago by admin	Pending	View details

< >

5. We can review image ownership and its signatures using `docker trust inspect`:

```
$ docker trust inspect --pretty
<DTR_FQDN>[:DTR_PORT]/myorganization/alpine:signed-test

Signatures for <DTR_FQDN>[:DTR_PORT]/myorganization/alpine:signed-test

SIGNED TAG DIGEST SIGNERS
signed-test
cb8a924afdf0229ef7515d9e5b3024e23b3eb03ddbba287f4a19c6ac90b8d221
<MY_USERNAME>
```

```
List of signers and their keys for
<DTR_FQDN>[:DTR_PORT]/myorganization/alpine:signed-test

SIGNER KEYS
<MY_USERNAME>  c7690cd8374b

Administrative keys for
<DTR_FQDN>[:DTR_PORT]/myorganization/alpine:signed-test

Repository Key:
63116fb0f440e1d862e0d2cae8552ab2bcc5a332c26b553d9bfa0a856f15fe91
 Root Key:
69129c50992ecd90cd5be11e3a379f63071c1ffab20d99c45e1c1fa92bfee6ce
```

We have mocked this output and other output seen in this chapter, but you will receive similar output. Your user should be shown under the SIGNER KEYS section (we have <MY_USERNAME> in the previous command's output).

6. There is also an important topic related to signing. Users can delegate image signing. This concept will allow other users to sign for us or share signing within a team. If we need to impersonate another user's signing process, we need to import their key. Therefore, we require the other user's key.pem key file. We will load this key in keeping with the steps covered previously:

```
$ docker trust key load --name <MY_TEAMMATE_USERNAME> key.pem
Loading key from "key.pem"...
Enter passphrase for new <MY_TEAMMATE_USERNAME> key with ID ......:
Repeat passphrase for new <MY_TEAMMATE_USERNAME> key with ID .....:
Successfully imported key from key.pem
```

We mocked the users' names and IDs.

7. We then add our teammate's public key to our repository:

```
$ docker trust signer add --key cert.pem <MY_TEAMMATE_USERNAME>
<DTR_FQDN>[:DTR_PORT][/ORGANIZATION][/USERNAME][/REPOSITORY]
Adding signer "<MY_TEAMMATE_USERNAME>" to
<DTR_FQDN>[:DTR_PORT][/ORGANIZATION][/USERNAME][/REPOSITORY]...
Enter passphrase for repository key with ID ......:
Successfully added signer: <MY_TEAMMATE_USERNAME> to
<DTR_FQDN>[:DTR_PORT][/ORGANIZATION][/USERNAME][/REPOSITORY]
```

8. Now, we can sign using both signatures:

```
$ docker trust sign
<DTR_FQDN>[:DTR_PORT][/ORGANIZATION][/USERNAME][/REPOSITORY][:TAG]
Signing and pushing trust metadata for
<DTR_FQDN>[:DTR_PORT][/ORGANIZATION][/USERNAME][/REPOSITORY][:TAG]
Existing signatures for tag 1 digest
5b49c8e2c890fbb0a35f6...................
from:
<MY_TEAMMATE_USERNAME>
Enter passphrase for <MY_TEAMMATE_USERNAME> key with ID ...:
Enter passphrase for <MY_USERNAME> key with ID ...:
Successfully signed
<DTR_FQDN>[:DTR_PORT][/ORGANIZATION][/USERNAME][/REPOSITORY][:TAG]
```

9. Now, we can conduct a further inspection and we will see both signatures:

```
$ docker trust inspect --pretty
<DTR_FQDN>[:DTR_PORT][/ORGANIZATION][/USERNAME][/REPOSITORY][:TAG]
Signatures for
<DTR_FQDN>[:DTR_PORT][/ORGANIZATION][/USERNAME][/REPOSITORY][:TAG]
SIGNED TAG DIGEST SIGNERS
1 5b49c8e2c890fbb0a35f6050ed3c5109c5bb47b9e774264f4f3aa85bb69e2033
<MY_TEAMMATE_USERNAME>, <MY_USERNAME>
List of signers and their keys for
<DTR_FQDN>[:DTR_PORT][/ORGANIZATION][/USERNAME][/REPOSITORY][:TAG]
SIGNER KEYS
<MY_USERNAME> 927f30366699
<MY_TEAMMATE_USERNAME> 5ac7d9af7222
Administrative keys for
<DTR_FQDN>[:DTR_PORT][/ORGANIZATION][/USERNAME][/REPOSITORY][:TAG]
Repository Key:
e0d15a24b741ab049470298734397afbea539400510cb30d3b996540b4a2506b
 Root Key:
b74854cb27cc25220ede4b08028967d1c6e297a759a6939dfef1ea72fbdd7b9a
```

To delete the repository's DCT, we will use `notary delete`
`<DTR_FQDN>[:DTR_PORT][/ORGANIZATION][/USERNAME][/REPOSITORY]` `--remote`.
You will require the `notary` application's binary in your host.

Remember that all client actions can be forced to be secure using `export DOCKER_CONTENT_TRUST=1`, to enable content trust as regards all the commands executed in the current shell.

Content trust can be integrated into CI/CD with process orchestrators and other automation tools. To avoid a user's interaction as regards image signing procedures, we can use the following variables:

- `DOCKER_CONTENT_TRUST_ROOT_PASSPHRASE`: Will be used for the local root key passphrase
- `DOCKER_CONTENT_TRUST_REPOSITORY_PASSPHRASE`: Will be used for the repository passphrase

As we have learned, users will be available to sign their images using their Docker bundle from UCP. It is also possible to generate keys using `docker trust key generate` command, but these will not be included in DTR.

DTR ships with Notary built in so that you can use DCT to sign and verify images. For more information about managing Notary data in DTR, refer to the DTR-specific notary documentation.

The following section will show us how we can integrate Docker Enterprise into our CI/CD pipeline using DTR's built-in features.

Integrating and automating image workflow

DTR provides built-in features aligned with CI/CD pipeline construction logic. We will have webhooks that can be triggered to inform other applications or processes regarding certain events, such as a completed image scan or a new image/tag arrival. We also have image promotions. This feature will retag images between repositories. The following diagram shows a simple workflow for building, distributing, and executing an application. We are including some of the features provided by DTR:

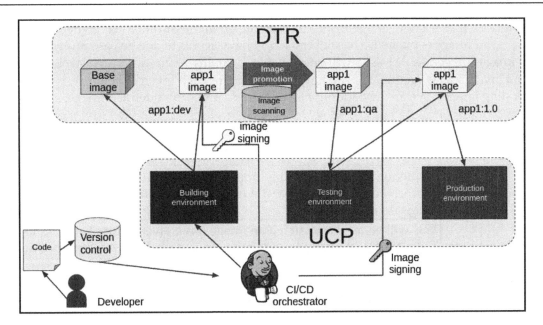

This workflow represents how to implement DTR in several development stages. Promoting a scanned image for testing will ensure its security before going to production in this example. Toward the end of this section, we will also be reviewing image mirroring. This is a feature used to share images between different DTR environments.

Image promotion

DTR allows us to automatically promote images between repositories. Promotion is based on repository-defined policies. Therefore, policies are defined at the repository level. When an image is pushed to this repository, policies are reviewed and, if the rules match, a new push is done to another registry.

Image promotion is very useful in CI/CD pipeline stages. It is easier to understand with the help of a quick example. Let's imagine a development repository for a frontend application's component. Developers will push images to this development/frontend repository. They manage all the updates in this repository. In fact, no one apart from them has access to this repository. They will develop new updates with fixes and new features. When a release has to be deployed to production, they will prepare a release version. They will include a release string in this image's tag. A policy will match this string and a new image will be created on the Quality Assurance repository for the application's component.

This process creates a new image to be tested by the quality assurance team when the `release` image is pushed. These users do not have access to non-release images. Only those images tagged as `release` will be available to quality assurance users. We know that only an image's ID is unique. We can have many tags for each image. Therefore, we are not duplicating images. We are just adding new tags and names for a defined image.

We can define policies based on the following attributes:

Attributes	Description
Tag name	We define a matching string for a repository's image's tags. Matching tags can be equal, or can start with, end with, contain, or be one of the image-defined ones.
Component name	This will be used to match if an image has a given component and its name equals, starts with, ends with, or contains, or is one the specified ones.
Vulnerabilities	We can define how many critical, major, or minor vulnerabilities (or all vulnerabilities) will be monitored to promote an image to another repository. We will use comparison expressions such as "is greater than," "greater than or equal to," "less than or equal to," "equal," or "not" with the defined value and the image will only be promoted if the equation is satisfied.
License	This rule will match if the image uses a license. This is usually used in relation to Microsoft Windows images.

We can apply more than one attribute to this policy's rules. Once we choose which criteria will be applied, we can set up the new repository and tag. There are a number of templates for the names of new image tags. These allow us to include an image's source tag or timestamps.

DTR webhooks

DTR has a series of integrated webhooks that will be triggered under special circumstances. When some events occur, DTR will be able to send webhooks to third-party applications. This is vital to integrating DTR in your CI/CD pipelines. DTR webhooks can be secured using TLS if the receiver backend also has this feature.

We will cover most of the important webhooks, but this link provides an accurate list of the current ones: `https://docs.docker.com/ee/dtr/admin/manage-webhooks/`:

Webhooks	Description
`TAG_PUSH`, `TAG_PULL`, and `TAG_DELETE`	Repositories' tag events will generate webhooks when someone pushes or pulls on a repository or when it is removed.
`SCAN_COMPLETED` and `SCANNER_UPDATE_COMPLETED`	Scanning is key to ensuring security. We will send notifications when the image-scanning database is updated or when a repository's scan has ended correctly.
`PROMOTION`	Whenever a promotion policy is applied, we will send a webhook. This will help us to follow DTR images' internal workflow.

We must have administrative privileges on a repository to be able to configure its webhooks using either DTR's web UI or its API. The web UI allows us to test defined webhooks by clicking **Test**.

The following screenshot shows a repository's webhook configuration:

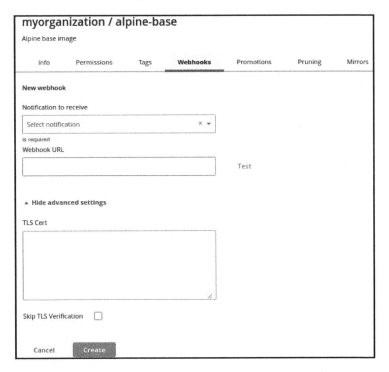

The following section will show us how to implement registry mirroring.

Mirror images between registries

Registry mirroring can also help us in our CI/CD. When images get pushed into repositories and there is some mirroring configuration, DTR will push them into another defined registry. This helps us to distribute repositories on different registries, with high availability.

Mirroring configuration is based on the promotion logic covered previously. We will first configure mirror direction to define which action will be used: pull or push. DTR mirroring allows us to integrate Docker Hub with the on-premises Docker Enterprise DTR environment.

We need to understand that DTR's metadata is not synced between registries. Therefore, image scanning and signing information from the first registry will not be available on the second one. All these actions must also be executed on the mirror registry. We can integrate scanning automatically when images are pushed to the second registry. Image signing requires external integrations. The following screenshot shows the mirroring configurations for a repository:

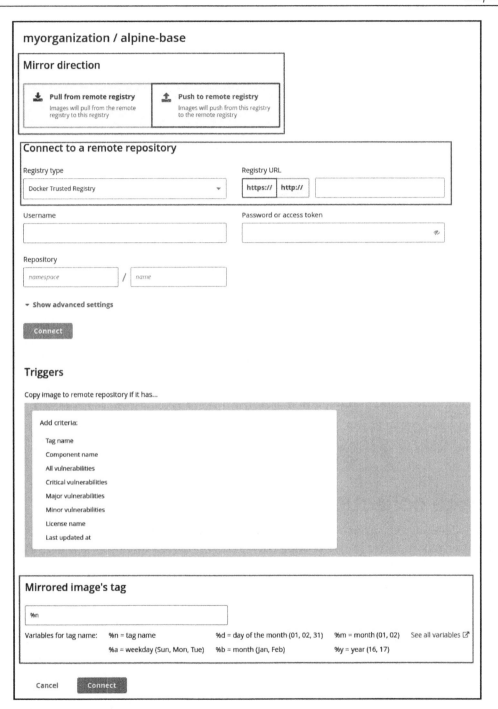

Now that we have learned about the built-in features for automation, we will review registry caching with a view to improving a developer's work.

Registry caching

Registry caching will help us to manage images on distributed environments. Users from remote locations can have latency problems and big images can take forever to load. We can deploy intermediate registry caches to decrease pull times.

Caches are transparent to users because they will use the original DTR's URL. When a user pulls an image, the DTR will check whether it is authorized and it will then be redirected to a defined cache. This cache pulls an image's layers from the DTR and keeps a copy for users. New requests do not require an image's layers to be pulled from DTR again.

To deploy a registry cache service, we will use the `docker/dtr-content-cache:<RELEASE>` image.

Registry caching help us to manage distributed environments. Docker clients must be configured in order to use this feature. We will add `"registry-mirrors":` `["https://<REGISTRY's_MIRROR_URL>"]` to the `daemon.json` configuration file or configure users to use it by using the **Users Settings** page. For this to work, it is necessary to register the deployed cache with DTR's configuration using DTR's API. Detailed instructions can be found at the following link: `https://docs.docker.com/ee/dtr/admin/configure/deploy-caches/simple/`

We will now learn about DTR's automated garbage deletion.

Garbage collection

Garbage collection will remove unreferenced layers and manifests from DTR. Registry data can consume a lot of space in our storage backend. This is not only a problem for storage resources. Security can be compromised if unsecured layers remain. It is recommended to remove all unused layers (also known as **dangling images**).

This process runs in two phases:

1. DTR's garbage collector will search all registry manifests. Those with active content, and image layers included within other images, will not be deleted.
2. The process will scan all the blobs. Those not included in the first phase's list will be removed.

Garbage collection can be run manually from a registry's container using `bin/registry garbage-collect`. We will usually apply scheduled tasks integrated into DTR's web UI. Garbage collection options will allow us to configure the removal of unreferenced layers periodically using cron-like logic. We will also establish for how long we will allow the removal process to run because it can take a significant amount of time. The following screenshot shows the **Garbage collection** configuration page:

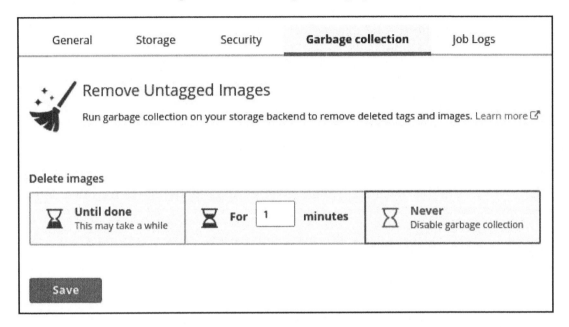

In the next section, we will learn how to deploy DTR's backup.

Backup strategies

DTR's backup procedure does not result in any service interruption. A backup process can be executed from any of the cluster nodes. It is recommended to create all backups from the same replica. This will help us to recover at least this replica. We will be able to recreate the full DTR's cluster environment using this replica.

The following list shows which content will be stored as part of your DTR's backup TAR file:

- DTR configurations
- Repository metadata
- User access control and repository configurations
- TLS certificates and keys required for DTR communication
- Images' signatures and digests, including the integration of Notary
- Images' scan results

The following content will not be included within your backups:

- Images' layers
- Users, teams, and organizations
- The vulnerability database used for image scanning

Take care of the content of images because users, teams, and organizations will be included in UCP's backup and the vulnerability database (CVE and reports) can be recreated whenever we need it.

By default, DTR's web UI will show a warning message if we haven't performed any backup.

We will find the healthy replica's ID by using `REPLICA_ID=$(docker inspect -f '{{.Name}}' $(docker ps -q -f name=dtr-rethink) | cut -f 3 -d '-') && echo $REPLICA_ID` and we will then execute a backup using this ID:

```
$ docker container run \
--rm \
--interactive \
--log-driver none \
--ucp-username <UCP_USERNAME> \
--ucp-password <UCP_PASSWORD> \
--ucp-url <UCP_COMPLETE_URL> \
--ucp-ca "$(curl -s -k <UCP_COMPLETE_URL>/ca)" \
--existing-replica-id <REPLICA_ID> > dtr-backup.tar.gz
```

Remember, this file does not include an image's blobs or meta-information. We need to include third-party backup solutions for DTR's storage backend.

> We can use either `--ucp-ca` with a valid UCP CA certificate or `--ucp-insecure-tls` to connect to UCP.

To restore DTR, we will use the same `docker/dtr` image release. We will use `docker container run docker/dtr:<RELEASE> restore`:

```
$ docker container run --rm --ti docker/dtr:<RELEASE> restore \
  --ucp-insecure-tls \
  --ucp-url <UCP_COMPLETE_URL> \
  --ucp-username <UCP_USERNAME> \
  --ucp-password <UCP_PASSWORD> < PREVIOUS-DTR-BACKUP.tar
```

This command will not restore images' blobs and meta-information as the backup only provides information to recover all of DTR's processes and their configurations.

The following section will help us to understand how to monitor DTR's health.

Updates, health checks, and troubleshooting

DTR application upgrades can sometimes integrate database modifications. Therefore, you must ensure the correct upgrade path between releases. The `upgrade` command can be executed from any node as we will execute this command against all DTR replicas. We will use the replicas' IDs or interactive mode to upgrade each DTR replica. The upgrade process will replace all replica containers.

 It is recommended to review Docker's documentation relating to updated procedures at the following link: `https://docs.docker.com/ee/dtr/admin/upgrade`

DTR uses semantic versioning. This is key for following upgrade paths. Downgrading is not supported because sometimes, an upgrade can modify database objects.

Upgrades between different patch releases can be skipped if a minor release is applied. Patches do not modify the database, so CA can be applied without an object's data changing.

On the other hand, upgrades between minor versions must follow the version number, although we can skip intermediate patches, as has been mentioned.

Major version upgrades require upgrading to the latest minor/patch release before going to the next major release. This procedure will implement a host of changes and you must ensure that you have a valid backup before this upgrade. Remember to verify a valid image's data backup.

To monitor DTR, we will use a common container's monitoring procedures. We can also use UCP's stacks view because DTR is deployed as a multi-container application. All replicas will be displayed. We can then click on each replica's link and inspect its resources.

DTR exposes the following endpoints for monitoring. We will use them to verify its health:

Endpoints	Description

`/_ping`	This endpoint shows a replica's status. We can verify status using third-party monitoring tools. If the replica is fine, we will obtain `"Healthy":true`:
	`$ curl -ks https://<DTR_COMPLETE_URL>/_ping`
	`{"Error":"","Healthy":true}`

`/nginx_status`	This shows us the common open source `nginx` status and statistics page.
`/api/v0/meta/cluster_status`	For all replica statuses, we will use this endpoint. This requires authentication because we will be accessing DTR's API. We will use any administrator's access. An overall cluster state and a list of replicas with their statuses will be shown.

We will also search for errors on DTR's container logs. In this case, we will usually integrate these logs in third-party logging management applications.

Logging

As standard, DTR's container logs will show all application errors. DTR also includes a view in its web UI with all job logs. We will have detailed information regarding the many actions executed within the environment. This log view provides useful audit information because it contains all images' management actions executed in DTR.

The following section will show us how to recover an unhealthy DTR environment.

DTR disaster recovery

DTR is deployed using a high-availability strategy. Therefore, we have a variety of situations, depending on how many replicas are unhealthy.

Some replicas are unhealthy, but we keep the cluster's quorum's state

In this case, the majority of replicas are healthy, so overall, the cluster's state is healthy. We will remove unhealthy replicas and add new ones as soon as possible. It is important to only join replicas after unhealthy ones have been removed. We will execute this procedure step by step, removing an unhealthy replica, adding a new one, and so on. This will keep the overall cluster's state intact. We will only remove unhealthy replicas that have been identified, so we will first need to identify which replicas are in a failing state using `docker ps --format "{{.Names}}" | grep dtr`. Once identified, we will execute `docker container run docker/dtr:<RELEASE> remove` to delete the replica in question:

```
$ docker container run --rm --ti docker/dtr:<RELEASE> remove \
 --existing-replica-id <HEALTHY_REPLICA_ID> \
 --replica-ids <HEALTHY_REPLICA_ID> \
 --ucp-insecure-tls \
 --ucp-url <UCP_COMPLETE_URL> \
 --ucp-username <UCP_USERNAME> \
 --ucp-password <UCP_PASSWORD>
```

Although the `--replica-ids` argument will allow us to remove a list of replicas, it is recommended to follow this procedure on each unhealthy replica, adding a new one with each removal:

```
$ docker container run --rm --ti docker/dtr:<RELEASE> join \
 --existing-replica-id <HEALTHY_REPLICA_ID> \
 --ucp-insecure-tls \
 --ucp-url <UCP_COMPLETE_URL> \
 --ucp-username <UCP_USERNAME> \
 --ucp-password <UCP_PASSWORD>
```

This will join a new replica. Always wait until synchronization has finished before continuing with a new one.

The majority of replicas are unhealthy

If the majority of replicas are unhealthy, the cluster's state will be unhealthy because it will have lost its quorum. However, if we still have at least one healthy node, we can repair the cluster using this replica. We will execute an emergency repair procedure using `docker container run docker/dtr:<RELEASE> emergency-repair`.

We can find the healthy replica's ID using `REPLICA_ID=$(docker inspect -f '{{.Name}}' $(docker ps -q -f name=dtr-rethink) | cut -f 3 -d '-')` `&&` `echo $REPLICA_ID` and we will then execute the emergency repair procedure:

```
$ docker container run --rm --ti docker/dtr:<RELEASE> emergency-repair \
  --existing-replica-id <HEALTHY_REPLICA_ID> \
  --ucp-insecure-tls \
  --ucp-url <UCP_COMPLETE_URL> \
  --ucp-username <UCP_USERNAME> \
  --ucp-password <UCP_PASSWORD>
```

This process should recover a replica completely and we will then add new replicas to recover a cluster's consensus.

All replicas are unhealthy

In this situation, we cannot recover the cluster without an existing backup. We will use `docker container run docker/dtr:<RELEASE> restore`. It is critical to have a valid DTR backup:

```
$ docker container run --rm --ti docker/dtr:<RELEASE> restore \
  --ucp-insecure-tls \
  --ucp-url <UCP_COMPLETE_URL> \
  --ucp-username <UCP_USERNAME> \
  --ucp-password <UCP_PASSWORD> < PREVIOUS-DTR-BACKUP.tar
```

This command will not restore Docker images. We have to implement a separate procedure for this data. We will use the normal filesystem's backup and restore procedures. Once we have a healthy replica, we will be able to join new ones in keeping with the procedure described previously.

Summary

This chapter covered DTR's features and components. We learned how to implement DTR in production using a high-availability strategy. We reviewed different solutions available for storing images securely.

We also covered image scanning and signing. Both options allow us to improve image security by integrating with UCP's application deployment platform. Users within organizations will have different levels of access to images thanks to DTR's integrated RBAC system.

CI/CD environments have changed the way we create and deploy applications nowadays. We have reviewed different features built using DTR that help us to integrate image building, sharing, and security in CI/CD pipelines. We also learned how to mirror repositories and improve users' experiences with registry caching.

Knowledge of DTR and UCP is required for the exam. We need to know their component distributions on cluster nodes and how they work. We also need to understand their installation processes and how we can ensure their health.

This is the last chapter related to the Docker Enterprise platform. Later chapters will cover the content that is required for the exam, with some quick topic reviews and further questions and answers.

Questions

1. Which features are included in DTR?

    a) Repository load balancing
    b) Repository mirroring
    c) Repository signing
    d) All of the above

2. How many DTR replicas do we need in order to provide high availability for Docker images' layers?

    a) We will need at least three DTR replicas to provide high availability.
    b) DTR does not manage the high availability of data. We need to provide third-party solutions for DTR storage.
    c) DTR manages volume synchronization when we deploy more than one replica.
    d) All of the above statements are true.

3. Which processes are part of DTR?

    a) `garant`
    b) `jobrunner`
    c) `notary-client`
    d) `auth-store`

4. Which of these statements are true in terms of how to deploy DTR with high availability?

   a) Configure a load balancer as a transparent reverse proxy. We will forward all requests for DTR's FQDN to any of the replicas.
   b) Deploy shared storage to allow all DTR replicas to store an image's data and meta-information at the same location.
   c) Deploy the first DTR replica with previously created shared storage on one node. Then, add at least two more replicas on different nodes.
   d) All of the above statements are true.

5. Which content is not included in DTR's backup?

   a) Repository metadata and images' layers.
   b) RBAC configurations.
   c) Image signatures.
   d) All of the above statements are true.

Further reading

The following links will help us to understand some of the topics covered in this chapter:

- Content trust integration in DTR: `https://docs.docker.com/engine/security/trust/content_trust/`
- Deploying the registry cache: `https://docs.docker.com/ee/dtr/admin/configure/deploy-caches/simple/`
- Authentication and authorization in DTR: `https://docs.docker.com/ee/dtr/admin/manage-users/`

4
Section 4 - Preparing for the Docker Certified Associate Exam

This section will focus on the DCA exam. This book covers all the exam topics and this section will summarize the book's content to help you understand what you need to know in order to pass the DCA exam.

This section comprises the following chapters:

- Chapter 14, *Summarizing Important Concepts*
- Chapter 15, *Mock Exam Questions and Final Notes*

14
Summarizing Important Concepts

In this chapter, you will learn which topics are most important for the exam and you will get a good idea of the knowledge required to pass the **Docker Certified Associate (DCA)** exam.

We will recap all the topics we have learned regarding orchestration, image management, Docker platform component installation and configuration, networking implementations for standalone and cluster environments, and security features and data management strategies in container-based applications. All these concepts were already covered in different chapters.

We will summarize the following topics in this chapter:

- Reviewing orchestration concepts
- A brief summary of Docker image concepts
- A summary of the Docker architecture, installation, and configuration topics
- A summary of the networking topics
- Understanding security concepts and related Docker features
- Quickly summarizing Docker storage and volumes

By the end of this chapter, you will be ready for some exam-like questions, which have been prepared for you in the next chapter. Before looking at some sample questions, let's start talking about the orchestration concepts we have learned.

Reviewing orchestration concepts

Orchestration is an important topic for the DCA exam. It represents 25% of the questions you have to pass to get this certification. In the second section of the book, we introduced orchestration and we covered Docker Swarm and Kubernetes.

Orchestration concepts were covered in `Chapter 7`, *Introduction to Orchestration*, `Chapter 8`, *Orchestration Using Docker Swarm*, `Chapter 9`, *Orchestration Using Kubernetes*, `Chapter 10`, *Introduction to the Docker Enterprise Platform*, and `Chapter 11`, *Universal Control Plane*.

This is a quick summary of the Docker Swarm features. We recommend you read this summary to remember the concepts we have learned:

- We started talking about multi-container applications before introducing orchestration because it is the first approach to container orchestration. They work locally, using Docker Compose (the `docker-compose` tool) and application components, and their interaction is described using `docker-compose.yml` YAML files. Multi-container applications run all of their components together on a Docker host, but we can scale their components up and down, as well as interacting with them and reviewing their logs.
- Docker Swarm orchestrates Docker services to provide them with resilience, internal discovery, and load balancing in cluster environments. Our applications' workloads will be distributed cluster-wide.
- We will use two kinds of node roles within Docker Swarm—managers and workers—which can be modified.
- We will deploy more than one manager and more than one worker to provide high availability to the cluster and workloads deployed on top of it.
- One of the managers is also the leader of the cluster and will update all cluster resource changes in an internal database, synced between manager nodes. Docker Swarm uses the Raft algorithm to update changes, hence a quorum between managers is required before changes are committed.
- Docker Swarm has a management plane, a control plane, and a data plane. The management and control planes can be isolated from the data plane, and they work encrypted out of the box. The data plane can also be encrypted but not by default (we have to encrypt each custom network).
- Docker Swarm issues and maintains an internal **Certificate Authority (CA)** and manages certificates for all cluster components. We can lock this information to keep it safe.

- A minimum of (*number of managers / 2 + 1*) healthy manager nodes is required to maintain the cluster health. If we have less than the required number, no changes can be made within the cluster but application workloads will continue working. If a service fails, it will not be recovered if the cluster is unhealthy.

- Docker Swarm uses the Raft log to maintain internal key-value store synchronization between nodes. Therefore, an odd number of managers is required to keep a quorum. This also applies to Kubernetes, but it uses `etcd` as a key-value store.

- All nodes can run application workloads, but we can change this behavior whenever we need draining nodes or to disallow new workloads without interrupting already-running ones.

- Cluster workloads are declared as services, with a required number of instances or replicas to be healthy. These resources are tasks and they will run one container.

- Docker Swarm does not manage containers; it only manages services. Therefore, we deploy applications based on services. We do not deploy standalone containers.

- Services receive one virtual IP address by default and this address does not change during their lifetime. Tasks run only one container; they do not have an associated IP address, and they always keep their names. If a task's container dies or needs to be modified with some updates, a new task will be created with the original name. The container will receive a new IP, but the internal load balancer will associate it as a backend endpoint for the service.

- We can scale up or down the number of tasks required for a service whenever we need to. However, Docker will not manage our application behavior under these circumstances.

- Tasks are scheduled automatically on healthy nodes if they have enough resources to run associated services' tasks, but we can force a task location on specific nodes.

- Docker provides some template tools to help us format, filter, and create unique resources using Docker Swarm variables.

- Networking in Docker Swarm uses bridged interfaces, as we also learned with Docker containers. We deploy overlay networks distributed cluster-wide using VXLAN technology to provide communication between containers running on different hosts and other network features.

- Docker Swarm provides a router mesh as a default strategy to publish cluster services for users and other applications. By default, services' ports will be published on all cluster nodes even if they do not run any services' tasks. Internal routing guides service requests to appropriate backend containers. We can change these behaviors with common Docker Swarm command options.

- As we learned with Docker Engine, services are not published to be consumed by default. We need to manually publish service ports and processes.

- Publishing applications to the world can be done using the router mesh on Docker Swarm, or Interlock in Docker Enterprise. Interlock provides an integrated and automated reverse-proxy solution to secure your application's backends. We just publish the `interlock-proxy` component while the Docker Swarm services receive requests internally. Hence, no additional publishing is required for services; just configure a few labels to inform Interlock about the required forwarding for an application.

- We can create as many overlay networks as required and they will be isolated from each other, as we also learned with custom bridge networks.

- Orchestration introduced some new concepts, such as secrets and configurations, to provide stored information that is distributed cluster-wide. Secrets are secured and encrypted by Docker Swarm and we use them to configure passwords, certificates, or tokens using on-memory filesystems. Configuration objects help us to distribute configurations on containers running on different hosts without having to sync files between nodes manually.

- In Docker Swarm, we deploy an application using Docker stacks. These resources allow us to deploy multi-service applications that are distributed cluster-wide. We will define all the required application resources (services, secrets, networks, configurations, volumes, and so on) in a `docker-compose`-like file and we will use these files to deploy the complete application. All changes or updates in application components should be written in these files because it allows us to manage the application's deployments as code.

- Application component updates are managed using rolling updates. We can deploy changes manually or using Docker stacks. In both cases, we can deploy changes smoothly, avoiding service interruption and user impact. If an update goes bad, we can easily execute a rollback to run the previous service configuration.

- We also reviewed the Kubernetes orchestrator because it is included in Docker Enterprise. This orchestrator has many differences from Docker Swarm, although both manage containers at the end. We learned all about Kubernetes components and their interactions.

- Docker Enterprise deploys full vanilla (non-customized) Kubernetes for us out of the box, including Calico as a **Container Network Interface** (**CNI**) by default. All worker nodes (DTR requires dedicated workers) can be set to run either Docker Swarm, Kubernetes workloads, or even both orchestrator workloads.
- Pods are the smallest scheduling unit in Kubernetes but they do not provide resilience. We need to integrate them on orchestrated templated resources, such as ReplicaSets, DaemonSets, or deployments.
- Kubernetes provides a flat network. This means that all pods that are deployed will see each other. Service-to-service communications are always allowed by default. To ensure security in this situation, we need to deploy NetworkPolicy resources to allow only specific component communications.

 Although Docker stacks and multi-container applications using `docker-compose` use the same type of YAML files, some keys are only valid for one of them. For example, keys such as `depends_on`, `build`, or `volumes_from` are only available for Docker Compose multi-container applications; therefore, we will receive a warning message indicating this issue when we try to use them for Docker stacks.

Let's review the required topics for the exam.

Required knowledge for the exam

The exam will verify our knowledge of the following topics, among others:

- Completing the setup of a Swarm mode cluster, with managers and worker nodes
- Describing and demonstrating how to extend the instructions to run individual containers into running services under Swarm
- Describing the importance of a quorum in a Swarm cluster
- Describing the difference between running a container and running a service
- Interpreting the output of the `docker inspect` commands
- Converting an application deployment into a stack file using a YAML compose file with `docker stack deploy`
- Manipulating a running stack of services
- Describing and demonstrating orchestration activities
- Increasing the number of replicas

- Adding networks and publishing ports
- Mounting volumes
- Describing and demonstrating how to run replicated and global services
- Applying node labels to demonstrate the placement of tasks
- Describing and demonstrating how to use templates with `docker service create`
- Identifying the steps needed to troubleshoot a service that is not deploying
- Describing how a Dockerized application communicates with legacy systems
- Describing how to deploy containerized workloads as Kubernetes pods and deployments
- Describing how to provide configuration for Kubernetes pods using ConfigMap and secret resources.

These topics are extracted from Docker's official study guide, which can be found at `https://success.docker.com/certification`.

A brief summary of Docker image concepts

Images are fundamental to creating containers, and this topic represents around 20% of the DCA exam questions. We covered Docker images in depth in `Chapter 2`, *Building Docker Images*, but we also talked about them in `Chapter 3`, *Running Docker Containers*, `Chapter 6`, *Introduction to Docker Content Trust*, and `Chapter 13`, *Implementing an Enterprise-Grade Registry with DTR*. In this chapter, we will quickly review all of the concepts seen in those chapters as a summary.

Let's review the most important concepts, features, and actions associated with Docker images before getting into the required knowledge section:

- Images are based on copy-on-write filesystem strategies. They are based on different overlapping layers, applied using different union filesystems and storage drivers. Currently, the most used filesystem driver for containers is `overlay2`. Docker Engine chooses the most adequate graph driver for our system, although we can change it.
- Containers are just isolated processes running on Docker hosts. We use images as templates to provide a root filesystem and meta-information to control processes' behavior.

- There are three methods for creating images:
    - **Using a Dockerfile**: This file contains all the steps required to install our application with all its dependencies, as well as how it should be started. We also provide which ports and protocols should be used to communicate with the container's processes. This method is reproducible and it provides infrastructure-as-code behavior.
    - **Running containers and committing**: In this case, we run a container, and inside, we run commands to install and configure our applications. When all the changes are made in the container's filesystem, we commit those changes to make an image. This method is not reproducible. We usually use this workflow when application installation cannot be automated, for example.
    - **Images from scratch**: In this case, images are lightweight because they just include an empty root filesystem with application binaries and dependencies. This root filesystem does not include any non-required operating system files. We add our binaries using Dockerfile copy keys.
- Multi-stage building can also be included as an alternative method for creating images. In this case, we declare different build processes in just one Dockerfile. We define a descriptive name for each one and we define a workflow, copying files from different builds. This allows us to define a phase to compile an application using the required compilers, headers, or libraries on an application-development image and just copy the final development product to another phase, with a runtime environment. As a result, the runtime image is much smaller than the development one.
- Dockerfiles create images by executing containers. Each container makes changes in its root filesystem and these changes will be committed (stored) for subsequent containers, using the previous container's layers for execution.
- Smaller images are more secure because having non-required binaries, libraries, and configurations inside images is risky. Images should only contain the required content for our application.
- There are a few important practices to follow to build better images:
    - Never add debugging tools or compilers to production images.
    - Declare all required resources on your images, such as exposed ports, the user required for the main process execution, and the directories that will be used as volumes. These will help other users to easily understand how your application works and should be used.

- Do not use root on your application's images unless it is strictly required by processes to work.
- Build your images to run just one process per container. With many processes per container, it is hard to maintain and verify their health.
- We always have to choose between the portability of layers between images and the images' sizes. There are cases where it is better to have fewer layers, while at other times it is better to have more layers because others will reuse them. Image layer caching is key to speeding up the image building process.
- Always add health checks inside your Dockerfiles to help Docker Engine verify the container's health.

- Docker provides all of the required commands for building and shipping Docker images. We can also inspect their content or build history to help us debug their processes or create new images.
- It is key to understand that dangling images, unreferenced layers from previous builds, will stay in your Docker hosts until you remove them. Administrators should keep the Docker platform clean to avoid hosts degrading due to disk space being lost.
- Good image tagging is fundamental on container platforms. We can also use labels on Dockerfiles to add meta-information to Docker images. You should try to uniquely identify images by their tags, but remember that only an image's ID will really identify an image uniquely. An image can have many names and tags, but only one ID.
- We can include variables inside Dockerfiles. This will help us to build images with special features for different stages. We can deliver a production-ready image into production systems while having debugging and instrumentation tools on testing images. They will still have common application binaries but we will use a debugging version to review some specific problems. Variables can also be modified as arguments for the `docker build` command line.

Let's get an idea of the topics required for the exam.

Required image management knowledge for the exam

The exam will verify our knowledge of the following topics, among others:

- Describing the use of a Dockerfile
- Describing options, such as `add`, `copy`, `volumes`, `expose`, and `entrypoint`
- Identifying and displaying the main parts of a Dockerfile
- Describing and demonstrating how to create an efficient image via a Dockerfile
- Describing and demonstrating how to use CLI commands to manage images, such as `list`, `delete`, `prune`, and `rmi`
- Describing and demonstrating how to inspect images and report specific attributes using `filter` and `format`
- Describing and demonstrating how to tag an image
- Describing and demonstrating how to apply a file to create a Docker image
- Describing and demonstrating how to display the layers of a Docker image
- Describing and demonstrating how to modify an image to a single layer
- Describing and demonstrating registry functions
- Deploying a registry
- Logging into a registry
- Utilizing search in a registry
- Pushing an image to a registry
- Signing an image in a registry
- Pulling and deleting images from a registry

These topics are extracted from Docker's official study guide, which can be found at `https://success.docker.com/certification`.

A summary of the Docker architecture, installation, and configuration topics

The installation and configuration of the Docker platform are key to every Docker Enterprise administrator. These topics represent 15% of the exam content. They were covered in multiple chapters for standalone and cluster environments. We learned about these concepts in Chapter 1, *Modern Infrastructures and Applications with Docker*, Chapter 8, *Orchestration Using Docker Swarm*, Chapter 10, *The Docker Enterprise Platform*, Chapter 11, *Universal Control Plane*, and Chapter 13, *Implementing an Enterprise-Grade Registry with DTR*.

This is a quick summary of special characteristics and tips for the installation and configuration of the Docker platform. We recommend that you read this summary to ensure you remember the concepts learned:

- **Docker components on standalone and cluster environments**: We should have a good idea of Docker Enterprise component distribution and features.
- **The installation processes for each component on different platforms**: We have seen that installation is easy in both the Docker Community and Docker Enterprise environments. Review the installation processes for the different platforms and ensure that you have a good idea of the configuration file locations.
- You must know all the components' requirements and the steps required to deploy a **Container-as-a-Service (CaaS)** enterprise-ready solution, with high availability on core components.
- Chapter 1, *Modern Infrastructures and Applications with Docker*, showed many configuration procedures for Docker Engine. By default, Docker will choose the best storage driver for your Docker layers. Remember that we used `overlay2` because we should be able to change it if our installation has different requirements.
- Ensure that you have a good understanding of what files are under the `/var/lib/docker` directory (or the one configured) and what should be stored in your Docker Engine's backups. You also learned about the procedures to create **Universal Control Plane (UCP)** and **Docker Trusted Registry (DTR)** backups and the steps and cases where restoration is required.
- Only Docker Enterprise and Kubernetes provide role-based access. We covered basic Docker Enterprise permissions and configurations for UCP and DTR in Chapter 11, *Universal Control Plane*, and Chapter 13, *Implementing an Enterprise-Grade Registry with DTR*, respectively.

- Review how we configured TLS communications for client authentication when we do not need different levels of authorization. This was covered in `Chapter 1`, *Modern Infrastructures and Applications with Docker*.
- Cgroups and kernel namespaces provide container isolation. These are key to ensuring processes have enough resources without any non-authorized communication with other processes running on the same host.

We will now review which topics should be known about for the exam.

The knowledge required about the Docker platform for the exam

The exam will verify our knowledge of the following topics, among others:

- Describing sizing requirements for installation
- Describing and demonstrating the setup of a repo, the selection of a storage driver, and the installation of the Docker engine on multiple platforms
- Describing and demonstrating the configuration of logging drivers (`splunk`, `journald`, and so on)
- Describing and demonstrating how to set up Swarm, configure managers, add nodes, and set up the backup schedule
- Describing and demonstrating how to create and manage users and teams
- Describing and demonstrating how to configure the Docker daemon to start on boot
- Describing and demonstrating how to use certificate-based client-server authentication to ensure a Docker daemon has the right to access images on a registry
- Describing the use of namespaces, cgroups, and certificate configuration
- Describing and interpreting errors to troubleshoot installation issues without assistance
- Describing and demonstrating the steps to deploy Docker Engine, UCP, and DTR on **Amazon Web Services (AWS)** and on-premises with high availability
- Describing and demonstrating how to configure backups for UCP and DTR

These topics are extracted from Docker's official study guide, which can be found at `https://success.docker.com/certification`.

A summary of the networking topics

Networking is one of the core components of microservice application architecture. Faster networks allowed the evolution of distributed architectures. High availability and resilience can be provided using modern infrastructures, even on cloud or cloud-hybrid architectures. Containers work like small virtual nodes and they get virtual interfaces. We learned that network namespaces allow us to isolate processes on the same host, even if they use the same bridge interface to communicate with the real network, out of the host's network namespaces. Distributed networking on clusters is also simple because Docker Swarm manages all the internal infrastructures and processes required to allow communication between containers on different hosts. Overlay networks in Docker Swarm, distributed cluster-wide, use VXLAN to encapsulate traffic and can even be encrypted. By default, the Docker Swarm control plane's components are secured using **Mutual TLS (MTLS)** communication and we can isolate application data from network management.

All of these topics were covered in multiple chapters on Docker Engine, Docker Swarm, and Kubernetes. We learned about these topics in Chapter 4, *Container Persistency and Networking*, Chapter 8, *Orchestration Using Docker Swarm*, Chapter 9, *Orchestration Using Kubernetes*, Chapter 11, *Universal Control Plane*, and Chapter 12, *Publishing Applications in Docker Enterprise*.

In Chapter 9, *Orchestration Using Kubernetes*, we learned how Kubernetes implements network features cluster-wide. We also reviewed these features side by side against Docker Swarm implementations to have a good idea of how we can use both or make container workloads that can run on any of them.

We also learned that containers can expose their application processes internally. Other containers can consume their services but we need to publish their ports for external users and applications. This is very important because security is ensured in Docker Swarm for containers working in the same network. They are isolated, hence we can publish only frontend applications' components.

Let's look at some network topics as a summary:

- Docker Engine networking is based on bridge networking, although we can use MacVLAN interfaces (with real IP addresses), underlying the host's networking (using its network namespace), and can even extend default behavior using plugins. We can use default or custom bridge networking. Custom networks also deploy internal DNS facilities, hence, containers running on these networks will know each other by their names. In some special cases, it is useful to deploy containers without networking features.

- Networking in Docker Swarm is easy because Docker creates new virtual networks (overlay networks) and deploys VXLAN tunnels to encapsulate all hosts' traffic. Containers deployed for services' tasks can see each other if they are working on the same overlay network.

- The Kubernetes network model is even easier. It is based on a flat network where services and pods are always reachable by default. For this to work, we need to integrate a CNI. Each CNI has its own implementation of this flat network model and Docker Enterprise deploys Calico (`https://www.projectcalico.org/`) by default.

- A flat network is unsecured by default because applications' components are not isolated. We will use network policies to isolate applications, grouping them by namespaces, labels, and so on. NetworkPolicy resources manage connection rules to allow or disallow specific pods' connections and hence their traffic.

- Docker Swarm nodes use encrypted TLS communications by default (mutual TLS). Docker manages all of the required certificates. Users' communications with the cluster are not secure, but we can also create secure communications manually (we have a complete example explaining all of the required steps in `Chapter 8`, *Orchestration Using Docker Swarm*) or use UCP-integrated **Role-Based Access Control (RBAC)**. UCP provides users with bundles, containing all the required files to create secure TLS tunnels.

- Kubernetes also encrypts its control plane. Docker Enterprise does all the deployment work for us and a fully functional Kubernetes cluster will be up and running after its installation. Certificates will be used to deploy TLS tunnels between Kubernetes components and users by default.

- Internal DNS is deployed for local custom bridge and overlay networks. Therefore, containers and services can be discovered by their names. Containers use an internal DNS and an external resolution will be forwarded to a specific external DNS. By default, containers receive the host's DNS configuration, but we can change this behavior.

- Kubernetes also integrates an internal DNS. In this case, the `kube-dns` component will manage all service entries.

- Internal load balancing is also deployed in overlay networks. Remember that services can be replicated or global. In both cases, `vip` mode is used by default, and services get an IP address in the special ingress network. This IP address is registered and the internal load balancer will route requests to all available services' replicas. We can avoid this behavior using the `dns-round-robin` mode.

- Kubernetes' internal load balancing has similar behavior. All services will receive an internal virtual IP address by default (a ClusterIP). Services in Kubernetes are logical groups of pods and services' requests will be forwarded by default to all associated pods.

- As mentioned before, an application deployed within containers will not publish their ports unless we declare this behavior. Publishing ports on Docker Engine is easy and we can ensure that only specific IP addresses will listen on a published port on multi-homed nodes. Bridge networking uses NAT for publishing an application's ports. Docker creates all of the required hosts' firewall rules to allow and route this traffic. If we use the host's networking, all container-exposed ports will be published and applications will be directly accessible.

- We also learned that services in Docker Swarm will be published by default in all nodes, even if they do not run any services' tasks. This feature is known as a router mesh and application ports will be available in all of the clusters' hosts. Internal load balancing will also be applied using an ingress overlay network and instances in different hosts will be reachable. This can be insecure because all application ports will be accessible on all hosts.

- Kubernetes' `NodePort` services have equivalent behavior to Docker Swarm's router mesh. Services declared as `NodePort` will publish their ports on all cluster nodes. However, Kubernetes also has the `LoadBalancer` service type. These services will be published directly using infrastructure load balancers. This integration only works on some cloud providers.

- UCP provides Interlock as a solution to avoid unsecured router mesh publishing. We have learned about Interlock's components and deployment and how we publish applications using this tool. Interlock's ports must be published, but all other applications' services can be accessed through Interlock. Therefore, we do not need to publish applications' ports. This improves security because Interlock acts as a reverse proxy, providing TLS security, host- and content-based services routing, and sticky sessions, among others. The Interlock proxy component will be updated using services' labels; therefore, only services with specific labels will be published. We have learned about these required labels and reviewed a few examples of their usage.

- Kubernetes can integrate ingress controllers to avoid `NodePort` cluster-wide application publishing. Ingress controllers deploy reverse-like proxy features to route requests to appropriate services matching specific headers or content rules. This improves security because services should not be published. We just publish ingress controllers (using service strategies, for example), and ingress resources manage the necessary rules for reaching out to the desired services, although they are not externally published.

As mentioned, networking is critical in cluster environments. Let's review some of the topics required to pass the exam.

The Docker networking knowledge required for the exam

The exam will verify our knowledge of the following topics, among others:

- Describing the container network model and how it interfaces with Docker Engine and network and IPAM drivers
- Describing the different types and use cases for built-in network drivers
- Describing the types of traffic that flow between Docker Engine, registry, and UCP controllers
- Describing and demonstrating how to create a Docker bridge network for developers to use for their containers
- Describing and demonstrating how to publish a port so that an application is accessible externally
- Identifying which IP and port a container is externally accessible on
- Comparing and contrasting host and ingress publishing modes
- Describing and demonstrating how to configure Docker to use an external DNS
- Describing and demonstrating how to use Docker to load balance HTTP/HTTPS traffic to an application (configuring L7 load balancing with Docker EE).
- Understanding and describing the types of traffic that flow between Docker Engine, registry, and UCP controllers
- Describing and demonstrating how to deploy a service on a Docker overlay network
- Describing and demonstrating how to troubleshoot container and engine logs to resolve connectivity issues between containers
- Describing how to route traffic to Kubernetes pods using the ClusterIP and NodePort services
- Describing the Kubernetes container network model.

These topics are extracted from Docker's official study guide, which can be found at `https://success.docker.com/certification`.

The next section will help you by presenting the required knowledge in relation to security on the Docker platform.

Understanding security concepts and related Docker features

Security is crucial when you are running applications in production. We have learned about many security features provided by Docker and its components. We started by reviewing how containers are isolated from other host processes and we also learned how we can ensure security in Docker Engine. Then, we moved on to Docker Swarm, where security must be applied cluster-wide. Users' access must also be managed and we need to provide authentication and authorization mechanisms. Docker Enterprise provides a higher level of security. It includes a complete RBAC environment, which allows us to manage fine-grained permissions to objects and cluster resources.

All of these topics were covered in multiple chapters on Docker Engine, Docker Swarm, Kubernetes, and the Docker Enterprise platform. We learned about security in Chapter 1, *Modern Infrastructures and Applications with Docker*, Chapter 2, *Building Docker Images*, Chapter 4, *Container Persistency and Networking*, Chapter 6, *Introduction to Docker Content Trust*, Chapter 8, *Orchestration Using Docker Swarm*, Chapter 9, *Orchestration Using Kubernetes*, Chapter 11, *Universal Control Plane*, Chapter 12, *Publishing Applications in Docker Enterprise*, and Chapter 13, *Implementing an Enterprise-Grade Registry with DTR*.

We have to remember that containers are created using images, so securing images is also critical. Following good practices is key to developing safe images. Docker Enterprise provides several strategies to validate image precedence, immutability, and content security.

Let's review some of these security topics:

- Docker is a client-server application. The server will publish its API on local (by default) and remotely accessible sockets. We can limit Docker Engine access by limiting access to these sockets. Locally, only users with filesystem permissions to a defined socket file will be allowed to run Docker commands on the local Docker engine.
- Docker Engine can be integrated with operating system-provided security modules, such as SELinux or AppArmor. Docker provides integration and default profiles to use with our containers. Docker also integrates with the Linux kernel to allow the adding or removing of specific system calls using capabilities. There are also simpler security tips, such as using read-only root filesystems and non-root users within containers, that will also help us to provide secure applications.

- Images should be secure to create secure containers. Images should only contain the required binaries, libraries, and configurations for our processes. Everything irrelevant to the application should be avoided. Docker Enterprise provides an image's content security scanner. It compares relevant content file hashes against a database of well-known published vulnerabilities and exploits (internet **Common Vulnerabilities and Exposures (CVE)**). We learned how this process works and how we can integrate tag promotions to ensure that only allowed users get the appropriate access to their images. These are some of the DTR features.

- We can also sign images. This process ensures image content immutability and ownership. If we integrate image building into our continuous integration and continuous deployment, we can ensure that images were created using an appropriate workflow. We can also improve our CaaS security, allowing only containers based on images signed by specific teams or users within your organization.

- We learned about all the automatic steps to be followed to sign an image and all the keys integrated into the process. Image signing is based on Content Trust logic, and we learned how it is integrated in Docker in `Chapter 6`, *Introduction to Docker Content Trust*.

- We mentioned some simple practices that increase security in our workloads, such as running read-only root filesystems or using non-root users for applications (or user namespaces). We should review an image's specifications using `docker image inspect` to have a good idea of exposed ports, applications' users, and commands that will be executed inside containers.

- As mentioned in this chapter, neither Docker Engine nor Docker Swarm have any RBAC integration. On the other hand, Docker Enterprise components have integrated role-based access. UCP provides different accesses to Docker Swarm resources based on roles, grants, and collections. We can configure fine-grained access to volumes, secrets, configs, networks, and so on, so users will only be able to execute allowed actions on their resources. Users will connect to the cluster to execute, review, and modify their resources by using either the provided web UI or their Docker command line, using their Docker client software and their UCP's bundle. This compressed file contains user certificates and environment scripts prepared to help users connect easily to the cluster.

- DTR has its own RBAC environment, isolated from that of UCP. DTR is a registry, therefore its RBAC environment is dedicated to managing access to the images stored within your CaaS. We have fine-grained permissions to allow a group of users to use or modify images, while other images are public within teams or the full organization.

- DTR and UCP are integrated by default in a single sign-on solution, although we can change this behavior. We can also integrate them into our organization user management solution, Active Directory, or any compatible **Lightweight Directory Access Protocol (LDAP)**.

- We learned how to deploy Docker Enterprise components and how to manage users, roles, and different levels of access to resources and images. They will be deployed with high availability using an odd number of software nodes and we will require an external load balancer to provide users' access. We can integrate our corporate certificates, but we can also use autogenerated ones. In this case, we will need to integrate DTR's CA in our organization server and client hosts.

- Although Docker Swarm requires UCP to integrate user management, Kubernetes implements its own RBAC system. We will be allowed to authenticate and authorize users using tokens and certificates. Kubernetes RBAC will work for applications and users and it is integrated into Docker Enterprise.

- Docker Swarm and Kubernetes provide secure storage for certificates, passwords, tokens, and so on. Both provide secret resources to manage any file (or variable) that should be protected from suspicious users. But while secrets are encrypted in Docker Swarm, they are not encrypted in Kubernetes by default. Secret resources are encoded using Base64 in Kubernetes, and additional configuration must be performed to encrypt them.

- Kubernetes has advanced features regarding security, such as PodSecurityPolicy resources, which allow us to force security on pods, allowing or disallowing specific behaviors (root processes and read-only filesystems). Admission controllers can also be implemented (there are a few already configured by default in UCP's Kubernetes deployment) to force pod security policies and other security features by default to any workload deployed in our Kubernetes cluster.

- We will use RBAC for either UCP and DTR user accesses. First, we will ensure only authorized users will be able to manage and use cluster resources for their applications. DTR's RBAC will protect images, allowing only authorized users to manipulate and update their content.

The next section will highlight the knowledge required to pass the exam.

The knowledge of Docker security required for the exam

The exam will verify our knowledge of the following topics, among others:

- Describing security administration and tasks
- Describing the process of signing an image
- Describing default engine security
- Describing Swarm default security
- Describing MTLS
- Describing identity roles
- Comparing and contrasting UCP workers and managers
- Describing the process of using external certificates with UCP and DTR
- Describing and demonstrating how an image passes a security scan
- Describing and demonstrating how to enable Docker Content Trust
- Describing and demonstrating how to configure RBAC with UCP
- Describing and demonstrating how to integrate UCP with LDAP/AD
- Describing and demonstrating how to create UCP client bundles

These topics are extracted from Docker's official study guide, which can be found at https://success.docker.com/certification.

Quickly summarizing Docker storage and volumes

Using Docker containers requires different storage solutions, as we have learned through this book. Images and containers are created using multiple-layer filesystem strategies. However, we also have to manage persistence in our container-based applications. This persistence can be associated with application data, but we also have to be able to manage configurations and states cluster-wide.

We learned about security in Chapter 1, *Modern Infrastructures and Applications with Docker,* Chapter 2, *Building Docker Images,* Chapter 4, *Container Persistency and Networking,* and Chapter 13, *Implementing an Enterprise-Grade Registry with DTR.*

This is a quick summary of the topics looked at in this book regarding storage and volume management within containers. We recommend you read through this summary to ensure you remember the concepts learned:

- We learned that containers are based on different filesystems and solutions with a common feature – copy-on-write. This allows us to create multiple immutable layers to group files. Each layer is the base for another, and file modifications will be stored in the last layer where they were changed. All immutable layers are considered as the image for the creation of new containers. We will add a new read-and-write layer for the container. These layers rely on host storage. This storage is known as graph storage and we will use different strategies to manage it, depending on the host operating system. Docker will choose the best driver for your host according to your kernel features and installed drivers. The most popular and most widely used today is `overlay2`, which is the default graph driver for many Linux distributions. `docker info` provides information about the driver used.

- We have also learned that images are stored locally for fast usage on your host. When these images must be shared with cluster nodes, things get difficult, although we can export and import image layers. We will use image registries to store images and share their content with hosts and users. We learned how to deploy Docker Registry (Community Edition) as well as DTR, which is recommended for enterprise environments. We can use different storage solutions for registry volumes, depending on whether we are using cloud environments or on-premises installations. As reviewed in `Chapter 13`, *Implementing an Enterprise-Grade Registry with DTR*, object storage is quite good for storing images based on big layers, which is the most common way of creating images.

- Images can occupy a lot of space in your host. We should take care of this and review dead containers and unused images that are consuming space with `docker system df`. We should remove dangling images not used as a layer within any other images. We also have to take care of the space on our registries. Only keep required images, but remember to verify which containers or applications will use different old image versions. We learned how to filter this information in `Chapter 2`, *Building Docker Images*.

- Volumes, on the other hand, are different from image and container storage. They are used to bypass container storage. These help us to improve performance when a lot of disk I/O is required, and also allow us to store persistent data. By default, we can use on-memory filesystems, a host's local directories (bind mounts), NFS, and Docker volumes for storage. Docker volumes are associated with a container's life cycle when they are created during their execution.

- As mentioned, Docker provides some volume solutions by default. We can extend them using plugins and third-party integrations. Using distributed storage with Docker Swarm and UCP is critical if we need to provide high availability to our applications using resilience. If one cluster host dies, another will take its workloads by default, but storage must follow this behavior.

- Kubernetes has a different approach to persistent data. We talked about volumes and persistent volumes (`persistentVolumes`). The former are used to share and manage data associated with pods' containers. On the other hand, persistent volumes are used to manage and persist data cluster-wide. There are different retention policies to manage their recycling cycles. Persistent volume claims (`persistentVolumeClaims`) are used to link pods with volumes using labels and required space among other parameters. Therefore, instead of using persistent volumes directly attached to pods, we will use `persistentVolumeClaims` inside pods' configurations as volumes. Administrators should create these resources, but they can avoid this behavior by using `storageClass` resources. They will just configure `storageClass` resources using labels, storage providers, and other advanced profiles to allow dynamic storage allocation for persistent volumes.

- We learned that Docker provides `Config` and `Secret` objects to allow us to manage information in cluster nodes. These help us to configure applications and ensure that applications' containers receive appropriate configurations, passwords, certificates, and so on. Kubernetes has its own configuration and secret resources. To manage configurations, we will use ConfigMaps for storing an application's configuration files and managing environment variables. Secret resources are used to store secured data, but they are not encrypted by default in Kubernetes. They are stored using the Base64 format and can be used for either storing keys and values or files.

Storing data and states is quite important and is part of the exam. Let's review what concepts you are required to understand to pass the exam.

The storage and volume knowledge required for the exam

The exam will verify our knowledge of the following topics, among others:

- Identifying the correct graph drivers to use with various operating systems
- Describing and demonstrating how to configure a device mapper

- Comparing and contrasting object and block storage and when they should be used
- Describing how an application is composed of layers and where those layers reside on the filesystem
- Describing the use of volumes with Docker for persistent storage
- Identifying the steps to take to clean up unused images on a filesystem and DTR
- Describing and demonstrating how storage can be used across cluster nodes
- Describing how to provision persistent storage to a Kubernetes pod using `persistentVolume` resources.
- Describing the relationship between container storage interface drivers, `storageClass`, `persistentVolumeClaim`, and `volume` objects in Kubernetes.

We will look at some final notes and sample exam questions to help us prepare for the DCA exam in the next chapter.

Summary

This chapter was a summary of the topics required to pass the exam. We reviewed the topic distribution and their approximate value in the exam. This should give you a good idea of what sections are more important than others. We recommend that you review this chapter before reading all the exam-like questions set out in the next chapter.

We covered a brief summary of orchestration's most important topics. We also reviewed some of the installation and configuration tips required for Docker Engine, Docker Swarm, and Enterprise components. We looked at a summary of the features and processes involved in the creation of images. Security is always critical and we looked at a summary of the features provided by different Docker components that help us to provide a CaaS platform in production. Container networking and the different storage implementations for containers and images and for data management were also reviewed. It is recommended that you review any chapters that were not clear in these summaries and review the labs provided in this book to reinforce your knowledge of all the exam topics.

The next chapter provides some exam-like questions that will prepare you for the exam.

15
Mock Exam Questions and Final Notes

This chapter presents some final notes with some mock questions. We will look at a brief summary of the exam specification, how it is delivered to you, and what topics are more relevant than others.

The mock questions prepared for this book are similar to the ones you will get during the exam. Please read them carefully because some are multiple-choice. Multiple-choice questions will appear in the exam and you should know how to answer them.

By the end of these questions, you will have a good idea of the format of the exam, what kind of questions you will get, and what topics are more relevant than others.

Docker Certified Associate exam details

At the time of writing this book, the exam is based on the Docker Enterprise platform. Please refer to Docker's site, `https://success.docker.com/certification`, to obtain the latest information.

The Docker Certified Associate exam will validate your Docker Enterprise professional skills and usually requires a minimum of 6 to 12 months of platform experience. This book teaches these required skills with labs that help you understand the platform's concepts and usage.

You can pay for and take this exam online, but it is only available in English. Although the Docker site shows that results will be delivered immediately, sometimes results can take 24–48 hours to be delivered.

The exam consists of 55 questions and the topics covered in this book have different values. We recommend you use the Docker Enterprise platform's 30-day free-trial, as there will be many exam questions about Docker Enterprise components and management. It is also recommended that you have good knowledge of Docker's command-line actions and options, including how to obtain and filter information about Docker resources. These are the topic weights at the time of writing this book:

- **Orchestration**: 25%
- **Image creation, management, and registry**: 20%
- **Installation and configuration**: 15%
- **Networking**: 15%
- **Security**: 15%
- **Storage and volumes**: 10%

This gives you an idea of each topic's importance and the question distribution. In the next section, we will provide some questions to help you prepare for the exam. They are exam-like questions. Take care because many of them have more than one correct answer and you should choose all the right ones. The answers to all these questions can be found at the end of this book, in the *Assessments* section.

Mock exam questions

1. How can we limit the number of CPUs provided to a container?

   a) Using `--cap-add CPU`.
   b) Using `--cpuset-cpus`.
   c) Using `--cpus`.
   d) It is not possible to specify the number of CPUs; we have to use `--cpu-shares` and define the CPU slices.

2. How can we limit the amount of memory available to a container?

   a) It is not possible to limit the amount of memory available to a container.
   b) Using `--cap-drop MEM`.
   c) Using `--memory`.
   d) Using `--memory-reservation`.

3. What environment variables should be exported to start using a trusted environment with the Docker client?

  a) `export DOCKER_TRUSTED_ENVIRONMENT=1`
  b) `export DOCKER_CONTENT_TRUST=1`
  c) `export DOCKER_TRUST=1`
  d) `export DOCKER_TRUSTED=1`

4. How can we increase the number of replicas of a service running one instance (mark all the correct answers)?

  a) This is not possible for global services.
  b) By updating the number of replicas with `docker service update --replicas <NUMBER_OF_REPLICAS> <SERVICE>`.
  c) The number of replicas can be increased using `docker service scale <SERVICE>=<NUMBER_OF_REPLICAS>`.
  d) We can use `docker service scale up` to create a new replica.

5. How many replicas does a global service run on nodes if we specify the `node.role!=worker` constraint?

  a) Worker and manager nodes will run one replica.
  b) Only workers will run one replica.
  c) Only manager nodes will run one replica.
  d) No nodes will run any replicas.

6. How do we stop all replicas of the service web server, which is currently executing three replicas?

  a) Using `docker service stop webserver`.
  b) Using `docker rm service webserver`.
  c) Using `docker service update --replicas 0 webserver`.
  d) None of the preceding answers are correct.

7. If we publish a service on port 8080 using -P, which nodes will expose port 8080?

  a) No node will expose a service on port 8080.
  b) All nodes will publish port 8080.
  c) We should use privileged containers to expose port 8080.
  d) We must use `--network=host` to publish ports below port 30000.

8. What step should we follow to remove the leader node from the cluster?

   a) Ensure all tasks run on other nodes by executing `docker node update --availability=drain <LEADER_NODE>`.
   b) Remove the node from the cluster as the leader by executing `docker swarm leave` on the node.
   c) Demote the leader node to a worker and then execute `docker swarm leave` on the node.
   d) Once the node is out of the cluster, we can remove it completely using `docker node rm <OLD_LEADER_NODE>` from any available manager.

9. Where do we specify that DevOps users can run a container using only images signed by the admin group from our Docker Enterprise registry?

   a) On **Universal Control Plane's (UCP's)** RBAC, we allow DevOps users to run their images.
   b) On DTR's image repository, we add image pulling access to DevOps.
   c) Image access should be configured on **Docker Trusted Registry (DTR)**, and DevOps users should be able to at least read this repository. On UCP, we allow only images signed by the admin group on the cluster and add at least scheduler access for DevOps users to their private collection.
   d) This is not possible on Docker Enterprise.

10. What step is required to access images stored on a secure registry that is using a self-signed certificate?

   a) We can configure our registry as "insecure" in Docker Engine's `daemon.json` file.
   b) We should disable Content Trust to allow image pulling from unsecured registries.
   c) The best option is to trust self-signed certificates. We will add DTR's created **Certificate Authority (CA)** into our system's trusted-CA list.
   d) We cannot use self-signed certificates, therefore we always require an Enterprise-signed certificate.

11. *User A* executed `docker service scale --replicas 5 webserver`, while *user B* executed `docker service update --replicas 3 webserver`. How many replicas will be running after both executions?

    a) None of the commands will work.
    b) The `webserver` service will run three replicas.
    c) The `webserver` service will run five replicas.
    d) The `webserver` service will run eight replicas.

12. Which of these lines creates a volume named `DATA`?

    a) `docker volume create --driver local DATA`.
    b) `docker create --volume DATA`.
    c) Volumes must be created during container execution.
    d) None of the options are valid.

13. How can we ensure that a minimum of memory is available to run a container using soft limits?

    a) We cannot ensure a minimum of memory is available for a container.
    b) Using `--memory`.
    c) This must be configured on your operating system.
    d) We use `--memory-reservation`.

14. What is true about Swarm networking?

    a) All overlay networks are encrypted by default.
    b) Control Plane nodes use mutual TLS encryption to secure traffic.
    c) An internal DNS can be consumed externally exposing its service.
    d) All of the preceding options are true.

15. Which concept routes requests to containers running for a deployed service?

    a) An `ingress` overlay network is used to route requests to different services' backends using a round-robin endpoint by default.
    b) A `docker_gwbridge` network is used to communicate with containers on different hosts.
    c) An `ingress` overlay network is used to route requests to different services' backends using the service's virtual IP by default.
    d) We must use a host network to route requests to containers.

16. Which of these sentences are true about signing images?

    a) Image signing ensures image ownership.
    b) Images can be signed using `docker trust sign <IMAGE>`.
    c) All images will be signed if we set the Docker client to use Docker Content Trust on every command.
    d) Image signing is based on the following keys: the owner key, the repository key, the snapshot key, and the timestamp.

17. What happens if we have a cluster where nodes have `myapplication` images locally but images have different hashes?

    a) If we do not specify the image hash, each node will run tasks with its own image.
    b) To ensure all nodes run the same image version, we will need to use `with-registry-auth` for remote registries.
    c) We will use signed images and Docker Engine on nodes that will use trusted content.
    d) It is not possible to ensure that nodes will use the right image version.

18. Which of the following is true about global services?

    a) Global services will only run one replica of the defined service on each node.
    b) Global services will not provide high availability based on resilience.
    c) Draining a node will not remove global services.
    d) All of the preceding sentences are true.

19. Which of the following sentences are true about replicated services?

    a) We need to specify the number of instances during service creation because it cannot be changed later.
    b) Replicated services are the default service mode and they will run one instance if none was specified.
    c) Replicated services can be stopped by setting the number of replicas to 0.
    d) All of the preceding options are true.

20. Which of the following steps are required to create a Swarm backup?

    a) Stop Docker Engine on any manager to ensure files are static.
    b) Copy the `/var/lib/docker/swarm` directory content for backing up Swarm.
    c) Raft logs should be backed up apart from normal files.
    d) All of the preceding steps are required.

21. What have you learned about Swarm networking?

    a) Overlay networks are deployed using UDP VXLAN tunnels.
    b) By default, all service replicas will be equally reachable by an internal load balancer.
    c) The internal DNS will allow all services to reach each other running on the same overlay network.
    d) All of the preceding options are true.

22. We tried to create a service with five replicas but it is not working. We cannot reach the reconciliation phase because we get the following error: `1/1: no suitable node (scheduling constraints not satisfied on 5 nodes)`. What could be wrong?

    a) The service's image does not exist.
    b) We were using a private image and we did not provide authentication credentials.
    c) We used constraints for deploying the service's tasks on specific nodes but none of them have the required labels.
    d) None of the preceding options are true.

23. Which of the following is true about locking a Docker Swarm cluster?

    a) The control, management, and data planes are secure.
    b) A passphrase is required to unlock the `/var/lib/docker/swarm` data.
    c) Executing `systemctl restart docker` will require the locking passphrase.
    d) If a node reboots, Docker Engine will not restart automatically, hence we have lost the Docker Swarm quorum.

24. Which of the following is true about replicated services?

   a) They will run one instance on each node.
   b) Only replicated services can be upgraded using the rolling update feature.
   c) They can be stopped using the Docker service update: `--replicas 0 <SERVICENAME>`.
   d) We will use Go templates to be able to provide unique resources, such as volumes or hostnames, inside containers to ensure all replicas use their own resources.

25. Which methods are allowed to publish applications on Docker Enterprise?

   a) We can use Interlock.
   b) We can use an Ingress Controller.
   c) We will publish each application container.
   d) We can use the `host` mode to publish applications as if they were running directly at the host level.

26. Which of the following is true about Kubernetes' integration with Docker Enterprise?

   a) Docker Enterprise provides Kubernetes out of the box.
   b) We must choose which orchestrator to use in cluster nodes because only one is allowed at once.
   c) We can run hosts in mixed mode to allow Kubernetes and Docker Swarm workloads, although it is not recommended for production.
   d) We can upgrade Kubernetes components with common Kubernetes installation commands.

27. What is the difference between `docker image import` and `docker image load` for uploading an image to a Docker host?

   a) There is no difference between the commands.
   b) Both import the same image content.
   c) `docker image import` will only retrieve image layers containing binaries, libraries, and configurations for the process but without any meta-information about how to launch the process, what volumes to use, what ports should be used, and so on.
   d) We can only use `docker image import` to create new images.

28. How can `docker build` avoid the use of cached image layers?

    a) Docker will always use cached information. It is not possible to avoid using image caching.
    b) By default, image caching is disabled, therefore we need to apply `--use-caching` to ensure caching is enabled as it will speed up the building process.
    c) To avoid image caching, we can use `--no-cache`. This way, the build will not use any previously saved layers.
    d) All of the preceding sentences are wrong.

29. How can we download all of the images from a repository?

    a) It is not possible. We need to make a list of all the images with their tags and retrieve them one by one.
    b) Every time we execute `docker image pull`, we download all the images and their layers, regardless of whether we are going to use them or not.
    c) We can use `docker image pull --all-tags` to retrieve all repository-associated images.
    d) None of the preceding sentences are right.

30. How can we filter running containers based on a specific image?

    a) There is no option for this. We use the Linux `grep` command to filter specific base images for containers.
    b) We will use the `ancestor` key to list all the running containers using a specific image.
    c) We will use the `image` key to list all the running containers using a specific image.
    d) None of the preceding sentences are right.

31. How can we push a locally built image to a remote registry?

    a) We need to know the registry's **fully qualified domain name (FQDN)** or its IP address.
    b) We tag the image with the registry FQDN or IP, the username or group, and the repository where the image will be stored.
    c) If the registry uses TLS/SSL certificates, we load its CA in our system to be able to trust them or we can configure it using the `insecure-registries` key.
    d) All of the preceding sentences are correct.

32. Which option will bind an already-created `DATA` volume inside a container, under the `/data` directory?

    a) `-v DATA:/data`
    b) `--mount type=volume,source=DATA,target=/data`
    c) `--mount DATA:/data`
    d) `--volume type=volume,source=DATA,target=/data`

33. How do we expose a web server container on the host's port `80` (the `nginx:alpine` image exposes port `80`)?

    a) `docker container run --cap-add NET_ADMIN -p 80:80 -d nginx:alpine`
    b) `docker container run --net=host -d nginx:alpine`
    c) `docker container run -P nginx:alpine`
    d) `docker container run -d -P 80:80 nginx:alpine`

34. Which of these keys requires a passphrase to unlock it while signing images?

    a) Timestamp
    b) Target
    c) Snapshot
    d) Root

35. What is a Docker bundle and what is included inside those ZIP files?

    a) A Docker bundle provides client binaries and configurations for administrators.
    b) All users have their own Docker bundle and it includes all the environment files required for the user.
    c) A Docker bundle includes only environment scripts and we will ask administrators for certificates.
    d) A user's Docker bundle includes all the environment files and certificates required for using the CaaS platform.

36. Which is the best node distribution if we have to deploy a cluster with seven managers with distributed high availability?

    a) Four manager nodes in a data center and three manager nodes on a different one.
    b) Two managers in a data center, two managers in a second one, and three in another.

c) All managers should be in the same data center.

d) We cannot manage distributed availability with 7 nodes; we need at least 9.

37. Which concept is responsible for managing external to internal load balancing for Docker Swarm services?

    a) Router Mesh
    b) Ingress Controller
    c) nodePort
    d) clusterIP

38. What are the differences between the COPY and ADD Dockerfile primitives?

    a) COPY adds files in read-only mode.
    b) COPY can be used to download files from external services.
    c) ADD can be used with packaged and compressed files and they will be decompressed in the layer's root filesystem.
    d) ADD and COPY are completely equal, but ADD is newer.

39. How can we deploy two applications using the same docker-compose.yaml file?

    a) We cannot deploy two applications using the same docker-compose.yaml file.
    b) Docker Compose can deploy two applications using projects to ensure applications run using different volumes and ports.
    c) We can use environment variables for fixed resources to avoid any resource usage conflicts.
    d) The only option to avoid application component conflicts is to deploy applications on different clusters.

40. What is required to deploy DTR?

    a) A Docker Enterprise license from Docker Hub and an appropriate repository URL
    b) Docker Enterprise Engine and Docker UCP
    c) Docker Engine, a DTR license, and Docker Content Trust
    d) All of the preceding options

41. How do we enable debugging on Docker Engine?

    a) By executing the Docker daemon with the `-D` argument
    b) By setting the `debug` key to `true` in the `config.json` file
    c) By enabling experimental features in `daemon.json`
    d) None of the preceding options

42. How do we only list containers created from an `alpine:3.10` image?

    a) `docker container ls image=alpine:3.10`
    b) `docker ps --format ancestor=alpine:3.10`
    c) `docker container ls --filter ancestor=alpine:3.10`
    d) `docker container ls --filter image=alpine:3.10`

43. Which of the following is true about privileged containers?

    a) Resource limits will be avoided (CPU, memory, and disk I/O).
    b) They always run the container as the root user.
    c) These containers run with all available capabilities.
    d) They run using the host's kernel namespaces.

44. Which of the following is true about Swarm join tokens?

    a) Once created, we have to store them in a secure place because they are not recoverable.
    b) We can generate new ones to get new values for new nodes if we lose them using `docker swarm join-token recreate`.
    c) We can recover them whenever we need them using `docker swarm join-token`.
    d) Join tokens will be automatically updated on all nodes once they are regenerated.

45. Which endpoints are provided to verify DTR and UCP nodes' health?

    a) DTR provides `/_ping`, `/nginx_status`, and `/api/v0/meta/cluster_status`.
    b) DTR and UCP provide `/status`.
    c) DTR and UCP provide `/_ping`.
    d) DTR provides `/status` and UCP provides `/_ping`.

46. Which command allows us to review and recover lost space due to "dangling images" and dead containers?

    a) `docker system rm`
    b) `docker system prune`
    c) `docker image rm --filter="dangling"`
    d) `docker container rm -a`

47. Which primitive combination creates the command line that will effectively finally run inside a container?

    a) `ENTRYPOINT` will set the script or binary to be launched and `CMD` will be used if `ENTRYPOINT` is not defined.
    b) `CMD` always overwrites the `ENTRYPOINT` definition.
    c) Using a combination of `ENTRYPOINT` to define the script or binary to be launched and `RUN` as arguments.
    d) `CMD` will add arguments to the defined `ENTRYPOINT` only if `ENTRYPOINT` is configured using the `exec` format.

48. Which of the following is true about secrets?

    a) They will only be available on manager nodes, so workloads with secrets must run on these nodes.
    b) They are ephemeral and deployed on on-memory filesystems.
    c) They are encrypted even for administrators, so they cannot be recovered from the control plane.
    d) If we need to change a secret, we need to create a new secret and update the service with this new one.

49. How can we ensure that a specific image is deployed in production?

    a) By using the image's hash for deploying containers.
    b) Signing images will ensure their tagging and provenance.
    c) Specifying the right tag is enough to ensure its content.
    d) By using `docker image history` to review commands used to generate the image.

50. Which of the following sentences about container isolation are true?

> a) The host's hardware resources, such as memory and CPU, are granted using cgroups.
> b) To ensure a container's limits, we need to use operating system security modules.
> c) Only the root user is allowed to deploy containers with unlimited resources.
> d) Privileged containers will avoid defined process' capabilities and execution user.

51. How can we ensure an image's content immutability?

> a) By using signed images.
> b) Defining immutable tags in DTR.
> c) By using image scanning.
> d) Images cannot be immutable.

52. Which of the following sentences are true about overlay networks?

> a) DTR deploys an overlay network, `dtr-ol`, to route a cluster's internal communications.
> b) Overlay-defined networks are only present on manager nodes when there is not a task connected to them.
> c) `interlock-extension` connects to services' defined networks to route requests to appropriate backends.
> d) Docker Swarm overlay networks are encrypted and deployed using VXLAN.

53. What does the `HEALTHCHECK --start-period=15s CMD curl --fail https://localhost:8080 | exit 1` line in a Dockerfile do?

> a) It will execute the defined `curl` command every 15 seconds, and if it fails three consecutive times, it will mark the container as unhealthy.
> b) It will wait 15 seconds for the first execution and then Docker Engine will run the defined `curl` command every 30 seconds, and if it fails three consecutive times, it will mark the container as unhealthy.
> c) This line does not do anything; health checks must be configured for each container.
> d) Docker Engine will run this probe every 15 seconds and if it fails, it will restart the container.

54. Which of the following is true about Docker Engine access?

    a) By default, only owners of a Docker socket are allowed to run containers on a standalone host.
    b) We can allow users to run containers allowing their access to either Docker Engine's Unix socket or the API's TCP port (enabled by default).
    c) Anyone allowed to log in to the host is also allowed to run containers.
    d) Only the root user is allowed to run privileged containers on a host.

55. How can we modify ports published on an already-deployed service?

    a) It is not possible; we have to remove the service and create it again.
    b) We can only change ports if the service is running using the host's network (`--net=host`).
    c) We use `docker service update --publish-add <NEW_PORT> --publish-rm <OLD_PORT>`.
    d) None of the preceding answers are correct.

56. How can we ensure that the web server Docker service runs one instance of NGINX on all cluster nodes?

    a) By using `docker service create --type=global --instances=1 --name=webserver --image=nginx:alpine`.
    b) By using `docker service create --mode=global --name=webserver nginx:alpine`.
    c) UCP can ensure that administrators run any service on all nodes in the cluster with a tick on `allow run on manager nodes`.
    d) `docker service create --name=webserver --image=nginx:alpine` is enough for executing one instance on all nodes.

57. How do we set a repository named `myregistry/myorganization/baseimages`, available for internal users, where images are owned and managed by DevOps group users?

    a) We need to create an organization with the name `myorganization`.
    b) We will create `myregistry/myorganization/baseimages` as a public repository.
    c) We configure DevOps team users as admins of the `myregistry/myorganization/baseimages` repository.
    d) The `myregistry/myorganization/baseimages` repository will be created as private for `myorganization` users.

58. How can we review ports published for a container named `webserver`?

   a) Using `docker container ls --filter name=webserver`.
   b) Using `docker container port webserver`.
   c) Using `docker container inspect webserver --format="{{ .NetworkSettings.Ports }}"`.
   d) All of the preceding answers are correct.

59. Which concept is responsible for managing internal load balancing for Kubernetes?

   a) Router Mesh
   b) Ingress Controller
   c) Interlock
   d) `clusterIP`

60. Which resources are used to link pods with Kubernetes' defined volumes?

   a) `persistentVolume`
   b) `persistentVolumeClaim`
   c) `storageClass`
   d) `persistentDataVolume`

61. Which labels are required to deploy a service with Interlock?

   a) `com.docker.lb.port`
   b) `com.docker.interlock.port`
   c) `com.docker.interlock.hosts`
   d) `com.docker.lb.backend`

62. How can we publish services externally in Kubernetes?

   a) Using Interlock
   b) Using Ingress Controllers
   c) Using the `nodePort` service
   d) Using a `clusterIP` resource

63. How do we know how much space is used by containers and volumes in our system?

    a) By using docker system prune
    b) By using docker system df
    c) By using docker container df
    d) By using docker volume df

64. Which role should be set in UCP for the DBA team to allow them to create their own volumes?

    a) Scheduler.
    b) View Only.
    c) Only UCP administrators can create volumes and other cluster resources.
    d) Restricted Control is enough to create volumes on their private collection.

65. Which flag should be used to configure all available FQDNs for UCP?

    a) --san
    b) --external-name
    c) --external-url
    d) --ucp-url

66. A user cannot push images to our DTR internal registry. What should we verify?

    a) Docker login access.
    b) That the DTR CA certificate should be trusted.
    c) We should verify whether the image's repository does exist.
    d) That the image has vulnerabilities and DTR's image scanning rejects the user's image.

67. Which internal networks are deployed for DTR?

    a) docker_gwbridge
    b) dtr-ol
    c) ingress
    d) dtr-internal

68. Which Kubernetes resources provide an application's resilience?

    a) `Deployment`
    b) `ReplicaSet`
    c) `Pod`
    d) `Replicated`

69. What does the `docker swarm --force-new-cluster` command do?

    a) It is used to recover a cluster in failure situations. It will set all managers as workers, leaving just one manager node.
    b) This command will destroy the cluster. It is used to remove the entire cluster.
    c) `--force-new-cluster` should be used to stop all services deployed on worker nodes.
    d) An application's services will not be impacted by this command. This command just affects the control plane.

70. Which sentences are true about Docker Swarm and Kubernetes networking?

    a) An ingress overlay network will be encrypted by default.
    b) Mutual TLS communications ensure control-plane security in Docker Swarm.
    c) A Kubernetes network is isolated with `networkPolicy` resources out of the box.
    d) Kubernetes uses certificates to ensure security for user access and the internal control plane.

 For some mock questions there is more than one correct answer.

Summary

This was the final chapter on our journey to becoming a Docker Certified Associate. We covered all the topics learned in previous chapters with some mock exam questions. As mentioned before, some of these questions are real questions posed in old exams.

The journey to becoming a Docker Certified Associate is not easy. We started this book from the very beginning, understanding why containers are so popular these days when we talk about microservices architectures. Then, we described how containers are executed using Docker Engine, integrating various isolation strategies to ensure security between container-embedded processes. As containers are based on images, we learned how to build and maintain them using Docker tools. We learned about different Docker objects and how to deploy applications using different networking methods, volumes, or security approaches. We learned how to deploy microservices applications, where every component is running containers. We learned the differences between running all components on standalone and cluster-wide distributed environments. Orchestrators are key in distributed environments. They keep applications healthy and help us develop microservices faster to provide features to update applications' components without service interruption. We studied Docker Swarm and Kubernetes because both are part of the Docker Enterprise platform. Finally, we introduced Docker's enterprise-ready CaaS platform, Docker Enterprise. We learned about all its components and features and how they help us to deploy applications, as well as improving their security.

This was a brief summary of all the topics covered in this book. If you followed this workflow, you are ready to take the Docker Certified Associate exam. This book should also be used as a command reference, although we know that technology changes quite fast these days. Now that you are ready to take the exam, take a deep breath and schedule your exam at `https://prod.examity.com/docker`. Good luck!

Assessments

Chapter 1

1. b and c: We can run more than one process per container, but it is not recommended because Docker Engine will only manage the main container process. We will need to manage additional logic between processes to start and stop everything at once. It is not easy and you can leave "zombie" processes in your hosts. Microservices are based on minimal functionality for each application component, which fits with containers very well.

2. b: Control groups, or cgroups, will manage the host resources provided to each container, but it is very important to understand that, by default, containers will run with unlimited resources.

3. a and b: Containers will run as root unless the source image has a non-root user definition or we specify a non-root user upon container creation. User namespaces allow us to use the root inside containers, although a real user outside the container can have a non-root ID. This is useful when processes require UID 0 to work.

4. d. All of the above sentences are true: Windows hosts will run two different types of isolation. We can run Linux containers on Windows, but this is not true in reverse.

5. a, b, and c: We can use `systemd` unit files or `/etc/docker/daemon.json` to configure the Docker daemon on Linux. On Windows hosts, `daemon.json` is located in the `%programdata%\docker\config\` directory. In both cases, Docker daemon remote access is not secure by default.

Chapter 2

1. b: The image ID is the only identification of uniqueness when listing or managing images. We can have one ID with many names, including the registry part, and tags.

2. d: All the methods described are valid.

3. b: Using a Dockerfile is a reproducible method as we describe all actions to add software, execute commands, add files, and more, in order to build a new image. We can automate and use templates to build images with Dockerfiles and this is the preferred method.

4. a and c: Only `RUN`, `CMD`, and `ENTRYPOINT` instructions admit shell and exec formats.

5. a: Using the shell format, the container main process, as defined by the `ENTRYPOINT` key, cannot be modified with arguments.

Chapter 3

1. a and c: `build` is only available for image objects, and `destroy` does not exist for any object.

2. b: This is not true. The Docker daemon will wait a defined amount of time (10 seconds, by default) before issuing a `SIGKILL` signal to the container's main process.

3. b: `docker kill` will immediately send a `SIGKILL` signal to the container's main process. Not all processes will be killed if they were executed in the background; for example, inside the container. It can leave zombie processes if they do not have parent-child dependencies. As we learned, containers must be removed by hand and `docker kill` will not remove them.

4. b: `docker container update` will only change the container restart policy and its access to host resources.

5. c: We have launched a privileged container; therefore no resource limits will be applied, although we have used `-memory` to confine memory usage. The privileged mode does not affect the filesystem. It will only modify the main process behavior, but in this case, we used a non-root user to create a new file on a directory owned by root and, as a result, it could not be created.

Chapter 4

1. c: Each container will use its own filesystem unless we declare a shared volume for them.

2. a, b, and c: There are different types of volumes and it is not only allowed on container creation or execution.

3. b: Docker volumes can be removed along with their associated container using the `--volumes` (or `-v`) option. A Docker volume purge will remove all unused volumes; those not associated to any container. But Docker will never remove a bind mount volume content (a local directory mounted on a container).

4. c: Only custom bridge networks are attachable after container creation. If we create or start a container and we want it to be connected to the default bridge network, we need to recreate it and attach it to that network on container creation.

5. b: Using `--publish-all` or `-P` will associate a random port between `32768` and `65535` to internal container port `80`. A NAT rule will automatically be created by the Docker daemon to allow this communication. You can disable the Docker daemon iptables management, but it is enabled by default.

Chapter 5

1. a: Docker Compose will run all application components just in one host. We will also use `docker-compose` files for deploying Swarm orchestrated applications with their components distributed on different hosts, but that requires a cluster running. In that case, we will not use the `docker-compose` binary to deploy the application; only the definition file will be valid and we will use it with the `docker stack` action. In Docker Swarm, we deploy swarm services, not containers.

2. d: Docker Compose provides all required actions to build, share, and deploy multi-container applications.

3. a and c: Docker Compose will review whether project images are present in the host. If they are not, the Docker daemon will try to download all not-present ones. Once the Docker daemon has all the required images, it will start all project containers and our terminal will be attached to containers' standard and error output unless the `--detach` or `-d` argument is used.

4. a: Docker Compose will allow us to scale the number of containers associated with a service. By default, Docker Compose will create a bridge network for our deployment, therefore an internal DNS will be associated and will manage all application IP addresses and names. In scaled services, we will receive one of the IP addresses of the replicas each time we ask for the defined service name. It uses round-robin DNS resolution.

5. d: In this case, we could say that answer c is almost right, but it is incomplete. Docker Compose will remove all containers. If containers were running, they will be stopped before they are deleted. All associated resources created during the application execution will also be removed.

Chapter 6

1. c: Docker Content Trust is based on **The Update Framework (TUF)** and this framework was created to ensure the release of content between updates using different keys. It is possible to validate the trustfulness of a package or any other content using TUF.

2. a and d: Docker Content Trust will use Root, Targets, Snapshot, and Timestamp keys to ensure content.

3. c: We ensure image freshness using Content Trust, but it is true that we cannot ensure that the image tagged as "latest" in a given repository is actually the latest one created. We can only ensure that the image tagged as "latest" will be used. It is always recommended to use tags avoiding the use of "latest".

4. b: We tried to sign a version of a non-public write repository. We are not allowed to modify root repositories at docker.io.

5. d: We can recover the key if we have a backup. If it is not possible, we can generate a new one or let Docker generate one for us on first signing. Although we will be able to sign images after the new key has been generated, all our previously signed images will be untrusted because we changed our signature.

Chapter 7

1. a: Orchestrators will not know anything about your application logic. On the other hand, we have quickly reviewed the interfaces that use orchestration to ensure that containers get the appropriate volumes of data on distributed environments.

2. c: Orchestrators will not manage application data, nor do they know anything about your application logic. The orchestrator will take care of the application components' health and will run a new instance if one of the required instances dies.

3. a and b: Distributed environments will help us to deploy applications with high availability and improved performance. But on the other hand, we will have new challenges because we need to be able to distribute application logic and components' interactions on different nodes.

4. a and b: Answers a and b are correct, while c is not, because application components can be managed one at a time. Therefore, upgrades will only impact one application component if the application logic knows how to manage the situation.

5. c: All sentences are correct. We learned that we can define container limits and the required resources. Orchestrators will review these specifications and will deploy them on nodes with enough resources to ensure their correct execution. We can guide orchestration to choose labeled nodes, for example, to ensure application disk I/O, along with many other features. Each orchestrator will manage different rules and workflows to choose the best node for each workload.

Chapter 8

1. a: Docker Swarm is built into Docker Engine, but we have to enable Swarm mode for it to work. We can deploy other orchestrators such as Kubernetes, but it will involve extra work to deploy them. Orchestrators allow us to deploy applications on clusters, hence Swarm will deploy distributed applications.

2. d: Docker Swarm provides service discovery via DNS, internal load balancing for services and their tasks, and overlay networking for services and containers distributed on different nodes.

3. b: Each cluster has only one leader node. The leader is elected from the available managers. When we initialize a cluster, the first node will be the leader until a new election is required. All managers will run workloads unless we specifically avoid them using service constraints.

4. d: Roles can be changed as we require, such as for maintenance, for example. We need to always maintain the defined number of odd managers to avoid cluster instability.

5. a and b: By default, Docker Swarm will deploy stacks on its own network, unless others are specified. Everything related to the application to be deployed must be configured in the Docker Compose stack file. We can add externally created components, but they must exist before the stack is deployed and we will set them as external in the infrastructure-as-code stack file.

Chapter 9

1. a and b: Kubernetes requires etcd to work. Most of the Kubernetes deployment solutions will deploy etcd for you, but it is an external application and therefore it is up to you to manage and ensure that the key-value solution provides high availability. Kubernetes internal networking will work out of the box, but communications between components deployed on different hosts rely on external plugins (the CNI standard). Therefore, we will need to choose and deploy ourselves a solution to provide this kind of communication.

2. b and c: We will deploy pods in Kubernetes, hence these are the minimum unit of deployment. We can deploy more than one container in a pod. The container density is higher in Kubernetes. Scaling pods will replicate all their components at once.

3. d: All sentences are true. All containers in a pod share the same IP address and localhost. They also share pod volumes. **Container Network Interface (CNI)** is not required for connections between pods running on the same host. They all are accessible using their virtual IP addresses.

4. a, b, and c: ReplicaSets allow us to manage replicated environments. Deployments create ReplicaSets and allow us to scale application pods both up and down. They will also maintain the application health based on the required running pods. DaemonSets will ensure one replica on each cluster node.

5. a: The ClusterIP service type will only provide internal access to a service. The assigned IP is not available from the cluster nodes.

Chapter 10

1. c: Docker Machine is maintained by the Docker community.

2. a: Docker Enterprise provides a supported and enterprise-ready CaaS platform, with supported Kubernetes, **Universal Control Plane (UCP)**, and **Docker Trusted Registry (DTR**, based on the Docker Registry community). We can deploy Docker Swarm in production even with Docker support using Docker Enterprise Engine.

3. a, b, and d: Docker Enterprise provides Kubernetes out of the box when we deploy UCP – we do not need to install Kubernetes manually.

4. d: We will use fixed IP addresses for all components. We will use an external load balancer to forward traffic to all manager nodes for UCP and all worker nodes with DTR running for the registry. Forwarding traffic to just one node will not provide high availability if it fails. The Docker UCP installation will deploy Calico by default for Kubernetes, but we will need to review `pod-cidr` and `service-cidr` to ensure that the subnets defined by default will be valid in our environment.

5. c: To provide high availability for workloads, we will deploy at least two Linux nodes. Although it is possible to run DTR on UCP managers, it is not recommended because managers need to have enough resources for control plane tasks and image scanning can affect cluster stability. We will also need to choose different ports for the applications' frontends because both use port `443`.

Chapter 11

1. b: As we have learned, Docker Enterprise Engine is required to install UCP. It will not be installed automatically for us. We can use Web UI, the UCP bundle, and the UCP API to manage our workloads and cluster configurations. UCP's RBAC system will manage authorizations, but it is true that it will also authenticate users if no external authorization source is configured or it is not available.

2. b and d: Docker provides a complete UCP backup and restore solution with the `docker/ucp` image, but remember that we should take care of Docker Swarm's filesystem because it is not part of UCP's backup. We should use the appropriate `docker/ucp` image release for our environment. In fact, we will use the same installed release for any action other than upgrading. UCP removal can be executed from the `docker/ucp` image and this will remove UCP components from all nodes in the cluster. We should then remove the `docker/ucp` image. The upgrade process can be achieved automatically using the `docker/ucp` image, but this may impact your users. We will usually upgrade UCP managers automatically and then execute upgrade steps manually on worker nodes.

3. a and b: We can use `--controller-port` and `:-kube-apiserver-port` to modify the UCP controller and Kubernetes' API server ports. We can also isolate the control plane from the data plane by choosing different interfaces in multihomed hosts using `--data-path-addr`. **Subject Alias Names (SANs)** will add alias names to UCP's certificate. We can add all required aliases for our environment using `--san` multiple times.

4. a, c, and d: UCP deploys a Kubernetes cluster with high availability on top of Docker Swarm. As UCP is deployed on Docker Swarm, we will need at least three nodes to provide high availability. All managers will run the same control plane processes and an external load balancer is required to distribute access between them. This requires a transparent proxy configuration to allow managers to manage encrypted communications. We will use the `/_ping` endpoint to verify manager nodes' health and it can be used on load balancers as a backend health check.

5. a and c: UCP provides **None**, **View Only**, **Restricted Control**, **Scheduler**, and **Full Control**. We can create new roles, but there are no privileged or administrator roles by default. Docker Enterprise administrators are not defined as roles. There is a checkbox in the user's properties to enable this feature. Only administrators can create grants, users, teams, organizations, and collections.

Chapter 12

1. b and c: There are two labels that are always required. We will need to ensure Interlock forwards the service's requests using `com.docker.lb.hosts` and `com.docker.lb.port`. These will have all the required information, but `com.docker.lb.network` is recommended and required if the service's instances are attached to more than one network. We need to specify which network should be used as an ingress.

2. b: The Interlock solution is based on a main process named `interlock`, a process for managing external proxy services and configurations, and an `interlock-proxy` service that will run inside the Docker Enterprise environment if no external load balancer is specified. These three processes run as services within Docker Swarm and they are prefixed with `ucp-`. `ucp-interlock-controller` does not exist.

3. d: By default, only the `ucp-interlock` service will be located by the node's roles. All other components can run anywhere. We will use location constraints to run the `ucp-interlock-proxy` and `ucp-interlock-extension` components on worker nodes.

4. a, b, and c: Interlock allows us to either manage SSL/TLS tunnels on `ucp-interlock-proxy` or configure it as a transparent proxy. In this case, our services' backends should manage SSL/TLS certificates. Interlock interacts with the Docker API and all changes will be updated automatically on Interlock's proxy component. Interlock is a Layer 7 load balancer; reverse proxy, TCP, and UDP protocols should be published using a routing mesh or host mode.

5. a and b: Ingress controllers and Interlock have a common logic, using a few published ports. They will manage all ingress traffic using load balancing and reverse proxy features. We will not publish applications directly. No application's service has to be exposed directly. The ingress controllers (and Interlock) will be exposed and they will route requests to the application's defined services. Interlock has to interact with the application's services, hence it has to connect to their networks. This will happen automatically. Docker Enterprise will connect the `interlock-proxy` service to our application's networks.

Chapter 13

1. b: This list only shows one valid feature. DTR provides repository mirroring. Neither repository load balancing nor repository signing are valid features. We do not sign repositories. We sign repositories' images/tags.

2. b: DTR does not manage images' data with high availability. Deploying more than one replica will provide high availability for DTR's processes. DTR replication requires data sharing between replicas, but we must include third-party solutions to provide high availability for our storage.

3. a and b: The DTR installation runs the `dtr-garant` and `dtr-jobrunner` containers. The first will manage user authentication, while jobrunner will execute DTR's maintenance tasks to remove unreferenced layers. `dtr-notary-server` and `dtr-notary-signer` will be deployed within DTR to manage Docker Content Trust metadata.

4. d: All the question's sentences describe required steps for deploying DTR with high availability.

5. a: DTR backups do not include images' layers. This can constitute a great amount of data and is the key to recovering your images. You should prepare third-party solutions for this data. On the other hand, repository metadata, RBAC configurations, and images' signatures will be stored within your backup TAR file.

Exam answers

1 - b and c

2 - c

3 - b

4 - a, b, and c

5 - b

6 - c

7 - a

8 - a, c, and d

9 - c

10 - a and c

11 - b

12 - a

13 - d

14 - b

15 - c

16 - a, b, and c

17 - a, b, and c

18 - a

19 - b and c

20 - a and b

21 - d

22 - c

23 - b, c, and d

24 - c and d

25 - a, c, and d

26 - a and c

27 - c

28 - c

29 - c

30 - b

31 - d

32 - a and b

33 - d

34 - b and c

35 - d

36 - b

37 - a

38 - c

39 - c

40 - a and b

41 - a and b

42 - b and c

43 - a and c

44 - c

45 - a and c

46 - b

47 - d

48 - b, c, and d

49 - a and b

50 - a

51 - a

52 - a, b, and c

53 - b

54 - a

55 - c

56 - b

57 - c and d

58 - d

59 - d

60 - b

61 - a

62 - b and c

63 - b

64 - b

65 - a

66 - a, b, and c

67 - b

68 - a and b

69 - a

70 - b and d

Other Books You May Enjoy

If you enjoyed this book, you may be interested in these other books by Packt:

Learn Docker – Fundamentals of Docker 19.x

Gabriel N. Schenker

ISBN: 978-1-83882-747-2

- Containerize your traditional or microservice-based applications
- Develop, modify, debug, and test an application running inside a container
- Share or ship your application as an immutable container image
- Build a Docker Swarm and a Kubernetes cluster in the cloud
- Run a highly distributed application using Docker Swarm or Kubernetes
- Update or rollback a distributed application with zero downtime
- Secure your applications with encapsulation, networks, and secrets
- Troubleshoot a containerized, highly distributed application in the cloud

Continuous Delivery with Docker and Jenkins

Rafał Leszko

ISBN: 978-1-83855-218-3

- Get to grips with docker fundamentals and how to dockerize an application for the CD process
- Learn how to use Jenkins on the Cloud environments
- Scale a pool of Docker servers using Kubernetes
- Create multi-container applications using Docker Compose
- Write acceptance tests using Cucumber and run them in the Docker ecosystem using Jenkins
- Publish a built Docker image to a Docker Registry and deploy cycles of Jenkins pipelines using community best practices

Leave a review - let other readers know what you think

Please share your thoughts on this book with others by leaving a review on the site that you bought it from. If you purchased the book from Amazon, please leave us an honest review on this book's Amazon page. This is vital so that other potential readers can see and use your unbiased opinion to make purchasing decisions, we can understand what our customers think about our products, and our authors can see your feedback on the title that they have worked with Packt to create. It will only take a few minutes of your time, but is valuable to other potential customers, our authors, and Packt. Thank you!

Index

Made in the USA
Coppell, TX
07 March 2021